The Transport Problem

Revised edition

C. D. Foster

⅌ Croom Helm paperback

THE TRANSPORT PROBLEM

THE TRANSPORT PROBLEM

2nd REVISED EDITION

C.D. FOSTER

CROOM HELM LONDON

First published 1975
© 1975 C.D. Foster

Croom Helm Ltd
2-10 St. John's Road London SW11

ISBN 0−85664−172−3 hardback
0−85664−177−4 paperback

Printed and bound in Great Britain
by Redwood Burn Ltd, Trowbridge and Esher.

CONTENTS

APPENDICES

ACKNOWLEDGEMENTS TO THE FIRST EDITION

I wish to thank the Institute of Transport for establishing the Senior Research Fellowship in the Economics of Transport which has given me the opportunity to write this book; to the East Hendred W.E.A. with whom I first discussed many of the problems raised in it; Dr. M.E. Beesley, Mr. A.J. Blackburn, Mr. R.F.F. Dawson of the Road Research Laboratory, Mr. W.A. Eltis, Mr. D.L. Munby, and Mrs. M.E. Paul for reading it in typescript and making many helpful suggestions; Mr. D.S. Barrie, Assistant Secretary-General and Mr. D.M. Dear, Head of the Traffic Costing Service of the British Transport Commission, for help on certain points; and my wife for encouragement.

Jesus College,   *C.D.F.*
Oxford,
August, 1963

ACKNOWLEDGEMENTS TO THE SECOND EDITION

My acknowledgements now to many who have advanced the state of transport economics since 1963; and in particular to Mr A.J. Harrison who has helped me evaluate my earlier work, without any responsibility for my opinions.

London School of Economics   *C.D.F.*
October 1974

INTRODUCTION TO THE SECOND EDITION

When it was suggested that there should be a new edition of this book, I was uncertain how far to revise it. I have made some substantial alterations. I have completely revised several sections of the original Chapter 6 to extend the analysis and meet criticisms which were made of it. Several of the figures and some of the examples in the book have been updated. There is new material in the postscripts to the chapters and two of the appendices. I have changed passages where I thought this would clarify their meaning and I have dropped some paragraphs, and an appendix, which now seem to me less relevant, but much I have kept unchanged. My reason for this treatment is that the book was, and is, an introduction to the principles of transport economics; and the economic principles needed to analyse transport problems remain the same. Many of the issues discussed here are still basic: how does one define the economic objectives of road and rail, and then evaluate the efficiency of the two modes? What are the appropriate pricing and investment criteria? What can one say about competition, and the coordination of transport policy? Moreover, the current problems of road and rail are not dissimilar from those of ten years ago. There has been development, but one can best understand the current position, I believe, through an appreciation of the recent history of the railways and the roads programme.

The traditional 'transport problem' of road and rail never seems to be solved completely. The 1968 Act was intended to provide more sensible legislation within which transport might operate: to give the railways (and other nationalised transport) clearer economic criteria and a framework of financial discipline within which they could fairly demonstrate their efficiency, or lack of it. It is already clear (1974) that the railways have failed to meet their targets, but this does not mean their financial framework was wrong, or that its principles should be changed. If as time passes the railways are able to run progressively fewer services profitably, then more will require specific subsidies. There seems to be the greatest reluctance among politicians and the public to cut out any passenger rail service, however high the subsidy per passenger journey. Even if this is so it must still be better for the nation to know from time to time whether it would not save resources on at least some services and use them to meet other social objectives. To go back to large-scale cross-subsidisation, hidden subsidies and deficit grants must be inefficient and obscurantist.

In recent years there have been major advances in the application of economics to highway problems. This is especially true of highways outside major cities where there is greater agreement on the investment criteria to apply. The criteria have been improved, adapted to handle more complicated situations, and made easier to use. There has been substantial research to investigate the empirical relationships that are needed to support the predictions that investment appraisal requires. There has also been substantial progress in research on methods of pricing. In cities the techniques are not yet quite adequate to deal with the problems, but progress has also been great during the last decade. Even so, I believe that what I wrote more than ten years ago remains more than a useful examination of highway economics. Many of the problems then identified have not been solved. Progress is still needed towards making the highways organisation of the Department of the Environment into an enterprise (or a collection of enterprises) which is accountable, operates with clear economic criteria and provides objective tests of its performance.

The plan of the book was to discuss principles of transport economics in their application to the actual transport problem of the early 1960s. As a result what will strike many readers is the relative lack of reference to the problems of urban transport and the environment. This can be defended. (1) The road-rail problem, which is at the heart of this book, remains important. (2) Urban transport problems require more complicated and powerful techniques; it would be over-ambitious to introduce anyone to transport economics in its application to cities. (3) Postscripts and references lead on to a discussion of urban and environmental applications. Neither are environmental conditions as crucial for inter-urban as for urban policy.

The postscripts are a commentary on the first edition and serve three purposes:

1. In the last ten years the theory and practice of transport economics have developed rapidly, but there are no advanced texts to which readers can be referred as a sequel. Whenever it seemed helpful I have referred to subsequent literature so that the reader may follow up these advances if he wishes.

2. I have also used the postscripts to consider how time has treated the original arguments and to refer to a number of criticisms.

3. When I wrote this book, I had no expectation that I would have any practical part in attempting to solve any of the problems discussed. However, as a civil servant at the Ministry of Transport from 1966 to 1969, I had the chance of making my contribution to the preparation of the 1968 Transport Act and other policy-making. In some of the postscripts I have used my later experiences to reflect on the ideas of 1963.

6

INTRODUCTION

It is on the law, on the response of the public to proposals for large schemes of expenditure to be undertaken on their behalf, and on the attitude of legislators and administrators to current economic problems as much as (or more than) on technical improvements in the arts of carriage and on the structure of the industry that the future efficiency of British transport will depend.
G. WALKER and C.J. SAVAGE[1]

This book is written not only for economists but for all those seriously interested in working out a coherent national transport policy, and also for those who, though not particularly concerned with transport are interested in the problems of the public sector and the nationalised industries. Nevertheless it is an economist's book treating of economic ideas and facts. Though not among the most difficult in economic theory, several ideas are not easy and will be unfamiliar to many readers. I have tried to explain them without assuming any previous knowledge of economics or accounting. When economic terms are used — and it would be absurdly long-winded and unnatural to avoid them — their meaning, I believe, is clear, or will have been explained.

Where everyone is a sufferer from the transport problem and has an opinion, it is fair to make it clear at the start what kind of a book this is. It is principally about Government policy, discussing the issues raised by decisions the Government has to make, particularly in two capacities: through the Ministry of Transport for roads and through the Ministry and the British Railways Board for railways. It is concerned with what I take to be in most people's mind the transport problem, the internal one. It does not touch on the problems of shipping and external airlines because to this they are almost wholly irrelevant. Neither is it concerned directly with the decisions which have to be made to resolve problems private operators face in the transport industry. If the Government formulates a deliberate, consistent policy for the road programme and the railways, many other problems will fall more easily into place. The Government has other responsibilities besides road and rail, but these do not present the same difficulty for policy. We will only consider some factors affecting public policy for other means of transport in Chapter 12, where it is essential we should do so.

Therefore this is not a technical book. When we chafe in a city rush-hour it is a natural outlet for our impatience to think technically —

7

of the fly-overs, under-passes, clover-leafs and dual carriageways which should get us out of the traffic jam, and possibly to look forward to a city under a net of overhead expressways and monorails. Similarly, the inadequacies of the railways tend to make us think first of how they could be improved technically without much regard to cost. As one would expect, suggestions of all kinds have been made by experts and non-experts, and it would be easy to fill a long book with a discussion of the most interesting.[2] Neither is it my purpose to try to take the more plausible technical solutions to road and rail problems, for example, alternative proposals for London ring roads, dieselfication versus electrification, and assess their relative profitability. To be worth doing it would have to be done in great detail, but my principal reason for not attempting that kind of treatment is that it would not be putting first things first.

Strictly it would be impossible to make such judgements except in rough approximation to nobody knows quite what yardstick of efficiency. To use a crude metaphor, which perhaps does not have to be any better at this stage in our argument, one cannot tell what the quickest and cheapest route is until one has decided where one is going. We cannot decide where and how to spend the public money available for road building and improvement until we have agreed on the criteria to be used for evaluating road building and improvement. Similarly, solutions to rail problems do not make sense until we have decided what policy the railways are to be required to follow. And, lastly, until policy has been decided consistently for road and rail, and for other competing forms of transport, there will be no criteria by which we can decide the most important question in transport: whether it is more desirable to invest in roads or in railways or, to put it more rigorously, how far it is more desirable to invest in one than in the other.

The first and most obvious reason why most of us have some interest in the transport problem is that we suffer from the inadequacies of the transport system, but there are other reasons for thinking the transport problem important which will be of unequal appeal to different people. It is not only the physical transport situation — the atmosphere of traffic jams and late trains — which has brought about the present ferment over the transport problem. There has also been a growing feeling that something must be done about the performance and policies of the nationalised industries, among which are the British Railways Board, the London Transport Board, the British Transport Docks Board, the Inland Waterways Authority, the regional railway boards and British European Airways, which operates internal airlines. And, though not formally the subject of a nationalised industry, the management of the road programme (by the Ministry of Transport) presents many of the same problems.

The nationalised industries are beginning to pull out of the first, or

Micawber, period in their history. Micawber said 'Annual income twenty pounds, annual expenditure twenty pounds nought and six, result misery.' His policy, or habit, of balancing on the knife-edge dividing solvency from insolvency brought him more often than not to disaster. Making their policy that of breaking even, taking one year with another, and not salting away sufficient reserves, the nationalised industries have been Micawberish, partly of their own will, partly from regulation, legislation and political pressure. While they break even, they do not have a care in the eyes of the world. Come the first year, and more certainly the second and third year, in which they have a deficit, when their expectations turn down and nothing turns up, and it becomes harder to convince anyone they will eventually break even in the end: result misery. Recently deficits (of the National Coal Board, British Railways and BOAC) and, of course, division of opinion over nationalisation in the Labour Party, have drawn the sharp fire of all kinds of critics who would scarcely have bothered if there had been a profit, however small. But the general public could bay at the nationalised industries for years, as indeed certain sections have done since they started, without effecting any real change in their behaviour and policies. What makes the difference is a change of attitude within the industries themselves or in the ministries to which they are wedded. The crucial conversion to a new point of view does seem to have to be that of a ministry, and there does seem to have been such a change of attitude at the Ministry of Transport *in relation to railways*. There Micawberism may have had its day with three vices of, first, over-optimism, showing itself in the choice of insufficient or non-existent risk premia in making investments; second, a hazy notion of what one's costs are; and, third, somewhat indiscriminate generosity by way of subsidy to various deserving classes of users who do not pay what they cost. As the Permanent Secretary to the Ministry said in 1959, 'I think that when the financial situation gets worse it does create a new situation in which the Ministry has to consider whether it must not ask more detailed questions than it has perhaps asked in the past.'[3]

Although over the last decade there has been what can loosely be called a toughening of national policy to the nationalised industries, it is still doubtful just what the principles are to be on which they are to be run. Certainly a large part of what is required is more rigorous methods, such as have been worked out for the nationalised industries of France and for water resource allocation in the United States, especially for investment.[4] But, again, it does not make too much sense to use rigorous methods without having first decided in some detail what policy should be. According to the policy adopted, rigorous methods will give on occasions different answers on what should be done. For example, it is, I think, in most cases a valid criticism of nationalised industries that they have not been able to identify their costs sufficiently; but an essential pre-requisite to the identification of costs is a decision on what are to be counted among the costs of a public enterprise, which need not be identical with what a private firm calls costs. To decide on policy, we need to go back to first principles and ask what nationalised industries, or if the answer is to be different for different nationalised industries, what the enterprises in which we are interested are *for*. Even those who think they see clearly that the nationalised industries should be run on principles no different from private firms, the upholders of commercialism, are frequently confused and self-contradictory in detail. When we have decided the function of transport public enterprises, we can work out in detail the appropriate rigorous methods for price and investment policy. The transport problem therefore has wider implications in that it entails some of the policy problems which face most of the nationalised industries.

When world and national governments have their overwhelming problems there is a tendency for the lesser ones to be forgotten, shelved or botched. We could go on for years, perhaps for ever, without a consistent, coherent transport policy, muddling on. Apart from any feelings one may have that all problems are worth serious consideration, there are two main reasons why it would be a pity to shelve or botch the transport problem. First, there is considerable waste involved in the present inadequacies of our transport system, which can be related (at least in principle, though the actual amount is hard to hazard because of poor statistics) to the rate of growth of national income. There is a level and a distribution of transport expenditure which would lead to a higher rate of growth. It is not improbable, because of the immediate impact and great publicity transport has, that something will be done; but this could easily be lavish expenditure on roads to keep up with the Joneses on the Continent, erratically distributed, and rather less lavish expenditure on the railways. It has to be admitted that this would be a *solution* which would satisfy most of us immediately, because the majority of the public are not concerned very much whether there has been an efficient use of scarce resources and whether public money has been used as efficiently as possible in the most desirable way. Nevertheless the waste which could be brought about by too much expenditure, unwisely spent, on transport, would be as unfortunate as the present inadequacy. Rich countries can afford to be slapdash in the allocation of public money for investment. A country which is as hard pressed as Britain cannot easily afford to be as approximate in the use of funds for investment. In general, given the level of consumption needed to encourage private firms to invest in new productive capacity, we are less able, verging on the shabby genteel as we are, to waste funds available for investment. In particular, the public sector has many calls upon the resources it has available for investment and it is important that we should weigh fairly precisely the advantages of investing in a new school, rocket or road.

Another reason for bothering is that if we manage to work out the policy for transport, where it is relatively easy to present the issues and to reach agreement or comparatively clearcut and therefore viable disagreement, we shall then be better equipped by experience to modernise the policy-making of other branches of government, where the elaboration of criteria and policy is likely to present greater difficulties. In short the argument is that it is timely for us to attempt to improve and make more efficient our methods of conducting public business (just as it was timely for the joint stock company to succeed the partnership and the decentralised firm of the fifties and sixties of this century to succeed the rather more centralised firm of inter-war years) and that it would be quite sensible to begin this process in transport.

Still the first solution which comes to many people when confronted by an organisation which is not working well is reorganisation.* This book suffers from the economist's vice which I believe a virtue, that it is more important to decide what to do than to bother about the institutional framework within which it is done. It therefore contains very little about organisation, on which so much has been written. It would not be quite fair to say that the reorganisation which has and is taking place is as unimportant as shaking a kaleidoscope or switching queen's with king's rook, but certainly the emphasis given to it does seem misplaced. The trouble is that many of those who talk most about reorganisation are the victims of slogans such as 'centralisation' and 'decentralisation'. There is plenty to be said for decentralisation, much to be said for centralisation; but to equate the first, as often seems to be done, and the virtues of free enterprise, competition and private business, and the latter with socialism, planning and the top-heavy leviathan, is extraordinarily naive. The fundamental error, which would have appalled Burke, is that organisation seems to be regarded in abstraction from what is organised: the people in the organisation, its policy, what it has to do. And if one is going to abstract from the whole it is surely more sensible to begin by considering policy,

*cf. 'What problems have we to solve? First, organisation: what is the best organisation for the railways and for the commission's other undertakings and for their relationship to one another? Second, management: what improvements can be made in management? Third, modernisation: do we still pin our faith on modernisation . . . Fourth, restrictions: ought the railways to be freed from the restrictions put upon them when they had a monopoly? Fifth, property: how can the best use be made of the commission's property? Sixth, are fundamental financial changes required? Seventh, how can we achieve viability?' Mr. Marples on the B.T.C. in the House of Commons.[5]

and, once that is decided, asking them what are the least possible changes in organisation that are necessary, than to begin by making an abstraction of mindless organisation. Anybody can play the game of sitting down to a sheet of paper and redrawing boxes and lines between them under the influence of some slogan; but, for it not to be a dangerous pastime for those who have authority to impose their will, there must be a real feeling for the needs of the situation. Reorganisation without a strong sense of policy and purpose is surgery without diagnosis.[6]

Although two-thirds of my feeling against this approach is distrust of mindless organisation and economist's bias, another third is conservatism. Drastic reorganisation such as the British Transport Commission has experienced is to a public or private corporation like revolution to a state. 'The science of government being . . . so practical in itself, and intended for such practical purposes, a matter which requires experience, and even more experience than a man can gain in his whole lifetime however sagacious and observing he may be, it is with infinite caution that any man ought to venture upon pulling down an edifice . . .'[7] There has not been 'infinite caution'. There has not been reasonable foresight. It is hard to believe that those who have so lightly advocated the considerable reorganisation which has now been undertaken realised at all what should have been obvious to them, that it entailed a great deal of work. A large part of the commission's time has been taken up with the difficult and intricate legal and financial problems of decentralisation: the division of assets between area boards, the definition of the legal and accounting relationships between the new entities, the redrawing of a multitude of documents which have to be altered slightly. These are almost wholly irrelevant to the real problems of the railways and divert effort from their solution. It is like asking someone who is having a great struggle to keep his business going, to move house, divorce his wife and reinvest his securities at the same time as well.

The only positive proposal of organisation that seems to me to be of the first importance is that the present administration of the road system should be reorganised as a national roads authority, that is as a nationalised industry or public corporation comparable to the British Transport Commission.

There is another approach to the transport problem and indeed to the problems of the nationalised industries in general which finds no echo here. This is that a chief problem is to define the *relations* between Minister and Board of a nationalised industry, Minister and Parliament, Parliament and Board: the problem of *accountability*. Who is to have the power in relation to the nationalised industries? How is it to be divided between Parliament, Ministers and the Boards of the industries? How is it to be exercised? In detail, should there be greater freedom for MPs to ask questions about the nationalised industries? Should there be more or improved committees of the House of Commons with more powers of investigation? What rights of directive should the Ministers have, etc.?

Without entering far upon this topic, again the province of the political scientist, it does seem to me that the difficulty in communication between Parliament, ministry and nationalised industry, which is often apparent as one reads Hansard or the reports of the Select Committee on the Nationalised Industries, is not so much one of channels of communication and definition of powers as lack of clearly defined policy. It is not that Parliament and the ministries cannot impose their will but that they frequently do not know quite what it is. The problem of accountability arises from vagueness of thought and language and the muddled floundering after tests of efficiency and rigorous methods, which are the result of not knowing one's own mind. That the formulation of policy is the essence of the problem of accountability seems also to have been the view of one of the greatest chairmen of public corporations, Lord Reith, who wrote: 'As to accountability, the instrument of establishment should not only say what the corporation has to do — obligations and limitations — but as clearly as possible should specify the nature, degree, occasion and method of accountability.' In other words accountability ought not to be an everlasting conversation but based on a clear statement of what should be done, and what reports are to be made, reducing *as much as possible* to a set of rules and a routine.

One last point. Although this is a book about policy — about what ought to be done rather than 'what is' — I have no particular axe to grind. This is not, I think, a partisan book, unless it is partisan to think that whatever axe is used should be sharp and to the point. My purpose is to explain the meaning and implications of certain divergent policies which it seems to me reasonable to suppose that substantial bodies of opinion might want to pursue. There are in fact four different basic policies which I examine in some detail, while indicating in passing how those who wish can elaborate modifications.

POSTSCRIPT

As one might expect the introduction made several points that were expanded later and will be commented on in their place, but there were three which were not:

1. Though true that new technology should not affect the criteria to be adopted, it does affect practical decision-making. It makes it harder to predict the traffic pattern of the future and its distribution

13

between modes. It is harder to assess the return on investment in a new mode. Intensive research on demand forecasting has attempted to estimate people's responsiveness to various 'abstract' characteristics of transport modes — speed frequency, reliability, etc. These findings are then used to synthesise the predicted characteristics of new modes.[1]

2. My experience has shown me that I was right to suppose that what makes the most effective difference to nationalised industry performance is the sponsoring Ministry's attitude. Vacillation in that attitude is a prime cause of variable performance. In Britain, neither directly nor through the Select Committee on Nationalised Industries, does Parliament get down to enough detail or figures to provide an effective discipline. What I did not appreciate in 1963 was that I had read too much into the words of the Ministry's witnesses to the Select Committee and that the 'toughening of national policy' towards the railways had not gone very far. Elsewhere I have compared the Ministry's attitude to that of a trustee who expected to allow the railways to employ additional capital, provided the railways said that in their best judgement the investment was necessary or profitable.[2] Even as late as the mid-'sixties the Ministry of Transport showed its anxiety by asking more questions and delaying approval rather than by exercising any decisive financial discipline.

3. I had not appreciated the significance of reorganisation as an administrative technique. For many administrators the principal evidence that something needs reform is often that decisions are difficult to make, rather than any objective test of the quality of the decisions taken.

A body which has in the past settled certain 'classes of decision', slows down the decision-making, multiplies its meetings or fails to take important decisions, passing on more decisions unresolved to a higher level, ever perhaps so as to take up more than what is felt to be its rightful share of ministerial time. Of course even where nothing of the kind disturbs routine it is possible for someone to decide that policy needs changing, but an administrative log-jam is much more likely to lead to a policy review than anything else is, unless it be a collision with strongly expressed public opinion or the will of a Minister. In such circumstances, a reorganisation may seem the right answer: to change the membership of the body to bring new interests on to it, to superimpose a co-ordinating committee, or to change its status and make it a body with more or less powers. All these may break the log-jam. Such reorganisation need not be 'mindless'.

There are, I believe, three main reasons why reorganisation figures so large in schemes of reform:

1. It is practically impossible to express policies in statutes or White Papers as clearly as an economist would like. The words the

Parliamentary draftsmen use, and civil servants prefer, are scarcely ever precise as an economist knows precision, simply because civil servants (and ministers) wish for enough ambiguity so that policies *can* be altered significantly without it being necessary to face all the problems and costs of having to pass new legislation, given the queue of impending Bills. Similar difficulties arise with internal policy statements. Therefore policies can never be imposed with very great clarity.

2. Quite often Ministers and civil servants do not have the time, as they think, to get policies clear. So rather than think things through they would prefer to reconstitute a body or set up a new one – and for it to provide the definite policy. Given their priorities there are other activities they prize more than clarity; and they reorganise in the expectation that if they give some policy guidelines there will be some change for the better.

3. One can reword the policies completely and yet so strong may be organisational inertia and habits of mind, that, unless they themselves want to change, most bodies may continue to do much as they have always done despite the redefinition of their objectives – changing the description of what they do rather than the actuality. At best they are likely to react slowly. While the very least one can say of a substantial reorganisation is that it forces some change to take place if only because it breaks one network of relations and substitutes another. None of this, however, affects the proposition that the shallower the policy analysis the less predictable will be the consequences of reorganisation.

It follows from what I have said that in 1963 I oversimplified the problem of the relations between Minister and Board. While accountability should be based on a 'clear statement of what should be done and what reports are to be made, reducing as much as possible to a set of rules and a routine' unfortunately this is not all that is needed to achieve economic efficiency. It matters more to decide what action Government is to take when there are significant differences between net revenue forecasts and out-turn; and what protection the Boards, or for that matter the highways, should have against Government policies which reduce their efficiency without compensation.

PART I

THE FRAMEWORK

1. THE SHORTCOMINGS OF SOME SIMPLE SOLUTIONS TO THE TRANSPORT PROBLEM

We are not spending enough on our roads. Few would dispute that. The difficult questions are 'how much more?', 'where first?' and 'what is the railways' part to be in the transport system of the future?' Finding answers to these questions is the essence of the internal British transport problem. It is tempting to fall for one or other of the easy solutions to the problem. The more respectable are superficially plausible, easily understood and comparatively straightforward to effect quickly. The type of solution developed in this book is complicated and not particularly easy to follow, requiring preliminary investment in what a private firm would call market research and cost analysis. It would mean a radical change in overall transport policy. Speed and simplicity are important practical advantages of the simple solutions. Therefore we must begin by arguing their shortcomings and making the case against them. The general nature of the objection is that they are arbitrary, wild stabs at a solution, possibly preferable only to drifting as we are. If we adopt a simple solution such as we are pressed to do by many disinterested and vested interests, we ought not to be surprised if the country is landed with a road system which on hindsight seems too small or large, a compromise or a showpiece, probably but not inevitably the latter.

SIMPLE SOLUTIONS TO THE ROAD PROBLEM

These can conveniently be divided into two categories (1) the largely arbitrary (2) those based on international comparisons.

The Largely Arbitrary

We may mention first the actual amounts spent on the road system in the past by central and local government (see Fig. 1.1). On reflection these amounts seem less than desirable in most years, yet they were intended to be the right amounts to 'solve' the road problem in the sense that more would have been too much, less too little in the opinion at the time of the central and local authorities responsible for determining them. The fact was of course that they were governed by (a) short-term considerations and (b) unfortunate theories of public finance.

(a) Road expenditure in any given year was affected by the

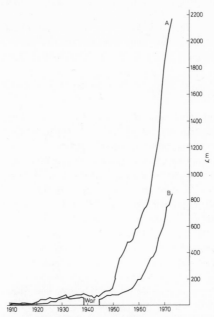

FIG. 1.1a: Annual expenditure on roads by central and local government

     b: Annual receipts from motor vehicle licences, petrol tax and purchase tax on motor vehicles (Local authorities did not keep proper accounts accounts (1939–1945)

immediate problems of chancellors (and local authorities). One year it was easier to balance a budget, and more was spent on roads. In another constraint would mean roads expenditure was cut. Expenditure was little determined by any long-run conception of the national need for roads.

(b) Roads expenditure got the worst of two schools of economic thought. Between the wars the classical view was generally accepted that budgets should be balanced even in a slump. Although some roadbuilding schemes were promoted to relieve unemployment, illogically on this view, the overwhelming tendency was to place roads well down in the priority list, among dispensable public expenditure items which could wait their turn for prosperity. (Mussolini and Hitler uninhibited by classical economics built more roads.) Since the Second World War roads expenditure has been kept down until recently for the opposite reason. Keynesian economics indicates that public works expenditure is one way of helping to lift an economy out of a slump. Roadbuilding is particularly suitable. Therefore governments postponed a major road programme until the next slump. Because there has been no slump, only slight recessions, roadbuilding has never caught up on what it has lost during the long postwar boom. Recently

19

it has become plain that it is foolish to delay a road-building programme for a slump which Government policy should be able to prevent ever happening.[2] Consequently expenditure on the roads has increased markedly. This is the problem: the Government knows that expenditure is moving in the right direction, but it does not know where the upward movement should level off — at £200m. a year, £250m., £300m.? Past policy and practice has nothing to tell us what the level of expenditure should be, once it is agreed that this level is to be governed by long-term considerations.

The most popular simple solution moves on a step. It would relate what is spent to what road-users pay in taxation. The argument is that road-users are overcharged, and that they have the right to have spent on roads what they pay for their use. When Lloyd George first taxed motorists in 1909 he established the now notorious Road Fund. The new taxes were to be paid into it and should be used only for roads. That was his promise. The promise was broken. The fund was raided to help pay for the First World War; it was raided by Winston Churchill in 1926 and 1927, and by Neville Chamberlain in 1935 and 1936, for general purposes of Government expenditure. The fund was formally abolished in 1955. 'What with raids and one thing and another,' said Mr Henry Brooke, then Financial Secretary to the Treasury, 'the Road Fund has had a chequered career. It was . . . fed by hypothecated revenues from motor taxation up to 1937 but since 1937 no hypothecated revenues have been paid into the fund. Instead the fund has been fed directly from the Exchequer. In other words the Road Fund was originally like a tank that was fed by a particular stream. Now for the last eighteen years that has ceased to be so and the Road Fund is a tank connected with the main, and the money flows through the tank from the Exchequer and is used for road expenditure.'[3] Abolition did not remove but rather sharpened the sense of grievance felt by many motorists and the motorists' associations. A glance at fig. 1.1 shows that apparently they have not been getting their money's worth since 1932. The surplus of taxation over expenditure has grown rapidly since 1949.

Alleged overcharging is made up of two sums: (a) arrears from past years and (b) the present annual surplus of taxation over expenditure. Some argue road-users have a moral right to (a) and (b). Some would be satisified with (b). This simple solution is therefore that roads expenditure should be increased by (b), or by (a) plus (b). We must disentangle the issues.

Road users have no right to these sums. Like all indirect taxes all or any part of them can be regarded as contributions to the general expenses of government. Parliament has the right to use taxes for any purpose it pleases. If it is argued Lloyd George promised this taxation would be used only for roads, the proper rejoinder is he had no right to try to bind his successors in this way. Churchill gave two valid though, as it happened, mutually exclusive reasons for 'raiding the Road Fund' in 1926.[4] The first was that all expenditure incurred on the sum 'raided' would cover the extra expense on police for which the motorist was responsible. The second was that he proposed to regard the part of taxation kept in the Road Fund as payment for the use of roads, and the part he was transferring as the proceeds of a tax on luxury. At different times British parliaments have regarded varying proportions of this taxation as a contribution to the war effort, a general purchase tax, a tax on luxuries, a method of redistributing income, of restricting the use of imported oil and simply as a means of raising money when it could not be raised in some other way. Parliament being sovereign there is nothing more to be said about the supposed right of the British motorist to (a), or (a) plus (b).

Nevertheless there are good reasons for returning to Lloyd George. Although Parliament is the law unto itself and for us all, it would be more sensible if as a general rule motor taxation were regarded as a price paid for the use of roads.[5] Indeed this is a prerequisite of an economic solution of the road problem. Some form of accounts must be drawn up relating what is spent on the roads to what is paid for the use of the roads. In so far as taxation is payment for the use of roads, it should be separate from taxation of vehicles, fuel, etc. levied for any other purpose. (We will consider how we should work out the details of such a pricing system in Chapter 10.) If we do use taxation as a charge for the roads, there is a strong case for relating it to the costs of providing the roads. It follows we should rid our tax system of taxes which bear especially hard on motorists compared with other sections of the population and distort the allocation of resources. (By contrast the rationale behind special taxation of tobacco, entertainments, betting, is clear enough whether one agrees with it or not. But why tax someone who spends money on using the roads more *pro rata* than someone who buys a refrigerator?) This does not imply that all taxes levied on road-users must be spent on roads, but that if it is decided there should be a purchase tax or luxury tax on certain commodities of which travel is one, motorists should not be taxed differently from anyone else in this respect. This is the case for keeping these other taxes which are not a charge for using roads formally separate, their purpose explicit, and preserving the bookkeeping convention of a road fund which publishes accounts similar, let us say, to those of a nationalised industry.

If we were to ignore these difficulties and accept that taxation of road-users should be and always should have been equal to expenditure on behalf of road-users, there are other reasons why the actual figures shown in fig. 1.1 are worthless. First the basis of the figures given for expenditure, those usually quoted, is inadequate. It includes such items as maintenance, improvement and new construction of roads by the Ministry of Transport and local authorities; cleansing, watering and snow clearing; the provision and maintenance of police vehicles used on traffic duty; some research and traffic surveys; trunk road lighting; salaries and establishment charges of surveyors. It does not include other items which have as much reason to be in. A figure can be put to some of these, for example the expenses of local authorities in registering vehicles and collecting duties (£2.7m. in 1957-8) and expenditure on street lighting (£23.8m. in 1958-9.) Other items are not separated out in the public accounts: for example police costs, other than for police vehicles, in respect of traffic; the administrative costs of the road system, which are borne on the Ministry of Transport vote or by the general expenditure of local authorities: that part of the Road Research Laboratory's costs which is met on the vote of the Department of Scientific and Industrial Research. A conservative estimate of these three only, might be about £70m. a year. There are certainly other items that should be included. Our present position is rather as would be obtained if a private firm should casually omit one item in three in working out the costs. In case anyone should be interested, counting all these in is not likely to eliminate the surplus of taxation over expenditure unless two controversial items are brought in: the cost of road accidents (estimated at roughly £220m. in 1959) and the cost of congestion, a cost imposed by road-users on each other (perhaps £630m. in 1961). If these are admitted or an equally controversial rent is charged for the use of land embodied in roads, 'expenditure' would exceed tax receipts. (We will examine the case for and against considering these as costs to be met by road-users in Chapter 9.)

The argument does not all go one way. The figure given for taxation is dubious for reasons other than those given earlier. There is a false antithesis: taxation of motorists against expenditure on behalf of road-users. Not all road-users are motorists. In fact some road expenditure is financed out of rates (£97m. in 1960-61). And most of the accident and congestion costs are not Government expenditure. Some expansionists conclude from this that the proper contrast is between motor taxation and that proportion of expenditure not financed out of rates; that is, central Government expenditure which given the expenditure figures of fig. 1.1, increases the extent of 'overcharging' considerably. (This is usually put as the proposition that only 15 per cent of what motorists pay is returned to them in expenditure.)[6] Others would argue that the wrong proportion of road expenditure is financed out of rates and that some different proportion should be used to work out the extent of 'overcharging'.

The fact remains that there are many views which can be taken on *what* receipts should be matched with *what* expenditure. The surplus shown in fig. 1.1 is based on one definition of relevant receipts and relevant expenditure. And, what is very important, the *right* definitions are not wholly a matter of fact. They are partly a matter of judgement. (This is a point we will develop in general terms in Chapter 3.)

Lastly, if we had figures for receipts and expenditure which satisfied us, the simple solution would still be worthless. What do we assume? The level of taxation is right, and expenditure should be increased to equal it. This is to argue in a circle. We have no reason to believe the present level of motor taxation and the proportion of rates spent on the roads is desirable. The revenue from these sources is arbitrary in amount and no indication of what anybody wants to spend on the road system. We might as well argue that the level of expenditure is right, and that taxation and other revenue should be reduced to equal it. (Besides, if we took this seriously, we should have to say that those who have contributed a bigger surplus over cost, for example, users of moderately utilised, poorly maintained country roads, deserve to have a larger proportion invested to their benefit. This would mean that more money would be invested where, by most standards, it would be agreed that there was least need for road improvement and vice versa.)

A third sort of solution relates what should be spent to the cost of congestion or to the cost of congestion *and* accidents. This is a less arbitrary solution than those we have considered, and indeed it takes us towards the type of solution we are to develop in this book, but, as it is usually argued, it has its limitations. For example in 1960, Mr. Philip Noel-Baker asked Mr Marples in the House of Commons if he would recall that the cost of congestion on the roads was now estimated at £500m. a year and the cost of road accidents was at least £200m. a year. He asked Mr Marples to calculate the capital sum on which £700m. was interest. Mr Marples replied: 'Many people make these calculations and I notice there is an astonishing variation between the highest and the lowest cost. I do not accept them at their face value.'[7]

Many people do. These figures are commonly used. What is the argument? The more traffic there is on a road the more it costs each vehicle that moves along it. The reasons are obvious. Each journey takes longer, and time is money for most people. Fuel and oil consumption, tyre and brake wear per mile increase. It was estimated that in 1956 £510m. were lost on the roads of Britain in that way. A more recent (1961) figure is £630m.[8] For the sake of this example let us assume that the Government can borrow for road improvement at 6 per cent. £630m. is roughly 6 per cent of £10,000m. Therefore, the argument runs, it is profitable to invest any amount up to £10,500m. in road improvement because the return − the elimination of £630m. worth of congestion − would be more than the interest charge on the capital invested. The highest estimates of the cost of completely modernising the British road system are less than £10,500m.: perhaps £2,000m. in London, £3,000−£4,000m. in other cities, £2,000m. on rural motorways, but not more than £8,000−£9,000m. in all. So it is argued there is a *prima facie* economic case for investing so much, but there is a fallacy in the argument. Its validity depends on the assumption that that much expenditure would get rid of congestion but, as roads are priced at present, this is not so. We have the experience of Los Angeles. Some of the most congested roads in California are expressways built recently to relieve congestion. Build a new expressway and it attracts new traffic on to the roads which later tends to offset the initial decongestion. The effect of this secondary round of 'generated' traffic, as it is often called, must be taken into account in working out the return on road investment; and this the simple argument does not.[9]

But there are other objections to using this argument. We are postulating a standard relationship between the total cost of congestion and the total cost of building improved road systems; and this may be misleading. It does not allow for the possibility that in many instances the cost of improving a roadwork may be less than the cost of the congestion it causes in its present state, and therefore desirable by this criterion, whereas in others the cost of improvement will be considerably greater than the cost of congestion and therefore not desirable by this criterion. This may be true especially of certain kinds of projects in cities. The moral is that the comparison of rounded global figures is not a substitute for the examination of any project on its merits. The simple solution is simple only because the overall figures can be based on deduction from sample surveys. Otherwise we must evaluate every investment separately, as a private firm evaluates every investment separately. If this is not done we are likely to go seriously wrong.

In contrasting the cost of congestion and the cost of building a road system one does not necessarily consider the possibility that the beneficiaries may not be those who pay for the improvement. As we shall see, this may be important.

Lastly in this kind of argument, as it stands, one ignores a factor which is perhaps the most important of all. We do not ordinarily invest in any project unless the rate of return expected is greater than the cost of borrowing (the rate of interest). This neglects one important dimension: the amounts of funds available. It is often convenient to assume that private firms are able to borrow as much money as they can profitably use at market rates of interest. But this will not do when we think of the sources of funds for public investments. Moreover roads have not been the only neglected part of the public sector. No doubt one could present arguments why money should be invested in education, particularly technical education, hospitals and prisons, for example, as strong as those for investing in roads. Making sense of the transport problem is part of the general problem of making better sense of public investment. This is another reason why it is necessary to break down the global figures and consider projects on their merits, so as to be able to compare their claims for funds with those of roads and other objects of investment. In particular this kind of simple solution avoids meeting the question whether it might not in some instances be as, or more, desirable to invest in other forms of transport, perhaps even the railways.

The fallacy in the similar argument that we should invest to eliminate accidents is still more obvious. It is suggested that we should capitalise £200m. as the annual cost of accidents. Without questioning whether this is the true value of road accidents to the community, £200m. is 6 per cent on roughly £3,300m. Again it is suggested that any sum less than this is worth investing. But it is not hard to see the fallacy. The validity of the argument depends on the proposition that any sum less than £3,300m. would eliminate the cost of accidents, that is get rid of road accidents altogether. But that is absurd. It is most unlikely that there is any possible level of investment which would make our roads accident-free. Therefore this sort of solution is much too simple an answer to the question: what should we invest in accident prevention?

Solutions Based on International Comparisons

These will not keep us long. The only available statistics — like many transport statistics — are inadequate. First, it is not possible to make comparisons over any length of time because the information is not available. Second, the definitions on which they are based appear to vary from one country to another.* The values showing total expenditure on roads (maintenance, improvement and new construction) as a proportion of gross national product at market prices, given in Table 1, cannot be relied on in detail but they are quite accurate enough to demonstrate one point without fear of contradiction. This is that the United Kingdom spends a lower proportion on roads than does any of the other countries listed.

*This is certainly true of a comparison which is often quoted of the ratio of investment in roads to Gross National Product in various European countries, which are rendered almost worthless because of this variety in definition.

Table 1.1 Total expenditure on road network including maintenance

Expenditure on roads as proportion of gross national product at market prices. The figures to the left of the double line are average figures for the year shown. Figures to the right of the line are from a different source and are not strictly comparable. Present statistics do not permit representation of comparable series over this period of time. There is also a problem in that countries do not always define expenditure on roads in the same way. It is therefore necessary to take these figures as as rough indications of the proportions spent.[10]

* Not available				† 1953-4 only.		

Country	1950-2	1952-4	1953-5	1956	1957	1958
Sweden	1.34	n.a.	1.74	n.a.	n.a.	n.a.
Luxembourg	1.25	n.a.	1.57	n.a.	n.a.	n.a.
Switzerland	0.93	n.a.	1.18	n.a.	1.19	1.39
Finland	n.a.*	n.a.	2.48	n.a.	n.a.	n.a.
Denmark	1.11	n.a.	1.24	1.49	1.45	1.33
France	n.a.	1.16	n.a.	1.05	n.a.	n.a.
United Kingdom	0.71	n.a.	0.71	0.55	0.60	0.66
Norway	n.a.	1.39	n.a.	n.a.	n.a.	n.a.
West Germany	1.08	n.a.	1.31	1.48	1.62	1.50
Ireland	1.51	n.a.	1.96†	1.94	1.85	1.64
Austria	1.61	n.a.	1.79	n.a.	n.a.	n.a.
Italy	n.a.	n.a.	1.22	n.a.	n.a.	n.a.

But we have no means of deciding from these figures what percentage of our gross national product we should spend on roads. Let us assume first for the sake of argument that these figures are comparable, referring to exactly the same items. It would be wild surmise to suppose that the right solution to our road problem would be to keep up with the Joneses, that is, to aim at some mean derived from these percentages. This would be a particularly absurd policy, because none of these countries are more rational in their road economics than we are. Their figures are arbitrary. They happen to be higher than ours. They may suggest to us that we should increase road expenditure. But that we know already. They cannot be used sensibly to fix a percentage of gross national product to be spent on roads.

Besides, such facile comparisons ignore possibly important differences in national circumstances:

(a) *Countries with a lower density of population might spend more per head on transport and roads than countires with a higher density;*

(b) countries with a higher real income per head might spend more in certain forms of road transport and therefore require more roads;

(c) since the total demand for transport is comparatively inelastic, countries where road building (and railway building) is expensive, because of the terrain, might spend and invest more per head of population;

(d) conversely the building and magnificence of motorways has been governed to some extent by motives of prestige in many countries, therefore countries in which labour and land are cheap might tend to spend proportionally more on this;

(e) countries with national or regional unemployment might spend more on roads as unemployment relief;

(f) countries with a relatively good though now old-fashioned road system currently might spend less proportionally on road investment*;

(g) this low investment might also occur in countries which have inherited a relatively large railway system.

In considering the proportion countries spend on their road systems it is also relevant to consider:

(h) different design specifications laid down as Government policy and

(i) relative road and railway rates – also partly determined by Government policy – in their effect on the proportion of gross national product spent on road transport and therefore on the road system.

Last we might mention:

(j) particular factors affecting the expenditure on roads of different countries, for example one would expect Western Germany to have invested more than usual in recent years because of the north-south realignment of her communications resulting from partition. [11]

These are only hypotheses: the data do not exist to check them. Unfortunately international road comparisons are in their infancy. All we need say is that it would be remarkable, when due allowance is made for national differences, if any group of these countries have the same need for roads. None of these reservations affects the general conclusion that these comparative figures indicate that the United Kingdom is spending a surprisingly small proportion of gross national product. But they do indicate it would be absurd to base the proper size of expenditure by comparison with what is spent abroad. The

---

*This hypothesis, it might be thought, could be tested by relating road milage possessed by countries over the years to the proportion of gross national product spent on road investment. OEEC states that the figures of road mileage cannot be used for this purpose because of the different ways in which roads are classified and in some instances different definitions of what constitutes a road.

sensible conclusion is surely that international comparison is no substitute for working out our own needs and policy.

SENSIBLE SOLUTIONS TO THE RAIL PROBLEM

Most of the objections we have made stand against the equivalent rail solutions. We may treat these briefly and in general terms.

The Largely Arbitrary

The amount of money which it was decided to invest in modernising the railways in 1955 when the modernisation plan was set going was arbitrary in the sense which means most economically. 'The British Transport Commission are convinced that an efficient and modernised railways system is essential to the economy of the country . . . This plan aims to produce a thoroughly modern system able to meet both current requirements and those of the foreseeable future.'[12] It was fixed as the sum which the commission estimated was needed to modernise the railways. The only economic check was that it was then believed that this investment overall would yield a 5 per cent rate of return. Since then the Government has had second thoughts about its wisdom in authorising the plan. (We will consider the modernisation plan further in Chapter 5.)

Quite often one comes across statements of a comparable crudity which say that the country must have a modern railway system judged by certain standards of efficiency and technological progress. Both kinds of argument are open to the same objection. They do not inquire whether the money could not be spent more profitably in some other way, roadbuilding for example.

Solutions Based on International Comparisons

One also finds arguments that investment and modernisation are lagging behind in the United Kingdom as compared with some other countries. As with roads we may wonder what conclusion to draw from such comparisons. Again most other countries do not have any better thought-out railway policy than we do. And there are also some special points to be made. (a) The operations which are included within the definition of a railway and those which are performed by outside bodies under contract vary considerably from one country to another and affect these comparisons. (b) The cost of operating railways varies considerably between countries. (c) The advantages of operating railways 'especially in relation to distance between stops' vary between countries and differently in respect of freight and passenger traffic.

Solutions Based on Internal Predictions

It is more dubious to argue that investment in railways should be a constant proportion of national income or of expenditure on rail travel. The first begs the question whether the railways should be allowed to decline. The second will be met by the rejoinder that investment is needed to win traffic back to the railways.

It is also beside the point to argue that there has been under-investment in the railways over the past half century. Once it might have been the case that more railway investment would have paid off and put the railways in a much stronger financial and competitive position than they are in today, though such investment was inhibited by the illogical system of railway legislation in force and, perhaps, by the undue timidity of the old railway companies. But this is irrelevant to decisions which must be made now — bygones are bygones.

SUMMARY

There is, however, no simple economic solution to the road and rail problem. The policy we adopt must depend on the overall policy we choose, and this is the most difficult aspect of our problem.

A decision must be made on what criterion nationalised transport undertakings and formulators of the road programme (which, though not formally the responsibility of a nationalised industry, raises the same question) are to be required to adopt to decide the output of goods and services they produce, the prices they charge and the investments they make. This is a difficulty that cuts deeper than the economics of transport alone, many of the factors affecting the decision being general considerations concerning the policy a public enterprise ought to pursue. To what end the Government and other public authorities engage in transport and the provision of roads? Efficiency? But what does it mean here? To further the public interest? What does that mean? To be commercial, some might suggest where, because of economies of scale or other reasons for fearing monopoly, or historical accident, private enterprise cannot, will not or must not be allowed to do the job. Others would argue that the function of public enterprise is to behave in some sense differently from private firms, and that this should be reflected in pricing and investment policy where appropriate. Various policies which can be offered as motives for nationalisation are considered in the next chapter. Two of them are selected because they appear at present to have considerable support from public opinion and to be particularly relevant to the transport problem. These are designated our basic criteria. The argument of the rest of the book is developed on the bases of making the alternative assumptions that the nationalised transport undertakings and road programme should be required (a) to maximise profits, possibly subject to certain constraints, and (b) to maximise consumers' surplus.

Anyone who is prepared to accept the one or the other as a basis for working out a solution to the transport problem either because he is already persuaded or is ready to take the argument on trust, may omit the next chapter and proceed to Chapter 3, where the relationship between the two criteria is examined. Anyone who believes that profit maximisation is the proper policy for the railways may find what interests him in Chapters 4, 5 and 8, omitting Chapter 7, where the problem of defining and using a consumers' surplus criterion for the railways is discussed. Anyone who is ready to accept consumers' surplus maximisation for the road system on the grounds that a commercial policy is not feasible, whatever its underlying theoretical foundation may be, will find what interests him in Part III, omitting those passages, if he pleases, where an attempt is made to devise the machinery by which the operation of the road system could be made commercial.

In Chapter 12 another change is rung to make our basic criteria four: profit and consumer's surplus maximisation each with competition, or coordination of transport.

POSTSCRIPT

There are many figures in this chapter which could have been up-dated; and in some cases more recent instances could have been taken of some of the fallacies criticised. However, the point of the chapter was to criticise the rationale of such arguments which are made no less wrong by up-dating. I have confined myself to adding more recent figures to fig. 1.1, and to adding some more recent figures (Table 1.2) to supplement Table 1.1. These show that no longer is Britain bottom of the league![1]

The chapter's opening sentence and a number of statements throughout the book suggest that ten years ago it was obvious there was under-investment in highways. As the revised fig. 1.1 shows, the increase in highway expenditure has continued to grow rapidly. It is far less obvious that there is now under-investment and more probable, especially in Scotland, the North, and in many towns, that the return on marginal investment is too low. This cannot be proved. The fault is neither the public's nor the academic's, but

30

Table 1.2 Total Expenditure on Road Network including Maintenance

Expenditure on roads as proportion of gross national product at market prices. The figures are from various sources and are not strictly comparable.[1]

Country	1967	1968	1969	1970	1971
Denmark	1.79	1.92	2.14	2.00	1.66
Ireland	3.89	3.55	—	—	—
France	1.39	1.38	1.36	1.40	1.42
West Germany	2.29	2.10	2.17	1.67	1.35
Great Britain	1.38	1.51	1.62	1.69	1.58
Italy	1.09	1.17	1.03	1.15	1.11
Norway	2.80	2.79	3.11	—	—
Sweden	1.87	1.81	1.57	1.55	1.45
Switzerland	3.05	3.01	3.02	3.17	3.22
USA	1.77	1.89	1.68	1.80	—
Japan	2.29	2.16	2.11	—	—
Australia	—	2.20	2.12	2.16	—

the Government's. In the last seven or eight years much has been done to improve and apply more widely techniques for highway investment appraisal (see the postscript to Chapter 11). It is possible to know the return on inter-urban road schemes and in an increasing proportion of cases they are calculated. But they are not normally published so that no one outside is able to judge the economic return on schemes. Neither is there any published back-checking of predictions. The calculation of urban rates of return is more complex but what evidence there is suggests that at least in very large cities the return on large schemes are low and that if one could quantify the environmental impacts these would on balance also be negative.[2]

A much more comprehensive analysis of highway costs was done in *Road Track Costs*.[3] It is interesting to compare the range of costs given there for 1965/66 of £625m. — £450m. (depending principally on how capital was treated) with the British Road Federation figures for that year of from £360m. — £380m. The *Road Track Costs* figures were:

Table 1.3   Public Roads Costs 1965/66

	£m Current Expenditure basis	£m Public Enterprise basis
1a Capital: New roads and major improvements	179	—
1b Capital charges	—	390
2 Maintenance	96	
3 Cleansing	23	
4 Lighting	9	
5 Policing	52	
6 Administration	40	
7 Accidents	15	
Total: Current Expenditure Basis	450	—
Public Enterprise Basis	—	625

But no Government annual series is available on this basis.

2 THE POLICY OF A PUBLIC ENTERPRISE

POST-WAR EXPERIENCE

It is difficult not to oversimplify our experience of nationalisation since the Second World War and only too easy to be partisan, but I think it would be generally agreed it has been something of a disappointment to those who were its advocates. The principle of nationalisation has been attacked by non-socialists and some socialists.[1]

Socialists who still believe in it passionately draw a distinction between it as it is, and as it ought to be to realise the wider aims of socialism. Disappointment — or relief — is not inconsistent with the opinion that nationalisation has succeeded in a more limited sense. Most authorities agree that it has made possible the rehabilitation of the fuel and power industries, that the Atomic Energy Authority and the nationalised airlines and many of the fringe nationalised industries are not inefficient: the BBC, British Road Services, the Bank of England. But this achievement looks less impressive than it would have done between the wars, because private industries have made equal or greater strides in efficiency. If we ask why most private firms are more efficient than they were then, the most important reason is full employment and the confidence and prosperity created by it. Scarcely anyone would now claim nationalisation as a panacea for industrial inefficiency; on the contrary, many would claim that nationalised industries tend to be less efficient than private firms.

If we consider the problems in efficiency which have replaced those of the inter-war years, we do so largely in terms of the rate of growth of firms and national income. Again there are two schools. Some blame our low rate of growth principally on the comparative inefficiency of some industries. This school tends to argue that harder work, better management, fewer trade union restrictions, better industrial relations and possibly more scientists and business education are needed. The second school — not all socialists — believe that some more planning is essential to coordinate investment plans and control the distribution of income. Both had their counterparts before the Second World War but, by contrast, nationalisation does not now have a real place in either of their programmes. Only a small wing of the second school argue that there are industries which should be nationalised in the interests of efficiency, and these are usually industries especially important for investment — machine tools, because of their low importance in the capital goods industries, and insurance, because of its command of enormous funds for investment. But the great majority of both schools would think nationalisation irrelevant to these problems of national and industrial efficiency; because, as Alan Day has said, 'the true commanding heights, in these post-Keynesian days, are held by any government which is willing to use its power to tax, its power to spend and its power to tell people not to do things'.[2]

The non-socialist — and socialist — arguments for nationalisation to control monopoly have also declined in influence. There has been a realisation over the last thirty years that it is not that there are isolated pockets of monopoly in an otherwise freely competitive economy, but rather the reverse: virtually all firms have some monopolistic advantage. Nationalising firms with monopoly power would mean nationalising most firms. Furthermore, hostility to monopoly has declined greatly. To achieve economies of mass production and distribution, firms have tended to grow until there are too few firms in most markets for effective competition. Many would argue that competition would not be worth the sacrifice in efficiency that would follow the splitting up of large firms; and many might argue that large firms are not 'irresponsible' in this sense, especially if scrutinised by a vigilant monopolies commission. Even those non-socialists who are most aware of the dangers of large monopolies scarcely ever nowadays advocate their nationalisation.

Neither is it difficult to see why the specifically socialist arguments for nationalisation have been disappointed. Nationalisation has not brought about significant equalisation of income. Taxation has. Industrial relations are no better than in private industry. Neither are they different in kind. Working conditions are not better than in private industry. Workers in nationalised industries are just as moved by the profit motive. They are not keener on participation in management. They get no more satisfaction from their work than workers do in private industry. There has been no radical change in the type of directors appointed. Nationalised industries are no more egalitarian than private industries. Although managements get lower salaries than in private industry, there is less equality than one would expect from socialist principles. Nationalisation has not abolished income from capital, because shareholders were compensated by the issue of Government stock. It has also been argued that nationalised industries are more amenable to Government control than private industry.[3] Private businessmen are not as 'irresponsible' as they used to be because they know it pays them to cooperate with the Government's economic policy to some extent; while chairmen of nationalised industries have sometimes been able to get their own way in spite of Minister or Parliament. It is significant that the Conservative Government feels that it has to interfere more often in the running of the nationalised industries to impose its will than the Labour Government did.

Nationalisation, in short, has failed to achieve its wider aims and, in disappointing most of the hopes of its friends, it has also disappointed most of the fears of its enemies. If one takes this as the last word, then one is likely to be led to the opinion that it really does not matter much what policy a nationalised industry is required to adopt and that it might as well behave as a private firm, that is, be commercial.

But even considering the wider aims of socialism and national efficiency, this view can be challenged. A nationalising socialist might argue that nationalisation has not been tried and found wanting, but that it has not really been tried. Very little thinking had been done on ways and means when the Labour Government came to office in 1945 committed to nationalisation. 'I immediately took up the task of preparing legislation for nationalisation of the mines' (Emanuel Shinwell has written in a frequently quoted passage). 'The miners expected it almost at the wave of the ministerial wand. The owners were hardly less anxious to get out of the pits — on terms. For the whole of my political life I had listened to the party speakers advocating State ownership and control of the coal mines and I had myself spoken of it as a primary task once the Labour Party was in power. I had believed as other members had, that in the party archives a blueprint was ready. Now as Minister of Fuel and Power I found nothing practical and tangible existed. There were some pamphlets, some memoranda produced for private circulation and nothing else.'[4] Other schemes of nationalisation suffered from similar lack of preparation, which meant delay before nationalisation could be put into effect. During the few years between nationalisation and 1951, when Labour was replaced by a Conservative Government, nationalised industries were fully occupied in administrative reorganisation and internal technical coordination, and were too busy to attempt any wider aims. By 1951 the opportunity was lost. Other nationalising socialists might argue nationalisation has not been given a chance because not enough industries were nationalised. These are some of the ways in which a socialist might argue that, despite recent experience, nationalisation is still a necessary or desirable means of achieving socialist aims; but to be convincing he would first have to answer two objections: his socialist opponents' objection that a government can impose its will without nationalisation because it occupies the 'commanding heights'; and the objection of those further to the Left that neither our society nor our State is minded to be socialist, and that the apparatus of public ownership has adopted the motives and behaviour patterns of a propertied ruling class. So to extend nationalisation would not change the distribution of power, the motivation of individuals and class differences, but only their outward form. Nevertheless, it is possible that nationalisation may come back as an essential ingredient in somebody's well-thought-out plan to achieve socialism, and it would be rash to assume that it will not. But at present it is, I think, reasonable to maintain that nationalisation does not have this importance in socialist thinking, despite the current (June 1963) greater prominence given to nationalisation in Labour Party polemic.

It would also be rash to assume there will never again be support for non-socialist or socialist nationalisation, in the interests of national efficiency. As we have seen, both socialists and non-socialists who believe that more planning is necessary to get us out of our present troubles tend to argue that a modern Government has all the political power it needs to enforce its economic policies. It is probably true that a Government now has all the power it needs to cure unemployment though we have not had a slump to prove it. Fortunately it is in almost everyone's interests that there should be a high level of employment, so that one would expect Government policy to gain cooperation and be easily enforceable once it is understood. But it is not the same with the problems which are now crucial. It is true that a higher rate of growth of national income is in some sense in most people's interest. Inflation is in the interest of some and, with any known cure for inflation, as soon as any means of attaining it is suggested, a conflict of interests is disclosed; some sections will be hurt, others benefited. The same is true of the correction of balance-of-payments crises. The measures taken are not in everyone's interests. And in recent years monetary policy has turned out to be rather disappointing in its results. It is not at all clear that the Government holds the heights which command those problems which matter most. Now it may happen that we will be able to improve the kind of controls the Government is using, but it is also conceivable that it will not be possible to solve these problems effectively without some extension of public ownership. A nationalised concern is potentially more amenable to Government direction than any private firm. The issue would arise whether further nationalisation was too high a price to pay to solve the problems of inflation and payments crises, just as it was once an issue whether Government intervention of a Keynesian kind was too high a price to pay for the elimination of unemployment. If the issue were to present itself, and it would be a rash man who would be sure that it would not, then once again many non-socialists might favour nationalisation. At present these are all open questions.

Now if we were to believe nationalised industries had some special contribution to make to national policy, whether in terms of national efficiency (the maintenance of full employment, the rate of growth, balance-of-payments problems, etc.) or to some other social end, then it might be that we would require some special definition of benefits, costs and appropriate rate of return of the kind to be described in the next chapter. If it seems sensible, and I have argued that it is, to make the *interim* assumption that a nationalised industry has no special contribution to make, then we do not need to postulate costs and benefits or a rate of return which departs from normal at least for those reasons. This exclusion simplifies our problem.

We could say that this elimination of special criteria is justified by public opinion but for one point: this is that the Government does make special use of the public sectors in one respect. As it happens this seems to be a most unfortunate discrimination. When the Government wants to restrict excess demand for consumption or investment goods in the private sector, it uses some mixture of the following policies: raising the bank rate, open-market operations, letters to bankers recommending that they restrict overdrafts, the calling in of special deposits from the commercial banks, payroll taxes, etc., and some direct controls restricting credit, notably on hire-purchase. But in the public sector the Government makes direct cuts in investment, requiring nationalised industries to reduce or postpone their investment, and it can also prevent prices and to some extent wages rising in the public sector in the interests of an anti-inflationary policy; whereas it does not do either of these in the private sector. In effect this means that Government policy bears much more harshly on the public sector than on the private. Government control of private investment and consumption is at present comparatively ineffective. Government control of the public sector, especially of the nationalised industries, is effective.

All that need be said now is that there has been an additional cost, in the sense of the argument of the next chapter, which has had the effect of retarding investment in the public sector and causing it to lag behind that in the private sector. This result is not obviously in the public interest. Once upon a time it was argued that much Government investment, particularly in roads, could be postponed until it could be made as a Keynesian corrective to a slump. This has been a reason for holding back certain forms of public investment, particularly in roads, since the Second World War. But we have not had the slumps in which public investment could catch up so as to keep its place in economic growth. If we do not have significant cycles, we should not try to manipulate major programmes of public investment as a counter-cyclical measure. To cut public investment more than private investment in the boom, without any compensation in recessions, means that public investment does not make up on the recessions what it loses on the booms. There seem to be two sensible views on this problem, and we do not here have to decide between them. The first is that since it is unnecessary to treat the private and public sectors differently to achieve the national economic objectives in question, the same policy should, as far as practicable, apply to both. The second postulates that it is necessary to put a specially severe brake on the public sector to achieve certain national objectives. On this assumption, the Government should compensate the public sector, and particularly the nationalised industries, by a balancing incentive to invest more at other times so as to maintain the required rate of growth (one way of doing this would be by adjustment of the interest rate at which the public sector borrows).

Although the Government still treats the public sector differently in this respect from private industry, Government thinking has recently come round more to the view that this kind of interference is to be avoided if possible. The 1944 White Paper on employment stated that 'for the purpose of maintaining general employment it is desirable that public investment should actually expand when private investment is declining and should contract in periods of boom'. Commenting on this the 1960 White Paper on public investment said that 'there is a large proportion of public investment where it would not be sensible to try to engineer short-term variations in momentum to match changes in economic circumstances as rapid or as relatively mild as those experienced in recent years.'

With the possible exception of the control of investment, our elimination of special factors seems to be justified by the present state of public opinion, but it is exclusion of the wider aims of nationalisation which has brought many people to believe that it does not really matter too much what policy a nationalised industry should be required to have, and therefore it might just as well be commercialised. This is to ignore the choice still left to us—a narrower range, but not unimportant. Because there are still many possibilities it is essential that we should again simplify our discussion, and this we will do once more by calling on public opinion. There are, so to speak, only so many basic policies 'in the air' which command serious support. Four seem worth considering. We will reject two and keep two.

PRESENT ALTERNATIVES

The first opinion which is still heard is that transport, or more often just the road programme, should be run as a public service. In ordinary usage this term is vague. From all the ideas which hover about this concept we want to single out the essential. It is surely not that we should think that work or management in a nationalised industry is more honourable than in a private firm.[5] It is not just that we expect the quality of the service or product provided to be better or the industry's honesty to be greater. Public service does not seem to be synonymous with a policy of running an industry in the consumers' interest (see p.41). Neither, though this is getting closer to the root conception, is a nationalised industry a public service because it lets just a few groups of consumers, perhaps the aged poor or country-dwellers, have their service at less than cost − a partial departure from the basic policy which we will consider below. A public service is surely one in which the basic policy is to provide all its services or products at less than cost, possibly even free. Typical examples of a public service are the National Health Service and education. Government undertakings which are not in this sense a public service are the General Post Office and the nationalised industries.

A service can be provided at less than cost or even for nothing and yet its output and investment policy can be determined by economic considerations. On the other hand a public service might imply the provision of some service of which the standard is determined solely by non-economic criteria. For example it might be said that a certain standard of health must be maintained whatever the cost. There is no need to explain why, if the undertaking is sizeable and the standard is pitched moderately high, it is often impossible to maintain this absolute value above all economic considerations. We do have to decide at times whether a limited amount of resources should be spent on health or on something else, and so depart from an absolute valuation.

The argument against running any part of transport as a public service in this sense is straightforward. First, there is no self-evident reason why people should be encouraged to use more transport than they can ordinarily afford, or why any section of the community, the rich possibly through taxation, or the road-user or ratepayer or anyone else, should subsidise the use of transport in general or some form of it in particular (though there are intelligible arguments why health, education, the police, or even labour exchanges should be subsidised, whether one agrees with them or not).

Second, a public service policy is likely to confuse the whole nature of the transport problem; for, even if it should be decided that there is some reason for providing transport below cost, there is no obvious reason why any one form of transport should be favoured in this respect. Traditionally it has been the custom until recently to provide roads at less than their cost to the road-user. If the Government were to subsidise roads now and not subsidise railways this would be unfair to the railways. The distribution of traffic between the two would not be related to differences in cost but would be affected by a difference in treatment, which I suggest it is hard to justify intuitively. The same, of course, would apply if railways were in this sense treated as a public service and not the roads.

Whatever policy we adopt for one there is surely a strong case for adopting the same policy for all forms of transport. Therefore it would be wrong to treat one branch as a public service and another differently. But there is no obvious reason for treating any transport as a public service. Therefore the assumption is made in what follows that users of transport are to pay the total costs of their use of transport facilities as far as is practicable. There may be good reasons for running certain transport facilities as public services for certain people but that is a separate question.

A policy which was once popular in socialist thinking and has been revived recently is that a nationalised industry should be run by and for the workers in it. This is a form of public enterprise which can be found for example in Yugoslavia. Let us try again to catch the essential conception here and translate it into costs, benefits and rates of return. One would expect a concern which was run in the workers' interest to maximise its profits, so far as it was able, like an ordinary profit maximising firm, though of course its profits would be distributed among the workers and not among the shareholders. An efficient firm adopting this policy would therefore be one which maximised its profits. Its policy might however diverge from that of a private profit maximising firm for either of two reasons. First, there might be payments it makes on behalf of its workers which a private firm would regard as costs but which it classes as benefits, or it might have to choose between investment opportunities where the real cost differed for labour because of differences in discomfort, difficulty, etc. It is therefore possible that in choosing between investment opportunities such a firm might decide differently from a private firm if the alternatives were weighted differently in this respect.

Secondly, history shows that workers' co-operatives tend to think only of themselves and not to consider the interest of workers elsewhere. Translating this into more precise terms, we might have the rule that the firm should act as to maximise the profits for its present labour force. A situation might arise when a private firm would make one investment which would necessitate the hiring of additional labour and a firm following a workers' surplus policy would make another more profitable to the existing labour force. Normally one would not expect to find an important divergence from ordinary profit maximisation for either of these reasons. Because it is more unlikely that such a policy would be required of any nationalised industry, and also because of its closeness to ordinary profit maximisation, we will not give it separate consideration.

We now come to those two policies which seem to me to be the most worth considering and making precise. The first is that which would seem to be implied in the actual way in which most nationalised industries have been required legally to conduct their business. The break-even principle was originally produced by Sidney and Beatrice Webb as the correct way in which to run municipal trading. Most of the Acts setting up postwar nationalised industries, including the setting up of the British Transport Commission in 1947, contained a clause requiring them to break even over a period of years, taking one year with another.[6] They were not forbidden to make a profit, but the interpretation put on the Acts has been that they should not. In general they should anticipate a profit by lowering prices.

This policy has been taken to be the normal and natural one for a nationalised industry, almost without question. We can see how a socialist might reach it unquestioningly just because of his objection to the profit motive. Another argument for this policy is that it appears to rise naturally from the anti-monopoly reason for nationalising industries. Such industries must be nationalised, it used to be suggested, because they are so large that they are able to exploit the consumer and make monopoly profits. Therefore it might seem that the Government would be breaking faith with the public if it continued to make profits after nationalisation. Neither of these arguments appears logical. Private profits may be an evil, but these should look different when they accrue to the State when they can be used for the public good.

These traditional reasons for requiring nationalised industries to break even perhaps have little to recommend them. We can nevertheless give a simple and direct justification. This is that it is a policy of running an industry in the consumers' interest. There are no shareholders. When costs have been met, all the benefit is passed on to the consumers in the form of lower prices. This, one can say, is how consumers receive their dividends, if there are any dividends to pay. This is a policy which seems sensible and intelligible to many with no need for further justification.

This is a policy which is compatible with the retention of some profits to form reserves. The reason for holding a reserve is to meet unforeseen contingencies. It can be argued that it is just as important for an industry pursuing this policy to have reserves for this reason as it is for a private profit maximising firm. If it has no reserves and runs into difficulties it must borrow or raise its prices to meet its obligations. A reserve is therefore a protection of the consumers' interest, just as it protects the shareholders of a private firm.

It is a policy compatible with the use of profits for self-finance. When a private firm decides how much of its profits after tax to distribute and what proportions to plough back in investment it decides what is in the shareholders' best interest. We can imagine the board of a nationalised industry faced with a similar decision. It must decide whether in its opinion it would be more in the consumers' interest that profits should be passed on to the consumer now in the form of lower prices or whether they should be reinvested to make yet lower prices possible in the future (or to forestall or diminish a possible rise in prices because of expected increases in costs).

This policy does not conflict with any obligation a nationalised industry may have to pay interest on borrowed money, for this is one of its costs. And we are assuming that the policy we have in mind requires the industry to meet its costs, taking one year with another. There is a rate of return appropriate to this policy which will be described in Chapter 3 as the consumers' surplus rate of return. This is the rate of return which is logically implied by the notion of running an industry in the consumers' interest, making on balance neither profit nor loss. It is more difficult to calculate than a profit maximising rate of return. Nevertheless it is possible to make some reasonable approximation. If we have our rate of return, we have our measure of efficiency. An enterprise which has this policy is at its most efficient if there is nothing more it could do to increase the consumers' surplus caused by it, just as a profit maximising firm is at its most efficient if there is nothing more it can do to increase its profits. Measures for increasing consumers' surplus or profit are of course change in output, change in prices, buying more cheaply, making use of new techniques, improving management, employing more scientists or improving the organisation.

What we have said in this last paragraph is the most important point of this chapter for, if we have a rate of return and a measure of efficiency, then this makes it possible to clear up the confusion which has made the policy of nationalised industries so incoherent since the war.

It has been realised since the beginning that one must gauge efficiency in public and private enterprise in different ways. One can say that a private enterprise is efficient by looking at its balance sheet and at its profits. One cannot do this with a public concern. More often than not a wrong reason has been given for this difference. This is that one cannot tell if a monopoly is efficient by looking at the dividend it is able to pay out; because as we have seen when considering railways in the nineteenth century, a railway may be inefficient in the sense that, if it were more efficient and no legislation forbade it, it could make larger profits than it does. Yet its monopoly position enables it to declare a dividend. But it is not because a nationalised industry is a monopoly that one cannot tell if it is efficient or not. It is simply that it is absurd to judge the efficiency of a consumers' surplus enterprise by the standards of a profit maximising firm. The reverse would also be absurd.

The realisation that the profit maximising test of efficiency would not do in the public sector has led several writers to look for indirect tests of efficiency. Many methods have been suggested of measuring and correcting the efficiency of nationalised industry meant to be run on a break-even principle. But all have been necessarily imperfect. They fall into two classes. The first calls for the use of non-economic indexes of the type considered in Chapter 1 — anything from the time taken to get an answer to a letter to, more sensible but scarcely less wrong-headed, measures of output per head or per unit of capital employed, or others based on such inter-industrial or international comparisons. Sidney Webb was one of the first to consider the problem, writing that 'what is needed is the systematic organisation with regard to each nationalised industry of comparative statistics of output or results in the various parts of the service, of detailed costing, of continuous test audits and of sample inspections; and with all this there should be associated not only the organised study of analogous administrations but also original research into the subject matter with a view to new discoveries.' But as one commentator has said, 'so far as we know nowhere did he quite say what he proposed to measure and how he proposed to measure it. And that is still the problem'.[7] As we have noticed, these are imperfect substitutes for an economic appraisal. They have a long history. There may we let the matter rest. Such tests are not analogous to profit maximisation as a test of performance. They are not designed to yield any rates of return. They do not make the distinction needed between investment and reorganisation opportunities.

The other type of test does not make this mistake, but is no more helpful because it is vague or incoherent. To give an example of a policy or test for nationalised industry which was only superficially valid, Professors Florence and Walker argued that some profits were compatible with, and were some test of the efficiency of a nationalised undertaking. (They argued, however, that the word 'profit' because of its overtones should be replaced by 'surplus'.) They then said that any surplus was acceptable provided it was not the result of exploitation, that is, monopoly power; but, as we will notice, all profits in an economic sense are made possible by the existence of some monopoly power. No monopoly, no profits. They also argued that the money costs used in nationalised industry accounting must 'not neglect social costs' but, as we will see in the next chapter, it is not practicable to consider all social costs, nor possible to decide what are to be counted social costs without choosing a policy. As it stands the proposition is vacuous.[8] The so-called 'policy' is vacuous unless it be interpreted to mean, against its authors' intention, that a nationalised industry should not make profits. Since its point is that the making of a surplus is some indication of efficiency, the test fails utterly. It becomes no better than the many declarations which state simply that a nationalised industry is to be run in the 'national interest', a turn of phrase which, as Professor Robson has said, is 'so vague a concept that it can be extended to cover almost every conceivable reason for granting or rejecting or modifying a proposal.[9] Neither has clarity of official expression improved. Consider the *Reorganisation of the Nationalised Transport Undertakings* White Paper. Nationalised transport 'shall be *soundly* based both in organisation and finance providing *efficient* services to industry and the public, and giving a *good* livelihood and *worthwhile* jobs to those who work them . . . The *practical* test for the railways as for other transport is how far the users are prepared to pay *economic* prices for the service provided. *Broadly* this will *in the end* settle the size and pattern of the railway system . . . increases in railway fares and charges must, *where and when appropriate,* make their *due* contribution *towards* meeting railway costs . . . As an *essential first* step, there must be radical changes in the organisation, financial structure and statutory framework.[10] All this vagueness typical of such statements proceeds either from inability to make up one's mind or from a failure to appreciate that if an industry is to be run in the consumers' interest then the appropriate rate of return must be used. The principal task of the next chapter will be to clarify what is meant by a consumers' surplus rate of return.

We can attribute much of the inconclusiveness of thinking about the problems of the nationalised industries to this confusion. It explains partly why the problem of accountability has dominated the discussion. If we have not decided what is meant by the public interest, or by the interest of the consumer, there will be a tendency to shift the problem so that it becomes one of who should share responsibility for the nationalised industries, and to what extent. Frank Pick said that politicians were irresponsible as interpreters. D.N. Chester has suggested that some solution of the problem would be to transfer power from the boards of nationalised industries to the Civil Service: 'Were the business manager to be told that as a general rule he must be guided by something called "social" or "public" policy rather than by production costs I cannot but feel that he would be rather out of his depth. The Civil Service is organised for that kind of decision, business management is not.'[11]

Yet the Civil Service has come no nearer to a working definition of the consumers' interest than anyone else. Others see the solution in terms of more ministerial or parliamentary control, for example the setting up of select committees or broadening of the scope of questions which Members of Parliament can ask about the nationalised industries. Another suggestion has been that the powers of consumer councils and consultative committees should be increased on the grounds that since they are meant to represent the consumers' interest they will find the proper formula for satisfying if empowered. It has also been suggested that the Central Transport Consultative Committee should be made responsible for the overall examination of the British Transport Commission's operations and for assessing their efficiency.[12] However there is no evidence of their effectiveness in this respect. In any case, in so far as the problem of accountability arises from inability to formulate an agreed notion that nationalised industries should be run in the consumers' interest, this defect is easily remedied by explicit recognition of such a policy. It should be no more difficult for a nationalised industry, however it is organised, to follow a consumers' surplus maximisation policy or any other expressed in the terms of the next chapter than to follow a profit maximisation policy.

Another effect of this inability to *formulate* any policy other than profit maximisation has been a gradual edging of public opinion towards the view that nationalised industries should be 'commercialised', tenable in itself, but often this has been combined with a view that they should not maximise their profits. For example, let us suppose that British Railways has been revived by closing lines and modernisation, so that it makes a profit after it has paid its capital charges. If this were the case many would argue that prosperity should be passed on to the consumer rather than go as a dividend to the Treasury. Let us suppose that this advice prevails and that the average rate per passenger mile is reduced from $3d$. to $2d$. By intention this is less than the railways could get for their services. In other words they are paying a subsidy of a penny a mile. In this situation it would be ridiculous to compare the rate of return on the railways' capital with that earned by a private firm which did try to maximise its profits. Now let us suppose that it is asked whether some station should be modernised and a rate of return is worked out on the investment. Part of the return is to come from lower costs of operating the station. This will yield a 4 per cent return on capital. Another part will come from passenger business. The yield arising from that is expected to be 5 per cent — 9 per cent in all. If we were then to compare the rate of return on this investment with one of equal risk contemplated by a private firm on which the return was expected to be 10 per cent we would be comparing the incomparable. It might be the case that the rate of return would go up to, say, nearly 12 per cent if the passenger rate per mile were increased to $3d$., which we will take to be the rate which would maximise profits. Then we would be comparing like with like, but to compare the 9 per cent and the 10 per cent is plainly absurd, since British Railways by assumption has chosen to charge less than it could. Many arguments supporting the commercialisation of the railways are illogical in just this sense.

Last, there is the alternative that a nationalised industry should be run commercially in the strict sense, that is that it should also attempt to maximise its profits. There is much that can be said for this view. An influential section of public opinion is moving in this direction. The profits would go to the Exchequer, who would use them to reduce taxation or increase Government expenditure. The public sector would then be an estate from which the Government would draw income. The public would be benefited as taxpayer, rather than as consumer. If the nationalised industries were to adopt this policy straightforwardly one would expect that their prices would rise; but, if this were balanced by cuts in taxation, the change would not be inflationary. If it were used to finance extra Government expenditure then it might have inflationary effects, because consumers feeling the effect of higher prices might pass it on by demanding higher wages or raising the prices of goods they sold. On the other hand if it were decided that the public was ripe for increased Government expenditure then it might be more feasible than higher taxation. At present it can be argued that consumers of the products and services of nationalised industries are being specially favoured, indeed this is what a consumers' interest policy means, and that it would be preferable for the community to gain according to some other distribution of the benefits of lower taxation or higher Government expenditure.*

One type of objection to this policy which needs to be overcome is that nationalised industries would make exorbitant profits because of the high degree of monopoly they possess. Here we need to make these points only:

(a) If this were so, there would be less need to worry about their size since the profits would go to the Exchequer.

(b) If their profits were judged exorbitant there would then be justification for some restriction on their freedom to make profits. (This point will be developed further in Chapter 12.) It is not an argument against their making any profits.

(c) It is doubtful if there is a higher degree of monopoly in the nationalised industries than there is in the bulk of private firms of comparable size. Gas, coal, electricity and oil compete for most purposes. Various forms of transport — private and public — compete, so that the danger of making so-called exorbitant profits is exaggerated.

*It cannot be argued that everyone gains from low prices for the products of nationalised industries because their cost enters into everything. Even if it were the case, for example, that the cost of transport were strictly proportional to the value of product throughout the economy, we could not assume that a lowering of the cost of transport would benefit everyone. We may suppose a firm which is in some monopoly position. Its costs fall for this reason. It will lower its prices somewhat but some of the benefit will be retained in the form of higher profits. So the benefits of a low cost of transport may not be spread evenly.

Lastly we must mention that the economist has another conception of the consumer's interest which does not imply average cost or break-even pricing, but marginal cost pricing.

Marginal cost pricing is the answer economists have usually given to the question: 'on what principle should the economic policy of a nationalised industry be based?' Nationalised industries are criticised by economists in so far as they depart from it. Even those economists who have been most aware of the theoretical difficulties and the possible ethical and political objections to it have tended nevertheless to use it as the basis of the practical advice they give. The principle implies if the price of any product or service is greater than its marginal cost, increase output until they are equal; if the price is less than marginal cost, reduce output until they are equal. The marginal cost of supplying something is the total addition to the expenses of an enterprise resulting from the production of the last (marginal) unit of output. As will be argued later it can be shown that any other pricing policy than marginal cost pricing involves a welfare loss. In contrast the equality of all prices to marginal cost is a necessary condition for the optimal allocation of resources. This will result in overall consumers' surplus maximisation for the economy as a whole, in that no possible change in the use of resources (or in pricing) could result in a higher level of real income. This is beyond dispute (though there is no reason why a lower level of real income should not be preferred if it implies a more politically acceptable distribution of of income.)

While many economists have favoured marginal cost pricing – while recognising theoretical difficulties – it has found almost no acceptance among practical men or politicians. In some cases it implies public enterprise making a profit, in others a loss and in others breaking even.*

What has happened therefore is that where marginal cost pricing would have implied profits as in coal, all the objections to its use were those we have listed above as those which have been made to profit-making and the profit motive. Where marginal cost pricing would imply a loss one gets the more pragmatic objection that 'every tub

*Where there is an increasing-cost enterprise – costs increasing more than in proportion to an increase in output – then marginal cost, as defined, will be above average cost. Therefore total revenue (marginal cost x output) will be greater than total cost (average cost x output) and the enterprise will make a profit. It would perhaps be easier to persuade a government to use marginal cost pricing if this should imply a profit, though in the past even with this expectation it has usually been unacceptable, for example in the case of coal. The difficulty arises when marginal cost pricing implies permanent subsidisation of an enterprise. In a decreasing-cost industry, as the railways are often held to be, in which costs rise less than in proportion to output, average cost will be more than marginal cost.

should stand on its own bottom', that is, a common sense judgement that whatever economists may say it is simply wrong, immoral and discouraging for management if all costs are not at least met from receipts.

While there will be further discussion of the economist's case for marginal cost pricing, the objection to using it as the guiding principle for solution of the transport problem is that there would seem to be no chance of its political acceptance.

If the real reason for rejecting marginal cost pricing is that there seems no chance of its acceptance by Parliament or public opinion, the sensible course of action is surely to select some basis, or bases, acceptable to substantial bodies of public opinion and draw out their economic implications. This is the method adopted in this book. It means taking a view on the strength and direction of public opinion. It is not, I think, particularly about transport policy that there is a difference of opinion on what is required of a public undertaking. The controversy is about what policy should be required of nationalised industries in general. It is here that the fundamental difference of opinion lies and where we must pick and choose among alternative policies before we can begin to think out a logical solution to the transport problem.

Various arguments have been given in this chapter for not adopting a policy other than *profit* or *consumers' surplus maximisation* as a basis for arguing the solution of the transport problem. Profit maximisation is the ordinary or conventional criterion of the textbook. We know or can easily find out what rules an enterprise should adopt so as to attempt to maximise its profits, but it is necessary to demonstrate that consumers' surplus maximisation is capable of formulation as precise and as useful. In one form and another, this will be the principal topic of Chapters 3, 6 and 11 and of those parts of Chapters 9, 10 and 12 concerning consumers' surplus maximisation. To some demonstration of the nature and resolution of this problem we now turn.

POSTSCRIPT

Post-War Experience

The biggest change since 1963 is the decay of our optimism in our ability to control the economy. The 'heights' are not so easily 'commanded'. Yet that aside, I do not find too much I want to change. Richard Pryke has argued that the achievements of the nationalised industries in increasing their efficiency have been under-rated.[1] He does not argue this of the railways. Stuart Holland has pointed to the Italian Institute for Industrial Reconstruction (IRI) as an example of how a government can use public enterprise to promote investment regional policy and other political initiatives.[2] The IRI may be imitated in Britain by a state holding company set up to maximise profits, subject to all these political constraints, but even in Italy the more traditional public enterprises are not expected to profit maximise. On the left there is ten years later as much a resurgence of interest in nationalisation as there was in 1963, but it still remains as true that it has to be demonstrated how, as they have developed in Britain, nationalised industries can become instruments of left-wing socialism. In spite of the intentions of the Heath government in 1970, there has been little de-nationalisation and much more extension of the public sector. There has been no serious attempt to work out what would be implied for its economic objectives of introducing workers' control on the Yugoslav model for any part of any British nationalised industry. In the economic literature there has been considerable research into the pricing and investment criteria of such enterprises.[3]

The belief that taxation either has been, or easily could be, the sole instrument needed to redistribute income now seems over-optimistic. There has also been much more interest in the use of public enterprise to redistribute income, though again most of all in underdeveloped countries because of the difficulties of redistribution there through fiscal means.[4] In Britain as elsewhere there has been growing interest in the redistributive impacts of major transport investments especially in cities where the poor often tend to lose more environmentally and through undercompensated relocation; and also from the withdrawal of rural rail services and the general decline of bus transport.[5] One must be careful to distinguish between myth and reality. Those that benefit from unprofitable branch railways are generally far from among the poorest. The case for subsidising such services in practice tends to be much more that those concerned have a right from precedent for such a service, and will use their political influence to enforce this, irrespective of their income which in many cases may be inversely related to their political power. Concessionary fares to the old in cities may be efficient and need not be in effect a subsidy. Many of the proposals for flat fares, and no fares for urban transport, confuse efficiency and distribution arguments; and in general the major beneficiaries of such proposals would not be the poorest. Those who will gain most tend to be those whose journeys are longest and those who commute furthest.

Present Alternatives

Leibenstein has argued that in general what he calls X–efficiency is more important than allocative efficiency.[6] By this he means that the loss of efficiency from misallocation of resources at the margin tends to

49

be small compared with the gains in technical efficiency which can be produced by technical innovation or otherwise in increasing the physical productivity of factors of production. Richard Pryke has adapted the same arguments to claim the relative unimportance of financial deficits and low rates of return in public enterprise.[7]
This amounts to a more sophisticated revival of the arguments used by the Webbs and by Professors Florence and Walker. To some extent there is a false antithesis.

Technical progress can achieve much greater improvement in efficiency than ending to equate marginal rates of substitution and transformation. But they do not have to be alternatives. An enterprise can attempt both.

However much it may have increased its technical efficiency an enterprise unable to sell its output at a price which will provide an adequate return on capital cannot demonstrate that its consumers value is enough to make an adequate return possible. Over-investment of this kind in one industry within a sector may have a serious effect in distorting the pattern of consumption. It may destroy the market for its rivals even though in the long run investment in its rivals would have proved more efficient. To argue that attempts to improve allocative efficiency actually hinder the achievement of X-efficiency requires more empirical testing than has been undertaken.

Marginal Cost Pricing
The original wording was too strong against the possibility of marginal cost pricing; though experience at the time did suggest that there was little hope of persuading government to adopt it. However during the 1960s marginal cost pricing came more into favour — especially in electricity where a highly inelastic demand made market pricing unfeasible without the possibility of earning very high monopoly profits. Thus a principle of (long-run) marginal cost pricing was adopted plus a mark-up to avoid losses since electricity supply is a decreasing-cost industry and would otherwise make a profit. An apparent success for the marginal cost pricing principle was the 1967 White Paper on the financial and economic objectives of nationalised industries which recommended it as a pricing rule. Even so the wording of the recommendation is obscure, particularly when it discusses the possibility that the principle could imply persistent deficits.[8] The argument that 'each tub should stand on its own bottom' still seems practically compelling. Neither are increasing cost nationalised industries allowed to earn profits.

As a result of attempts to hold back nationalised industry prices as an instrument — almost certainly of little actual effect — to check inflation, more and more nationalised industries are making losses, being forced into them by government policy.

When a civil servant I was also surprised to find how strong was opposition to nationalised industries profit maximising. Though their statutory objectives do not prevent them making as large a profit as they can, I found widespread the belief that this was an improper objective for public enterprise, even where it was clear the nationalised industries had little monopoly power.

The need in principle to agree pricing and investment rules for public enterprise expected to break even and not to engage in cross-subsidisation remains important. Therefore the interest and importance of a consumers' surplus maximisation policy for public enterprise remains. This is what is attempted in Chapter 6.

What has made it easier to accept MC pricing as a basis for transport policy are changes in our understanding of the relevant facts:

1. As will be discussed in the postscript to Chapter 4, if railways were to have efficient investment (and disinvestment) policies there would not be the scale economies as implied, for example, by the footnote on p.47.

2. Similarly, as will be discussed in the postscript to Chapter 10, the probabilities are that the road system in most countries will *on average* be subject to increasing costs, though this will depend on the proportion of urban roads. MC pricing on roads overall is unlikely to imply a loss, except in rural undeveloped countries, but it may imply a profit.

3. Various authors have shown that a short run MC pricing policy with prices reflecting congestion will break even — if associated with an efficient investment policy — when there are constant returns to scale; will make a profit where there are increasing costs, and a loss only when there are decreasing costs. Because both road and rail — under efficient investment policies, approximate to the first — or in the case of roads — the second of these, but not the third, there are less likely to be practical objections to MC pricing.

This means that one can define consumers' surplus maximisation as approximately compatible politically with MC pricing. That the highways are not organised as a statutory public enterprise may help on this as there may be less inhibition against their earning profits. But of course should MC pricing lead to politically unacceptable deficits or profits, then the considerations of Chapter 6 will again become relevant to transport policy.

3 THE BASIS FOR AN ECONOMIC SOLUTION

Popularly economic problems are supposed to be alike. They are to do with making money and avoiding money loss. Actually they do not have to conform to this pattern though it is of course the usual one. An economic problem is a choice between alternatives: How much investment? Where? How many trains? When? The most profitable level of fares? How wide a road? What level of petrol taxation? etc. The ordinary impulse is to look for the most profitable alternative: the most profitable investment, the most profitable number of trains run at the most profitable spacing in time, the most profitable level of fares . . . And then one wonders if one is starting to talk nonsense . . . The most profitable width of a road? The most profitable level of petrol taxation? It is natural to believe there is no *economic* solution to a problem if all possible ways out of it would result in money loss. If it is decided, notwithstanding the certainty of loss, to say, modernise a railway, on this view the economic solution is to select the least unprofitable method of doing it.

We are so accustomed to commonsense economics, and rightly, that it is tempting to assume we cannot use the apparatus of economics, costs, revenue, rates of return, etc., unless we are discussing economic problems narrowly defined in this fashion. That is wrong. Economics may be used to work out the logical implications of any policy fulfilling three conditions. The policy must be, first, consistent and, second, well defined so that there is no doubt as to what are defined as the advantages, or *benefits,* and disadvantages, or *costs,* to be accounted for in coming to a decision. (For example, profit maximisation is a fairly definite policy. 'Serve the public interest' is so indefinite that it is practically useless.) Third, it is convenient if these advantages and disadvantages — benefits and costs in economic language — can have a money value set on them. We do not need to inquire in what circumstances, if any, this kind of measurement is not possible. If we know what are to be accounted benefits and what costs, if these can be given a money value and if the classification is kept consistently then we draw up the profit and loss account appropriate to the policy and to the situation.

It may seem a paradox, but it is not their status as benefits or costs — revenues or expenditure — which determines their place to left or right in a profit and loss account.

Their place in the profit and loss account determines their status as benefits and costs. They are normally drawn up on one principle. They can be drawn up on others. Profit maximisation, which common sense calls commercialism, is one possible policy. To adapt a phrase of Alfred Marshall's for modern times: 'profit maximisation is the leading' – because most familiar – 'species of a large genus'. A few of the other species are interesting and important in their own right, particularly when we have public enterprise in mind.

It is here that we need a general theory of the principles of economic decision to help us. We must examine the meaning of what the textbooks call economic rent or surplus in general, and in one of its manifestations: monopoly profits. This excursion into theory is not a digression. Rather it is a necessary stage on our journey. The approach is practical and is intended to rough-out an apparatus through which can be made rules as precise in an economic sense as those which state the ordinary commercial principles of profit maximisation. It is normal to draw up the accounts of a concern – private or public – as if its purpose were profit maximisation. If its aim is not profit maximisation, this is illogical and can be confusing. A result of our argument will be to indicate the method by which accountants should attack the problem of drawing up the accounts, especially the profit and loss accounts, of these abnormal enterprises.

The approach is sensible because it asks the right question. The right method is not to lay down some universal law such as 'long-run marginal cost pricing' or 'long-run marginal social cost pricing', which are dogmas resting uneasily on unsafe foundations. It is to get behind such maxims and ask the first question first. 'In whose interest is the enterprise to be run?' The second question is: 'If there is more than one party, how are the interests of the several parties to be combined (weighted)?' When we have decided these we then develop the appropriate set of rules. We will find that to serve someone's or some number of persons' interest, when a money value is set on it, is to attempt to maximise a rent – a surplus of some benefit over some cost. This is definitional.

RENT, SURPLUS AND ECONOMIC INTEREST

We can illustrate more easily what is meant by economic rent if we begin by a distinction: (1) On the supply side we have rents (or surpluses) gained by factors of production; (2) On the demand side we have consumers' surpluses (or rents). The old division everyone knows between supply and demand is a convenient expository device. By describing (1) and (2) separately, the fundamental similarity of all forms of rent is more easily demonstrated. We will use rent and

surplus synonymously. The common, though not invariable, usage —
rents on the supply side and consumers' surpluses — has historical
significance only.

Rent

If we want a single name for all species of rent on the supply side,
the most illuminating is *factor rent* since they all are gained by
factors of production. The archetypal form of rent is land rent. In the
economic sense rent is the difference between the payment a
landowner gets for his land and the least he would receive rather than
let it go out of cultivation. If all land were of the same quality, and able
to satisfy all purposes equally well, every acre would simultaneously
gain the same rent *or* would be on the margin of cultivation gaining
no rent *or* would be disused. Rents vary because land varies in quality
and convenience — nearness to markets, suitability for building etc. —
and this is why we are able to talk with some plausibility of the existence
of marginal land. If the demand for land rises, more land is brought
into use somewhere in the world and it becomes profitable to invest
more capital and labour on land where it has not been worth it before.
If demand falls some land goes out of use and other land is used less
intensively. Rent does not enter into the cost of production of the
produce of land — crops, buildings or anything else — since intramarginal land would be used in the same way if it were to become
marginal. Truly in this sense rent is a surplus, not a necessary cost.

We have considered land rent in what might be called the large sense.
It is useful to look at it also in a smaller. In the large sense the rent
on a piece of land is the difference between its market value and
the marginal value. In the small sense it is the difference between its
market and next best or alternative use values. If the income received
from land in one use should decline and fall below the alternative
use value, it pays to change it to that alternative use. Let us assume
that initially railway operation is the most profitable use of a certain
piece of land. There is a change in circumstances, the demand for
railways falls in that place and the railway income from that line
declines. If the decline is sufficient it becomes worth while at some point
to convert the railway into, let us say, a road — the alternative use.
If someone maximises his rent in the most profitable present use for
his land in the small sense he will simultaneously be maximising rent
overall in the large sense.

In summary, rent is gained by land, first, because of the superior
profitability of some land over land at the margin; second, because of
the level of demand for land, which determines the margin. These are
necessary but not sufficient reasons for the existence of rent. Third,

land must be scarce. If there were enough land, if it were what economists call in infinitely elastic supply, rent would be at most a temporary gain. Its existence would be a sign to other landowners that it would be profitable to come on to the market and compete the rent or surplus away. Rent is possible in so far as competition is absent. Competition does not compete rent away because land is fixed in amount.

If we ask why rent accrues to a certain class of persons, this is because they own it. Rent could accrue to others: to a peasant cooperative, to moneylenders or to the State through taxation. It is in the interest of landowners, or of anybody who receives rent, to maximise it. That is the definition of their economic interest as landowners. They may have other interests — everyone has more than one economic role — which can conflict with their interest as landowners.

Rent can be obtained by the owners of other factors of production which are scarce under the same conditions. This needs no elaboration. Anything — iron ore, a railway engine, a patent, labour or capital — can earn rent.

There are the monopoly profits gained by a firm. With perfect competition these would not exist. A firm gets the profit or a quasi-rent because of an unexpected boom in demand or because of some new technological process it has invented or acquired. Other firms enter the market and compete this profit away. Competition will continue until profits are normal. Competition will also reduce differences in profit from one industry to another. Firms will leave the industries where profits are lower than average and enter where they are higher. Thus there is a tendency for equalisation of a rate of profit at the level of normal profits. These are named misleadingly. Normal profits are to a firm what the margin of cultivation is to a landowner. If profits are subnormal it will pay a firm to find an alternative use for its resources or go out of business. If profits were everywhere subnormal, and this were expected to persist, it would pay part of the economy to revert to a pre-capitalist type of production. It is as confusing to call normal profits simply 'profits' as it would be to call the earnings of marginal land 'rent'. True profits are always monopoly profits and always rent. It is because competition is imperfect that monopoly profits exist. It was characteristic of the classical economists that they saw economic existence as a war between two forces. On the one side there were men and firms trying to maximise profits and, on the other, there was competition working inexorably to reduce these profits to zero. They saw the world as a battle-ground in which firms struggled to keep alive. Contemporary economists see the economy as less of a battle-ground, less competition and more monopoly profits.

It is therefore possible to talk about firms attempting to maximise profits, their producers' surplus to use another term, without seeming to suggest that they are striving after an *ignis fatuusi,* something they could never permanently possess. Nowadays there are many frictions and institutional arrangements that impair the workings of competition.

Consumers' Surpluses

On the demand side there are consumers' surpluses. Their definition is very close to that for factor rents. It is the difference between the price someone pays for a thing and the most he would pay for it, given that his income does not change. The consumers' surplus on a particular railway journey is the difference between the fare the traveller pays and the most he would pay rather than forgo the journey. If we think of any commodity or service on the market it is almost certain that there are some marginal purchasers of it. If they buy one unit only they would no longer consume the commodity or service if the price rose. If they buy more than one, they would buy less, giving up those on which they had no surplus at the old price. Everyone must make marginal purchases, buying things on which he has no surplus. This is quite certain. Let us suppose some railway fare goes up and that a particular traveller had a surplus on the journey. He will pay the increase. His income has not changed. He must cut some expenditure elsewhere to find the money; and he will cut down as far as is necessary on marginal purchases, where he has no surplus. It might be a less important railway journey, but it could be anything: saving, smoking or buying the *best* quality bulbs for his garden. It follows that there is always something that a person buys on which he has no surplus, simply in the sense that faced by a price rise among the things he buys, he would give it up. It is marginal to him. And this is, of course, not only true of private consumers. All entities with money to spend — governments, firms, etc. — have consumers' surplus. It is a necessary consequence of their having priorities, an order of preference, governing what they buy. A consumer who gained surplus on nothing he bought would be someone utterly indifferent to what he bought, or living at subsistence-level.

We have a large family of rents or surpluses about which, to generalise our argument, we can make three connected propositions. The first is that all rents can be expressed either as a difference between actual payment received and the least payment beneath which the factor would not stay in that employment or as an analogous difference between what is actually paid for something and the most the consumer would pay rather than go without. The second is that no rent or surplus is gained in respect of something or somebody that is in perfectly elastic supply. Third, it is possible for a more powerful entity to expropriate what was initially another's rent or surplus. This was what Karl Marx called exploitation, which he saw principally as the exploitation of the proletariat by capital. But anyone who gets a rent which might be someone else's is an 'exploiter'. It could be exploitation of the landowner or worker by the Government, the exploitation of a retailer by a wholesaler. It is just another effect of monopoly power which enables someone to expropriate another's surplus. Since there are always many interests whose owners *could, mutatis mutandis,* be the beneficiaries from any source of rent, if rent exists, then exploitation in this sense must always be present. The social problem is to decide who is to be the beneficiary, 'the exploiter', and then see if the social will can be imposed at this point.

We have in this notion of surplus, or rent, a useful apparatus for clarifying and formalising economic policies. Any economic policy is meant to be in the interest of someone or a number of people in one or more of the roles they play. Therefore by assumption it is intended to maximise a rent or some nexus of rents. Rent maximisation is the very meaning of economic interest. Rent or surplus is benefit received less the cost involved in receiving it. If benefit equals cost then the person is on a margin of indifference, whether it be between life and death, or between moving to a job in Messrs X and staying on the railways, or between driving to work and going by bus, or whatever else it may be. Our classification of kinds of rent is of course incomplete. There is a surplus which describes every man's economic interest for every part he plays in economic life. And there are all the surpluses relevant when the economic interests of individuals are compounded in groups. The family of surpluses is infinitely large.

From a family of surpluses we can draw a family of surpluses criteria with which to make economic decisions, of which profit maximisation, the maximisation of one kind of producers' surplus, is the most familiar: a special case of a general possibility, a policy motivated only to maximising one kind of rent.

PROFIT MAXIMISATION

When a firm sets out to maximise its profits this is equivalent to an admission that the only beneficiary of its operations in which it is interested is itself *as* profit-maker* The actual beneficiary or beneficiaries may have different identities. In one firm the entrepreneur

---

*The profit maximising rule is that a firm should fix price and output so that marginal cost equals marginal revenue. This is often explained by use of the equivalent of fig. 3.1. (Compare with the consumers' surplus maximisation diagrams of Chapter 6.) We assume a firm selling one commodity at a single price.

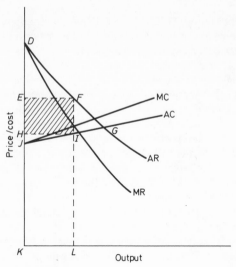

FIG. 3.1: Profit maximisation

Output is measured on the horizontal axis, costs and prices on the vertical. AR is the average revenue, or demand curve. (AR equals total revenue divided by the number of articles sold which equals price.) From the standpoint of the firm it describes the price to be expected from the sale of any given output. AC is the average cost or supply curve. (AC equals total cost divided by the number of articles produced.) It shows the average cost of producing, and the lowest cost at which a firm can sell, without a loss, a given output. The AR curve is falling from left to right, which is the normal assumption: a fall in price is needed to sell a larger output. Another way of saying the same thing is that marginal revenue is falling. (MR is the additional revenue earned by selling an extra unit of output.) It falls because price must fall to sell an extra unit of output. The MR curve can be derived from the AR curve. (It is the partial derivative of it in respect of an output change.) Similarly the MC curve represents the addition made to total cost by producing an extra unit of output. In our example average cost and therefore marginal cost is rising, meaning that it costs more to produce every additional unit of output than the one before. But in any given case, the AC curve might be constant or falling; or have different segments of falling, constant and rising costs. The curves in the diagram have been drawn for a hypothetical enterprise. In fact their slopes will depend on the particular circumstances of an enterprise, but such a diagram can in principle be drawn for any enterprise. The assumption does not have to be made that it knows exactly what its demand would be at any given price or its costs at any given output. The AR and AC curves represent the best guesses it can make and the MR and MC curves are derived from them.

It will maximise profits if it sells the output, *KL,* at the price, *KE; EFIH* is the largest rectangle which can be inserted in *DGJ* and represents (price × output) minus (average cost × output), or in other words the greatest possible *difference* between total revenue and total cost. Thus the profit maximising price and output is determined by the intersection of the MR and MC curves. This can be proved — but it should be intuitively obvious. If a firm has more than one product, each selling at a single price, the analysis is the same. It will maximise profits if it sets MR equal to MC for each product.[1]

58

will be himself the owner: profit-maker and profit-taker. In another profits are distributed to shareholders. If it is owned by the State one expects profits to go to the Exchequer. What matters from our point of view is that all other payments are costs and that the only costs which go into a profit maximising firm's balance sheet are the money costs it incurs in its operations. The only benefits counted are money receipts. The surplus of receipts over costs is profits. The surplus expected to result from an investment can be expressed as a percentage rate of return on capital. The most profitable investment is that which is expected to yield the highest rate of return. We will follow traditional usage and call the costs a profit maximising firm takes into account private costs; the benefits, private benefits; and the profit maximising rate of return it uses to decide if a change in its price, output or investment policy would pay, the private rate of return. All commercial profit and loss accounts, whether the firm follows a profit maximising policy or not, are drawn up on this basis.

The principal topics we need to remind ourselves of in connection with profit maximisation are these. We will have to revert to them later when we consider the policies of British Railways and the road programme.

Profits

The dividend paid on ordinary shares should be the same as the rate of return in the profit maximising sense on the firm's capital. But profits as recorded in a profit and loss account are not the same as profits in a profit maximising sense. Some part of profits goes to the Government in taxation. This is in the economic sense a cost of being in business, though it is computed as a proportion of profits. True private profits in the economic sense are bookkeeping profits less tax. Another part of profits will often be put to reserve. Although this reduces the amount of profits distributed to shareholders, this is compatible with profit maximisation. One must ask why a given amount is put to reserve. If it is a profit maximising firm one would expect to hear one of two things:

(a) The reserve is needed to meet unforeseen contingencies. Without a reserve the firm runs the risk of being caught short in an emergency. This would cost it more in the long run than the cost of providing a reserve. Therefore it is a profitable insurance to keep such a reserve. It is of course possible that a given firm would maximise profits if it kept a smaller reserve than it does, or a larger depending on the circumstances of the case.

(b) The reserve is needed to meet foreseen contingencies, for example to pay for capital investment. The question which arises is

whether it is more profitable for a firm to keep reserves or borrow for this purpose, a question which can generally be settled by considering the firm's credit and the state and likely future of the money market.

In most firms another part of profits will be ploughed back as investment. Although it reduces the sum immediately distributed to shareholders this may maximise their profits in the long run. If the firm has a profit maximising policy which it follows consistently, this must be its intention. In the long run shareholders will gain from the investment. The only question is whether it will pay the firm — and therefore its shareholders — to borrow the money needed for investment on the money market or to plough in undistributed profits or in what proportions to do both. A profit maximising firm will make this decision so as to maximise the returns to its present shareholders in the long run. Indeed profit maximisation may be compatible for a time with the payment of very small, or even no dividends.

Production Costs

All other payments are costs — private costs. This means that such a firm will purchase what it needs in what it believes is the most profitable way for it. It will pay more for efficient labour rather than less for less efficient labour if it thinks this will be more profitable. It will raise the conditions of work of its labour force — build canteens, shorten hours, concede wage demands — if it thinks that these will be in the long run the most profitable course of action for it. A profit maximising firm may therefore pay high wages and give its workers the very best working conditions, short hours, etc., if it thinks that the alternatives — strike, slackness, a less cooperative labour force, a higher rate of labour turnover — would not pay as well. On the other hand it might decide that it would be profitable to pay low wages and provide bad working conditions. The right policy depends upon the facts of the case. The proper contrast is with firms who, for example, believe that wages and the conditions of labour should be bettered even if it should mean lower profits; and firms who refuse wage increases and improvements on some principle of not giving in to 'unreasonable demands' even if a 'moral stand' should lead to the sacrifice of some profits.

Costs of Increasing Revenue

Profit maximisation is not the same as revenue maximisation. This is a point which most businessmen know well but which has

60

sometimes to be pointed out to their critics. For instance a firm can without doubt improve the quality and scope of its costings and demand analysis, and the speed with which its statistics are forthcoming, by introducing an electronic computer. Thereby it can increase its revenue. But the decisive factor should be whether the expected increase in revenue will be greater than the increase in cost from hiring or buying and using a computer. On a much less complicated level the same argument is relevant. Quite crude calculations can maximise profits. A shopkeeper might set prices by mark-up, adding X per cent to the cost of all the goods he sold. It would be tempting to advise him to mark up prices more on those products where he had less competition to fear from rivals (the demand was inelastic) and by less where competition was greater (the demand was elastic). In almost every case this should increase his receipts. But the cost of making the better calculations might not make them worth while. When we come to consider improving the costing machinery of the railways and the demand analysis of the roads programme we will have to bear this two-sidedness of the problem in mind. It is a point particularly foreign to public enterprise which is often made to indulge in expensive and unprofitable costings.

Time and Reinvestment Opportunity

The same sum realised next year and ten years hence has not the same money value. Therefore, it is necessary that decisions involving time should be properly discounted. An enterprise has a choice between two investments. The first will realise X million pounds in 1964. The second will realise X million pounds in 1974. The first is worth more than the second because of the opportunity for reinvestment: X million pounds invested in 1964 at compound interest − the relevant procedure − will be worth more than X million pounds in 1974 whatever the rate of interest. Its exact value in 1974 will depend on what happens to the rate of interest during the next ten years. If it rises the value of the investment will rise. If it falls the value of the investment will be less. If it were possible we would want to know the exact pattern of interest rates to come. Then we should be able to work out the value of any investment, any part of whose returns accrue in the future. Since we cannot know this, the best we can do is to take a view discounting the future by those interest rates which we think will be the likeliest to obtain and which determine the opportunity cost of private firms. The further we peer into the future the more arbitrary our choice of discount rate will be.

Choice of Means for Achieving Profit Maximisation

Profit maximisation is a definite enough policy, but its adoption does not mean that anyone confronted by the identical facts in the same situation of choice must come to the same decision; as it would do if the selection of, say, alternative A was the only course a profit maximiser could take or be judged illogical or mistaken. The decision to be made may vary on one of two grounds: (1) a different valuation of uncertainty, and (2) a different valuation of time.

(1) We do not know the future. We use our experience of the past to try to predict it. On the basis of experience different men will vary considerably in their predictions of supply and demand conditions for the sale of any commodity or service. Because people and firms evaluate uncertainty differently they will frequently make different decisions in similar circumstances and yet all be sincerely bent on maximising profits. A pessimist will chose differently from an optimist, an experienced man from a novice, a practical man from someone who has his facts from books.

(2) Take a case where two men are faced with similar investment opportunities. In the discounted sense (as discussed in the previous section) they will both realise the same value of money over their lives. In one the stream of profits will be greater in the earlier stages. In the other it will grow towards the end. Therefore, although the discounted value will be the same and, by a mixture of borrowing and reinvestment it should be possible to realise the same income at the same time on either investment, yet the difficulties of borrowing and reinvestment may be such that an investor may have what is called time preference.[2] If he has *negative* time preference, money today will be more valuable to him than money, properly discounted, in the future. If he gave a reason he might say 'enjoy yourself while you are young', or 'tomorrow I might be dead'. If he has *positive* time preference he may believe he will grow wiser and that against his present inclinations, it would be better if he were provident. He would rather, let us say, have a pound in his old age than a guinea today. If he had to choose, that would be his preference. The rate of time preference to be selected by a society is an ethical problem of the first difficulty since it raises the problem of 'our generation's duty to the future'. How much should we forgo consumption today to make it is possible for our descendants to enjoy a higher standard of living? There is no consensus of opinion on this question except, perhaps, on avoiding extremes. Few would argue that we should tighten our belts so severely that, by our savings and exertions, our children will be able to enjoy a standard of living several times our own, though this degree of sacrifice seems standard in many Communist countries. Neither would anyone think it right for us to take no thought for the

morrow by consuming as much as we can and investing very little.

Last, we are not of course talking about what people and firms do, but about what they could do. Once upon a time it was thought that profit maximisation was the self-evident, only possible policy for an enterprise to adopt. It was held everyone acted from self-interest and therefore this implied logically the maximisation of his rent or surplus. For the landowner this was held to mean screwing the most rent he could from his tenantry. For the worker this meant bargaining for the highest level of money wages his bargaining position enabled him to exact. And for a firm this meant exacting any monopoly profits it could. For more than a century it has been realised that this is an economist's fiction. Many factors do not seek to maximise their money rent. This may be because they are not wholly selfish, but take other rents or surpluses than their own into account. Or because they are incompetent: they would maximise their profits if they could. Or because, while they are acting in their own self-interest, the ordinary private classification of benefits and costs misrepresents this self-interest. They are not interested only in maximising their money surplus. One possibility is that a man sets a value on a quiet life. The ordinary method of striking a profit and loss account on this occasion would exclude a decisive cost. On the debit side should go the valuation he sets on leisure and peace of mind, and any other relevant facts. These have a money value which can be discovered by a process of self-examination. The highest value he could set on these things would be *infinite*. This would mean that no increase in salary would compensate him for these non-pecuniary disadvantages, costs. Literally, he would rather die.

OTHER 'COMMERCIAL' POLICIES

A firm may have some end in mind other than profit maximisation. It is not germane to our argument to ask whether it ought to — whether, for example, if it is a joint stock company, it is not thus defrauding the shareholders. We accept that some firms do have other objectives. Someone investing money in such a company is quite logical if he is interested only in its prospects of profits, as it is presumably his sole interest to maximise the rate of return on his capital (straightforwardly as income or indirectly through capital appreciation). But the firm might be illogical if it did this. We take an example. There is a firm which regards the dividend it pays out not as a surplus but as a payment determined largely by what other firms pay. The firm is in fact run from our point of view in the interests of its management. We suppose that such a firm has a choice of two investments properly discounted for risk and time preference.

Investment A is expected to yield 15 per cent on a profit maximising basis, investment B to yield 12 per cent. A profit maximising firm would choose A. But our firm, if it is logical, should draw up the estimate for the investment in a different way. There are other costs and benefits which should appear, others possibly which should disappear. For example it can fairly be represented that the work of management in implementing B is more responsible and that as a result more management will be needed and top management will have to be paid more. B is also more attractive to management because it will be pleasanter for it: for example, it may involve pleasant travel, a pleasanter place to work in, more entertaining, or, if they are so minded, less travel, less entertaining. All these would appear in an ordinary commercial reckoning as costs. Here they might rightly be classed as benefits. Depending upon the amounts of these non-private benefits and costs and the weights given to them, B may or may not be preferred to A. Clearly the rate of return that is relevant is not the private one, but some other; and this possibility is often recognised in practice, though people making such decisions do not usually go to the extent of drawing up a special – the logical -- profit and loss account, or still less of estimating a precise numerical rate of return. (That is *possible*. Just as we can set a money value on someone's estimation of leisure and peace of mind, so a money value can be set on these things also and by the same method. If a money value can be attached, then it is possible to express the relative advantage of one investment over another as rates of return. What would be nonsensical would be to have some policy other than profit maximisation and yet let a profit maximising ordinary private or commercial rate of return dictate one's investment policy.

These are slight deviations from profit maximisation, but radically different economic policies exist, which can be logical and perfectly acceptable to those who accept the values on which they are based; where the usual apparatus of private benefits, costs and rates of return is wholly irrelevant.

THE SOCIAL SURPLUS CRITERION

We may as well turn at once to the policy that is often put forward as if it had some absolute value. An objection to profit maximisation and to other policies we might consider is that they leave out many categories of *social* benefit and cost and are therefore *incomplete*. It is often argued that these social elements should be taken into account: sometimes it is suggested that both private and public enterprise *ought to* allow for them; more frequently it is said that, although one cannot expect private firms to do so, public enterprises should because they are agents of society. That is why they ought to take into account all social benefits and costs, whoever gets or suffers them, wherever practicable. Similarly, when we have in mind an investment, the proper rate of return should allow for social benefits and social costs, the surplus of social benefits over social costs being expressed as a percentage rate of return on the investment. To use a social rate of return is, it is contended, to act in the interest of society (usually one's country) as a whole. Just as profit maximisation aims at maximising the profit, rent or surplus of a firm, so the use of this rate of return aims at maximising the profit, rent or surplus of society.

Take any economic event as an example: for example the upward revision of fares by a bus company. The private benefit is the rise in receipts the company hopes to get. Social benefit is any benefit (increase in surplus or rent) whoever gets it. *Private* is therefore a special case of *social* benefit. If the bus company were a profit-maximising concern the only private benefits it would recognise would be increased cash receipts. If it were not strictly profit-maximising, it might recognise benefits private to itself, such as an increase in leisure which, as we have seen, can only be measured indirectly. Similarly social benefits other than private ones can be direct money gains. (Let us suppose that one result of the fare increase is to cause a number of people to buy a car which they would not otherwise have bought. One effect of this could be to increase employment amongst car workers. From our point of view this is a social benefit, one accruing to someone other than the bus company, and it is a straightforward real gain.) or they can be benefits, other than cash, whose value has to be fixed, as we have seen, by self-examination: how much would I be ready to pay rather than go without this good thing which has happened to me? (Let us suppose that a result of the fare increase is that some buses are less crowded. It may be a trivial example but, in mass, this kind of thing can be important. There is a passenger with varicose veins who can now always find a seat. How much is this worth to him? Possibly considerably more than the increase in his fare.)

It is safe generalisation to say that nothing happens in economic life which does not create some benefits (and costs for that matter) other than private ones. We could choose many examples from transport. Their importance is particularly marked when we consider roads. As payment for use of the roads is made at present, the private benefit to the highway authority of improving a crossroads can easily be nil or negative. Receipts from petrol taxation can fall as congestion lessens. But there will be beneficiaries.

Neighbouring shops may gain because of an increase in trade. Pedestrians may find crossing safer. Road-users save, among other things, petrol, tyre wear and time, which is money. In a sense the community may gain in ways which are not always immediately obvious. For example a police car or an ambulance reaches its destination more quickly. If the improvement is beautiful or just more beautiful this will confer a social benefit, measurable, it must be insisted, by what those who value it — private person, local council, arts council — would be prepared to pay rather than make do with something uglier — if the machinery existed to make them pay.

Social costs have the same relation to private costs that social have to private benefits. The bus companies' private costs appear in its account. An upward revision of fares will cost it something in tickets and publicity at least. The social costs of the change are any costs borne by others. Because of an increase in fares some desert the buses for private cars and increase congestion on the roads. This is a social cost and may have some repercussions. An important rise in fares will affect prices and rents and surpluses throughout a large part of the economy.

Again we can find many other examples where transport is the cause of social costs. There is the noise of a marshalling yard at night. There is the separation of a farmer from some of his fields by a motorway, if he is not indemnified for this loss of free access. There is the cost inflicted on other road-users by one more motorist coming on to a congested road. All the road-users find their journey along the street costs them slightly more than it would have done if this marginal road-user were off the street. There is the cost suffered by business, particularly perhaps transport cafés and petrol stations, when a new road takes away some of their custom.

Formally the policy can be expressed as follows. Its aim is to maximise *social surplus.* In any situation where an economic choice is made this means the calculation of all benefits and costs expected to result to whomsoever they accrue. For any alternative, X, the social surplus equals expected gains in factor rents and consumers' surpluses *minus* any expected losses of factor rent and consumers' surplus.[3] If a money value is allotted to all these — direct or indirect — the social surplus will have a definite expected money value. The social surplus maximiser will choose the alternative expected to yield the highest social surplus. If it is an investment the social surplus maximiser will choose the investment possibility which will yield the highest social rate of return or dividend.

Anyone — let it be roads authority or railway — would often make a different choice if he used a private classification of benefits and costs instead of a social one. There is no presumption that the two would show the same balance of advantage. Similarly the outcome might be very different if the Government used a private, not a social, rate of return to allocate public money for investment between road and rail. There is no reason to suppose social benefits and advantages of road improvement and railway modernisation reflect the difference between the private return to be expected from each. *Prima facie,* as we will see, this is not so. And the same kind of difference might be expected when a Government ponders the pattern of investment in gen general, how much to invest in transport and how much, say, housing, defence, fuel and power and, perhaps other things outside the public sector altogether.

Now if anyone is persuaded that all costs and benefits *ought* to be taken into account just because they are costs and benefits, social or private, then he is likely to be led to this criterion as an ideal. One obvious objection to it is that it can only be an ideal. No one could spare the time to estimate the effect on every rent or surplus. If they could spare the time they could not possibly have the knowledge. As we have noticed it is partly guesswork for a firm to rough out its own particular demand curve and even sometimes its cost curve. To gauge the effect of anything it might do on all other interests in the community, it must know all the community's demand and cost curves, so that it could tell, for example, what the effect of rise in price of commodity A, which is indirectly a result of its choice of alternative X, would have on the demand for A, the profits of producers of A. and the consumers' surplus of consumers of A. The repercussions of one effect upon others would complicate the calculations enormously. And in fact there is no assurance that even if one had perfect knowledge that it would be possible to complete the calculation.[4]

All usable and used economic criteria are therefore more or less close approximations to the social surplus criterion, and omission of categories of benefit and cost clearly makes a difference to the so-called ideal character of the method. The calculations omitted may be more important, from the ideal standpoint, for the result than those included. The advice given to an investment analyst is therefore that he should list the unmeasurable factors; and let those responsible for the decision weight the unmeasured factors in the same balance as those measured, using their best judgement on the respective weight to be given to each.

A more fundamental objection is quite simply that we do not have to accept that it is *the* ideal. Its underlying principle is that a pound's worth of rent or surplus is to have as much weight (i) whoever gets it, (ii) whenever they get it and (iii) whatever they happen to have already. One might say 'One to count for, One wherever it is', a democracy of pounds sterling with no more weight given to one than another. As soon as we question the assumptions the ideal breaks up. We do not have to make them. We are not being illogical or immoral, but only different in our opinions, if we hold some other view.

(i) We do not have to accept that a pound is a pound whoever gets it. Imagine a situation in which there are two alternatives. If one is chosen, a million poor men will gain £5 a head and a few rich men will lose a few shillings. If the other is chosen one wealthy man will gain more than £10,000,000 and, to accentuate the agony, some poor men will lose several hundreds of pounds apiece. The social surplus maximisation criterion commits us to select the second. In any situation of the kind we can all think of many good reasons why the alternative yielding the lower social rate of return but proffering a better distribution of benefit should be chosen. In short there is no argument which can compel us to accept the weighting implicit in the criterion. If we wish to weight net benefits going to the poor or to consumers or to certain classes of people more than those which go to others, we can do this, choosing any system of weights we please. If we say a pound to a poor man is worth a million to a rich that is permissible. If we say a pound to a poor man is worth 25s. to a rich man that too is permissible. As long as we make up our minds and our values, our distribution policies can be whatever we care to make them.

(ii) The criterion implies that a pound's worth of benefit has the same value whenever it accrues. This means that an assumption of neutral time preference is built into the criterion. There is no necessity for this either. We can make a different basic assumption, and we can also make different assumptions for different people. From this point of view also there is not one social surplus maximisation criterion but an infinite number.

(iii) Last, the criterion seems to imply that a pound more or less is to count as much, however much or little money one has. Our first point was that we do not have to give a benefit or a cost the same weight for different people. We now say that we do not even have to give different pounds the same weight in our calculations for the same person. It is often true that the more money someone has the less value every additional pound he gets has for him, and we could if we wished in any given case modify our criterion to allow for this fact.

All usable and used criteria, or policies, fall short of the social surplus criterion we have described for one of two reasons:
(i) practicability, (ii) by deliberate omission. We may not be able to make the calculation we would like to make on practical grounds. We may not wish to put some social benefit or cost in quite simply because we do not wish to consider it. To generalise, the effects of any choice can be divided into three groups (i) the 'good', which are those to be

put on the credit side, (ii) the 'bad', which are to be put on the debit side, and (iii) the 'indifferent', which are to be left out. Whoever is responsible for making the decision is responsible for defining 'good', 'bad' and 'indifferent'. The social surplus maximisation criterion is one which lays down as an ideal that no effects should be judged indifferent and that all money gains — direct or indirect — should be judged good and similarly all money losses judged bad, using a particular system of weighting for both: one to count for one. It would be open to anyone who held the view to say that certain gains were in his judgement 'bad', and losses, 'good'. And if he was of a certain turn of mind he might say he valued a decline in income to a bookmaker twice as much as (or, if he pleased, the value he set on it might be the square of) an increase in income to an 'honest' tradesman.

Where does this argument land us? On our own feet or nowhere. Economics is not a science which makes up our minds for us, asserting there is a criterion which we should adopt, whether it be the 'ordinary' one of profit maximisation or the 'ideal' of social surplus maximisation. It helps us work out the precise logical implications of any policy we demand of it.

This is why we should put first things first and the first thing is to ask of an enterprise or project: 'in whose interest?' Then, unless the policy is well known, it is necessary to go on and define it precisely enough for it to work. Suppose that it is decided to run a nationalised industry in the *consumers' interest.* As an implication of our argument we can say that in principle a policy of running an industry in the consumers' interest is one which sets out to maximise their 'profit, surplus, or rent' — hence the term: consumers' surplus maximisation. The exact form of the criterion will depend on (a) whom we define to be the 'consumers' in question; (b) whether a pound's worth of surplus is to have as much weight (i) whoever gets it, (ii) whenever they get it, and (iii) however much benefit they already happen to have; and (c) on the definition adopted of the costs to be borne by these consumers — whether possibly the enterprise's private costs, less than these, or more, including some social costs. It will be convenient if we do not attempt to settle these questions, and some others needed to give precise content to this criterion, here, but in the particular context of railway operation in Chapter 6.

Quite apart from this there is a management reason for not attempting the comprehensiveness of the social surplus criterion. This is often referred to as the policy which would try to maximise the sum of all consumers' and producers' surpluses in the economy — 'consumers' referring to everyone in their capacity as consumers. But just as profit maximisation limits and simplifies the objectives of a private firm and makes it easier to evaluate performance, so one can argue that to give each public enterprise a social surplus maximising criterion is to define its aims so widely that it will be impossible to evaluate performance. The yardstick will be too complicated. On these grounds there is much to be said for defining the goals of public enterprise in relation to a particular set of surpluses – for example, its consumers' or its workers'; and leave society to legislate for the interests of others by regulation or subsidy (see Chapter 7 below) where these conflict with the interests of those in terms of which the enterprise's objectives are defined.

It so happens that social surplus maximisation implies marginal cost pricing. As was indicated in the last chapter setting all prices equal to marginal cost is a necessary condition for social surplus maximisation. If it is decided to modify the application of the social surplus criterion for the reasons stated in almost all cases this will result in some modification of marginal cost pricing. Since marginal cost pricing will result in surpluses and deficits for particular enterprises which experience suggests will be politically unacceptable this of course implies another practical objection to social surplus maximisation.

Nevertheless it is possibly apt to point out now some of the analogies between profit and consumers' surplus maximisation in principle by referring to earlier arguments in this Chapter. Just as profit maximisation is not the same as revenue maximisation, so consumers' surplus maximisation is not the same, and for the same reasons. The same amount of profits realised this year and ten years hence has not the same money value. Similarly, the same amount of consumers' surplus realised this year and ten years hence has not the same money value. It is as relevant to discount the future in pursuing a consumers' surplus as in a profit maximisation policy.

We now have an apparatus which we can use to discuss the transport problem, and which is capable of being made numerically determinate. Inasmuch as the transport system is amenable to public control, we assume that it is in the public interest that it is run to maximise either (a) profits or (b) consumers' surplus. These are the only two policies which we will work out in detail; the apparatus described will enable anyone to modify either policy as he pleases.

The method of argument will first be to discuss the rail and road problems separately. In Chapters 4 and 5 the implications of adopting profit maximisation as the railways basic criterion will be discussed. The subject of Chapter 6 is some special problems arising from the adoption of consumers' surplus maximisation. To prevent duplication of argument the treatment in Part III on the road problem will not be symmetrical. The profit maximising and consumers' surplus maximising alternatives will mainly be considered in parallel in

Chapters 9–11. Finally some questions posed by the transport problem as a whole will be considered in Chapter 12, and it will be argued there are good reasons for requiring all nationalised transport undertakings and the road programme to adopt the same criteria.

A last point. It is generally thought there are other factors which should influence the policy of a nationalised industry on occasions. For example it is often urged that certain types of consumers and occasionally certain groups of workers or producers supplying raw materials should be subsidised. Certainly there are often good reasons for giving subsidies. Recent thinking tends towards the opinion that any subsidy should be offset in the accounts of a nationalised industry by a specific Government subsidy to the industry. What really matters is:

(a) that subsidies and their amounts should be identified;

(b) that some agreed authority should decide whether the benefits gained by the subsidy are worth its cost;

(c) if the benefits are obtained at the lowest cost; and

(d) who should bear the cost of the subsidy, for example whether it should be the Exchequer or other transport users.

We will discuss this question further in Chapter 7, and also that of regulation.

POSTSCRIPT

Rent
There is a further discussion of the meaning of rent and surplus in E.J. Mishan.[1]

Consumers' Surplus
Depending on the existence of income effects, the actual measure of consumers' surplus need not be unique. This is of theoretical but rarely of political importance. See Mishan[2] and Currie, Murphy and Schmitz[3] for a very full treatment.

Other 'Commercial' Policies
There is now a large literature on objectives a firm may pursue besides profit maximisation.[4] Nationalised industries have as much incentive to maximise their size (or resist rundown) as have private firms. Size affects the salaries paid — though less than in private enterprise — as well as power and prestige.

The Social Surplus Criterion
On fairly stringent assumptions (see Appendix 1), it is social surplus maximisation which implies marginal cost pricing as its pricing rule.

Although there is nothing formally wrong with the distinction made between 'private' and 'social', it would have been useful to have noted the distinction between *pecuniary* and *technological* social costs and benefits. As used in the literature a 'technological' social cost or benefit represents a real cost or benefit. Thus environmental and congestion costs are technological or real, in that they represent charges in the real income of those affected. But the action of one enterprise which affects the profits or rent of another is not real because, as was argued earlier, rent does not measure the real cost. It is a transfer, because what the renter loses, someone else, usually the consumer, gains. Similarly a change of government tax receipts is not a real change because it is a transfer. Once again what the government loses (or gains) someone else gains (or loses). The only exception to this treatment of tax is where government gains or loses because there is a change in net surplus for the economy which is solely or in part gained as increased taxation.[5]

The problem of selecting the discount rate for public investment has been shown to be extremely complicated theoretically and to be interrelated with the problem of determining the shadow price of capital. Because of these complexities, the original Appendix has been dropped, but there is more discussion later. There is a useful selection of readings in Layard.[6] In practice in many countries the Government lays down the discount rates and the shadow price of capital to be used in the public sector. This is often sensible because their determination are matters to be settled for the economy as a whole and do not just rate as issues affecting transport.

One should mention the growing interest among economists in the use of property rights as a method of clarifying the attribution of costs. The point can be made quite simply. Has one man a right to make a noise in his vehicle or have those who live by a road a right to some degree of quiet? Unless this is decided by law, it is impossible to decide who should compensate whom if policies are introduced to reduce vehicle noise. If people are given property rights, so called, which entitle them to defined standards of quiet and freedom from pollution, they have a base from which to sue for damages.

PART II

THE RAIL PROBLEM

4   RAILWAY COSTS AND CHARGES: PROFIT MAXIMISATION

In this chapter we consider problems set by the requirement that the railways should adopt profit maximisation. To concentrate attention on this without distracting complications, it will be convenient to make five assumptions.

1. The form of the criterion is settled: the profit maximising criterion is the ordinary one, unqualified by any prohibition of price discrimination (See Appendix 3).

2. Not to complicate the argument at this point it is assumed we are considering a situation where there are no modifications of the basic criterion required by subsidy or regulation. This assumption will be relaxed in Chapter 7.

3. In particular, profit maximisation is not assumed to be under any constraint because of anti-monopoly policy.

4. Later we will consider modifications of the basic criteria made for a different reason — to establish some form of competition or coordination in the transport system. We abstract these complications also, reserving their discussion for Chapter 12.

5. Another assumption is needed. We need to know whether the railways are to be run as a single economic entity or not. It has not been made clear in any Government pronouncement I know of whether it is Government policy that decentralisation should mean that the various successors to the old British Transport Commission should be run as economically independent and competing units — one might say as independent firms — or as part of a combine. For example Western Region might have the chance of some new traffic profitable to it, the carriage of which might lower profits in other regions by more than Western Region gained. If something of this kind should occur, it would not be in the interest of the railway system as a whole that Western Region should take the traffic. If the regions are run as separate firms, Western Region would rightly be indifferent to possible profits or losses made by other regions and would think only of itself, just as independent private firms do not normally consider the interest of other firms. (In the language of Chapter 3 the definition of what is a private cost and private benefit differs in the two situations.) I assume — again for simplicity in argument — the railways will continue in this sense to be run *as a whole*. (In the past a region has been known to take business which reduced the profits of other regions more than it increased its own, but this has not been deliberate policy but

presumably inadvertence). On the other hand I assume the non-railway undertakings of the old commission are to be truly independent of the railways: British Railways, British Transport Docks, British Road Services and the Inland Waterways are in this sense to be regarded as separate firms. (I make no assumption about some of the smaller fragments of the commission which are in fact closely integrated with the railways in certain respects. They are sufficiently small for it not to be necessary to take a stand one way or the other about them. It is to be presumed from the *Reorganisation of the Nationalised Transport Undertakings* White Paper that packet ports and railway services 'which are extensions of the railway system', railway catering services and London Transport will be treated as part of the same economic entity as the railways. British Transport Hotels and Thomas Cook and Son Ltd. will act as independent firms. However this is not made explicit and it is, I think, a point on which one could have expected a definite ruling from the Government at that stage.[1])

The first need (relevant to any criterion) is that the railways should improve their costing (first section). In the second section the charging policy appropriate to profit maximisation is argued. In the third section the special problem of deciding on what charging policy should be when the railways are running at a loss is considered.

COSTS

Until recently railways had, by comparison with most industries, an exceptionally sparse knowledge of their costs. This comment of a parliamentary committee in 1882 would have given a fairly accurate impression of the state of railway costing at any time from the 1830s to the 1940s: 'The charge for conveyance (the railway managers informed us) was such a sum within the power of the company as they thought the traffic could bear, having regard to competition, both of other means of conveyance and of other districts and markets; or in other words, as much as could be got *and without reference to the cost of performing the service.* Indeed the managers examined informed us that they found it impracticable to determine with accuracy the cost of conveying any particular kind of goods between two stations.[2]

Most firms are interested in maximising their profits. Railways attempted to maximise their revenue. As they did not count the cost of what they were carrying, undoubtedly they carried a proportion of traffic at a loss though at the highest possible revenue. Another effect of cost unconsciousness was that in general the railways had a hazy idea of how they might cut costs and a hazier one of the relative profitability of cost-reducing investment.

Although inexact, it can be argued that railway costing was adequate.

There are three sound defences for poor costing:

(1) The enterprise would like to improve its costing. It does not know how to do it.

(2) Though it would pay, the firm is not interested. It has some monopoly power and does not have to be more efficient to survive. It could increase its profits by better costing but it would rather sacrifice some additional costing for the case of a quiet life. It decides not to to bother.

(3) It would not pay to do better. If it is thought likely that the cost of better costing itself would be more than the increase in profits (or reduction in losses) expected to result from it, plainly it would be foolish to improve costing.

All three are conceivable defences of railway costing as it used to be, their relative importance varying from one railway and, more significantly, from one period in railway history to another.

Railway costing involves practical and theoretical problems beyond the experience of most firms (point (1)). This was truer in the nineteenth century when the multi-product firm was less common – and the railways are and always have been an extreme example of the multi-product firm selling a wide range of different services. The railways would have found it difficult to improve their costing sufficiently to have been helpful without themselves undertaking theoretical research because the necessary refinements in economics and econometrics had not been made.

It is possible that when and where they were monopolies, their managers did not bother to improve costing (point (2)), but more important than either of these was the simple explanation that at more periods in railway history it would not have paid them to do so (point (3)). This can be argued on two counts. When they were making profits and could have increased them by better costing, there was little incentive to do so because of the pressure Parliament would have brought formally and informally to make them pass on increased profits in lower fares and charges. Second, when the railways were later tending to make profits less than the maximum that public policy might have allowed, they were enmeshed in a net of railway rate regulation which made it almost impossible for them to benefit from better costing, because they could not usually alter their charges or discontinue unprofitable services. It is an oversimplification, but in general the only costs the railway companies were concerned about were their own total expenses in relation to total revenue. In this they were Micawberish. With total revenue a decent amount above total expenses, they were or had to be satisfied. With less they were not, but there was little, especially by better costing, they could do about it.

The revolution in railway costing of the 1950s was another and essential element in the total railway situation and had the same causes: the realisation that the old hotch-potch of regulations was a wasteful and unintelligent method of controlling a monopoly, the realisation that the railways were no longer a monopoly and the knowledge by the railways that they had to change their ways to survive and this meant better costing. It is also possible that the fact of public accountability itself had some effect in making them wish to have more detailed costing.

The Traffic Costing Service was started in 1949. Since that date there has not been sufficient time to construct a perfect system of costing from virtually nothing. Most businesses have had costing systems which have grown and been adapted as the firms grew, the problems posed being solved as they appeared. The largest firms, if they had happened to grow up in a strong monopoly position where detailed costing did not matter, would have found it difficult to build up a satisfactory costing system, one suspects, in ten years, especially if their business was as complicated as that of the railways; and of course the railways are much larger than the largest private firm. Because of the peculiar problems set for costing by the nature of railway operations, it was more difficult for them to adopt wholesale the costing methods used by other industries. Quite as important was the lack of cost consciousness among railwaymen. Businessmen are trained to think of the cost of everything they do. Soldiers are not. Railwaymen have been more like soldiers than businessmen in this respect. That was why it was not possible to introduce comprehensive costing at all levels of management. Instead, a small cadre, the Traffic Costing Service, was set up with three purposes:

(1) to decide the principles and methods of railway costing.

(2) to find out as quickly as possible what the costs were.

(3) to circulate this information. (When every stationmaster and goods agent is familiar with costs and costing procedures and the system is working well, the Traffic Costing Service as a separate entity and ginger group may wither away.)

It is useful to recall this recent history to be just to the railways. It would be a severe criticism of the efficiency of any ordinary commercial business to discover that it had only an impression where its losses were made or that it was not sure if one of its component parts (Western Region) was operating at a profit or loss, but it is understandable why this should still be so on the railways.[3] The strongest criticism is perhaps that it is doubtful if enough has been invested in the Traffic Costing Service since 1950. Some one hundred officers or roughly one-fifth of 1 per cent of the railways' manpower is employed on costing. It is unlikely that the cost of the service is much more than £200,000 per annum or one-thirtieth of 1 per cent of the railways' working expenditure. Manpower has probably been more limiting than money. Men of the standard needed for the job are scarce in the railways — another result of the Galbraith effect in the public sector (This is the proposition that the growth of public expenditure always tends to lag behind that of private expenditure in a capitalist society.) However the proportion of both devoted to costing seems very small. One would imagine that the Traffic Costing Service is somewhere where both more men and money could be invested profitably.

That railway costing is in process of development should be remembered now that we come to consider the present state of the railway costing of goods traffic. It will be helpful to give a brief description of it so as to get some feel of the railways' self-knowledge of their costs and, more importantly, I think, so as to be able to appraise the principles on which this costing is based. There is, I think, no need to give separate attention to the costing of passenger traffic. The problems raised are much the same.

Let us imagine a goods agent in Yorkshire who is asked to quote a charge by a local trader for some new traffic which is to go from his station to one in Gloucestershire. The agent has two costing procedures open to him. These we may call *particular* and *generalised* costing. The first would be used *if* it were thought worth while to attempt to work out the particular costs of that traffic: for example if it were consignments offered by the trainload or a regular traffic of several wagonloads a week from A to B. In fact not all traffic which it would pay to cost particularly can be, because of the limited resources of the Traffic Costing Service. As a rough estimate it would probably pay the railways to cost in this way about 75 per cent of the traffic they carry measured on a tonnage basis. The actual proportion costed particularly is certainly much less than this. How much less than this it is difficult to say. However if the agent were offered traffic which he thought deserved particular costing he would suggest it to his traffic costing officer or traffic accounting centre. If it were decided to cost it particularly, the costing officer would normally first set about estimating its cost under eight heads:

(1) shunting at terminal stations.

(2) provision of terminal facilities and accommodation — that is local overheads and general yard wages at the stations of origin and destination.

(3) terminal haulage — haulage between station of origin and first marshalling yard and last marshalling yard and station of destination.

(4) provision and maintenance of wagon(s).

(5) provision of sheets and ropes.

(6) documentation.

(7) Marshalling.

(8) Trunk haulage — haulage between first and last marshalling yards.[4]

He would then cost each item separately. Normally he would cost the first six items as a standing charge per wagonload since they are held not to vary significantly with distance except that some proportion of (4) is treated as a cost per wagon-mile; (7) and (8) are costed per wagon-mile since they do vary with the distance travelled. To both the standing cost and the cost per wagon-mile he would add a percentage to cover the risk of damage or loss in transit. So he would get a figure which would stand as a minimum for charging. Track and signalling, and general administration would normally not be costed separately, but any amount the traffic could earn above the minimum would be set against this cost. This is the usual procedure of what I have called particular costing, though there will be variations if, for example, the traffic is carried in owner's wagons or to private sidings, or if some of the track, for instance, to a colliery is only used for the traffic being costed.

If our goods agent decides that particular costing is not worth while, or if the Traffic Costing Services are unable to do it because they are fully employed, the simpler procedure of what I have called generalised costing is used. Let us suppose the consignment offered is a wagon-load of machinery once a week from the station in Yorkshire to one in Gloucestershire. There is first of all a different cost scale for general merchandise, minerals and coal. This, of course, would be classified as general merchandise. Second, within these classes there are separate scales for consignments of different 'loadability', which is, briefly, a measure of density. The principle is that the more nearly a consignment fills a wagon the lower the cost per ton, but the lighter the consignment the greater the cost per ton. The goods agent decides whether the consignment is of top-, middle- or low-class loadability, and selects the appropriate scale. This is normally as far as he will ordinarily consider the special characteristics of the goods offered, though if they are especially difficult or unpleasant to handle, he may use his discretion.

The same breakdown of costs into eight categories applies, except that the first three categories are united in a single cost for the beginning and another for the end of the journey. The six thousand goods stations in the country are divided into twenty-five groups ranging from the highest to the lowest cost. The goods agent will know into which his own station falls. He can find out the grouping of the station of destination. So he reaches the cost he must put into his calculations for the first three items. There is of course averaging of costs involved here. Within any group of the twenty-five there will be a range of costs from the lowest cost to the highest. (The range of costs overall is considerable.)

There is much more averaging in respect of the other items. Here there is just one figure for traffic of a given class (general merchandise, minerals or coal) and a given loadability (*A, B* or *C*). Important are trunk haulage and marshalling. Marshalling is worked out as a cost per wagon mile — the assumption being that the average wagon is marshalled once every thirty miles. As the railways themselves admit, the number of marshallings a wagon goes through in fact varies considerably. Sometimes there is considerably less than 30 miles between marshallings and sometimes very much more. However the one figure of x pence per wagon-mile is normally used for all consignments whatever the number of marshallings in fact. Similarly, the costs of trunk haulage can vary and here too a figure averaged for the whole railway system is used. The first six items are summed up to produce a standing cost per wagon again with the exception that a small proportion of the cost for provision and maintenance of wagon is treated as a cost per wagon-mile. It and the last two items sum to a cost per wagon-mile. To each again is added a fixed percentage for risk of damage or loss in transit which does not vary except between general merchandise and mineral or coal traffic. Again this calculation sets a minimum for charging. Any charge he can make above the minimum is a contribution towards track and signalling and general administration, which are not separately costed.

That is the essence of the procedure used by the railways for costing freight. The second procedure, generalised costing is, as we have seen, subject to a considerable amount of averaging. Particularly in respect of marshalling, traffics which in fact must be responsible for very different costs are in practice costed at the same rate,

However if we look at the data on which the costs for generalised costs are based there is more averaging and guesswork than has yet appeared. In 1955 the British Transport Commission presented their railway merchandise charges scheme to the Transport Tribunal, where it was argued for forty-four days. This was a consequence of the 1953 Act and was the first major breakaway from the old principle of railway charging. The Transport Tribunal had to be persuaded that the scheme did not violate any clauses in the 1953 Act designed to protect the interests of the consumer. In the course of the proceedings the Commission presented much evidence on its costs and costing procedures and sources, much more, one is tempted to suggest than any other British business has ever published. The Commission is unlikely to be required to publish anything as detailed again. The principle is coming to be accepted that it has no more obligation to publish its costs than any commercial firm. Also this responsibility of the Transport Tribunal before which it gave this information has been ended except in London. Therefore we have to use this 1955-6 information as a basis, but it is possible to bring it up to date from other fragmentary pieces of information in so far as there has been improvement in railway costing.

Let us consider the data under the eight heads.

(1) *Terminal shunting*. In 1955 the information available was based on a detailed study of 28 stations and a week's analysis of 2,000 stations out of a total 6,000 for a week. Since then a detailed study has been made of all 6,000 stations. The cost used in generalised costing for station X is therefore based on a detailed study made within the last five years. Every two or three years, this figure will be revised by a detailed study of a representative sample of these 6,000 stations and the figure for X — which of course may or may not be one of the sample — will be revised accordingly. Other changes in the figure will only be made if there is an increase in costs for the railway system — for example, an increase in wages — which will be passed on as a percentage increase in the labour content of station X's shunting cost.

(2) *Terminal accommodation and facilities* was based in 1955 on a detailed study of an unspecified small number of stations, some ordinary non-financed returns made by stations and the same week's analysis of the 6,000 stations. Since then detailed studies of the 6,000 stations have been done in this respect also and the present position is the same as for terminal shunting.

(3) The *terminal haulage* cost in 1955 was based on a sample of 153 terminal haulages which were chosen as 'representative'. The detailed studies of all stations made since have included a study of the average cost of terminal haulage from that station to the first marshalling yard. The present position is therefore the same as for (1) and (2).

(4) *Provision and maintenance of wagons*. The cost figure used here is an average found by dividing the number of wagons in service by the average number of journeys made by each wagon and dividing this into the total cost of providing and maintaining wagons. The only distinction normally made for generalised costing is between merchandise and mineral wagons.

(5) *Provisions of sheets and ropes*. This relatively unimportant item is found by dividing the total expenditure on sheets and ropes in a year by the number of wagon journeys made by merchandise wagons.

(6) *Documentation* is based on the same detailed study of the 6,000 stations and the present position is as for (1), (2), and (3).

(7) *Marshalling* is the most interesting. In 1955 it was based on a sample survey of 16 marshalling yards out of a total of 900 and on regular returns of the number of wagons marshalled from 322 yards. The samples are larger now, though I have no definite information on this. But there has not been a detailed study of every marshalling yard.

One can presume that the samplings are revised about every two or three years.

(8) *Trunk haulage* was based on a sample of 120 trunk-haul train freights in 1955 and on a week's test of freight loadings. Presumably the sample is larger now.

(9) *Risk of damage or loss* is not worked out separately for different kinds of traffic except that a different percentage is used for general merchandise and for mineral and coal traffic.

(10) All *track and signalling* is classified on a track-mile basis into four categories for costing purposes. Within these categories there must be considerable averaging of costs. The costs here are, broadly, maintenance and repair of track and earthworks, and operation, maintenance and repair of the signalling system. The present system of classification has not changed essentially from what it was in 1955.

By the railways' own evidence there was in 1955 considerable variation in costs and there is no reason to suppose that the range of costs has narrowed. For example marshalling costs varied from under 2*s*. to over 6*s*. per wagon detached from one yard to another, but these were themselves average figures. Different wagons would incur different marshalling costs at the same yard. Some wagons would have to be marshalled more than once at the same yard, others would go through in the same train without being detached, etc. All such variations are concealed in the average figure used for generalised costing. (The range of costs for marshalling was not as great as for some other items. Documentation for example varied between 1*s*. 6*d*. and approximately 21*s*. per transit.)

It is inevitable to wonder whether this costing is sufficiently detailed. One's reaction to it as the generalised costing procedure of a large multi-product firm will depend, I suspect, on the reader's background. An economist will perhaps be more sceptical than he should. Some businessmen will feel that they would not like to run their firms on such a basis. Some may not be surprised. Certainly the coverage and frequency could be improved. The first two defences for seemingly poor costing cannot be offered. We cannot say that railways do not know how to improve their costs or that they are a monopoly. Even if they were, a public enterprise should not, one supposes, be privileged to be slack if better costing would pay. It is this third defence — whether it would pay to improve costing in this respect or not — which is still possible; and it is a point which cannot possibly be decided from without.[5] We know what tests would be needed. For instance one needs to test to find out if it would pay to quote a figure for each marshalling yard to all goods agents, so that they can sum average figures for each marshalling yard to be passed through by any wagon despatched. If the financial gain from extra provision was less than the additional cost of providing the information, then it would not be worth it. The outsider cannot have a reasonable opinion on what the results of such tests would be. He can only note the facts of railway costing.

It is regrettable that the 1963 proposals for the *Reshaping of British Railways** — the 'Beeching Plan' — do not make it clear what improvements there have been in the railways' knowledge of their own costs during the last few years. It seems that the categories of costs are still the same, and it is probable that the cost estimates given in the report are still based on considerable averaging. But one cannot tell to what extent the averaging of costs has diminished. What is new are total cost figures for more classes of traffic — e.g. general merchandise traffic — analysed by distance, terminal conditions, etc. (An example is general merchandise and minerals traffic of over 12 tons and up to 16 tons travelling between 101 and 150 miles.) Valuable though such information is it leaves obscure the costing process used.

Although that point cannot be pressed, a serious criticism can be made of the principles on which railway costing is based. The principles seem fallacious, because they appear to have the effect of keeping traffic off the railways which it would be profitable to carry — by either of the basic criteria. Or to link this point with the argument of Chapter 3, railway costing is based in part on a wrong, irrelevant and illogical definition of costs. The fallacy turns on the old question of the allocation of joint or, as the railways call them, indirect costs, which has always been a special problem for railways. One of the difficulties in clarifying the issues is linguistic. Railwaymen talk of direct and indirect costs. Businessmen tend to talk of prime and supplementary costs or overheads. Economists use a wide range of terms, costs and joint cost, short-run and long-run marginal costs, escapable and inescapable costs, divisible and indivisible costs. Sometimes there are subtle and important differences in meaning between the terms. Sometimes there are not. It is helpful I think, to define a few terms.

But first we must not forget that it is not just academic but bad economics to advocate a refinement in costing which would not pay. It will be sufficient objection to any of the refinements to be suggested to say that it would not pay to use them. However, it would seem to me, and this is a point which will be developed, unlikely that it would pay best to leave the principles of railway costing as they are.

There are first of all what might be called true or unavoidably joint costs. The classic example is wool and mutton. They are joint products. You cannot produce one without the other. There is no cost of mutton or cost of wool, only cost of sheep. If one asks the crucial question

*H.M.S.O. (1963)

what real resources would be saved by not producing wool (or mutton) the answer is none unless at the same time the production of mutton (or wool) is also stopped. Then what is saved are the real resources used to produce sheep. If the cost of rearing a sheep was £10 it would be nonsense to attempt to subdivide and say, for instance, that the cost of rearing wool was £6 and the cost of rearing mutton £4, since if one neglected the existence of the wool altogether the cost of sheep would still be £10; there is no possibility of sheep without wool and vice versa since one cannot rear wool without mutton. (In fact this example is not quite as good as at first appears because it is possible to vary to some extent the proportions of mutton and wool on a sheep by breeding. However the *principle* holds.) Furthermore if for the sake of example we suppose wool- and mutton-buyers are two groups of people, that wool-buyers maintain that the cost of rearing wool is £6 and that there is suddenly a slump in the price of mutton lowering the price to something near zero, it would be foolish of the wool-buyers to stick blindly to the point that they will not pay more than what they consider, wrongly, to be the cost of producing wool: £6. What concerns the sheep-farmer is that he should at least cover the cost of production: £10. If he cannot he will stop rearing sheep. If in fact it would pay the wool-buyers to pay more for wool so that costs of rearing sheep are covered rather than go out of the wool business, it would be mulish of them to cut their own throats because of an utterly fallacious conception of cost.

Similarly it is often suggested that if goods traffic pays for almost all the track and signalling costs jointly used by goods and passenger traffic while passenger traffic makes a 'small contribution', goods traffic is *subsidising* passenger traffic. The assumption is that passenger traffic cannot afford to pay a higher proportion. As we have seen subsidisation means the incurring of costs which it would pay the enterprise not to incur. If goods traffic were to pay a lower proportion both would be worse off, since by assumption, the cost of track and signalling could not be covered. Therefore it is not subsidisation.

The defining characteristic of true joint costs is that their jointness is a fact of nature — or technology — and exists at all points in time: before as well as after the relevant investment is made. Someone who would invest in producing mutton knows that it is a fact of nature he will be producing wool also.

There are a number of examples of true jointness on the railways though not as many as are often supposed.[6] Most of them are the effects of time.[7] For example it is a fact of technology that one cannot conjure up the fabric of a station only on alternate Saturdays or only during the hours of peak travel. So far as its fabric is concerned, the output (use) of a station is available at all times. There would be no point in trying to attribute a station fabric cost to peak hour traffic and others to off-peak, evening or early morning trains. This a joint cost.[8] In this type of case it would only be possible to attribute a cost if it could be shown that to use the station for one sort of traffic would be to reduce its availability for other sorts of traffic as follows: suppose it is a fact that if a station (building) were to be used only for peak traffic it would wear out in sixty years, and that if it were to be used for peak and offpeak traffic it would wear out in fifty years. If this were so we could attribute a station fabric cost to the offpeak traffic in terms of the shorter station life, but in fact the difference made to the life of a station thus is negligible, compared with the effect of deterioration due simply to time and to obsolescence, that to all intents and purposes we can regard the output of a station as a joint product in respect of *time* (though it may not be a joint product as we shall see in respect of other things).

Other joint costs of the same kind are in respect of marshalling yards, goods depots, locomotive depots, etc. Much the same can be said of the provision and maintenance of wagons. The railways argue that their deterioration is negligibly an effect of use and almost entirely an effect of age and obsolescence. Therefore their costs are joint in respect of time also. With rather less confidence the same can be said of passenger coaches, locomotives, cranes and other equipment which is less durable than buildings normally are. A slightly different example is the joint cost of labour. It is a fact of industrial relations that it is usually impossible to hire men for less than a full day's work at a time. (For various reasons shift-splitting is rarely practicable on the railways.)[9] As there are two peaks in Britain – more than eight hours apart – this means that labour is available in general for sixteen hours. It is not possible to provide labour for the peak without providing it for these other times also. Therefore the cost of this labour is properly a joint cost of all uses made of it at different *times*. All these examples which I believe are the most important are the effect of time but the most famous transport example is really the effect of the one-dimensional character of length distance. This is that it is impossible to provide a capacity for a journey from A to B without providing it for the journey back. (This has to be modified when triangular and similarly more complicated patterns occur but the principle is the same.) There is not a cost of providing capacity for each leg of the journey but a joint cost of the round trip.

The other kind of joint costs exists only in the *short run* – a definition which is circular: as the short run is defined as that period during which these costs are joint or fixed. To illustrate by example, suppose British Railways decides to build a marshalling yard. To keep the argument as simple as possible we will assume that two kinds of traffic will use the yard — x, which is a certain kind of mineral traffic from X, and y, a certain kind of merchandise traffic to and from Y — these meet at the marshalling yard where they are marshalled to other parts of the country. (The calculations will be more complicated if we assume more traffics, but the principle will be the same.) We can draw up a table as follows:

Table 4.1 Capital cost of marshalling yard (£m.)

Number of tons of x marshalled per annum (thousands)	0	10	15	20	25	30
0	0.19	0.25	0.29	0.34	0.39	0.40
10	0.31	0.37	0.38	0.39	0.44	0.46
15	0.33	0.39	0.40	0.41	0.46	0.48
20	0.39	0.45	0.48	0.49	0.50	0.53
25	0.40	0.46	0.49	0.51	0.52	0.54

Here we have a range of possibilities: the range of feasible marshalling yards which are of optimum economic size for the various expected combinations of the two traffics. Taking all costs into account, not only these capital costs, the problem is to decide which it will be the most profitable to build — according to one's criterion. In this context of investment it makes sense to talk of separate marshalling yard capital costs for x and y as it did not for wool and mutton. Suppose we take the plan of a marshalling yard which is optimum for 15,000 x and 20,000 y and ask the crucial question: what real resources would be saved if it were decided not to provide facilities for, say, 500 or 5,000 tons of x per annum? The figure which is the (marginal) cost for 5,000 tons can be read off the table: £0.01m. Given any volume of either x and y we can ask what would be the separate cost of providing it, because while the yard is in the planning stage, it is still possible to alter the plans and vary the proportions of the two traffics.

Once the decision to build the yard is made irretrievably, and certainly when the yard is built, all this changes: the provision of marshalling-yard facilities for x and y have joint costs. If we ask the crucial question what real resources would be saved by discontinuing the provision of facilities for x (or y) the answer is *none* — as far as the capital or fixed costs are concerned. It is now nonsense to talk of separate marshalling-yard capital costs for x and for y. It is also nonsense to talk of an average marshalling-yard capital cost for all wagonloads irrespective of whether they were x or y. If the traffic should use the yard in the proportions predicted when the size of yard built was chosen, then one would expect, other things being equal, that the two sorts of traffic would contribute to the costs of the marshalling-yard as predicted. But if the demand pattern should change and, say, the proportion paid by x increases and the proportion paid by y decreases, again there is no question of x *subsidising y,* for however much y contributed to the joint costs of the marshalling both would be worse off if it contributed less. What matters once more is that the cost should be covered and the cost is the one cost, the joint cost.

All capital installations on the railway fall into this category. Most labour costs fall into this category in practice for some period of time since labour cannot be hired or fired immediately in response to any increase or decline in the volume of traffic.

Joint costs of the second kind, if not of the first, exist inevitably in all businesses. What makes them a special problem for the railways is their magnitude. During the course of the inquiry into the railway charges merchandise scheme, counsel for the Traders' Co-ordinating Committee on Transport asked why there was such an objection to costing on a cost-plus basis.[10] This − the commonest ordinary commercial procedure − calculates separately any costs which can be specifically related to a consignment, but treats all joint costs as overheads and averages their cost over all traffic, the direct cost being increased by a percentage to cover them. The then director of the Traffic Costing Service, Mr Tait, gave an entirely proper logical answer. It would not be practicable or profitable to do this because of, first, the high ratio of joint costs or overheads to direct costs and second, the great diversity of the services provided by the railways. What the railways were being asked was whether our third and only remaining defence of apparently inadequate costing − that it would not pay − were not a valid reason for cost-plus. The extra flexibility a firm would gain by refining its costing procedures so that it could allocate its overheads and estimate its actual profit margins more accurately, would not be worth the extra cost in many cases. Furthermore a firm which had no great diversity of products with overheads in common would find it difficult to extract different contributions to overheads from different customers. As an extreme case the single-product firm would be unlikely to be able to do so because of competition. If it charged different prices − discriminated in its price − for the same product or service, it would run the risk of the low-price buyer reselling to the high-price buyer.

The representatives of the railways were in fact impeccable in their understanding of the issues raised by the existence of joint or indirect costs. On many occasions they refused to accept the argument that there was subsidisation because different traffics were making different contributions to overheads and it was made quite clear that it was their policy to take any traffic which would 'at least cover the direct costs and make a contribution to the indirect costs'.[11]

It is here that we come to our criticism. The fundamental error made in railway costing would seem to have been in the definition of what are and are not joint or indirect costs. The line between them was drawn wrongly. It can only be a rough estimate, but it would seem that the British Transport Commission treated about 40 per cent of its costs as indirect or joint and 60 per cent as direct or specific,[12] whereas, as far as it is possible to tell from the 1955 figures (there is no more recent information), roughly 84 per cent of its costs were in fact joint and only 16 per cent direct. (Or, to allow a margin for error, 79-89 per cent are joint and 11-21 per cent are direct.)*

Some idea of what is involved can be given by an example. The figures used are entirely imaginary but possible. Let us suppose that a flow of traffic is offered of moderate size and it is decided to use *generalised* costing. (The same objections, however, it would seem could be made against the methods of particular costing.) The minimum cost worked on the lines indicated earlier in this section is 250s. standing charge per wagonload and 9d. per wagon-mile. This covers what the railways call direct costs. Indirect costs — the cost of track and signalling and some of the costs of general administration are to be met by charging over and above this what the traffic will bear, but the traffic will not be taken at a charge less than that which will cover direct costs by this definition. I suggest that on the basis of the correct distinction between direct and indirect costs, the minimum cost beneath which it would not pay the railways to take the traffic is more like 17-34s. standing cost per wagonload and 4-6d. cost per wagon-mile. Any amount above this would be a valued contribution to joint costs. (Even if this should be an underestimate, which I do not think it is, the difference between it and the figures the railway would use in the circumstances is substantial.)[13]

*Perhaps the most serious criticism which can be made of the 'Beeching Plan' *(Reshaping of British Railways)* is that its proposals seem at least to perpetuate the false distinction between direct and indirect costs. Criticism is made difficult because although the terms 'direct costs' and 'indirect costs' are used freely and frequently they are not defined, and it would seem they are not always used with the same meaning throughout. (How do we reconcile the following two items in the report? On p.9 we read that the 'total cost of providing the route system which it should be emphasised excludes the costs of associated sidings, yards, stations and depots . . . is a fixed cost, in the full sense of the term, all the while the route system remains unchanged'; and on p.101 in the Table on 'Examples of Assessments Made of the Annual Financial Effect of Withdrawing Typical Passenger Services' there is a column heading 'Direct track and signalling expenses'.) Although the Board may be able to defend in detail the closures of lines they propose, their argument would have been more convincing if it had been based on relevant and more exact distinction between costs of various degrees of escapability.

But there is a reservation which should be made. There is one kind of direct cost which does not show up as it should in the costs we have analysed; and which may mean that in fact it would not pay the railways to lower charges to the extent I have suggested. Although there is excess capacity in most parts of the railway system, there is evidence that there are also crucial bottlenecks: marshalling yards and terminal stations where short-run marginal costs are high because additional wagons cause congestion. Experience over the last few years has shown that it often does not pay the railways to lower freight charges and this is almost certainly the reason. This fact is, however, no justification of railway policy. If costing had been better these bottlenecks would have been shown up and would have merited, as they have not, very high priority for modernisation. If for this reason the ratio of direct costs to indirect costs is higher than our analysis indicates, traditional railway costing does not disclose it. The railways know very little about their marginal costs.

Three points have been made in this section on railway costing:

(1) The first is a tentative conclusion that it would have been profitable to have spent considerably more on costing since 1949 than was spent, and that it would be more profitable now.

(2) The second is not a conclusion but a doubt if railway costing on its own principles is based on sufficiently comprehensive and regular information.

(3) The third is a reasonably firm conclusion that their distinction between 'direct' and 'indirect' is invalid and produces results that are significantly erroneous. Instead of approximately 60 per cent, probably between 10 and 20 per cent are properly direct costs.

CHARGING

Profit maximisation: no special problems are set by this basic criterion. Price and output will always be selected so as to maximise profits. The principal part in fulfilling this policy will be played by the reactions of two sets of people to each other. There are first of all those whose business it is to fix fares or bargain with traders. They will have figures of marginal cost given and they know they must not quote a fare or charge less than these. Given that, they will attempt to settle fares and charges so as to maximise net revenue, or profits. (This does not mean that they will often take a quick profit. Their aim will be to maximise profits over a period into the future over which it is reasonable for them to foresee. So they need not sacrifice future profits for a quick profit now.)

The second set of people who have a part to play are those who fix the marginal costs for various classes of traffic for the separate component parts of the railway system — the stations, marshalling yards, track, etc. — and whose duty it is to see that these maximise their profits. To take again the example of a marshalling yard it is the manager's responsibility to see that its short-run marginal revenue is equal to its short-run marginal cost in respect of all its services. The marginal cost which he will quote the various types of traffic that use his yard will be to conform with this. For example if it should happen that the marginal revenue attributable to it is 3s. 6d. per wagonload, then it will pay him to reduce the number of wagons of this type marshalled; and the best way he can do this is to raise the marginal cost figure until sufficient wagons have been discouraged to bring about the equality of marginal cost and revenue and, therefore, by implication: profit maximisation. If *all* parts of the railways set out to maximise their profits in this manner, the profits of the whole will be maximised.

I have spoken of two sets of people but this was a figure of speech. In principle it is possible that all decisions should be taken at the centre, decentralised to the regions or taken at lower levels still. This should make no difference whatever provided that the same principles are adopted and that the decisions are made as efficiently.

It is sometimes suggested that it might be sensible to give station-masters, managers of marshalling yards, and anyone else who is responsible for a definable segment of the railway system, a measure of independence so that they bargain with each other, all attempting to maximise their profits, just as it is sometimes suggested that the workshops in a factory should buy and sell to each other. This should not in itself make any difference. The only disadvantage might be that it would tend to make people judge the efficiency of the parts of the system by the size of their profits. This would be fallacious because some parts would have much greater monopoly power than others, and as we know where there are differences in monopoly power profits are not an indicator of efficiency. Provided such false comparisons were not made, this kind of independence and bargaining might be stimulating, but it is not an essential feature of the policy.

A last point: another defence can be argued for the present distinction made between direct and indirect costs, namely that, owing to human nature, it is a wise charging policy whatever its defects. The argument is that it would be fatal to rely on commercial managers and goods agents to maximise railway profits by making the best bargain they can because they will inevitably tend to look on the floor not just as a minimum but as a reasonable charge and if they tend to do this joint costs will not be met. Put a man against a wall and he will fight. Give him the chance to retreat and he will tend to do so. After all they are not making money for themselves and are likely to be somewhat anxious to please those with whom they have dealings, quoting a price less than that which would maximise profits. If your selling agents were hard-faced profit-maximising men it would pay to set them the low ceilings of marginal or average short-run costs, but because they are not it will pay to set them a higher minimum. More will be gained because they will make fewer concessions than will be lost, because they could take some traffic profitably at less than the minimum given them. If this is a good argument it would be sufficient defence of something like the present distinction between direct and indirect costs (though it would make the method by which average direct costs were reached hocus-pocus). But it would be a pity not to try to get the best of both, first by educating commercial managers and goods agents in the new approach and, possibly, if this is not too revolutionary, paying them a commission; second, by circulating information on similar deals made; and third, by setting up some system of inspection to check, so far as possible, that the most profitable dealings had been made. (The problem of charging where there are joint costs is considered in more detail in Appendix 4.)

DEFICIT CHARGING POLICY

In the preceding section we have argued charging policies appropriate to an enterprise which is not in deficit. We have therefore been considering principles which might govern these policies in the long run. A deficit may affect the charging policies of the railways in two ways.

In the first place we may assume that the railways have broken even on revenue account but have an accumulated deficit behind them. What are they to do with *any profits* they may now begin to make? If the policy is profit maximisation it will make no difference, but, if the ultimate intention is consumers' surplus maximisation, the Government may demand either the repayment of the accumulated deficit as a first charge on profits or may prefer to leave the deficit invested in the railways as a fixed interest debenture in effect. When the time comes, a decision must be made. (If the policy is constrained profit maximisation it will have to be decided whether the constraint shall operate until the accumulated deficit is paid off — if it is decided not to leave it invested in the railways.)

Second, let us assume the railways are not breaking even on revenue account. There is no hope of them doing so, though all separable unremunerative lines and services are discontinued: the core of the railway system runs at a loss. If it is not to be subsidised, the difference between the two basic criteria of profit and consumers' surplus maxima is irrelevant. A distinction is wanted between *immediate costs* and costs which can be avoided for some longer period of time — *ultimate costs.* Immediate costs are those which must be paid if an enterprise is to be kept open at all. If revenue is insufficient to cover them, it would pay the enterprise to close down at once and release these resources for use elsewhere. Immediate costs for the railways include fuel (except in so far as they possess *stocks* of coal) oil, and labour.* The second category of costs could be avoided in part at least for a short time until the railway (or part of it) was unsafe to operate. These are mainly maintenance costs. The third category is the one that matters. These are replacement costs which can be avoided if the railway system or parts of it are not replaced. In so far as the failure to provide for replacement out of revenue means that there is no capital sum freed when the assets wear out, this is a burden which falls on the Government which has the obligation to continue interest payments to shareholders. But as long as revenue can cover costs of the first two categories and make any contribution to the third, the Government as creditor is better off than if the railways were closed down completely. They are being paid 'something' in the pound instead of nothing. If it should be decided that the railways are not going to be profitable and it is not worth investing in them to make them so, then one would expect that a charging policy of this kind might be adopted. Thus it would be best if the railways ran (down) at a loss, as it would be most profitable for all interests if they did so unless there were more remunerative alternative uses for their assets.

POSTSCRIPT

Costs

Falling demand has caused the chronic financial problems of the railways. Road transport is responsible for much of it, but the traditional coal and steel traffics have also declined.[1] The railways could not have had their fortunes reversed by better costing, but this could have raised the efficiency of the decisions they took as a consequence of falling demand: on investment, service withdrawal, and pricing.[2]

The railways have published no account as detailed of their improvements in costing during the 1960s. They would seem to have accepted that the old division between direct and indirect costs was inefficient and misleading. If one had taken it at its face value, then my demonstration that only some 10 to 20 per cent of costs were direct, was not far wrong. But it was a mistake to take the distinction between direct and indirect costs as if it related to one between marginal

*I have made some very approximate calculations of the proportionality of costs of different degrees of immediacy, though of course this will vary from traffic to traffic and line to line. (1) Immediate costs or current inputs: (a) Standing cost; 54 per cent (b) cost per wagon-mile; 62 per cent. (2) Repairs and maintenance: (a) 19 per cent (b) 9 per cent. (3) Renewals and replacement cost and interest: (a) 27 per cent (b) 29 per cent. [13]

and fixed costs. As Stewart Joy has pointed out, many of the so-called joint or indirect costs have subsequently been shown to be variable with output in the relatively short run.[3] However, the railways got into the greatest difficulty in allowing salesmen to charge down to marginal or direct cost. This was partly for the reason given that salesmen more often than not, did not try to fix charges as high as possible — so that overheads were not covered. A second was congestion. There were other direct or short-run costs of accepting traffic. Some new traffic taken on some routes or through some goods yards or marshalling yards caused congestion in the strict economic sense already referred to in Chapter 3. They added to the costs and delays of pre-existing traffic through slowing it down. Therefore the total, or systems, cost to the railways of carrying the traffic in question exceeded the *particularised* cost of carrying that traffic. A third was the effect of the incorrect arguments they were using on overheads or fixed costs. They assumed that these overheads were not variable with output, whereas many of them were. The effect of not pursuing an optimal disinvestment policy was that losses were unnecessarily large.

On principle, similar to those outlined in Appendix 4, the railways have set about analysing their joint costs.[4] Towards the end of the 1960s they set up profit centres — that is they sub-divided railway operations into a large number of more or less separable operations to each of which they allocated costs and revenues. This was relatively easy for workshops and other ancillary activities, but much harder for other operations where it was more difficult to attribute costs and revenues to particular stations or routes because of the problems of interdependence described in Chapter 4. Because there is no published detailed description, one does not know how successfully the traditional problems have been overcome. The railways have used systems analysis to synthesise costs. One of their earlier exercises was to analyse the effect on route costs of running trains of different mixes of speeds. Estimates have been made of the effect of discontinuing: (1) the carriage of particular traffics, or combinations of traffics, and (2) the closure of routes. By such means British Railways would hope to estimate the net savings of various charges, e.g. if it abandoned, say, the least profitable 10 per cent of traffic on a route.

It is far from clear how far statistical costing is used to check what costs really are and how these vary with output. System analysis based on synthetic or accounting costs (and revenues) is an improvement on what was described in Chapter 4, but it continues with a reliance on the use of average costs by categories which does not allow sufficiently for actual circumstance. It is here that econometric studies are most useful: to determine how far there are economies in operation or congestion.

A classic railways belief, reflected in this chapter, is that there are substantial scale economies in railway operation: unit costs would fall if volumes were increased because railway track and other assets are under-employed. Any systems approach which does not test for economies of scale or model congestion effectively will reinforce the traditional railways prejudice in favour of there being substantial economies of scale. This prejudice leads to assertions that the scale of railway operations should be maintained and that closures and withdrawals have a cumulative effect on the deficit.

Econometric studies of railway costs do not support the economies of scale thesis.[5] In the most careful study, Griliches argues there is no evidence of scale economies among larger American railroads, but that more detailed research is required to disaggregate railway operations to discover if disproportionate increases in traffics carried would result in scale economies. The large number of American railroads and the data they have to give to the Interstate Commerce Commission make it possible for outsiders there to perform such studies. Only British Rail has the data to perform them in Britain. However, there is fragmentary data which suggests that congestion is a major problem on British Rail, even though many of its route-miles and other assets are under-utilised.[6]

Quite as important as setting up profit centres has been costing to improve efficiency. The studies undertaken for the 1968 Transport Act made it clear that the railway had no viable future in most of its freight and much of its passenger traffic without vast improvements in efficiency. Unfortunately much of the investment in the Modernisation Plan which was intended to improve efficiency by cutting costs had not done so. To improve efficiency the railways had to achieve higher utilisation of its stock and its manpower. It has proved far better at the first than the second. It is possible that reduction in unnecessary and unproductive manpower could still make most of the railways financially viable. Reductions in stock and manpower can get rid of 'bogus' scale economies — that is economies which only exist because the railways had, and have, more assets than they need at actual output levels. The fixity of track itself has been regarded as a major reason for scale economies. A most important development since 1963 has been the realisation that even track costs are variable in the relatively short run.[7] Modern signalling methods can achieve greater flexibility of output on any given track, as well as achieve greater efficiency by reducing the number of tracks on a route. From an efficiency standpoint British Rail was found to have excess track capacity on most routes. Much of this survives. The realisation that the railways can tailor assets, manpower and track-mileage to suit the traffic offering in the relatively short run has meant that efficiently operated, the railways can be regarded as more like a *constant returns* industry. In the short run, a railway system which had followed an optimal investment (and disinvestment) policy would rightly consider congestion both in its investment and its charging policy. This means that the danger of a consumers' surplus maximisation policy (see Chapter 6) based on short-run marginal cost pricing, leading to persistent deficits is much less.

Charging

Broadly, profit maximisation has been adopted as the railway pricing policy as a result of the 1968 Transport Act. The exceptions are: (1) London and other unremunerative grant-aided services where the level of fares is determined by negotiation with the grand-aiding body. Therefore a grant-aiding body such as the Department of the Environment or a local Passenger Transport Authority may subsidise fares to any given extent. (2) Where rail traffics are competitive with coastal shipping, the latter may appeal to a special body set up by the Minister if they think rail rates are 'discriminatory'. The compelling argument here was that coastal shipping interests felt that rail costing was not above reproach and that some of the rail traffic they were competing against was cross-subsidised. No appeals have been made since the Act.

Profit-maximisation means here that railway rates are largely determined by rates on competing modes, usually road haulage. Railway costing aims to make sure the railways know the profitability of a given traffic at that rate (though the railways may charge a premium where they have a quality advantage). To compete, during the decade rail rates have had to come down relative to road rates.[8] Often traffic will only be profitable until certain assets have to be renewed. Railway costing also aims to establish this. A decision then has to be taken for investment or withdrawal.

Therefore the railways operate pricing policy which reflects short-run marginal costs, but in the long run they are expected to meet financial targets which imply they cover long-run costs. When, if ever, the railways are in long-run equilibrium, market prices may be expected to do this for them, because they are nearer a constant returns to scale industry than used to be supposed. Otherwise a policy of short-run marginal cost pricing might have implied a long-run deficit. On most traffics market prices are seldom much above marginal costs because the railways retain very little monopoly power on either freight or passenger services. Accepting profit maximisation as the rail objective also had the advantage that railway costing methods could not directly estimate prices based on marginal costs without so much averaging and arbitrary allocation that the result would have been far too inexact. The difference between this and the traditional railway policy of 'charging what the traffic will bear' is profound. As put forward by the nineteenth-century railway economist Acworth, provided total railway costs were covered, there was virtually no attempt to relate the costs of a particular service (or profit centre) to the revenues its traffic will bear.

The 1968 Transport Act and the explanatory statements issued relating to it implied that the railways were to maximise profits in their charging policies except where they received an explicit subsidy to provide unprofitable services. It is not clear what the effect of the 1974 Railways Act is intended to have on charging policy. The railways are now to receive subsidies to cover track costs. This would be more defensible if the Government and the railways had been able to produce evidence showing that this was justified by MC pricing because track costs were fixed overheads. But they have not attempted to meet Stewart Joy's argument that track costs can be varied substantially in the short run. If Joy is right, any track costs subsidy is not only unjustified but will discourage the railways from achieving an efficient quantity of track. Since their track costs will be met, their incentive to be efficient in that respect is diminished.

5   RAILWAY INVESTMENT: PROFIT MAXIMISATION

If profit maximisation is assumed to be the policy required of the railways — defined as at the beginning of the last chapter, how should investment be determined? And, first, what can we learn from the 1954 modernisation plan and its subsequent history, to improve investment decisions?

THE MODERNISATION PLAN

Between the world wars there was little investment in the railway except in electrification on the Southern Railway. During and after the Second World War the railways were used intensively and deteriorated because of insufficient maintenance and replacement. One good estimate is that the total disinvestment in the railways — that is, the capital that was run down and not renewed — between 1937 and 1953 amounted to £440m. at 1948 prices.[1] In the immediate postwar years greater priority was understandably given by the Government to investment in manufacturing business, fuel and power, and building. The railways were technically backward and inefficient by the early 1950s but it was only in 1954 that the British Transport Commission felt able to produce an investment programme with a chance of acceptance. This, the modernisation plan, proposed expenditure of £1,240m. over fifteen years, revised to £1,660m. in 1957 because of increased costs due to inflation; better calculation of costs and receipts; and some extensions of the plan (£160m.). If the total investment needed to fulfil the plan were now recalculated it must amount to more than £1,660m. because of further increases in cost from inflation, and possibly also for the other two reasons; but a result of the Commission's crisis has been a Government reappraisal of the plan and it has not as yet been decided (June 1963) how much in total is now to be invested in railway modernisation. The amounts which have been spent so far (see Table 5.1[2]) total £912m. but not all of this has been spent as part of the plan.

There have been strong differences of opinion between the Commission and the Ministry of Transport over the profitability of the plan. The Commission has argued from the beginning and still argues it is 'a sound investment from the country's point of view'[3] — the Ministry is sceptical. It has remarked on the continuing and deepening deficits. In 1955 the Commission predicted that the railways would

Table 5.1   1955 1956 1957 1958 1959 1960 1961

	1955	1956	1957	1958	1959	1960	1961
Investment expenditure (£m.)	70	87	124	140	168	163	160
as percentage of national gross investment	2½	2¾	3¾	4	4½	4	3½
public sector gross investment	5½	6¼	8½	9½	10½	10	9½

break even in 1960. That was the year of the greatest deficit so far. In 1956 it predicted it would break even in 1962 or 1963. In 1959 it predicted a surplus on working but not on capital account by 1963. Since then the deficit on working account has increased and it is implausible, short of drastic closure, that the Commission will break even on working account in 1963. Indeed the Permanent Secretary to the Ministry of Transport has said 'I find it difficult to understand how the whole of the modernisation scheme could possibly have the economic results forecast by the BTC in their last (1959) reappraisal'.[4] Indeed he went so far as to tell the select committee on the nationalised industries that he did not see how their expectation that they would break even in five years − by 1960 − could ever have been justified.[5] The Treasury representative before the committee criticised the rigour of the plan as well as its content. 'The 1954 plan was merely a hotch-potch of the things that the Commission was saying it was desirable to achieve by 1970, ill-qualified and not readily explainable.'[6] The Ministry blamed itself (or rather the officials in effect blamed their predecessors) for accepting the Commission's assurance that the plan would be economic without making detailed investigations. When they did investigate in 1959 they were 'shocked' to discover the criteria the Commission had applied.[7] The Commission came close to admitting that the original 1954 calculations had been dubious: 'There was no attempt made in the earlier estimates to make a precise calculation of the return'.[8] But they would have said that, although their first methods of computing its value had been rough, (a) they had improved on them greatly subsequently, and what was more important (b) their later, more sophisticated, calculations had proved them right in their first rough estimates. They had since been dogged by ill-luck. Prices had risen faster than expected, especially wages. Fare and rate increases had been held back. There had been a decline in freight traffic because of a national and temporary recession in production. And there had been an unforeseen slump in the demand for coal, which had also greatly affected them. It was quite illogical for the Ministry to assume that because they were still making deficits where they once predicted they would break even, that this indicated a failure in the modernisation plan. Rather it emphasised its necessity. And to this the Ministry's answer might be said to be another statement in evidence given by Sir James Dunnett. 'Certainly a difficulty is that the reappraisals were not very specific as to what the position was going to be from year to year. They did not break it down. So it is very difficult to compare exactly what is happening with what was behind their calculations.'[9]

If one can read between the lines the present state of official thinking would seem to be this. The modernisation plan in that form was a mistake, but now that so much has already been invested we must make the best of a bad job and spend as little as will complete modernisation. This will not be sending good money after bad. If we s stop investing now our losses proportionally will be markedly greater than if the scheme is completed. To avoid a failure like that of the groundnuts scheme, investment must be continued. This will reduce the burden which will fall on the public, the deficit. It is unlikely that it will eliminate it.

The two outstanding questions are: (1) was the modernisation plan a good investment on the best information possible in 1954-5?; (2) is it best that, having been persisted in so far, it should be abandoned or considerably curtailed? It should be admitted at once that we cannot answer these questions. The data are not available. In the evidence given to the select committee on the nationalised industries, the Ministry was more vehement that its judgement was correct, but confidence in their confidence is lessened because some of their criticism of the Commission's methods was confused and illogical. On the other hand the Commission, although clearly it had a better opportunity to make accurate forecasts, plainly has a vested interest in optimism. It is a severe criticism of the modernisation plan and its reappraisals, and also of the Ministry of Transport, that it is not possible to make an intelligent guess of its eventual profitability. But there are other criticisms which can be made.

The modernisation plan, as it was presented originally, should never have been accepted. With hindsight the Ministry of Transport seems to agree with this but for the wrong reasons. It now says it knows more about the methods and data used. But even without any further information than that presented in the original modernisation plan it should not have been approved. The Commission explained that it hoped for a return of *at least* £85m. or 6.8 per cent on the investment of £1,240m. It then considered what must be offset against this rate of 'profit'. 'Of the total outlay of £1,200m., it was estimated that some £400m. would be provided from internal sources such as depreciation provisions and so forth; the annual charge for interest and redemption on the external borrowings may be put at approximately £40m. In addition to this financial charge, it will gradually become necessary to meet increased depreciation charges amount to £15m. arising from the need to base these provisions on the replacement cost of new assets. In addition, to put the railways into a healthy state and rectify the present inadequacy of net earnings, the current net traffic receipts ought to be increased by about £25m.'[10] The working deficit was then £25m. Additional depreciation was estimated at £15m., interest at £40m.; total £80m., leaving an apparent margin of £5m.

A minor error was to calculate a return gross of some provision for depreciation. If we deduct the £15m. additional provision for depreciation, the return is reduced to £70m., and the rate of return to about 5.6 per cent.

The second objection which might have been made concerned the treatment of time. The plan itself was disquietingly vague. On the one hand it suggested that the investment might be made in fifteen equal annual instalments. On the other hand it said 'in the Commission's view the expenditure would *ultimately* attract a return amounting to at least £85m. a year'[11] and in the subsequent reappraisals of the plans there were references to the 'long haul' before modernisation paid off. What seems to have been implicit in the Commission's calculations was a time lag between investment and the expected 6.8 per cent on that investment. 'It is not possible to say how quickly the expenditures made under the plan will fructify but since they are all interdependent the full benefit will not be reaped for many years ahead.'[12] Such a time lag implies there are certain costs in the early years which must be recouped from subsequent profits if the venture is to be remunerative. There was no argument whether the eventual so-called surplus of £5m. was likely to be sufficient to cover these.

The first two mistakes in the formulation of the plan exaggerated the rate of return. The effect of the third mistake is less clear. The Commission was at first glance mistaken in counting only interest on borrowed money into its calculation. By either of our basic criteria or any known criterion, it is only sensible to reinvest depreciation funds in a business if it will pay to do so. If it would pay better to invest them outside the business one would expect the firm to do this. In this respect internal are no different from external funds. The Commission's arithmetic, by contrast, assumed that interest had only to be calculated for the external £800m. The explanation that a private firm might be expected to advance will not do without elaboration. If there is a firm earning a (satisfactory) 10 per cent say, per annum, and the time comes to replace worn-out capital, this replacement capital is not required to earn a rate of return above the 10 per cent. As the railways were making a loss and not a satisfactory rate of profit, this will not do as justification of their failure to impute interest or an income to the £400m. To save the explanation it would have had to be established that the loss would have been eliminated, and replaced by a satisfactory profit, if all or some parts of the railway not to be modernised were closed down. Then one could say what was to be modernised was earning a satisfactory rate of profit disguised by losses incurred elsewhere. If any part of the system to be modernised were unprofitable, it would not pay to invest there unless the expected return from the investment were high enough to make satisfactory the return from all the capital, replacement and new capital. If the Commission at the time held this was the explanation of their defensive reasoning, one might have expected them to argue the case, or have been made to do so by the Ministry of Transport, and not have left what is, as it stands, an illogicality in its argument.

What it did do was to try to offset that defect in logic by another. We have seen that one of the claims made for the modernisation plan was that it would wipe out the £25m. deficit of the railways of the time. That amount was set off against the 'return' before arriving at the 'surplus'. If it had been established that all this deficit had been incurred on those parts of the railway which were to be modernised and that it was the total deficit on those parts, the argument of the plan would have been capable of being made logical, but we have no reason to suppose either true. First, the deficit — which was then only on capital account — was not only incurred on those parts of the railway to be modernised. Losses on unremunerative branch lines and other services, which it was no part of the plan to modernise, must have been responsible for some, possibly most, of the deficit. And these deficits elsewhere are irrelevant to the return on modernisation. If a firm has a complicated business running at an overall loss, a decision might be made to invest in one part of it, and it might happen that the return of that investment would wipe out the loss on the whole. But the firm would be stupid if it let matters rest there. It would be more profitable if the loss-making parts of the business were eliminated, or invested in, where possible, to turn their losses into profits. If this were all there was to the matter, the plan would have underestimated to some extent the return from modernisation. But, there is another point. The £25m. was the total deficit on the railways at the time. Therefore the deficit on the part of the railways to be modernised could not have been more than £25m. unless profits elsewhere were disguising even greater losses there — which is unlikely. However, not making a deficit meant earning enough revenue to cover operating and maintenance costs, depreciation *and interest charges at a lower rate on average* than obtaining in 1954. Therefore there would have to have been an increase in earnings to justify replacement.

Let us attempt to put some figures to these things. Interest payable on the £800m. external borrowings was at 5 per cent: £40m. Let us assume that the assets to be replaced were intended to earn the equivalent of 3 per cent on their replacement value. Then we can say that an additional 2 per cent must be earned on the £400m. internal financing to make it 'pay', i.e. an extra £8m. Let us assume also that though the old assets were intended to earn 3 per cent in this way £10m. of the railways' loss of £25m. was incurred in respect of those assets to be modernised. Therefore another £10m. must be earned, making £58m. in all. If we predict that revenue minus depreciation will be £70m. then there should be £12m. surplus. But we do not know whether this surplus will survive a proper allowance for time. Twelve million pounds is 1 per cent of £1,200m. It is certainly quite possible that more than an extra 1 per cent would have to be earned on capital to pay off the interest liabilities accumulated during the early years of the plan before 'fruition'.

For these reasons the plan should have been returned by the Ministry for explanation. It is a serious criticism of the plan that it does not indicate whether the railways would break even or not when it operated, and that the actual returns suggested by the Commission are misleading for the reasons given above.

In 1956 the Commission made the first reappraisal of the plan. The overall figures were the same as in 1954. Eighty-five million pounds was the minimum hoped for from modernisation. Eighty million pounds was still the figure which had to be set off against it, but it was composed differently by 1956. The anticipated interest cost was still £40m., but the deficit of the railways which the Commission still thought relevant to the plan was also £40m. instead of £25m. What was elided from the reckoning was the additional provision for the depreciation of £15m. This had disappeared without comment. (If it had remained and it is not easy to see why it had gone — it reappeared as £14m. in 1959 — modernisation, on the Commission's own reckoning, would have had to yield at least £95m. to break even.) Besides this new curiosity in the Commission's formulation of the expected return on the investment, all the old objections still stood against the 1956 reappraisal.[13]

The 1959 reappraisal went further than the other two in confusing the profitability of investment in modernisation with the profitability of the railways as a whole. It is impossible to disentangle from the evidence a rate of return on the investment. Instead it was predicted that by 1963 there would have been a net improvement in railway revenue of between £45m. and £95m. per annum. By 1959 the capital cost of the plan had been increased to £1,660m.; but of this only £1,420m. would have been spent by 1963. If it is assumed that the whole of this increase in railway revenue is due to investment in modernisation, the expected rate of return would range from 3.2 per cent to 6.7 per cent. But it is quite clear, from the few figures given, that some of this increase in revenue cannot be attributed to the modernisation plan. First, the £14m. additional depreciation returns must be deducted. Second, a net increase of £10m. in working expenses — 'track, signalling, general administration, etc.' — must be almost wholly attributable to modernisation. (Inflation is ruled out by assumption as a cause of this increase.) Allowing for these two only, the rate of return falls by 1.5 per cent to 5 per cent. But this must still be too high since it is stated explicitly that the increase in net revenue is partly due to closure of lines, changes in charging policy and administrative reforms. If one were to make the not unreasonable assumption that only two-thirds of the net improvement is due to modernisation, the rate of return dwindles by 0.9 per cent to 3.3 per cent. The only factor which it appears might be brought to raise the return again is the possibility that revenue might be expected to rise after 1963, but the Commission said in the reappraisal that although 'the prospect is of continuing improvement after 1963, with increasing traffics and falling working expenses . . . the improvement in the working surplus may well be absorbed by 'rising interest charges and the repayment of deficit advances.'[14]

What conclusion can be drawn from this? I hope it is the importance of making clear exactly what is implied by such a plan when it is presented to a Government department, Parliament or for public reading. I do not want to appear to assert that my reading of the plan or the reappraisals is exactly the right one, but that it is a possible and plausible one; and that there should be several possible interpretations of such documents seems to me a serious criticism.

THE EXPLANATION OF THE SHORTCOMINGS OF THE PLAN

There are three possible explanations of the obscurities and deficiencies we have considered. First, the Commission may have had something to hide. Second, it genuinely did not know how to set out its calculations unambiguously and correctly. Third, it was so puzzled by the lack of data on which to support its calculations that it fell into well-intentioned confusion. The third of these is the most plausible. Why was it difficult for it to draw up an immediately intelligible document? The Commission was in a quandary. By 1954 it knew that the alternatives were modernisation, closure or growing decrepitude. It did not have the necessary costing and revenue data to tell with any accuracy just what should be modernised, what closed and what allowed to decay. At times it tended towards a non-economic solution: thorough modernisation of most of the system as a social need whatever the profitability or loss.* It resisted this temptation and tried to assess inaccurately what it would be profitable to modernise, close and let deteriorate. It was unfortunate, but understandable, that the plan and 1956 reappraisal should have given the impression that the data on which the estimates were based were better than they were. It has since become clear that the profitability of the plan was established not by a careful comparison of expected costs and expected revenue, so as to produce an ordinary economic rate of return, but on a cruder basis (not very different from that which has normally been used to work out investment priorities for road construction).† And it was not then revealed that the profitability of each scheme in the plan had not been estimated separately. The original calculation had been done approximately for the plan as a whole.

The information which was available for costing — and prediction of receipts — was worse in 1954 for working out the modernisation plan that it was in 1955 for the charges scheme. Sample surveys are not at the best of times very satisfactory evidence on which to decide the profitability of an investment. These deficiencies in information had principally three effects.

The Commission of course could predict reasonably accurately the cost of the modernisation plan and the cost of the separate schemes that composed the plan. They also estimated where possible the increase in receipts and reduction in operating costs expected to result from each scheme. It was therefore possible for them to calculate the expected rate of return on modernisation. They subtracted from the cost of investment what would be needed to maintain the *status quo* by replacing worn-out capital. For example, it was re-estimated in 1960 that it would cost £161m. to electrify the London-Manchester main line; and that the return on this, would be £8m. per annum — a return on the £161m. of just under 5 per cent — but this was not the figure

* The aim of the plan . . . may be simply stated: The Commission are determined to exploit the opportunities for re-equipment which modern science and techniques present, and to transform the operations of British Railways so as to offer the public a rail service second to none,[15] whilst deriving from the equipment the full economic benefit it can provide.' The idea that the railways should be modernised at all costs has been implied more frequently outside the Commission than in it, especially on the Left. The Government has opined recently that 'there has been a tendency for technical and operating factors to prevail over others . . . in financial and commercial matters'.

† Mr. Ratter, chairman of the BTC's technical committee: 'No attempt was made . . . to make a precise calculation of the return on electrification. It was done on the basis of a yardstick of the return that comes from a given tonnage carried over the line. This was well over the tonnage which is normally assessed as being that above which electrification is profitable . . . We have worked out now the anticipated return from this electrification'.[16]

used. Instead £48m. was subtracted from the £161m. as the amount which would have been needed to maintain the line as it was under steam by replacing worn-out locomotives, renovating the track, etc. The rate of return was calculated on the remaining £113m. at just over 7 per cent: a significant difference in the opinion of both Commission and Ministry.*

The Ministry opposed the Commission bitterly on this, maintaining in some confusion that the rate of return should have been calculated on the £161m. and not the £113m.[18] The disagreement was not resolved by the Commission and the Ministry. The select committee could not decide what was the correct procedure, and the discrepancy appeared important as affecting the soundness of the plan. The cause of the difference was partly confusion of mind among the Ministry's representatives but also underlying this there was a real cause: the Commission, and therefore the Ministry, had insufficient knowledge of costs and receipts. Some discussion of the issues will illuminate the most important effect of this lack of information.

The Commission have at times given three defences of their procedure. The first was that those parts of the railway system to be modernised would have had to be kept going anyway, as the public would not let them deteriorate or close. The only decision that had to be made was whether in addition it was worth modernising; and the profitability of modernisation depended on the cost of modernisation in relation to the net benefit (reduction in operating costs, increase in receipts) to be expected from it, so it was wrong, in the example of London—Manchester electrification, to include the £48m. since this would have *had* to be spent on replacement anyway.

The argument is valid provided its premiss is valid: that public opinion demands the service should be maintained even if it did not pay to do so — in the case of the London—Manchester line that it ought to be maintained as a steam line, worn-out assets being replaced, though it were more profitable to close it down altogether. Those who have used the argument have therefore implied the possibility (a) that the modernisation plan would not be able to make the railway system pay as a whole, and that a subsidy would be needed; or (b) that the system would only pay because such unremunerative services would be subsidised by the rest: cross-subsidisation. And on subsidisation we have nothing more to say than will be said in Chapter 7.

The second argument used is that it is only necessary to work out

---

*The calculation was in fact more complicated than this, since quite properly it made allowance for scrap credits, the value of displaced assets and the nuances of a complicated bookkeeping procedure,[17] but the complications do not affect the point which is as represented in the text.

a return on the capital invested in modernisation because it can be assumed that replacement would be profitable anyway. To take again the example of the London-Manchester line, the only question is whether it is profitable to electrify it (or modernise it in some other way). It can be taken for granted that the line is profitable under steam and that if there were no better alternative it would be profitable to keep it going as a steam line. Therefore deduct the £48m. and calculate the return on the £113m. The £48m. is already earning its return as current net earnings.

Again the argument is quite valid if its premiss is accepted, but to accept the premiss is to beg the question. We have already considered the premiss that the existing (1954) railway system as a whole was profitable and questioned its plausibility. We may be persuaded to concede that the London–Manchester line under steam is a profitable part of the railway and allow the Commission the validity of its procedure there, but to assume that all schemes which are part of the plan and all other investments put forward by the Commission are modernisations of service, lines, etc., which were profitable as they were, is not just reckless: it is patently and admittedly false.

The difference that this act of faith makes can be shown by an example. There is a worn-out marshalling yard. To replace it by a new one virtually identical, would cost £1m. Another £1.5m. would build a modernized yard with mechanical handling devices, etc. The rate of return on the £1.5m. is estimated at 15 per cent and is found by calculating the net benefits expected to result from modernisation. It has been decided on other grounds that investments should be made if expected to yield more than 9 per cent. Should the yard be modernised? The answer is not a straightforward 'Yes'. The £1.5m. cannot be spent unless the other million is spent also. If it could no doubt the investment should be made. As it is we need to know the profitability (or loss) of the line if merely renewed as its capital stock wears out. This will be the discounted future stream of profits in such circumstances expressed as a rate of return on the capital invested. Where capital is, and is to be, replaced in the period under consideration it must be valued from the date of replacement at replacement cost. The rate of return on this part of the investment can, in our example, be (a) more than 9 per cent; (b) between 9 per cent and 5 per cent, or (c) be less than 5 per cent, possibly even negative. If it is more than 9 per cent there is no question that the investment should not be made; and replacement like-with-like would be justified even if there were no question of modernisation. If it were between 9 per cent and 5 per cent, replacement would not be justified on its own account but the investment of the £2.5m. would be since the return on the whole would be more than 9 per cent, the standard required. If it were less than 5 per cent the investment should not be made.

The premiss the Commission makes is that all its investments fall in category (a) or (b): and this amounts to an act of faith the Ministry disputes: many fall in category (c) and are less profitable than the Commission's method of working out a rate of return makes them appear; others fall in category (c) and should not be undertaken at all. In principle it should be easy to settle the matter, by inquiry and calculation, but it is just this the Commission's inadequate data do not permit. (The Ministry seemed to suggest that the net benefit from *modernisation* should be expressed as a rate of return on the cost of *modernisation plus replacement* — the total investment; but that was their confusion. Unless the non-modernised line were making a loss this underestimates the return from the whole investment. If it were losing, it would overestimate the return, though less than the Commission's procedure would.)

When the select committee asked how profitable the London–Manchester line was under steam in 1960, it was told the Commission did not know because it was not possible to separate the receipts attributable to it from the total receipts of the region;[19] and the same would have been true of lesser schemes. Neither would the Commission have been able to isolate the costs, capital and operating. When the Commission were asked to give evidence on the profitability of modernisation already accomplished, they produced increases in receipts from modernisation for some thirty passenger schemes. Although gains of 30 per cent to 50 per cent were not unusual, as the select committee remarked, they did not 'indicate whether the line is now making a profit or a loss' because the Commission was unable to say anything about the previous profitability of the line.[20]

This fact is the most important reason why the financial future of the railways and the plan is doubtful: the state of costing and demand analaysis. Sample costing at least as practised by the railways was inadequate. Demand analysis — the analysis of the factors affecting the demand for railway services — had not got far enough.

The last defence of the railways' procedure is they do the best that can be done in the circumstances, given they cannot work out a proper rate of return on all capital invested. It would have been foolish to postpone modernisation in 1954-5 whatever the state of costing and demand analysis. I think this can be granted. The sensible action in such circumstances is not usually to do nothing but to make the best of bad information. The question is whether the railways made the *best assumption* in premising the underlying pre-existing profitability of parts of the system to be modernised. There was reasonable doubt about this which surely should have been reflected in a larger allowance for uncertainty than was otherwise necessary, and though costing has improved since then this would still seem to be necessary though to a lesser extent.

Some investments have had no return attributed to them. It has been said they *must* be done. Sometimes this means that they must be done even if they have to be subsidised: as public opinion, in the Commission's view, would not stand for it if they were not. They are unremunerative services in the sense of Chapter 7 and as such do not concern us further here. But 'must' is frequently used with another implication: the investment must be made if the line, service, etc., is to continue. One example of such an investment has been the rebuilding of the bridge at Victoria Station in London. If it were not rebuilt, the station would become unsafe for traffic and unusable. Therefore if Victoria Station is to exist, the investment must be made. The argument continues: if there is no choice but to rebuild, there is no point in working out a rate of return on the investment. All businesses make such investments whose necessity is so plain that the calculation of a rate of return would be an unprofitable elaboration.

Nevertheless it would seem that for projects of any size this common commercial practice is indefensible for the railways but, before arguing that, the objection must be met that it is often not possible to calculate a rate of return on an investment. This can be maintained on two grounds. First, there are no returns which can be attributed. Second, although there are returns so little is known or can be predicted about them that in that sense it is not possible to attach a rate of return. The first argument is false. The second in almost all conceivable cases insufficient. To take the example of the Victoria Station bridge, let us assume that we know the profitability of the station. It is yielding 20 per cent on its capital after allowing for depreciation at replacement cost. The bridge becomes unsafe. Victoria Station earns nothing (and to simplify we will assume that this is not mitigated by any increase in earnings at any other station). Let us suppose that this 20 per cent is £1m. In an economic sense this annual stream of net earnings can be imputed as a return to the rebuilding of the bridge. In an accounting sense this return would now be shown as a lower yield on a larger capital, the capital being increased by the capital value of the rebuilding of the bridge in so far as this has not been allowed for by depreciation. (The bridge is in fact the kind of asset on which the railways do not allow for depreciation and it is this fact only which distinguishes this argument from what has been argued in the previous chapter, p. 91 et seq.)

Suppose that the yield from Victoria Station is much lower than this, such that it is in fact yielding a rate of return on the capital invested in it which would be unsatisfactory for a new investment. Then the argument of the previous chapter applies. We assume the return required from new investment is 9 per cent. The yield on Victoria Station is 2 per cent or x pounds. Although x pounds is only 2 per cent on the capital invested in the station, it is more than 9 per cent on the capital required to rebuild the bridge. Therefore other things being equal, it will pay to rebuild the bridge as a satisfactory rate of return will be earned on that investment and something, which is better than nothing, will be earned to service the old capital invested in Victoria Station; whereas if the bridge were not built, the situation would be worse since nothing would be earned and no contribution would be made to the service of the old capital. If it should be predicted that further capital outlays will be needed to maintain the earning power of Victoria Station then the cost of these, properly discounted to allow for time, should be considered since they could make a difference to the profitability of rebuilding the bridge. And of course if there are profitable alternative uses for assets embodied in the station, these may affect the calculation too.

There are two reasons I think why it is indefensible that the railways should not attempt to work out a rate of return in such cases. Probably the more important is the old doubt whether there are not times when it would pay not to make the 'necessary' investment but to close down. This may seem implausible for Victoria Station, but there must be many lesser investments where there is reasonable doubt. Besides, such omissions gave a misleading notion of the profitability of schemes. It was maintained by the Ministry of Transport that the cost of London–Manchester electrification was not £161m. but £194m. because of the cost of 'associated works' including the rebuilding of Euston Station which is 'something you might have to do anyhow'.[21] Plainly there is something quite unsatisfactory here. It may be the case that whole investment — unnecessary and necessary — will be profitable showing a satisfactory yield when the true rate of return is computed, but who is to say if there is an utterly false distinction between investment and necessary investment which ignores the fact that there is always an alternative to 'necessary' investment: closure? And if 'necessary' investment should be unprofitable then it will have to be decided whether a subsidy is desirable. The best that can be said of the present situation is that it is misleading.

The other reason for working out a rate of return is that this involves the discovery of what traffic is expected to benefit from the investment (or suffer if it is not made). This makes it possible to charge the beneficiaries. There is a danger, more important for a consumers' surplus policy than profit maximisation, that if a rate of return is not worked out, the cost of such investments will be recouped from the earnings of the railways as a whole, or the region, and this of course implies cross-subsidisation.

The principal reason why there is this class of 'necessary' investments[22] may or may not be a decision of principle. The reason why in many cases it may not be possible to eliminate it, even where it would pay the railways to do so, is once more the inadequacy of costing and demand data — the second argument why the working out of a rate of return is impossible. Yet there must be cases where the estimates are not as firm as the railways like to use, but most probable figures would be more helpful than none at all.

The third effect of poor data and the reluctance to think in terms of probability has been underestimation of receipts. Possibly this has been the Commission's salvation. They maintain that they underestimated the return from the modernisation plan because they were overcautious in predicting increases in receipts resulting from modernisation. Invariably the gains from modernisation achieved so far have been more than was allowed for. Gains of 30 per cent, 40 per cent and 50 per cent have not been unusual. In one instance, the small Leeds—Barnsley route, there was a gain of 415 per cent. The Commission's view is that their bad luck elsewhere — their rashness in making the assumptions they did about interest rates, the level of economic activity, wage levels, etc. — has been more than balanced by overcautiousness here.*

It would surely be excessive to say that this justifies the Commission's procedure, in particular their treatment of risk. Even if it were the case that the Commission had said to itself that it would not allow for the chance of adverse circumstance in the assumptions it made about interest charges, wage levels, etc., but would allow for all risks by being overcautious in the estimation of receipts, that would scarcely have been a desirable method of hedging against risk. If it were not a nationalised industry and accountable to no one outside itself, perhaps it would not have mattered, but as the Commission is required to explain itself to the Ministry and, to a lesser extent, to the general public by the publication of plans and white papers, this as a deliberate method of providing against risk would be highly misleading, and would make it impossible for the Ministry or the public to appreciate properly the true merits of the various factors affecting the profitability of the plan. It is surely less misleading that the risk of predictions being

*Cf. this conversation between the Rt. Hon. Enoch Powell, MP and Sir Reginald Wilson (the BIC was then borrowing at 5¾ per cent): P: 'So you are bound to make a loss? . . . W: 'I doubt it very much . . . because it depends on the receipts' . . . P: 'But on the conservative estimate . . . there was no prospect of avoiding a loss at the rate of interest on which you were then borrowing?' W: 'That is so but perhaps I should now add that we are working on an average rate of 5 per cent. We are assuming that over the years we shall be borrowing at 5 per cent. We could of course be wrong about this.'[23]

falsified, for better or worse, should be estimated for each of the major factors: at the least on the demand side, the level of economic activity, the probable future demand for the more important commodities carried by the railways, receipts specific to the investment where important; and on the cost side, the level of wages, the cost of fuel, interest rates.

Another effect of underestimating receipts which one might expect is a bias in favour of cost-reducing investment, since savings of cost are usually firmer figures than increases in receipts.[24]

RISK AND UNCERTAINTY

One lesson of railway experience, and experience in other public undertakings, is the need to make proper provision for risk and uncertainty. The planning rate of return expected from an investment by nationalised industries is almost always lower than that used in the private sector. Nationalised industries have been in the habit of using a rate which is barely more than the expected cost of finance to them, say 5—6 per cent. Private firms tend to use a rate of from 10—20 per cent, well above the cost of finance to them or the dividend they expect to pay.[25] But we cannot generalise from this absolute difference, for example, to argue that the expected rate of profit used by nationalised industries should be the same as that used in the private sector. The rate used will vary according to (a) the degree of monopoly power; (b) difference in policy and (c) the riskiness of the investment.[26] But we can note differences in the factors considered by the nationalised industries and the private sector. Let us imagine a firm which expects to pay 5 per cent on, or for, its capital. It uses a 15 per cent rate of profit for investment, meaning by this that it will not invest unless it estimates it will get a return of 15 per cent. The margin normally exists for three reasons:

(1) The rate of profit sometimes but not always includes an allowance for the cost of replacement over and above its original cost, particularly as a hedge against inflation.

(2) To cover taxation of profits.

(3) To provide a premium against risk.

The first two are immaterial. Nationalised industries have in recent years taken account of (1) as indeed the Commission did originally, as we have seen in respect of the modernisation plan. In so far as a nationalised industry is liable to pay profits tax, they will make provision for it in calculating the return from it, but this is of course irrelevant for the railways.

Reason (3) is of the first importance. A sensible firm will allow some percentage difference between the cost of finance and the expected rate of profit to allow for the chance that it has read the future wrongly. A private firm will also have reserves to weather any loss which should result from miscalculation. The risk premium and the reserves are a cushion against actual loss, on the assumption that the firm is risk averse. The Commission, like most public corporations, has, as we have seen, no reserves for this purpose.

The Commission does not appear to use or to be required to use any risk premium.[27] An old argument was that it was not necessary for railways or public utilities as there was virtually no risk attached to their investment because of their monopoly position and the inelasticity of the demand for their services. But this argument no longer holds. Investment in railways is at least as uncertain as ordinary commercial investment. Failing that, it would have been, I think, a reasonable inference from the 1955 modernisation plan that the difference was one of appearance only. Instead of saying there is an $x\%$ margin between cost of finance plus special depreciation provision and expected rate of profit as a hedge against risk, it is said that the return is expected to be 'at least' £85m., which could be taken as implying that they had considered all significant factors likely to affect the return from the plan, and had decided that if the worst came to the worst the outcome could not be less than that. It was the worst outcome it was reasonable to assume. The 1956 reappraisal made it plain that was a mistaken inference. The Commission stated then that they expected to make a return of £85m. provided that:

(1) interest rates remained the same;

(2) there were no more delays in adjusting fares and charges to increased costs caused by the Transport Tribunal or the Minister;

(3) there were adequate investment resources to fulfil the plan;

(4) wage rates remained the same or increases were proportional to increases in productivity; and

(5) there was no interruption in the rate of economic growth causing a recession in traffic.

These were the more important suppositions. Whatever might be said of them as a statement of aims or requirements, they were quite unreasonable then as predictions. As one commentator remarked at the time, an investment programme which made such assumptions showed an enterprise 'insulated from the ugly current facts of life' and saw the assumptions as 'excuses for failure stockpiled in advance'.[28] It is incredible that they should have been made, but if one should be interested in asking who is to blame for subsequent deficits which might have been avoided by a more realistic calculation, the Ministry must bear as much blame as the Commission for accepting what the Commission told them; and therefore there is the less reason to commiserate with the Ministry and the nation for the deficits it has had to meet. Unless the calculation of return proved wildly pessimistic on other grounds, the prediction that the modernisation plan would enable the railways to break even in 1960 (1955 prediction) or 1961-2 (1956 prediction) was doomed from the start.

If this analysis is correct, the right criticism is not that the Commission failed to allow for risk and uncertainty but that they were unreasonably over-optimistic and at least in the original 1954 Plan, hid this fact. Far from sharing the risk aversion normal to a private firm, which wants to avoid an eventual fall in its share values and possibly bankruptcy, it is hard to escape the conclusion it was gambling.

Hirshleifer has argued[29] that risk should be discounted in the same way for public as for private investments. Against this however Arrow and Lind[30] have argued that this is unnecessary on certain not unreasonable assumptions. We may regard the public sector as a vast insurance scheme against risks. The risks are borne by the multitude of taxpayers. If the outcome of an investment like the Modernisation Plan is worse than predicted then each taxpayer faces an unanticipated increase in taxes. If the outcome were more favourable than predicted, then each tax bill would be reduced. Because there are so many taxpayers, the actual effect plus or minus of an individual investment outcome upon a single taxpayer will be small. The risks are pooled. Moreover there are many public investments and if, as seems reasonable, we assume their outcomes are independent, then the government is pooling risks to a much greater extent than is possible to private investors or firms. Arrow and Lind were able to show that the larger the number of taxpayers who were pooling risks the nearer a rational risk premium approximated to zero. Therefore the state does not need to require a risk premium on public investment. This implies that private planning rate of return or discount rate will exceed the public (unless as Arrow and Lind have suggested one tries to extend to the private sector some of the benefit of the state's ability to pool risks).

What was wrong with the Modernisation Plan was not a failure to allow for risk, but over-optimism expressed as a tendency to make unreasonably favourable forecasts of the likely course of interest rates, price increases, real wages and economic growth. If the state believes that a nationalised industry is consistently over-optimistic one tactic is to raise the rate of return required from its investment. The rationale is that if such a public corporation says that an investment will earn 10% then experience suggests that it will actually earn 5 per cent, so one requires it to earn, say, at least 15 per cent. But this is a crude method of adjustment. (1) If one requires a higher discount rate this will distort the time-stream of costs and benefits. (2) The enterprise has no incentive to stop being over-optimistic. (3) It does not get down to questioning the assumptions — like those listed above — which are responsible for an unrealistic anticipated return. A first step might be to require public enterprises to adopt the commercial system of estimating the most probable return, making an allowance for the probability of less and more favourable returns. There is a case for formalising the expression in terms of a probability distribution for a nationalised industry to help overcome the problem of communication or accountability between board and Ministry. The board should make an estimate based on the best information *available* — whatever its adequacy — of the probability of earning various rates of profit on the investment, for example

5 per cent chance of a return of   3—6 per cent
20 per cent chance of a return of   6—8 per cent
25 per cent chance of a return of   8—10 per cent
30 per cent chance of a return of 10—12 per cent
15 per cent chance of a return of 12—15 per cent
5 per cent chance of a return of 15—20 per cent

What is implied by this probability distribution, is, first, it is predicted that there is no plausible chance of the return being less than 3 per cent, or more than 20 per cent. Second, by weighting the average percentage in each bracket the percentage probability that the rate of profit will fall in that bracket, the most probable rate of profit can be found (the choice of which, as statisticians put it, will maximise mathematical expectations). In this example it happens to be just over 12 per cent. The Ministry, when it comes to approve or disapprove the investment, will also be interested in the probability that the scheme will make a loss.

One would expect such a probability distribution to be supported by calculations based on various assumptions about the level of wages, raw material costs, etc., the rate of inflation, the flexibility of charges, the level of traffic, the rate of growth of the economy, other rival means of transport, etc. The detail of such calculations will be governed by the nature of the evidence on which it is possible to base projections and the extent to which it is judged profitable to make such calculations. (The greater the care with which risk has been allowed for in calculating the various categories of revenue and costs, the less need there should be to allow for risk also in the expected rate of profit used. Indeed one must be careful not to allow for risk twice over — in the basic calculations *and* the rate of profit.)

Even this may be regarded as too much hidden and in important cases, the sensitivity of the outcome to changes in crucial assumption may be demonstrated. What would be the effect of assuming a lower rate of growth of Gross National Product; a higher growth in real wages or a relative fall in the price of another mode of transport? Such sensitivity analysis enables it to question and, if it feels it has the power, to alter

114

the assumptions made by public enterprise. Except for the largest investments – among which was surely the Modernisation Plan – it is not practical for governments to examine the assumptions public enterprise makes on all projects. Therefore one can take the pooling ideas to an intermediate stage, by asking a nationalised industry like the railways to work out the return on its whole capital expenditure programme; and then test the sensitivity of that to changes in underlying assumptions.

If the expected (most probable) rate of profit used should turn out to have been too pessimistic and the railways should make unexpected profits, these can always be returned in higher profits, or lower prices, according to the criterion in use. The present practice, because of the Government's responsibility in respect of railway deficits, puts an avoidable strain on the national budget. But if the Commission persistently exaggerates the profitability of its scheme it is sensible for the Ministry to react to correct such over-optimism.

Sor far it has been argued that, once a nationalised industry such as the railways is directed to maximise profits, it should:

(1) improve the presentation and logic of the investment proposals (the clearest way in which to set out an investment proposal is in the form of present discounted values)*;

(2) improve the data on which calculations are based;

(3) allow for risk in a way which works.

These three recommendations of course are valid whatever criterion is used, not only profit maximisation. But, last, in considering the implications of profit maximisation, we should examine what the policy of the Government should be in supplying capital.

THE RATE OF INTEREST

If the railways are to maximise profits for the Government, the possibilities would seem to be, besides self-finance, that (a) they borrow from the Government at a fixed rate of interest, (b) they borrow by raising equity capital from the Exchequer, or (c) they borrow from the public by issuing debenture or preference stock without Government guarantee. It would not be compatible with the criterion that the railways should raise equity capital on the market, since this would imply that the equity shareholders were entitled to the residual profit when other charges had been paid; and this would mean, subject to any restrictions, that the enterprise would be run in *their* interest to

---

* It is perhaps worth remarking that the latest considerable railway proposals published shows no advance in presentation. It is defective in logic and data. British Railways Board, *The Reshaping of British Railways* (HMSO, 1963), p.42; 'Liner trains'.

maximise *their* profits and therefore would in most respects be indistinguishable from a private firm. There is of course *prima facie* nothing impossible about such a proposal. It might appeal to an anti-nationaliser who wishes to denationalise a profitable public enterprise but does not wish to see the enterprise or its component parts sold outright to the highest bidder. Instead he would make service of the existing capital, pending redemption, a fixed charge on profits and require that new capital should be raised by the issue of ordinary shares on the market. But it is not a possibility we have considered and it is plainly incompatible with either of our basic criteria.

The difference between the first and second methods is formal only. In the first case the Exchequer gets both fixed return and any surplus profits; and the difference would only be a bookkeeping one if, with the first method, the enterprise was yielding a return of less than the fixed rate. It would be more straightforward if the second method was adopted rather than the first. There would be no need for the complication of suspense accounts and accumulated deficits partly composed of fixed interest charges unpaid.

The choice between either the first or second and the third method of raising finance would more obviously depend on the particular circumstances of the public enterprise and Exchequer at the moment — which would be more profitable and convenient. Besides raising money on the market by the issue of fixed interest or preference stock, a nationalised industry would also be able to borrow from the commercial banks, raise money on mortgage and plough back profits in reinvestment like any other commercial enterprise, subject to the requirement that residual profits should go to the Exchequer.

Traditional practice has been that nationalised industries should borrow on the market by issuing fixed interest stock with Government guarantee that the stockholder would get his return, the Government paying if the railways could not. Since 1956 it has been recognised that nationalised industries would find it difficult to borrow directly from the market on their own credit. They have therefore borrowed instead from the Treasury. If the railways are to become truly commercial there does not seem to be a case for continuing with Government guarantees. If the railways use a realistic discount rate, it should not be necessary. If they do not, then they should try to act sensibly as an enterprise intending to maximise profits. Neither should they borrow from the Treasury because it would be too expensive to borrow on the market unless the Treasury rates the railways' expectations of profit higher than the market does. It must be remembered that the only reason the Treasury invests in the railways on this criterion is because it believes it could not get a higher profit by investing anywhere else.

Whatever method is agreed on, it is necessary for the railways to take a view on the future rate of interest when starting an investment programme which will entail raising capital over a number of years. When the modernisation plan was worked out the Commission was borrowing at 4 per cent. They are now borrowing at 6 per cent. This is one other reason why the modernisation plan could not have succeeded, if the original calculation of revenue and costs had been correct, since the rate of return would have been less than the rate of interest which they had to pay. At present it is probably best to assume that the rate of interest on money raised by method (a) will be 6–7 per cent in the foreseeable future and, until the railways pull out of the red or unless special arrangements are made for the repayment of creditors, rather more by method (b), and certainly more by method (c). If the arguments for raising the cost of finance advanced in Chapter 4 are accepted it will be higher still.

Given the changes in the relative values of ordinary shares and gilt-edge which were already becoming apparent in 1954 (more especially in the United States) and the reintroduction of monetary policy to control the economy in 1951, both the Commission and the Ministry were perhaps unwise to assume that the rate ruling in 1954-5 would continue.

The object of this chapter has not been to appraise the profitability of actual railway investment, because that would have been impossible on the data available, but to criticise the way in which these schemes have been presented, in so far as they are obscure and illogical and therefore misleading. Whether the Commission in fact knew better than it expressed itself one cannot be sure. The causes of the obscurity have probably been an understandable reluctance to be honest about how little they knew about their own costs and profitability and a reluctance to think in terms of probabilities. If one should wish to point out where they would seem to have been most misleading it is, I think (a) the unsystematic treatment of time; (b) the evaluation of risk; and (c) the consequences of the fact they often do not know if services etc., to be modernised are running at a loss or a profit, and if at a profit, at a satisfactory profit. Other points which have been made are as follows.

Internal funds should not be reinvested in the railways unless it would pay to do so. Internal and external sources of finance are no different in this respect, but the modernisation plan required, or appeared to require, borrowed money alone to show a rate of return.

If it is argued that losses could be eliminated by closing some parts of the railway system, this is not enough in reckoning the profitability of a scheme. The probability that they will be closed must be estimated.

It is not clear why certain provisions thought necessary for replacement in 1954 were not thought necessary in 1956.

It is wise to allow a margin between the expected rate of return on an investment and the expected rate of interest payable as insurance against over-optimism. One might expect this over-optimism would be based on some estimates of the probability of changes in demand and costs. On the demand side, the most important factors would appear to be the level of economic activity and the demand for coal as well as any specific factors affecting particular investments. On the cost side a view is needed at least on the probable course of wages, fuel, the effect of Government policy in freezing increases in charges, and the future level of interest rates.

There is something to be said for the formal use of a probability distribution, not because it is impossible to think clearly without it, but because greater clarity in communication is impossible and this is especially important for a nationalised industry.

It would seem that the railways might either borrow from the Government or the market at a fixed rate of interest or from the Government as equity capital. The third would be compatible with profit maximisation only; but if that policy should be adopted it has much to recommend it.

Rates of return should be computed on all projects of any size. There are two undesirable effects of assuming that some investment is 'necessary' whatever the return. The first is that it may lead to an exaggerated notion of the profitability of interdependent schemes and at worst lead to a wrong decision whether to invest or to close a facility. The second is that it is liable to lead to what is in effect cross-subsidisation.

The Commission's practice of underestimating receipts though in a sense fortunate is not a defensible way of allowing for risk and can give a bias to cost-reducing rather than revenue-increasing investment.

POSTSCRIPT

The Modernisation Plan

Subsequent events seem to have borne out the criticism of the procedures and calculations underlying the Modernisation Plan. Since the Government allowed the railways to invest again substantially in the mid-1950s on average the investment record has remained bad.[1] They have consistently over-invested in relation to their actual and prospective earning power.[2] The railways have repeatedly expected that they could invest their way into a profit. Much of the responsibility lies with persistent over-optimism that demand would improve.[3] But there also has been a more or less continuous record of investment which failed to cut costs or stimulate demand sufficiently. It was estimated in 1967 that if one had imagined that the kind of services which were to be grant-aided under the 1968 Act had been grant-aided since nationalisation, then more than £1,000 million of public funds had been absorbed into the railways since nationalisation with on average a zero return. This is a way of saying that in spite of very substantial investment, the persistent tendency was towards deficit.

The Explanation of the Shortcomings of the Plan
The confusions reported in Chapter 5 are not only found on the railways — though rarely elsewhere to the same extent. From the Modernisation Plan onwards the railways were engaged in a kind of corporate planning, demonstrating its perils when improperly done. The railways in principle made a net revenue forecast assuming certain investment was not undertaken and then another, assuming it would be. They calculated the return on investment as related to the difference in the net revenue forecasts, the essence of what is often now called a Corporate Plan. Had net revenue grown as predicted, their wisdom would have been approved. It was their deficits that brought them blame. What subsequent events and the analysis in this chapter shows, however, is that their corporate planning was not sound. Even as such, there was no explicit allowance for the effect of the gestation period upon profitability; their treatment of depreciation and interest charges was confused; and they did not allow for real increases in the cost of labour.[4] Far more important, they had not worked out what services were profitable, what were the returns from individual investments, or what investment would in effect have been cross-subsidising loss-making services. Therefore the returns on investment in the profitable services would have had to be more profitable than indicated, if the railways were to maintain the loss-making services they meant to, given that some at least of the investment would have been in these (and *may* have been expected to yield a low return). A corporate plan which gives one no confidence that it is grounded on a real knowledge of what is, and what is not, profitable, is worthless. The unknown question is how far the new generation of corporate plans produced since 1968 are an improvement. As we have seen, the railways have much better cost data. They have also undertaken some market research and other demand analysis. They have a more systematic approach to the analysis of profitability. Whether the quality of their data and analysis has improved sufficiently for their corporate plans to be a sufficient basis for approving their investment plans is more doubtful. The Marsh Plan produced in 1973 had even less relevant data than the 1954

Modernisation Plan to justify public expenditure which threatens to be of more than Concorde proportions. But it is clear that not only as in the past does its profitability depend on a very high rate of growth of inter-city passenger traffic but also on that traffic being ready to pay a very high but untested premium for speed.

To summarise, the new Marsh Plan appears based on a number of old contentions, many of doubtful validity and many of which the railways have previously put forward in a variety of guises.

(1) It is argued that there are enormous overheads — of track and administration — which cannot be cut without traffic and revenue falling more than proportionally. This is contrary to what Joy has maintained and to what economists would normally think plausible, given good management. One would have hoped the railways would have tried to demonstrate its truth publicly, given its enormous importance.

(2) The railways now argue that revenue cannot cover these overhead costs; but that the nation must meet them or face the only alternative of eliminating most of the railway system. This follows only if contention (1) above is true.

(3) They then argue that a certain pattern of investment will minimise net losses. They do not try to demonstrate publicly at least what investments will be profitable, but wrap it all up with one overall investment programme as in the Modernisation Plan.

(4) They continue to make overoptimistic demand forecasts especially of the price people are prepared to pay for need.

One can conjecture that until the railways are ready to improve their costs and analyse the marginal costs of systems charge, as well as improve their demand analysis, there is no reason to suppose that the Marsh investment programme has any greater chance of success than the original Modernisation Plan and the investment in the Beeching Plan.

6 THE CONSUMERS' SURPLUS CRITERION FOR RAILWAYS

We begin where the argument of Chapter 3 ended. There the relationship —
the family resemblance — between the profit and the consumers' surplus
criterion, and the possibility in principle of using a consumers' surplus
criterion as the basis for drawing up a set of accounts, and determining
a rate of return, was argued. It is now necessary to consider in some
detail what kind of a consumers' surplus criterion we want — and also
how to set about using it — especially in the context of railway
operation.

DEFINITION OF THE CRITERION: BENEFITS

We must decide first what we mean by consumers — whether we mean
consumers in general (everyone in his role as consumer of goods and
services) or some group of consumers of which the most obvious are
the consumers of the products and services of the enterprise in question.
The former interpretation, though it has some traditional support, is
impracticable. Even if it were not, it is most certainly not what most
people would mean by running an industry in the consumers' interest.
Rather they intend the second meaning. Therefore we will define our
consumers' surplus policy as one in the interest of consumers of
railway services, that is, simply railway-users.

We move on a stage. An industry can be run in the interest of all
its consumers or there could be some exceptions. For example one
could adopt the position that foreign consumers might be required to
pay profit maximising prices: consumers' surplus policy at home,
profit maximisation abroad. In the past when coal was scarce this was
the kind of policy the National Coal Board could have pursued,[1] though
such a policy would have to contend with the difficulties that have to
be met by any attempt at price discrimination: the possibility that home
consumers buy the product at domestic prices and sell abroad at a profit.
This could be overcome in controlling the export of coal. This obvious
basis for excluding some consumers from benefits scarcely exists for
the railways — it would be difficult to charge different fares for foreign
and British travellers on the railways — and it is not easy to see what
other argument might be advanced for the exclusion of some group of
railway users from benefits. Therefore we will assume in what follows
that all railway users are consumer-beneficiaries in the sense of the
criterion.

121

When the coverage of the term 'consumers' interest' is decided, the next decision is whether all consumers are to be treated equally. It could be decided that greater weight is to be given to the preferences of the poor, or to country-dwellers or some other deserving group of railway users, so that a pound's worth of benefit to them is to count for more than a pound's worth of benefit to other consumers. I intend to assume that consumers' preferences will count equally in this sense:[2] and that if it is decided to confer extra benefits on certain groups of consumers, for example the users of country services, this will be done by explicit subsidy rather than by modifying the weighting of the criterion.

There are other questions we might want to ask. Recalling the argument of Chapter 3, do we wish to benefit one generation of railway-users more than another, that is, do we want to build in a non-zero rate of time preference into the distribution of benefits?[3] I assume that there is no strength of opinion that we should do either.

Therefore we are assuming that:

(1) only railway-users are to be beneficiaries;

(2) all railway-users, without exception, are to be beneficiaries;

(3) they are to be treated equally;

(4) generations are to be treated equally by assuming neutral time preference.

Analogous assumptions are implicit in the normal notion and practice of profit maximisation, that is: only shareholders are beneficiaries; *all* shareholders are beneficiaries, their benefits being in relation to the number of shares they own, as the benefits received by consumers are in relation to the amount they consume; in proportion to the shares they own, shareholders receive equal dividends; no special weight is given to the preferences of shareholders now or at any particular point in the future; and no account of income is taken in determining the size of the dividends received by a shareholder.

DEFINITION OF THE CRITERION: COSTS

Assume consumers are to pay the private costs of the industry just as they cover the private costs of a profit maximising concern. Then no one — the State or anybody else — is out of pocket because of the industry's existence. The enterprise is not to be run as a public service, all or part of the costs being borne by the community as taxpayers. But it is not to make profits. Profits are to be passed on to the consumer.

If consumers are required to meet the enterprise's private costs, this seems to imply that costs are defined identically for a profit maximising and a consumers' surplus maximising enterprise. Or, to put the matter in another way, one would expect to find the same items under the heading of expenditure in the enterprise's accounts as one would in the accounts of a profit maximising firm, except that instead of dividends one would find − if the enterprise were profitable − an item of 'profits to be passed on in lower prices'.

Such a consumers' surplus policy implies proper provision for depreciation, if receipts permit this. Otherwise the enterprise will not be covering its costs. A consumers' surplus policy is also compatible with the retention of profits to form reserves. The purpose of holding reserves is generally to meet unforeseen contingencies (or to act as bridging finance). It is as important for a consumers' surplus enterprise to have reserves for this purpose as it is for a profit maximising concern. If it has no reserves, and it runs into temporary difficulties, it must borrow or raise its prices to meet its obligations. A reserve is therefore a protection of the consumers' interest as it is a protection of the shareholders' interest. (When capital is guaranteed by the Government, the cost of the railways' failing to provide sufficient reserves falls on the Exchequer, as we have noted when considering profit maximisation. Therefore in these circumstances the proper provision of adequate reserves may be in the Treasury's best interest.) Similarly a consumers' surplus policy is compatible with the Treasury requiring the railways to use a risk premium when working out the rate of return on investment. Otherwise the railways may make a loss which would have to be met by drawing down reserves, raising prices where possible, or, under present circumstances of Government guarantee for railway stock by a subsidy from the Exchequer.

A consumers' surplus policy is also compatible with requiring consumers' surplus enterprise to pay tax analogous to profits taxation. As we have seen it hardly makes sense to charge a profit maximising nationalised industry, profits tax since all profits go to the Exchequer. But there is no obvious reason why the State should not tax consumers' surplus enterprises to the same extent it taxes private firms. If consumers' surplus accounting should reach a stage of precision so that it is possible to put a reasonably accurate figure on the consumers' surplus gained by its consumers over the year − their dividend, so to speak, the difference between what they have paid and what they would have been prepared to pay at most − then a profits tax could be calculated on the same basis for a consumers' surplus enterprise as for a private firm: as a percentage on profits. But this is to look much too far into the future. Indeed consumers' surplus accounting may never reach such a state of refinement, not because it would not be possible in principle, but because the practical difficulties and costs involved would be tremendous. Therefore some other method of profits (surplus) taxation would be needed, possibly a sales tax or turnover tax, intended to raise an amount roughly equivalent to what the same organisation would pay if profit-making. Whatever the means adopted one should not assume that just because it is a consumers' surplus organisation it should bear less tax than a similar private firm. One would also expect a consumers' surplus firm to be subject to any other taxes or rates incurred by a private firm.

Next, a consumers' surplus policy is compatible with requiring an enterprise to pay the interest costs of the capital it uses. On this two points must be made. First, the source of funds for a consumers' surplus organisation cannot be equity shares, because it is of the essence of equity shares that the residual profits, after all other obligations have been met must go to shareholders. And for the same reason consumers' surplus enterprise cannot borrow on equity terms from the Government. They must therefore borrow money at fixed interest. They could issue fixed interest stock, borrow on overdraft or from financial institutions at fixed rates. In certain circumstances they might raise money on mortgage. They could borrow on the market or through the Government as at present.

The second point concerns the rate at which they borrow. There is a short-term problem. The Government may or may not believe that the money already invested in railway modernisation will show a proper return to meet the payment of interest eventually. But if the railways were required to borrow from the market now, one can be sure they would have to pay a very high rate of interest indeed, unless backed by Government guarantee. A rate of interest of 10 per cent or more would hardly be surprising. However this is only a short-term problem because we may hope that Government policy and the transport consultative committees, whose duty it is to approve closures of lines, will make it possible for the railways to become viable. When the railways have solved their more important problems and confidence in them has risen, it might be possible for the railways to raise capital by issuing debentures. Normally one would expect that the rate of interest at which the money market would lend to the railways would be based on expectations of their future profitability. By analogy with commercial firms, it would seem highly probable that a consumers' surplus enterprise would have profits to pass on in the form of lower prices, even if it borrowed at market rates. But it might be necessary to face the fact that this might not work: which in theory is what one might expect if consumers' surplus enterprises are required to borrow from a (profit maximising) money market.

In such circumstances the question might be asked whether it was possible to have consumers' surplus enterprises in a free-enterprise economy. The answer to which the argument of Chapters 2 and 3 leads us is 'Yes' – provided that the Government does not compare incomparable rates of return on profit and consumers' surplus maximisation. If this situation should arise, and the Government should decide that it is in the public interest that there should be a consumers' surplus sector, then it would have to provide, or perhaps only guarantee, the funds, and this *might* mean subsidising investment in the sense that it could get more *profits* if it invested in *profit* maximising concerns. But it is just this comparison which the existence of two criteria makes illogical. It will be sensible if, as far as funds allow, it invests in consumers' surplus enterprises to the limit that investment is profitable as measured by the consumers' surplus rate of return. If the state of the money market is such that there is no difference between the market rate of interest payable and the consumers' surplus rate of return — an unlikely thing if the enterprises are sound — the Government might decide to subsidise the funds to the consumers' surplus sector either by giving a guarantee or, if this were insufficient, perhaps by providing funds at a rate of interest lower than the market rate. This 'subsidy' would be a measure of its evaluation of the relative worth of investment in the two kinds of enterprise — a comparison which, as we have said, cannot be established by direct comparison of rates of return. And indeed this is not a subsidy in the true sense. It would simply be the only way — a decision of principle — by which the Government can decide the relative merits of investment in two sectors when a different criterion operates in each.

Last, a consumers' surplus policy is also compatible with self-finance. When a private firm decides how much of its profits after tax to distribute, and what proportion to plough back in investment, it decides to do what is in the shareholders' best interest. We assume there is a profit maximising firm which has earned higher profits than it did in the previous year. It has the choice of paying all the increase as a dividend (to the Exchequer) or of ploughing some part or the whole of it back into the business. If it does the first the shareholder, the Exchequer, gets an immediate increase in income and, so to speak, the value of its shares rises. If it does the second, there will be a smaller, or no increase in the shareholder's income, but the higher rate of investment means that the capital value of the enterprise will increase and therefore that the value of the shares will rise. Since the investment would not be undertaken unless it were expected to be profitable, the company's profits will rise in future when the investment is fruitful. If the enterprise is rational and its expectations are fulfilled it should make no difference to the shareholder what proportion of investment is financed from profits and what from outside finance (except in so far as the absence of a capital gains tax or a wish to retain control of the company complicates the issues, but these are irrelevant in this instance). We can imagine the board of a consumers' surplus enterprise faced with exactly the same decision. It must decide whether in its opinion, it would be more in the consumers' interest to pass all profits on as a fall in prices or whether some should be retained for reinvestment. In both cases it is the same criterion, the consumers' interest, which should determine the choice.

The argument of the first two sections of this chapter has gone some way towards giving us a definite consumers' surplus criterion. On the benefits side we have said that the consumers mentioned in the criterion are all railway users without exception. And that a pound's worth of consumers' surplus is to have as much weight whichever consumer gets it, whenever they get it and however much or little income or surplus they already have. We have also argued that such a concern should be required to meet all private costs, including depreciation, provision of adequate reserves, any taxation required of it, and subject to some reservations, the interest cost of the capital it employs. It is now necessary to consider what is implied in respect of, first, charging and, second, investment by this definition of consumers' surplus maximisation.

PRICING POLICY OF A SINGLE-PRODUCT ENTERPRISE

The policy that maximises consumers' surplus for the consumers of the services of an enterprise sets price equal to zero. In fig. 6.1, if price is 0, output is OQ_5: and consumers' surplus is maximised, subject to the constraint that the consumer may not pay negative prices,

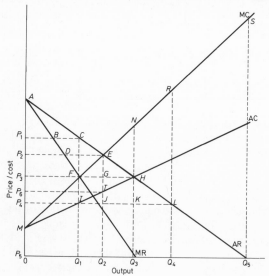

FIG. 6.1

126

that is, receive subsidies to consume. By assumption, the costs of production, represented by the area under the marginal cost curve, $OMSQ_5$ must be met by the taxpayer or someone else other than the consumer. Thus it does not meet the desiderata of our consumers' surplus criterion laid down in the last section.

However, the most efficient solution is to sell OQ_2. Just as the intersection of the marginal revenue and cost curves fixes the maximising output, OQ_1, and price OP_1, so the intersection of the average revenue and marginal cost curves determines the most efficient consumers' surplus output and price. To show this, consider the difference between this policy and the consumers' surplus maximising policy of the last paragraph. The inefficiency of that policy is measured by the area below the MC and above the AR curves, that is ESQ_5. For any output to the right of OQ_2 the marginal cost exceeds the benefit (measured by the demand curve or 'willingness to pay'). Therefore any reduction in output from OQ_5 towards OQ_2 saves more in costs than it loses in consumers' surplus. For example, relative to OQ_5, an output OQ_4 would mean cost savings of Q_4RSQ_5 exceeding the surplus loss of Q_4LQ_5. Any reduction in output beyond OQ_2, for example to OQ_1, the profit-maximising output, would be inefficient; the consumers' surplus loss, Q_1CEQ_2 exceeds Q_1FEQ_2. Therefore producing OQ_2 and setting price equal to MC is the policy by which the excess of consumers' surplus over costs, measured by AEM, is maximised. Thus we might imagine a railway with a single product maximising consumers' surplus net of private costs. (We will consider the multi-product case later.)

Only if AC = MC, and is horizontal, does this meet another of our desiderata, and break even. Otherwise this pricing policy implies that the railway makes a profit (as in fig. 6.1, where MC exceeds AC) or a loss (as in fig. 6.2, where AC exceeds MC). Except where AC = MC one can demonstrate the relative inefficiency of requiring that the railway at least breaks even. In fig. 6.2, AC pricing implies a price of OP_1, and output, OQ_1. By comparison with the efficient price OP_2, and output, OQ_2, there is a consumers' surplus loss, Q_1ABQ_2 and a reduction in costs, Q_1DBQ_2. The surplus loss exceeds the cost reduction by ABD. This is the measure of the relative inefficiency of average cost pricing. The judgement underlying the requirement that enterprises should at least break even, must be that political inefficiency, bad effect on management morale or whatever other reason is given for the constraint, must be worth at least ABD of lost efficiency.

When MC exceeds AC (as in fig. 6.1) the loss of efficiency from AC pricing, relative to MC pricing, is $Q_2ENQ_3 - Q_2EHQ_3 = ENH$.

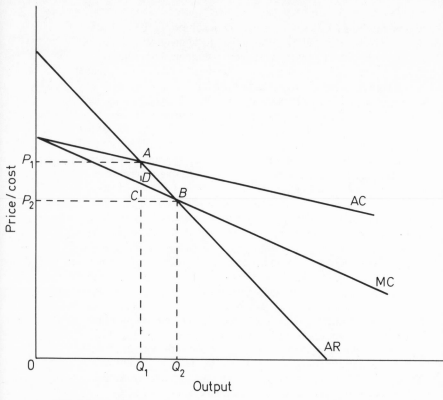

FIG. 6.2

If AC pricing is required so that a public enterprise should not make a profit, *ENH* measured the inefficiency of this. The next fifteen page contain more difficult material than elsewhere in the book. It is subordinate to the main argument which begins again on p.143.

One might imagine that with increasing costs (MC exceeds AC) one could produce the efficient (or MC) output, OQ_1. but sell it at the break-even or AC price, OP_1 (in fig. 6.3). This is unstable. At the price OP_1, consumers will demand OQ_2 but the average cost of producing OQ_2 is OP_2; and so forth. This will set up what is known as a cobweb. In the example of fig. 6.3(a), this will converge to a solution with price OP_3 and output, OQ_3. This will be stable, imply average cost pricing and mean that the railway makes neither a profit or a loss. However, the existence of such a convergence depends on the relative slope of the demand and AC curves[3]. For the cobweb to converge on a solution, the slope of the demand curve must exceed that of the AC curve exceeds that of the AR curve, the cobweb will be explosive and

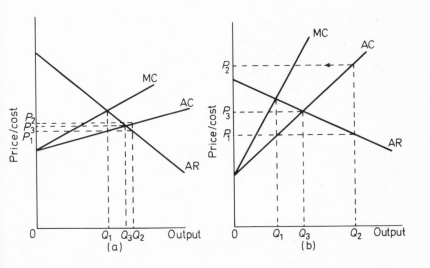

FIG. 6.3 (a & b)

there will be no progression to a stable solution. This does not mean, however, that if one is prepared to accept the inefficiency of a break-even solution, whatever the relative slopes of the AR and AC curves, that one cannot select an average cost pricing policy with output OQ_3 and OP_3. One can. What presents the problem is trying to sell the efficient output at the average cost price.

In the first edition, I argued that if the railway did not respond to the excess demand at OQ_1 by increasing output, but continued to produce OQ_1 at OP_1, there would have to be rationing and that this would probably be 'intolerable'. I was rightly criticised by Arrow, Merrett and Millward for not taking the analysis further.[4]

There are several possibilities.

1. There is a black market in tickets. Middlemen buy the tickets and sell them to the passengers prepared to pay most. In fig. 6.4, instead of the railways gaining a 'profit' which they would do had they set price equal to OP_2, the same profit P_2BCP_1 is made by the

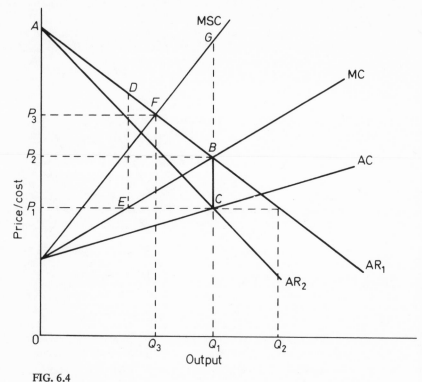

FIG. 6.4

middlemen. The effective price to the consumer which clears the market is indeed OP_2, so the railways' loss is the middlemen's gain. (In fact there will be some loss of efficiency, for the middlemen's costs must be deducted from their profits.)

2. A second possibility is that OQ_1 tickets are sold to the first OQ_1 passengers to reach the booking office, but the rationing procedures secure that *these incur no queuing costs*. If one were to assume that the first OQ_1 passengers were a random sample of the OQ_2 passengers willing to buy at the price, OP_1, then the effective demand curve would rotate to AR_2. By comparison with an efficient policy of setting price at OP_2 this would mean a surplus loss of ABC. Consumers would be better off in this event because ACP_1 exceeds ABP_2, but overall there would be a surplus loss because of the reduction in rail profits P_2BCP_1. ($ABCP_1$ exceeds ACP_1.)

3. It is more realistic to assume there are queuing costs. The

greater the ratio of excess to realisable demand (OQ_2/OQ_1) the longer a passenger must be prepared to queue to be sure of a seat. However, the steeper the slope of the MC and AC curves the more OQ_2/OQ_1 increases. Thus the average queuing time is a function of the slope of the MC and AC curves, relative to the demand curve. If the potential passengers arrive in sequence, and are served in sequence, it is not unreasonable to assume that all will have the same queuing time for any given ratio OQ_2/OQ_1. The time a passenger will queue will be limited by the maximum time he will queue rather than forgo the journey. For any given passenger, faced by a price, it will be some difference, DE, between that price and the maximum he is prepared to pay, measured on the demand curve. How long a person is ready to queue depends on the value he sets on his time. The greater the value, the less time a given DE will buy. If we assume that all potential passengers have the same value of time, then the length of the queue will be determined by BC since this is the value that clears the market. $OQ_2 - OQ_1$ value a ticket by less than BQ_1 so they will not queue. Passengers to the left of OQ_1 value it by more than BQ_1 but they do not have to queue for longer than the time valued by BC. Thus they still gain consumers' surplus. The net loss of this solution is P_2BCP_1 since the railways have lost a profit. Instead, every consumer has incurred an additional cost, BC, which sums to P_2BCP_1 for all consumers.

We can take this analysis a step further. BC is the additional queuing (or congestion) cost to the consumer at OQ_1 which results from trying to sell an efficient output at an average cost price (under conditions of increasing costs). But as we have seen the ratio of excess to effective demand is a function of the MC, AC and demand curves. The cost of queuing that clears the market is always measured by the vertical distance between the MC and AC curves for a given effective demand, OQ. It follows that in the presence of queuing, the market will always be cleared where the MC curve intersects the demand curve. The difference is that instead of the railway gaining a profit, the passengers collectively incur queuing costs of an equivalent amount. However, in the presence of queuing OQ is no longer the socially efficient output. We shall find in Chapter 8 that queuing or congestion is far more important for road pricing policy: but it will be useful to demonstrate the point here. Let us assume that the railway in our present relatively unimportant example decides to allow for queuing costs in deciding on an efficient price and output. Each additional passenger not only incurs a queuing cost himself, but adds to the time everyone else spends in the queue, so that the marginal social cost of his joining the queue exceeds BC. For the OQth person it is the sum of all the extra costs he causes to everyone in the queue including himself. In fig. 6.4 it is expressed in the MSC curve. The efficient output,

OQ_3 is where the MSC curves intersect the demand curve, sold at the price OP_3. When queuing or congestions costs are brought in, OQ_1 is no longer the efficient output. OQ_3 is, since the reduction in social costs, Q_3FGQ_1, exceeds the reduction in consumers' surplus, Q_3FBQ_1. The efficient output will therefore be lower than in the absence of queuing costs.

In the first two cases considered, (1) and (2), there were no queuing costs so the efficient output stayed at OQ_1 but there were income transfers and/or losses of surplus. In case (3) it is only if queuing costs are positive at OQ_1 and to the right of OQ_1, but zero to the left that the efficient output will remain at OQ_1. In the more normal case where congestion is a continuously increasing function of a rising MC curve, the efficient output will be to the left of OQ_1. The relations between these curves and other aspects of this problem are further analysed in Chapter 9. Thus stable equilibrium can rarely be reached with an efficient output and average cost pricing when marginal costs are increasing. Even, as in cases (1) and (3), where the price formally remains set at average cost, the effective price to the final consumer is determined by marginal private cost (in the absence of congestion pricing).[5] It is only in case (2) where we suppose that there is a *costless* rationing procedure that an efficient output can be sold at an average cost price. This is hardly a practical outcome because of the great difficulty of devising such a rationing scheme. Excess demand normally does cause queuing and it may result in other inefficiencies also.

In the first edition I considered another pricing policy intended to produce an efficient 'break-even' output under increasing costs, This was the 'co-operative' policy which seemed to embody the principles of the co-operative movement and had the advantage of being formally equivalent to profit maximisation both as a pricing and investment policy. The difference is in distribution, since the dividends go to customers who are members, and not to shareholders. The policy could be stated as: set out to maximise profits like any private firm. Invest to maximise profits. Determine dividends like any profit-maximising firm but return them to members in proportion to their purchases. Such a system on the railways would incur some administrative expenses. All rail travellers who were members (and presumably no one could be forced to be a member) would have share books and membership numbers. Every transaction, whether for passengers or freight, would have to be recorded twice — once for ordinary accounting and once for dividend purposes (unless stamps were issued as has become common among co-operative societies since 1963. Then the value of this year's stamps are likely to be related to last year's profits). There would have to be machinery for paying the dividends: and the nature of railway business with customers widely dispersed, especially passengers, would make it dearer to administer per member than for a co-operative society. (In practice one might issue encashable stamps to passengers while paying dividends to freight passengers to keep down administrative costs.)

What determines the effect of adopting such a policy under conditions of increasing costs is the difference made to consumer behaviour by reimbursement of the excess of selling price over average cost. (We will assume that the dividend not only returns the excess, but also covers interest on the loan the consumer is making the co-operative society between his purchase and the receipt of his dividend.) In fig. 6.1 this means the consumer is paying an immediate price of OP_1 but an ultimate one of OP_4. If consumers collectively are under no illusion, then at a real price of OP_4, they will demand OQ_4. If their dividend is received immediately by them as encashable stamps, there should be little illusion; and there will be a cobweb problem similar to that already analysed, if output is expanded. If output is not expanded beyond OQ_1, then the rationing problem will again be similar to that already analysed.

The differences arise if some or all consumers are misled by the situation into thinking the real price is indeed OP_1 or, at least, higher than OP_4. If all were to be misled into thinking it OP_1 then one would have found a method of combining an efficient output policy with a break-even pricing policy. Such a depth of illusion would seem implausible. It is much more plausible however that some consumers would be misled and therefore the actual output demanded would be less than OQ_4 if the real price were OP_4. The effective demand curve to the right of E would lie below the demand curve that would exist (AR) in the absence of illusion. Where output was constrained, illusion would similarly reduce congestion costs. Since illusion is itself presumably an inefficiency which is not easy to quantify, not much can be deduced normatively about the effect of illusion on the efficient price and output policy. Therefore it would only be if no customer thought the real price was below OP_2 that the objective of selling an efficient output at an average cost price would have been achieved.*

*In the first edition I stated that a co-operative policy would not maximise consumers' surplus by comparison with an average cost pricing and output policy. In a private communication, Millward has shown this need not be correct. His argument implies assuming the 'co-operative' policy is feasible without queuing costs.

Profit-maximising output and price consumers' surplus is $ACQ_1O - OMFQ_1$ or $ACFM$. With average cost pricing and output, it is $AHQ_3O - OMNQ_3$ or $AEM - ENH$. Consumers surplus with marginal cost pricing and output is AEM. Profit maximisation is more efficient than average cost pricing and output if, and only if, CEF is smaller than ENH.

What these arguments show is that, for a single-product enterprise, attempts to avoid making a profit and produce an efficient output normally fail if costs are increasing. To adopt an average cost pricing and output policy will lead to a demonstrable inefficiency unless there are constant costs. The justification for average cost pricing and output policies must be that the advantages exceed the inefficiency. The economic or management case for refusing to allow an enterprise under decreasing costs to make a loss must be that the disincentive effect of making losses on management results in an overall net loss in inefficiency. The political case for requiring enterprises to at least break even is based on some notion of 'fairness'. Whatever the reason behind the requirement of the British nationalisation statutes, that public enterprise should at least break even (as well as similar directives in other countries), many would accept this as an institutional constraint on public enterprise pricing and output policy.

More controversial is the requirement that nationalised industries should not make a profit. As Merrett says: 'The insistence that consumers must pay at least the average cost of the services they require is evidently a constraint which is imposed by the community as a whole, since it is the community which would need to make up any losses incurred by the nationalised industry. There is no self-evident reason why the community should insist on imposing consumers a *maximum* price equal to average costs, if some higher set of prices would maximise consumer surplus either now or over accepted future periods.'[6]

CEF, ENH are similar — having equal angles. Their relative size depends on whether *CF* is greater than, equal to or less than *NH*.

The elasticity of AR curve $\quad \left(\in_d\right) = \dfrac{\Delta q}{\Delta p} \left(\dfrac{p}{q}\right)$

for a price fall of *CF*, $\quad \left(\in_d\right) = \dfrac{Q_1 Q_3}{CF} \times \dfrac{OP_1}{OQ_1}$

$\quad \therefore \quad CF = \dfrac{Q_1 Q_3}{\in_d} \times \dfrac{OP_1}{OQ_1}$

Similarly the elasticity of the *MC* curve $\left(\in_s\right)$ for a price rise of *NH* is

$$\in_s = \dfrac{Q_1 Q_3}{NH} \times \dfrac{OP_3}{OQ_1}$$

$$NH = \dfrac{Q_1 Q_3}{\in_s} \times \dfrac{OP_3}{OQ_1}$$

If $CF = NH$, then $\quad \dfrac{Q_1 Q_3}{\in_d} \times \dfrac{OP_1}{OQ_1} = \dfrac{Q_1 Q_3}{\in_s} \times \dfrac{OP_3}{OQ_1}$

or $\quad \dfrac{OP_1}{\in_d} = \dfrac{OP_3}{\in_s}$

therefore, if $CF \lessgtr NH$, $\quad \in_d \lessgtr \in_s \dfrac{OP_1}{OP_3}$

This is distinct from the general argument for allowing public enterprise to plough back some of its profits rather than pass them on in lower prices. If we could assume a perfect capital market then one could argue that it would benefit consumers to plough back up to the point that the marginal return from investment in the enterprise equalled the return they could get from saving or investing elsewhere in the economy.* Merrett's point is that where capital to public enterprise is rationed so that for this reason the marginal return in the enterprise is always above that in the private sector, the consumers of the enterprise's products will always be better off if the enterprise sets out to maximise profits, and ploughs back all its profits, so long as the marginal return on its investment exceeds the marginal return in the private sector — that is, for as long as capital rationing is effective. Merrett assumes that government does ration capital to public enterprise, but as has already been observed in the Postscript to the last chapter, it is improbable that the railway marginal return on investment exceeds that in the private sector. Neither (Chapter 11 below) is it always plausible that there is capital rationing for highways. If one invests in the consumers' surplus enterprise even though the marginal return is lower than in the private sector, this in its turn creates an inefficiency measured by the difference in the two returns.

PRICING POLICY OF A MULTI-PRODUCT ENTERPRISE

Where an enterprise is producing a single product, the average cost price is obvious and can be read off diagrams such as shown in figs. 6.1 to 6.4. In each case there is a unique price implied by the zero profit and loss constraint.

Most enterprises have more than one product and can therefore meet the zero overall profit and loss constraint with an infinite number of price combinations. One can then ask what is the efficient combination of prices, defined as that which would result in the least loss of consumers' and producers' surpluses, or alternatively as Pareto optimal. It is the combination of prices which corresponds to the least social cost method of meeting the zero profit and loss constraint.

If one assumes two products whose demand and cost functions are

*This implies a capital market perfect enough for savings and investment to be equilibrated throughout the economy. Following on work by Feldstein and Marglin, it has become more usual to assume that there is a difference in the weight to be attached to public investment financed by borrowing and to that financed by taxation at the expense of consumption.[7] The second should be weighted more heavily because it displaces consumption. Because some public investment is so financed one would expect the average shadow price of capital to the public sector to exceed the price of capital in the private sector. (The reverse implication of this is that more weight should be given to lowering prices than to investment in a consumers' surplus enterprise.)

independent of each other (their cross-elasticities of demand are zero and they have no joint costs), then what determines the efficient pricing policy is the relative demand elasticities of the two products. In the case of two increasing cost products that would make a profit with marginal cost pricing, the price of the service with the more inelastic demand will fall more if the constraint is imposed. Similarly if both products are subject to decreasing costs, the price of the product with the more inelastic demand will rise the more when the constraint is imposed. The intuitive meaning of this can be shown in fig. 6.5a and b. For simplicity of exposition only, in each figure both products are assumed to have the same (but independent) cost functions. For a given price fall $(P_0 - P_1)$, the loss of surplus on the commodity with the more elastic demand is the revenue change (R) plus the surplus gain (CS) less the increase in costs (C):

$$= R\,(DEGF - ABDC) + CS(ABDC + BED) - C(DEGF + BED + BHE)$$
$$= BHE$$

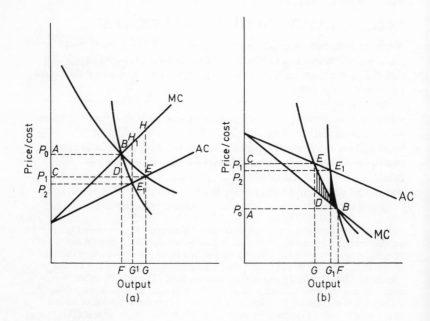

FIG. 6.5 (a & b)

136

It can be seen that BHE exceeds BH_1E_1, the corresponding surplus loss for the product with the more inelastic demand, even though the price reduction is greater, $(p_0 - p_2)$. Fig. 6.5b shows the equivalent comparison for the case where both products are subject to decreasing costs. The relevant triangles are shaded. The same principles apply for n products and for cases where some are subject to increasing and others to decreasing costs. The underlying principle is simple enough: the more inelastic the demand, the less the surplus loss from a given price change. Therefore the price combination which will minimise the loss of efficiency from imposing a zero profit and loss constraint will tend to be one which implies a greater divergence between marginal cost price and quasi-optimal price for goods subject to less elastic demand curves. Indeed if there are zero cross-elasticities of demand, then the percentage deviation of price from marginal costs will be inversely proportional to the demand elasticity of each. Where the demand cross-elasticities are not zero, it is still true that efficient pricing subject to the constraint will imply that outputs should be changed in the same proportion from the outputs that would be demanded if unconstrained marginal cost pricing were permitted. Even this requires modification since it does not allow sufficiently for the effect of output-related cost changes on the extent of inefficiency.*

---

*This proposition has a long history in economic literature. For a review and more detailed exposition see Baumol and Bradford.[8] As it would seem impossible to demonstrate the proposition geometrically, the following algebraic demonstration is adapted from them. I am grateful to Mr. A.D.J. Flowerdew of LSE for his help in improving this demonstration.

Let $p_1 \ldots p_n$ and $q_1 \ldots q_n$ be the prices and outputs of the n products of the enterprise. Let $W(p_1 \ldots p_n)$ be the consumers' surplus function to be maximised subject to $P = 0$, where P is the overall enterprise profit or loss.

We require to maximise $W - \lambda P$ where λ is a Lagrangean multiplier. Suppose p_i are the decision variables and the q_s are dependent on them. The first-order conditions are:

$$\frac{dW}{dp_i} = \lambda \frac{dP}{dp_i} \qquad\qquad i = 1, \ldots n \qquad\qquad (1)$$

Suppose demands for all products are independent: then

$$W = \Sigma_i \int_{p_i}^{\infty} q_i(p) \, dp_i \qquad\qquad (2)$$

so

$$\frac{dW}{dp_i} = -q_i \qquad\qquad (3)$$

From (1) and (3)

$$-q_i = \lambda \frac{dP}{dp_i} \qquad\qquad (4)$$

and since this is true for all:

$$\frac{1}{q_i} \frac{dP}{dp_i} = \frac{1}{q_i} \frac{dP}{dp_i} \qquad\qquad (5)$$

Total revenue $= p_i q_i$, so that MR_i, the marginal revenue for product, is given by

$$MR_i = p_i + q_i \frac{dp_i}{dq_i} \qquad\qquad (6)$$

Assuming $q_i(p_i)$ can be inverted, to give the function $p_i = p_i(q_i)$

137

P = total revenue − total cost, therefore

$$\frac{dP}{dp_i} = \frac{dP}{dq_i} \cdot \frac{dq_i}{dp_i} \tag{7}$$

$$= (\text{MR}_i - \text{MC}_i) \frac{dq_i}{dp_i} \tag{8}$$

which, from (6) $= (p_i + q_i \frac{dp_i}{dq_i} - \text{MC}_i) \frac{dq_i}{dp_i} \tag{9}$

substituting from (4), and multiplying both sides by $\frac{dp_i}{dq_i}$, (which equals

$1 / \frac{dq_i}{dp_i}$, by the property of an inverse function)

we have $\quad -q_i \frac{dp_i}{dq_i} = \lambda (p_i + q_i \frac{dq_i}{dq_i} - \text{MC}_i) \tag{10}$

and adding $p_i + q_i \frac{dp_i}{dq_i} - \text{MC}_i$ to both sides gives

$$p_i - \text{MC}_i = (1 + \lambda) (p_i + q_i \frac{dp_i}{dq_i} - \text{MC}_i) \tag{11}$$

$$= (1 + \lambda) (\text{MR}_i - \text{MC}_i) \quad (\text{from (6)}) \tag{12}$$

So the difference between price and marginal cost should be proportional to the difference between marginal revenue and marginal cost.
(11) may also be written:

$$- \lambda (p_i - \text{MC}_i) = (1 + \lambda) q_i \frac{dp_i}{dq_i} \tag{13}$$

or $\qquad \dfrac{p_i - \text{MC}_i}{p_i} = \dfrac{1 + \lambda}{\lambda} \cdot \dfrac{1}{E_i} \tag{14}$

where $E_i = - \dfrac{p_i}{q_i} \dfrac{dp_i}{dq_i}$

and is the elasticity of demand for the ith product
If all demand elasticities are constant, it follows that $(P_i - \text{MC}_i) / p_i$ must be a constant and hence that price should be proportional to marginal cost.

Write $\Delta p = p_i - \text{MC}_i$, so that (13) becomes:

$$-\lambda \Delta p = 1 + \lambda q_i \frac{dp_i}{dq_i} \tag{15}$$

or $\qquad \dfrac{dq_i}{dp_i} \cdot \Delta p = - \dfrac{1 + \lambda}{\lambda} q_i \tag{16}$

Second order conditions for a maximum are

$$\frac{d^2 W}{dp_i^2} - \frac{d^2 p}{dp_i^2} < 0 \qquad (\text{sufficient})$$

$$\frac{d^2 W}{dp_i^2} = \frac{-dq_i}{dp_i}$$

$$\frac{d^2 p}{dp_i^2} = (1 - \frac{d\text{MC}_i}{dq_i} \frac{dq_i}{dq_i}) \frac{dq_i}{dp_i} + (p_i - \text{MC}_i) \frac{d^2 q_i}{dp_i^2} + \frac{dq_i}{dp_i}$$

which is of indeterminant sign.

In other words it may well be optimal not to produce some products, and there will be a corner point maximum.

What is relevant here is whether or not there is cost interdependence between the products such that a change in output in one affects the marginal cost of producing at least one other. Where output changes would be substantial, the effects on the marginal costs of producing related products might be considerable. Suppose that under conditions of increasing cost, the constraint implied a substantial reduction in the price of certain passenger services for which the demand was inelastic, but that even so, the increase in volume resulting was large enough to imply it would be profitable to invest in certain track and signalling improvements which, even if optimal from the standpoint of the passenger trains, would reduce the operating costs of other off-peak passenger services using the same track. The costs of production of these off-peak services would fall and/or their quality of service would rise. The actual estimation of an efficient price combination in these circumstances would present severe problems. Nevertheless we may assume that there is in principle an efficient set of prices which would meet the zero profit and loss constraint.

In the first edition I produced an alternative solution to the average cost pricing problem where there is more than one product. *Ex hypothesi* it cannot be the most efficient solution. Its rationale was that it implied different distributional judgements. The ethical characteristic of the efficient solution is that like price discrimination it charges relatively more on those products where the demand curves suggest consumers have a relatively high inter-marginal valuation of the product: which is what an inelastic demand curve means. It has some affinity with a very old principle of public utility pricing, namely that it should be based on 'value of service'. There is nothing impossible in questioning the distributive implications of such a policy, though one would normally expect ethical and political attitudes to depend on circumstances. One would not be surprised to find the political process regarding differently a situation where the relatively inelastic demand and therefore high prices referred to long-distance main line traffic catering for businessmen and where it related to short-distance city commuting traffic by rail. One might expect to find attitudes towards pricing policy affected by whether the 'captive' public who pay more because of the inelasticity of their demand, are rich or poor, able or disabled, and so forth.

The alternative I put forward was akin to what the public utility pricing literature has called 'cost of service' pricing. It began with the proposition that the railway manager should make clear that his charges covered the short-run average costs (normally equal to marginal costs) of accepting the traffic. I then supposed that charging what the market would bear would result in politically unacceptable profits. The question then is what rules, alternative to the efficient rule already discussed, might the railways adopt to meet a zero profit (and loss) constraint, where there are joint costs, if the 'efficient' rule had unacceptable redistributive implications?

Where there are joint costs the solution is not as evident. Suppose we have a marshalling yard serving two traffics. The contributions made by the two traffics more than cover the total costs of the yard. For the sake of example let us suppose that all the costs are joint costs. How are we to define consumers' interest in respect of the surplus of revenue over costs? One ruling might be that it should all be devoted to improving the service at the marshalling yard so that its users get better facilities at the same price. Investment would continue until joint costs had risen to equal revenue. This solution would avoid several problems but it implies that the railway knows the consumer's interest better than he does. The consumer is not given the choice of spending this surplus as he wishes which may well be something other than railway transport. It is rather as if instead of giving an office-worker a rise the firm decided to give him a new desk and chair, which would not make him more efficient but would make him more comfortable. Most people would rather have the increase in salary. Most consumers it might be assumed would rather have the reduction in price.

Another ruling might be that all such surpluses accrue to the railway system as a whole and are reflected in a general reduction in rates and charges — for instance on an x pence per ton-mile or per passenger-mile — or since this would involve immediate problems of deciding how much should be distributed to passengers and how much to goods, let us modify the ruling and say that any surplus which is made on goods traffic should be reflected in a reduction in the charge per ton-mile throughout the system and similarly any surplus earned on passenger-traffic is to be reflected in a reduction in the rate per passenger-mile. The first difficulty about such a rule would be of course that there are certain surpluses which would be joint to both passenger and goods, for example earned by a station which handled both. Waiving that difficulty, there is a more important one. Such a procedure would imply cross-subsidisation. It would in fact be in the direction of a return to the old ideas of railway charging. Let us imagine a generalised case. The facilities serving suburban traffic are in general making a profit. The old system was that such profits were used to subsidise other parts of the railway system. This ruling would not have quite the same effect. The cross-subsidisation would be less. But profits made on suburban traffic would be used to lower the rate throughout the country, which would imply a measure of cross-subsidisation of other traffic by suburban traffic. Therefore unless we are to be inconsistent with the principles already laid down in the last chapter, this kind of solution must be ruled out. Of course if we are ready to accept cross-subsidisation this solution may appeal.

The only logical alternative to cross-subsidisation is that the profit should go back to those who have paid more than the cost of the services provided for them. The question which presents itself is how the profits should be passed on in price reduction.

There is a solution which may be acceptable in certain circumstances: long run average cost pricing, but only when, first, joint costs are short-run in the sense given on p.85 and, second, when there has been no considerable miscalculation affecting the proportion in which the joint cost facility is used by the various streams of traffic. Let us take an example which makes the point very simply. A goods line is being modernised. Involved in the reconstruction is the rebuilding of a number of bridges over the line. Most of the traffic on the line is expected to be of normal gauge requiring a normal clearance under bridges; but there is the possibility of a certain traffic using the line which will require wagons of greater than normal height. If this traffic is to use the line, bridges will have to be higher than they otherwise would be for these special trucks to pass under them. Let us suppose that the difference between modernisation with 'normal' and 'high' bridges is £1m. Then this £1m. is a cost which can definitely be attributed to the special 'high' wagons. It therefore seems reasonable that if the line begins to show a profit, a distinction should be made between the prices charged to the users of the two types of wagons. The users of normal wagons pay one long-run average cost price and the users of high wagons another (higher) long-run average cost price reflecting the difference in the cost of the facilities provided. It must be emphasised that this solution is not implied by our criterion since, as we have argued, once the investment has been made, no allocation of joint costs can strictly be made. It is just a value judgement which may well be acceptable as a basis for charging. But it is not difficult to imagine situations where the adoption of the rule will seem unfair. Suppose the railway authorities predicted that 10,000 wagons would use the line and in fact only 8,000 do: and yet the line makes a profit. Adopting the rule that each class of traffic should at least pay a charge covering the long-run average costs attributable to it might mean, let us suppose, that the users of 'high' wagons do not benefit from a reduction in prices at all since the same extra total costs are spread over a smaller than predicted number of users. Now if the bad prediction were the miscalculation of the railways this solution seems hard on the users of the high wagons, and in these circumstances a solution of the kind to be discussed below as appropriate to long-run joint costs may seem fairer. This is clearly not a matter which can be decided *a priori* from without but must be left to the railway to do what it thinks best in the circumstances, once the

141

principles of the decisions are explained.

In so far as there are 'true' joint costs (pp.83-5) the rule of long-run average cost pricing will not work because there is no meaning to be attached to average cost — where everyone contributes to joint costs as much as he can be made to pay. The solution which at first sight appears most like the solution which seemed obvious for an enterprise without joint costs is that the surplus should be averaged over the users of the service and be returned to them as a lump sum on every wagonload or passenger using the facility. In other words every user would have the same amount struck off the price paid per wagonload (or passenger) for the use of the facility. This solution would benefit most those who contributed least to joint costs since they would be relieved of a greater proportion of their payment. (One might draw an analogy between this and a progressive measure of taxation.) Another solution would set a ceiling. Goods agents and those responsible for fixing passenger fares would be told that on the basis of demand predictions it is estimated it would be unnecessary to charge more than a given maximum for the use of a facility. The fact about this solution is that those who would not have paid as much as the maximum will not benefit from it. (The analogy is with a regressive measure of taxation.) The rule which I suggest has the most obvious intuitive appeal is that the surplus should be returned in amounts proportional to what is contributed by them to costs. A profit made by a facility with joint costs would be passed back by cutting the revenue received from users of the facility by a fixed percentage. The purpose of our criticism is to treat consumers alike as far as possible. As the main purpose of the basic criterion is to treat consumers alike, this would seem to be the rule most compatible with that aim.

If this argument is accepted we now have a rule necessary to complete a consumers' surplus maximisation charging policy, not that this would be the only rule which could do so. If it should be Government policy to benefit certain groups of consumers more than others in these circumstances, then such a rule could be built into the pricing policy of nationalised industries. Some may feel that the formulation of a rule like this is not a question of economics and this is of course correct. It is a value judgement or normative rule. But this does not mean it does not have to be decided. There is an exactly analogous value judgement for the pricing policy of a single-product consumers' surplus maximising enterprise as we have seen. The only reason why that does not arouse comment is that we are not likely to notice it, since it seems obvious if there is one product or service that any profits should be passed on equally to all consumers by a uniform reduction in price, but this does not make it the only distributive rule which could be used or make it other than a value judgement. Similarly the analogous rule for profit maximisation — that profits should be distributed in proportion to value of shares held except in so far as there is preference stock, is so much a fact of commercial life that we do not stop to consider how it would be possible, for instance, for any enterprise to discriminate, if it chose, between classes of shareholders in the distribution of profits, perhaps paying a higher dividend to the poorer shareholders than to the rich. The decision of this rule is the only problem of importance arising immediately from the adoption of the basic criterion.

INVESTMENT

The crucial difficulty raised by consumers' surplus maximisation is over investment because, though many have attempted to make it such, average cost pricing does not always in itself provide a definite criterion for investment.[10]

To return to diagrams such as fig. 6.1 or fig. 6.2, these indicate that an enterprise is to move along its long-run average cost curves as the demand curve shifts to the right (or left). For this to be helpful, the enterprise's production function must be such that the most efficient output is achieved without discontinuous changes, that is without investment. In practice, as we know, the long-run cost curve of a single-product firm is more likely to be discontinuous as in fig. 6.6

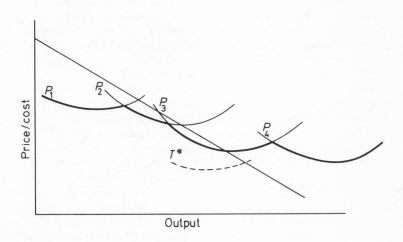

FIG. 6.6

where the envelope curve – the thickened line – illustrates the most efficient technical production possibility for each output level. Even without a shift in the demand curve, technical or managerial innovations may open up the possibility that investment may be profitable through cost reduction. Such a possibility is illustrated by T^*. Even this over simplifies the production problems of most enterprises. There are alternative production possibilities which could be chosen; and the firm must evaluate which it expects to be the most efficient. (The same problems arise if we imagine an enterprise moving along its long-run marginal cost curve if it is subject to long-run increasing or decreasing returns.) The maxim is unhelpful which advises 'choose the production technique which leads the enterprise to the lowest average (or marginal) cost output, given its pricing policy'. To choose between alternatives, the return from each must be calculated. Though there has been growing use of consumers' surplus investment criteria, one still hears that such a criterion is impractical.

Just as profit maximisation and consumers' surplus maximisation with (1) average cost pricing (2) marginal cost pricing do not imply the same outputs in terms of diagrams such as fig. 6.1 to 6.4, so the two criteria will often not select the same production possibilities as yielding the best return on investment. Let us assume that if one were to charge prices for the station which maximised profits a throughput of 2,000 passengers a day is anticipated. If an average cost pricing policy is pursued, 3,000 passengers a day would be expected. Let us assume as would be reasonable, that the optimal, must profitable station, for handling 3,000 passengers, would be different from that required for 2,000. Certain facilities would be provided which would not be provided for 2,000 passengers. In general platforms and exits would be wider, waiting-rooms larger, etc. Therefore it would be a mistake to select the modernisation scheme suitable for 2,000 instead of that suitable for 3,000.

However, there is another reason why use of the two criteria could lead to a different ranking of investment alternatives. Let us imagine that the profitability has been calculated of two quite different rail investments, for example, investment in new wagons and in modernising long distance coaching stock. To make the point, we will assume that the predicted profit maximising return is the same on both. As we have defined it, the consumers' surplus return on each may still vary. While profits are defined as (Price x Output) less total costs, the calculation of a consumers' surplus return requires calculation of an area under the demand curve. In fig. 6.7, this is the triangle BDE. $ABEF$ represents the reduction in cost to existing traffic of an innovation which shifts the cost curve from AC_1 to AC_2. But as a result of this reduction in cost, new traffic is generated $(OQ_2 - OQ_1)$.

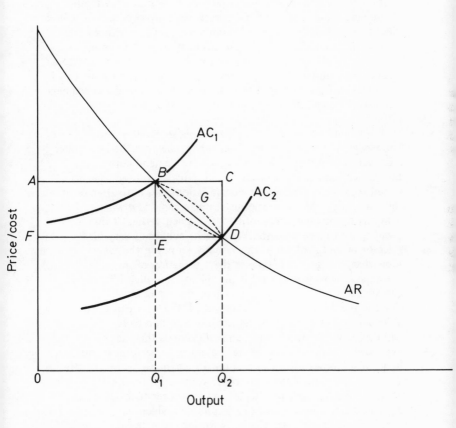

FIG. 6.7

145

BDE measures the benefits to these new travellers, being the difference between what they would be prepared to pay, and what they do pay, O*F* The size of this 'triangle' depends on the curvature of the demand curve. It follows that in principle two investments which have the same profitability may be predicted to yield different amounts of consumers' surplus because of differences in the elasticities of the demand curves over the relevant range.

It is when we talk of drawing demand curves that we come across the first common objection to the practicability of the consumers' surplus investment criterion: as soon as we attempt to measure areas under demand curves 'such a procedure . . . could yield a large variety of answers from which anyone with an axe to grind could take his choice.[11] The occupation of measuring areas, it is usually suggested is just not practical business, and to a businessman this may seem convincing, perhaps obvious, but this is only because he is not used to running a business in the consumers' interest. If he had, he would not have found it much more difficult.

The second objection is that it presupposes an unrealistic knowledge of demand curves. You cannot measure the area under a demand curve if you do not know your demand curve, that is, how much you can sell at any price. The suggestion would seem to be that profit maximisation does not suffer from this difficulty, because every businessman can know what it means to maximise his profits over a given period of time — meaning by this he is reasonably sure he could not vary his price or output profitably. But nobody knows in the same way what it means to maximise the satisfaction of his consumers. Money in the till is more knowable than bliss in the customers' eyes. Certainly businessmen do not normally think in demand *curves* and seldom draw them on paper, but a demand curve is a way of setting down certain facts and conjectures; and the facts and conjectures that can be expressed as a demand curve are present in some form to the mind of a businessman who sets out to maximise his profits. He asks himself whether there are other volumes of output which would be more profitable; and to answer that question he must hazard an estimate of the prices at which he could sell other outputs. The basis for his estimate may be past experience, some knowledge of his competitors' experience, market research, amateur psychology or something so unanalysable that it can be called instinct or intuition. The demand curve found in elementary economic textbooks is assumed continuous and certain, showing the price at which any output will be sold as incontrovertible fact. Such a demand curve never existed outside a textbook. The demand curves of real life are uncertain, based upon an assessment of probabilities, and they are discontinuous, points of probability, joined by lines of assumption. For example, we may suppose a businessman contemplating a new line of production who asks himself the price he is likely to get if he attempts to sell 1,000, 2,000, 3,000 and 4,000 units of the commodity. What is in each case the highest and the lowest he is likely to sell it for? He plots these points down on graph paper. He then asks himself for each pair what is the most probable price. He may guess that it is midway between the two. He may not. He plots these most probable price points and draws straight lines or fits a curve freehand between them. That is a demand curve. Even if he does not draw in the curve he always could do so. It will not be the most accurate demand curve he could estimate but it may be as accurate as he wants. If he is more sophisticated he gets someone to estimate his demand curve econometrically. If he is a profit maximiser he will be logical if he asks whether it is, or is not, likely to be worth producing anything more detailed.

The point is that information which is capable of being sketched out as a demand curve is needed for a private businessman or public enterprise which wants to maximise its profits. If the relevant information and experience is so inadequate that points cannot be plotted, it hardly matters what output and price are selected. Now the conclusion towards which this has been working is that one can exaggerate the difference between a consumers' surplus maximising enterprise and a profit maximising firm in respect of their demand curve. The railways contemplating investment can draw up a demand curve for each investment opportunity based on two, three or four points. They draw the curve freehand and then estimate the size of the consumers' surplus to work out the rate of return on investment. There is almost no reason why the information must be more accurate for this criterion than for profit maximisation. The only difference is that the consumers' surplus maximiser would like to estimate BD in fig. 6.7. The demand curve could take any path within the rectangle between B and D which did not intersect itself. (It is conceivable that its path is outside $ABCD$ and while still between B and D, but this is unlikely and can normally be ignored.) Therefore it is necessary to know the shape of the demand curve between B and D to calculate this second part of the gain in consumers' surplus accurately. This is information which one cannot expect a firm or nationalised industry to have and it is information which it would be difficult and dear to get. But unless there are special reasons for thinking that the demand curve has a markedly different shape the best thing a firm or nationalised industry can do is to make a rough assumption that DB is a straight line and calculate the second part of the gain in consumers' surplus as half $BCEF$. The total gain in consumers' surplus is therefore

$$ABEF + \frac{BCDE}{2}$$

or to generalise, $\frac{1}{2}\Sigma\,(q_1 + q_2)\,(p_1 - p_2)$

(If we were to put figures to these magnitudes, we might suppose that the fare had fallen by $3p$. a unit and that pre-investment number of journeys bought was 100,000 units. The first part of the gain is easily measured as $3p$. x 100,000 = £3,000. For the second part let us assume that the increase in output associated with the lowered fare is from 100,000 to 140,000 units. The gain in surplus is therefore:

$$£1,250 + 3p \times \frac{40,000}{2} \quad = £3,000 + £600$$

$$= £3,600$$

If we then suppose that the company has gone through a similar process in respect of another investment involving another of its products we can make the rate of return comparison. (Let us suppose that the investment in both cases wil cost £10,000: or £1,500 per annum on £10,000 is 15 per cent. The other we will suppose promises a yield of 13 per cent properly discounted for risk, on this basis.) The rate of return is less on the second investment. It would follow by this criterion that the first investment is to be preferred to the second. It is a modified consumers' criterion which is, as we have defined it, a consumers' surplus criterion, there being no such thing as the consumers' surplus criterion. It also follows that an enterprise would be contradicting that policy if it did not select the first investment opportunity. (If the demand curve happened to have the shape BGD between B and D, this would subtract something from the rate of return on the first investment and perhaps bring its yield below that on the second investment. The moral is that the closer together the rates of return are the more probable (and the less important) it is that such a mistake might be made. But this of course is a risk the investor takes if he makes the rough assumption).

Whether railway demand curves are similar enough in shape for this to be plausible is an empirical question requiring research. If a sample survey were to show that there was not much difference between the

148

elasticities of demand for, say, suburban services, improved marshalling yards, long-distance goods expresses and the other various projects which compete for investment funds, then there would be much to be said, on the grounds of simplicity, for adopting the rough approximation.

Intuitively one would guess this unlikely. For example, the demand curves for long-distance express goods traffic are likely to be different from those for holiday passenger traffic. An investment in improving the former may be expected to show an elastic demand (a considerable increase in demand for a moderate increase in prices) because traders who might use such a service might be expected to be sensitive to a change in prices and switch traffic from road to rail. On the other hand one might expect that an investment in long-distance passenger traffic would be met by a relatively inelastic demand (an unappreciable increase in demand for a moderate decrease in price) because, one might expect, businessmen are less sensitive and less likely to change their means of transport because of a change in price. Although in the absence of research one could not say much about it, it would be surprising if demand curves for railway services were of the same shape.

The practical point to be made is that one scarcely ever wishes to know the 'whole area under the demand curve'. Strictly that would be relevant if one wished to make an appreciation of what consumers would pay rather than go without the service altogether.

If it agreed that measurement of the *relevant* area under the demand curve is not inherently impracticable, one can either assume linearity, which is accurate enough for most purposes, or attempt to be more accurate.[12] There are three useful methods.

1. *Experience.* An obvious way of working out a demand curve for a contemplated investment is by using information learnt from the results of past investments which were sufficiently similar. Modernisation has already produced considerable data about the demand for different kinds of railway service.[13] Such information should give some knowledge of the variation in demand for different kinds of facilities and services. As charges become more flexible it may give some indication of the response of demand to difference in price. Though it should be tested experimentally, one might suspect that such information will never be sufficient to establish demand curves accurate enough for investment by either of the basic criteria, because of the great diversity of services provided. It will be profitable to supplement this by demand surveys which are basically of two kinds.

2. *Direct Inquiry.* If the first method does not yield enough information the next to consider is this one. A complete direct inquiry

would imply asking all railway users who are potential beneficiaries of the investment how much they would pay, if they had to, rather than that it should not be made. Such complete enumeration would be impossible and unprofitable, unless the potential beneficiaries were few. Instead a sample survey of them is wanted. Direct inquiry is the classical method of discovering the value of consumers' surplus.

Its merit is that those questioned set their own value on the benefit (or cost) they expect. They are given the opportunity of taking into account all the factors causing benefit of cost and these may be individual to them. Let us suppose the investment – a reconstruction of the refreshment room – is intended principally to make the food more varied and hot and the room brighter and more cheerful. Our hypothetical customer benefits from these and can set a money value on them – let us say threepence a visit. If called on, he would pay threepence a time for the benefits of the new over the old refreshment room on these grounds. But he has other factors which influence him which were not thought of by those who planned the new room. On the credit side he may put an exceptionally high value on speed of service because habitually he only has ten minutes between trains; on a bright white instead of a dim yellow light because he likes to read while eating; on a non-slip floor. On the debit side he misses the mahogany and cut glass of the bar and would, if given the chance, pay something to eat in the old room on that account only. So he reaches what the investment is worth to him – the amount summed over an agreed period of time. It is probable there are some benefits and costs which matter to potential users and will escape indirect inquiry.

The first disadvantage is that while this can be so, it need not be. Direct inquiry relies on those questioned evaluating all the factors. If he does not, if he makes a quick answer, or allows weight only to the first factors that come to mind, or if he is unimaginative, he may answer with a figure considerably different from that he would have given when the investment is made and he is using it. To some extent this difficulty can be avoided by careful structuring of the questionnaire.

The second and less important disadvantage is that there is no check on the honesty of the answer. Someone who knew what was at stake would realise that if he overstated consumers' surplus, and more especially if he could persuade others to overstate it, the more likely it is the investment will be made, unless those interested in other investments keep pace in this inflation. The influence of a local newspaper for example could make nonsense of a direct inquiry.

(In theory a passenger travelling on his own pleasure or business must be persuaded to think that if he was going to spend more on transport, he would be spending less on something else since there is no reason to suppose his income would increase; except in so far as profits earned by the railway, if it were profit maximising, would be returned to him in kind or cash as a taxpayer. If he were travelling as the employee of a business, or if we are considering the carriage of goods, the position would be more complicated, but in most cases this income effect via reduced taxation may be taken to be negligible. Therefore there is something to be said for putting the direct inquiry to a man as if his income were to remain the same.)[14]

3. *Indirect Inquiry* is a topic we will have to consider in more detail when we come to the roads programme since attempts have been made to estimate consumers' surplus there by this means. It would be impracticable to measure consumers' surplus on most commodities and services indirectly. Fortunately, the chief benefit from most investments in the railway system can be represented as a saving in time. The saving in time which can be achieved, say, by investment in a marshalling yard or new rolling stock can be measured directly without difficulty. It is then necessary to set a value on it. One method is to value time saved by passengers travelling on business by multiplying it by their wage rates. A survey establishes the various wages and salaries earned by a sample of passengers. The problem of valuing time-saving by passengers travelling in their leisure time and by goods traffic is difficult and will be considered more fully in Chapter 11. One advantage of this method of inquiry is that, for example, it is possible to make a sample survey of the valuation of time-saving in leisure time by passengers in general and use it to evaluate this element in all investments unless there is good reason for thinking a particular investment would have special characteristics. Besides savings in time, one might want to establish the valuation set on increased punctuality, more comfort, greater frequency by a sample of consumers in respect of most investments. But there is no need to go further into this now as long as the nature of the kind of demand surveys needed to implement a consumers' surplus investment policy has been indicated sufficiently.

It is not possible to guess how much the implementation of the policy would cost by comparison with profit maximisation particularly since trial and error only will show how detailed the surveys will have to be to be useful and profitable. It might be thought that there would be a tendency for railway representatives to exaggerate the consumers' surplus return on investments when presenting their schemes to the Government. If they do tend to do this they will of course be liable to make a loss. Experience should cure this fault. And it may well be the case that given a precise understanding of what they are after, that there would not be such a tendency, but if it were thought that the consumers' interest and the Government's as guarantor of the debt was jeopardised by exaggeration, then it might be profitable to set up an independent survey organisation to check on the conclusions of the railways by investigations of its own which need not, of course, be on the same scale.

Another objection is that one cannot tell afterwards if an investment has been successful or not by the consumers' surplus criterion; whereas one can by profit maximisation. The argument is that a businessman plans to get a given return from an investment. If he gets it he knows he was right. If he does not, he was not. An enterprise practising consumers' surplus policy has not got this check, as it has no money in the bank to show for what it has done, and the benefits have gone imperceptibly to a multitude of consumers. Since they had no part in making the investment decision, they never predicted how much they would benefit by it. To find out whether the investment has been successful it would be necessary to ask all those who were expected to benefit from it how much it has in the event been worth to him.

Again the answer is that the difference between the two criteria is not as great as it might seem at first. There is a test of the success of a consumers' surplus investment. Success will be indicated by the impossibility of selling the predicted output at the predicted price if less successful than was hoped; and the possibility of selling more than the predicted output at the predicted price if it is more successful. (For this not to be so all the shortfall or excess in consumers' surplus must accrue to intramarginal customers. The demand curve would have to intersect the average cost curve at the same point. In other words it would have to revolve on X as an axis. That this should happen is improbable. The possibilities are illustrated in fig. 6.8. D_1D_1 is the predicted demand curve, D_2D_2 is a demand curve which represents a less successful outcome and D_3D_3 a more successful outcome than predicted. D_4D_4 and D_5D_5 correspond to D_2D_2 and D_3D_3 but represent the queer cases where the failure in expectations is not reflected by a change in the quantity demanded or the price.)

Therefore there is a check on the success of an investment by this criterion. Second, this argument exaggerates the ease with which it is possible to prove success or failure when practising profit maximisation. Conditions will almost certainly have changed between the planning of an investment and its realisation. It is unlikely that the rate of return will be as predicted. It is quite possible with hindsight that one would have chosen an alternative investment. One would hope that one's investment would be successful within the limits set by the margin allowed for risk in one's original calculations; but if one should want to check whether the outcome one predicted had been achieved for the reasons given when making the decision, whether in fact the investment had been based on an accurate assessment, whether one did not in fact make assumptions which should be improved on when

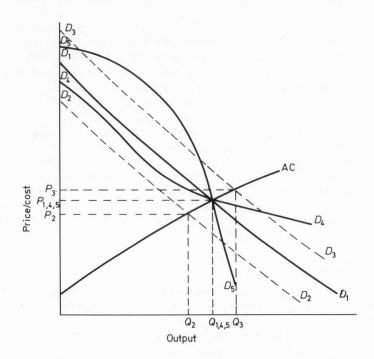

FIG. 6.8: Testing the success of consumers' surplus maximisation policy

the next decision is made, that requires a casual analysis of the factors affecting demand and costs which will not be different in kind from that needed to establish the success of a consumers' surplus investment. There is a difference in difficulty but it is not such a great difference. What one would probably do to test for success or failure in the consumers' surplus case, is to follow up the sample of consumers who were used to establish the demand curve in the first place.

SUMMARY

The principal points which have been made in this chapter are as follows.

1. It is necessary to decide who the 'consumers' are whose interest is to be considered and what weight is to be given to their preferences to make the criterion determinate.

2. The criterion adopted was one where consumers' surplus was maximised subject to the requirement that the consumers should pay the average private cost of any service they use.

3. Private costs were defined to include depreciation, provision for reserves, provision for self-finance, any taxation imposed on the

enterprise and the cost of capital. It was argued however that in certain empirically unlikely circumstances it might be the case that a consumers' surplus enterprise might be unable to pay the cost of its capital *and* pass on profits by lowering prices. In such circumstances the Government must decide whether to subsidise the consumers' surplus sector.

4. The inefficiency of average cost pricing was discussed. The chief charging problem for consumers' surplus which does not arise for profit maximisation, is the choice of method for distributing profits through lower prices when there are joint costs.

5. The methods by which a consumers' surplus rate of return could be used to decide priorities of investment was considered. This will be continued in Chapter 11.

It is necessary to improve costing and to remove illogicalities and obscurities in calculating the rate of return for consumers' surplus as it is for profit maximisation.

POSTSCRIPT

The third, fourth and fifth sections have been rewritten substantially to meet criticisms. Inevitably the chapter now seems of more theoretical interest than a practical guide to transport policy-making. If one were to return to a belief that the railways are a decreasing cost industry, and they were to be required to break even its argument might again become one of practical importance.

Definition of the Criterion: Benefits
Most cost-benefit analyses attempt to measure benefits and costs wherever they accrue. One definition of what we have called the social surplus maximisation approach is that it sets out to maximise the sum of consumers' and producers' surpluses. To talk about consumers in this context is another way of saying that everyone's interest should be taken into account when decisions are made. It does not seem unreasonable to expect public enterprise to evaluate the external effects, or social costs and benefits, of their actions wherever these seem significant. When deciding to site a power station or a noisy depot, public enterprise can reasonably be expected to evaluate the impact on the environment when choosing between sites. As public opinion gives more weight to externalities like noise, pollution, accidents and many environmental impacts, laws are introduced and physical planning procedures operated, so that private and public firms are rquired to allow for environmental impacts. These requirements may take the form of regulation or constraint on their actions or some other locus by which those affected can influence what firms do through a right to sue for damages or otherwise receive compensation. One method of some interest is the creation of property rights. These exist in Britain for those

who own portions of the banks of many rivers and streams. It is regarded as implicit in ownership that the water flowing past their property should not deteriorate through pollution. If it does, they may sue those responsible. Similar property-owners could be given rights to sue traffic or highway authorities which act so as to affect their environment.[1] Nevertheless one may suppose public enterprise may always be expected to consider external effects which private enterprise is not forced to.

The issue is whether one can reasonably run an industry and judge its performance, requiring it so far as it is able to maximise its contribution to the sum of all consumers' and producers' interest. This is not a question of economics — it is theoretically possible that it should be given such a social welfare function — but of management. To simplify management and make it easier to assess performance it is normal to narrow its objectives. A private firm is broadly judged by the profits it makes. By analogy a public enterprise may be considered to consider the interests of those it directly serves — *its* consumers — here those who use railways. If it is a holding company like the Italian IRI it will have distinct sets of consumers for its different activities but the principle could be the same. The management remit will be to run it in the interests of its consumers. As will be discussed in Chapter 7, other interests will be served by other constraints.

Definition of the Criterion: Costs

I suggested in 1963 that closures should bring the railways back to 'viability'. Closures have been shown to be relatively unimportant.[2] Discontinuing services and then disinvesting in track are probably more important. Reducing labour costs is probably more important still.

Since 1963 there has been extended discussion of the problems involved in determining the opportunity cost of resources transferred from the private to the public sector, which makes it possible to improve the argument here. As it stands, as Professor Arrow pointed out,[3] it is far from obvious how a subsidy to the consumers' surplus sector is to be relaxed for interest payments when it has been eliminated in the short run. It is not impossible that a government should wish to encourage a consumers' surplus maximising sector just as it might wish to encourage workers' production co-operatives by providing capital at a subsidised interest rate. But one can illuminate the issue by an analogy with those raised by Feldstein and other authors in another context.

The problem arises when the public sector has what economists call a different rate of time preference from the private sector. One needs to distinguish this concept from that of the social opportunity cost discount rate. As has been described earlier the latter represents the highest capital return earned in the alternative uses available. Thus to use an SOC rate of 10 per cent implies the judgement that a 10 per cent economic return could be earned by applying the resources elsewhere. The requirement that a project must show a positive present value when its benefit and cost streams are discounted at 10 per cent implies that it must earn a return, so measured, of at least 10 per cent. However the consistent use of SOC as the public sector discount rate implies a particular distribution of income between present and future generations, but like all questions of redistribution, it is an ethical or political problem to decide the distribution of income between generations. *Ceteris paribus,* a higher interest rate implies giving less weight to a pound in the future and therefore less weight to the interests of future generations; while a lower discount rate conversely gives more weight to future generations relative to the present. Thus to say that one is modifying the SOC rate by Social Time Preference is a way economists have of saying that the discount rate implied by SOC is to be modified upwards or downwards to give a different intergenerational income distribution. Therefore if the public sector has an (STP) discount rate different from the private sector's discount rate, it follows that the public and private sectors will make a different selection of projects if confronted with the same investment opportunities. If, as is common, the public sector has an STP rate which is negative, lowering the discount rate below that of the private sector, then there is a sense in which the existence of a public sector will lead to a lower overall return on national investment, when judged using the private sector's discount rate. This is because generally some investment will be judged worthwhile using the public sector discount rate which would not show a positive net present value using the private rate, or which would be shown to be inferior. There are similarly private sector projects that would not be preferred, if judged from the standpoint of the public sector and using its discount rate. Since the rates of time preference are different, there is no unique solution to the problem of deciding what share of resources should be invested in the public sector. Using the social time preference rate there would be a preferred investment programme if all resources were invested in projects ranked using it. *Mutatis mutandis,* similarly from the standpoint of the private sector, a different preferred investment programme would be selected using the private time preference rate.

It would be widely accepted that society's judgement should prevail over that of the private sector. As an alternative a number of writers following Feldstein have suggested the introduction of a new rule as a constraint on the transference of funds from the private to the public sector. This implies assuming that the value of resources transferred from private investment is the net present value of a perpetuity discounted at the social time preference rate. This ensures that no public sector project will be undertaken yielding less than the private sector marginal return when discounted at the private sector discount rate. Then it is logical to choose the mix of projects which yields the greatest surplus when discounted at the social discount rate, provided that capital resources are valued at their shadow price.

One could use the same procedure to ensure no investment is undertaken in the consumers' surplus sector unless it yields some surplus over the marginal return on investment in the private sector. In precisely the same way as before this could be achieved by using the same shadow price of capital, identically calculated. If a shadow price was chosen lower than this this would be equivalent to a 'subsidy' to the consumers' surplus sector and in need of justification.

The argument assumes that the resources used are diverted from private investment. If they are partly diverted from consumption this raises a new set of problems since the opportunity cost of such resources must itself be determined. One method is to divide this consumption into public and private. The public is then valued at the social rate of time preference. The private is sub-divided by income group and then the marginal borrowing/lending rate of each group is used as the discount rate. Among the difficulties of this approach are that such rates incorporate a risk premium and that it is difficult to distinguish average from marginal rates. Some would argue that the social value of the social time preference rate should override the private even for private consumption. The decision of this problem needs to be political.

Addendum (1974): I have argued that Dr. Joy's and other investigators suggest that if railways pursue optimal investment and disinvestment policies, it may not be unreasonable to assume that return to scale in railway operation are approximately constant. But the 1974 Railways Bill — first introduced by the Conservatives and then in substantially the same form by the Labour Government — introduces subsidy principles which only make sense if the railways marginal cost curve falls from left to right over its whole range (as in Fig. 6.2). British Rail have produced no evidence for this. To my mind Dr. Joy has not been proved wrong. But should British Rail be correct, the argument of this chapter ceases again to be academic and ought to be again of some practical importance.

7   REGULATION AND SUBSIDY

In this chapter we consider modifications of the basic criteria by
regulation and subsidy. Of course there may be some regulations
imposed by the Government on an enterprise which will not lessen
the profits or the consumers' surplus it will earn, and may even in
some cases increase profits and consumers' surplus by forcing the
enterprise to do something which is in its own best interest as profit
or consumers' surplus maximiser — though it had not realised it.
However the regulations we have in mind in this chapter are those
which for one reason or another do reduce profits or consumers'
surplus.

It will be useful to begin with definitions of regulations and
subsidy for (1) profit and (2) consumers' surplus maximisation.

Profit Maximisation. First, a regulation may be defined formally as
a requirement by the Government or by some other public body with
the necessary authority, whether statutory or otherwise, which has the
effect of making the enterprise regulated (a) forgo some revenue which
it might otherwise have gained and (b) incur some cost which it might
otherwise have avoided. Therefore by definition profits are less than
they otherwise would be. An example of (a) would be a law or
regulation preventing fraudulent description of a product, thereby
preventing the manufacturer making sales and earning revenue he would
otherwise have been able to. An example of (b) would be a labour law
controlling conditions of work and thereby putting up the firm's costs
and so reducing its profits. (If the labour law should have the effect
of increasing the productivity of labour more than its cost, that would
not be incompatible with, but conducive to, profit or consumers'
surplus maximisation.)

Second, a subsidy by a firm is any revenue which it forgoes
voluntarily or any cost which it incurs voluntarily which by assumption
has the effect of reducing profits. It is therefore a self-imposed
departure from profit maximisation. And this is, I think, an exact
representation of the notion we usually have in mind when we think of
a subsidy. If I charge you a price less than cost, that is a subsidy
(unless I should do it with an eye to future profits), but if I charge you
a price above cost but forgo some of my profit, that too is a subsidy,
a present. Similarly on the cost side, if knowingly I buy something for
more than it is worth, more than the least I could pay for it, that is a
subsidy or present. If an office worker is paid more than he is worth,

the firm subsidises him to that extent.

Consumers' Surplus Maximisation. The definitions are similar.
First a regulation may be defined as a requirement imposed on an
enterprise which has the effect of making it forgo some consumers'
surplus it might have gained or, as with a profit maximising concern,
incur some cost it might have avoided. The difference between profit
and consumers' surplus maximisation in this respect may be
illustrated by an example. A regulation may be designed to protect
the consumers' interest and has the effect, we assume, of reducing
profits somewhat. But a consumers' surplus firm has the consumers'
interest at heart, therefore the regulation may not be necessary if the
enterprise is conscientious. The facts may imply, let us say, that it
will not maximise consumers' surplus if it sells a shoddy product.
Nevertheless it *may* be the case that a regulation is needed in the
consumers' interest if the Government chooses to define this differently.
Suppose a concern maximises consumers' surplus by selling some shoddy
or dangerous product. Its customers like it. In their opinion it
maximises their surplus for the concern to produce the product – an
extreme example might be opium. But the Government decides that
the consumers' *real* interest should be defined differently and
introduces regulations to this end. What this means formally is that the
Government modifies the criterion in what it holds is the consumers'
real interest.

Second, under consumers' surplus maximisation, a subsidy is any
consumers' surplus forgone which it was in the power of the concern
to earn and which would have increased its overall consumers' surplus;
or any cost incurred which could have been avoided. Such subsidies
occur, for example, when a consumers' surplus enterprise gives more
weight to the consumers' surplus of certain of its consumers and
thereby sacrifices more than an equivalent value of surplus pertaining
to other consumers. An unremunerative or subsidised service here is
one where some consumers are subsidised, and this puts up the
average cost of the undertaking and therefore the prices the average
consumer is charged, thereby reducing the consumers' surplus of the
average consumer.

In both cases, subsidy and regulation can best be regarded as
departures from, or modifications of, our basic criteria. The cost of a
regulation or a subsidy can either be borne by the enterprise or by
someone else. If the first, we have what is commonly called
cross-subsidisation; if the second, a subsidy *to* the enterprise.

Cross-subsidisation as a word has a long history in transport, but its
use is often misleading. When railways in the nineteenth century
sought an Act of Parliament to permit them establish themselves in
an area, they were often required, or thought it wise to offer, to carry

various classes of passengers and goods at a loss so as to offset their monopoly advantages and appease Parliament. This was 'cross-subsidisation' — 'taking the rough with the smooth' — the idea being that the profitable traffic paid for the unprofitable. This was not an entirely correct account of the matter since the unprofitable traffic was subsidised not by other traffic but by profits. If the railways had not subsidised this traffic, or been required to do so, there is no reason why this should have had the effect of their lowering charges on the unprofitable traffic. Rather one would have expected them to raise charges on the unprofitable traffic and so by cutting costs or raising revenue to have increased profits so as to make the maximum of their monopoly advantages. But there is a genuine use for cross-subsidisation in relation to consumers' surplus maximisation: any departure from average cost pricing where a charge is raised on one traffic above average cost to subsidise another charged less than average cost. Here there is genuinely cross-subsidisation of one traffic to another.

Explicit Subsidy. The other possibility is that the cost of a particular subsidy within the railway system is offset by a subsidy to the railway system so that the railway makes no smaller profit or consumers' surplus (or is partly offset). The most obvious source is the Exchequer; but it is conceivable that a local authority may wish to subsidise the railways for some reason; or private persons as, for example, when a society is prepared to pay something towards the preservation of a railway building of architectural interest.

Regulation and subsidy raise several questions:

(1) In what respects are the railways impeded in maximising profits or consumers' surplus by regulations?

(2) Are these regulations justified?

(3) In what respects are the railways inclined to subsidise some railway-users at the expense of profits (or more realistically at present, at the expense of losses) or consumers' surplus?

(4) Are these subsidies justified?

(5) Should the cost be borne by other railway-users through cross-subsidisation or by the Exchequer explicitly if consumers' surplus maximisation is the policy adopted? (If there is profit maximisation, there is no choice. Directly or indirectly the cost is borne by the Exchequer as profits forgone or losses made good.)

The question of the extent and method of subsidisation is clearly of the greatest importance as the deficits of the British Transport Commission indicate. The activities of the Commission, principally the railways, have been subsidised by the Government to the extent of the deficits. This implies that a great number of railway-users must be getting services provided for them below average cost. It may be the case that cross-subsidisation is also present. Some railway-users are paying more than average

Table 7.1 The Financial Position of British Railways[1] (£m.)

	1938	1948	1958	1959	1960	1961	1948-1952	1953-1957	1956-1969
British Railways									
Gross receipts	164.7	346.3	471.6	457.4	478.6	474.7	366.9	464.1	478.0
Working expenses	137.7	322.5	519.7	499.4	546.2	561.6	340.6	462.2	518.3
Net receipts (or deficit)	27.1	23.8	48.1	42.0	67.7	86.9	26.3	1.8	40.3
Central charges	—	(28.5)	42.0	42.0	45.0	49.0	—	—	42.2
Surplus (or deficit)	—	(4.7)	90.1	84.0	112.7	135.9	—	—	82.5
British Transport Commission									
Overall surplus (or deficit)	—	4.7	89.0	73.8	100.9	122.0	6.3	31.2	76.3
Working surplus (or deficit)	—	40.8	28.1	12.6	36.3	53.4	41.8	25.6	17.0

From 1956 the central charges were allocated as between British Railways and other activities of the Commission. For 1948 it is assumed that the overall deficit of the Commission was due to British Railways.

The overall deficit of the Commission is calculated after the transfer of interest charges to Special Account under the 1957 Act (interest on railway revenue deficits from 1957-9 and interest on new railway borrowings for capital expenditure from 1959-60).

Values for the five-yearly periods are averages.

costs and therefore either they, or the Exchequer, in profits forgone, depending on the criterion adopted, are subsidising other railway-users. It is therefore most probable that the true extent of subsidisation on the railways is greater than the subsidy to the railways indicated by the deficit, possibly much greater.

The exact identification of all these subsidies must wait upon improved costing. However some of the more important and obvious instances of subsidy will be considered in later sections of this chapter.

As for *regulations* it is still the case that the railways are bound by certain regulations which do not affect ordinary commercial firms. It is unlikely that their removal would make a great difference to the railways' profit-making or consumers' surplus-making ability; but in so far as they exist they must make some increase in deficits. We may assume, I think, that any regulations which normally restrict the freedom of commercial firms — Factory Acts, Health Acts, etc. — ought to apply to the railways.

REGULATIONS AND RESTRICTIONS

Whether we like it or not, there is a strong and sustaining tradition of public service among railwaymen. It is admirable that many feel their duty is not just to make cash for themselves and their employers; and that a public service is something more than giving the public the worst it will tolerate. The trouble is not the spirit of public service but much of what is done in its name.

A public servant in most countries has it in common with a missionary or social welfare worker, that he is expected to work for less than it is to be hoped he could earn in a commercial firm. And since the ideal of serving the railways is not as compelling as the ideals of God and Humanity, the result is as might be expected: the quality of labour and the standard of service falls. Before the Second World War the security of railway employment made up for low wages. It no longer does. What is surprising is how many men do more and better work than can reasonably be expected of them because of their attachment to the railways and the tradition of loyalty and public service. But even allowing for these, wages and salaries are too low for efficiency. We may or may not regret that salaries are higher in private firms, but if they are it is foolish to penalise the public sector. At various times since the war the railways have not been allowed to increase their charges so as to pay higher wages. They have suffered from the Treasury's insistence that the public sector should set an example in every pay purse, whatever the cost in efficiency. There is no formal restriction on the salaries nationalised industries can pay, but there is an effective maximum since the Government fixes the salaries of full-time board members. A few recent appointments have departed from the principle of a maximum of £10,000 but still the great bulk of salaries have to be graded between a minimum of, say, £600, and a maximum of £10,000. The great size of the railways – they employ more than half a million – means that steps in promotion can only be matched by proportionately small increases in salary – not an incentive to the ambitious. Although the tradition of public service is perhaps strongest among management, it is not efficient to pay exceptionally low salaries; moreover, it is not the way to maximise profit or consumers' surplus.

As a public service the railways suffer other restrictions on their activities. The greatest part of these disappeared in the 1953 Transport Act but several remain rather oddly. One of the most important of these is that the railways are still not free to develop the property they own. The original idea was that the railways should not go into business that is not directly or indirectly related to the running of railways. Therefore they might build a hotel on top of a station, but not a block of offices. If they wanted to do that they must sell the building to the *minority* shareholder in a special development company. In practice this put the railways at a disadvantage in developing their land. The new 1962 Transport Act states that 'a Board shall not incur any substantial item of expenditure in developing their land for purposes which are not purposes of the business without the consent of the Minister, and the Minister may from time to time give directions to the Boards indicating what is to be treated for the purposes of this section as a substantial item of expenditure.'[2] It would be unfortunate if this were interpreted restrictively. The railways should be as free as anyone else to develop their land, not only because it would be profitable, but because it is generally in the public interest that such land is developed. And if they have the freedom they should not be thwarted because of their past lack of freedom. For example, and it is not an isolated example, the City of London Court of Common Council rejected permission for an office building over Fenchurch Street Station for the reason that it was zoned for railway purposes only and that it would be contrary to their policy of restricting office-building to the zones set aside for it.[3] One can guess why the Court of Common Council acted as it did. In recent years it has become alarmed at the spate of office-building and would use almost every measure in its power to stop it; but it is to take refuge in a technicality to argue that this particular office building should not be permitted because it was 'zoned for railway purposes'; and it is markedly unfair to the railways. If the rate of office-building is to be slowed down, the railways should be restricted neither more nor less than anybody else.

Another restriction is that they cannot manufacture for anyone else except under special licence.[4] The original purpose of this was to prevent competition between railway workshops and private firms. It is difficult to see why the restriction should persist, though most of the damage has been done. Many railway workshops have been closed down because they were unable to sell their products to other firms and this meant in practice that they could not achieve the necessary economics of scale or the economics of a continuous run of production. They are also, as one might expect, forbidden to export:[5] so they are unable to use their expertise where it might be most valuable to the developing railways in underdeveloped countries and where it would be profitable for them. In all fairness one would hope that public service would be freed from these regulations which distinguish it from private enterprise — these constraints on profit or consumers' surplus maximisation.

TAXES

All restrictions are not to the disadvantage of the railways. Some give them privileges, for instance, in respect of taxation. They do not pay rates as ordinary businesses do, but an annual lump sum in commutation: about £2¾m. This means that a railway property is not separately assessed unless the general public has access to it.[6] It is difficult to be sure that this means the railways have a lighter rates burden than if they were private enterprise, but this seems probable. There seems no obvious reason why the railways should not make the same contribution to the finances of local authorities as if they were a comparable private undertaking. Nationalised industries are now liable to profits tax at the standard rate. Under profit maximisation this would seem unnecessary since all profits go to the Treasury; but separate calculation might have the advantage of making comparison with the dividends paid by private firms easier. If a consumers' surplus policy is adopted there should be no profits and therefore no profits tax under present arrangements. If it were felt that a consumers' surplus undertaking like any other business should make its contribution to public funds, some method of computing a tax would have to be invented. The ideal would be some percentage of consumers' surplus earned, raised as a sales tax, but we are never likely to get a sufficiently accurate estimate of consumers' surplus to make this more than a dream. The most obviously workable tax would be a general sales tax.

There are other taxes for example which require different analysis. Railways do not pay tax on the Diesel oil they use. In so far as this represents payment for the use of roads, this is proper since the railways pay the costs of their own track; but in so far as it is a special tax on the use of the roads, it would seem right that all forms of transport should be treated equally.

SUPPLY OF FINANCE

Nationalised industries are also privileged in the terms at which they borrow money. Until 1956 they borrowed on the open market by the issue of fixed interest stock, though backed by a Government guarantee of interest payments. Since 1956 they have borrowed directly from the Treasury because it had become clear that nationalised industries' stock was not sufficiently attractive to draw the funds the Government thought ought to be invested in them. This development means, in effect, that the Government has been subsidising the nationalised industries: first, by allowing them to borrow at less than the market rate; second, by guaranteeing interest payments if the nationalised industries should not be able to pay it — at considerable cost to the Exchequer as it has turned out; and third, in various other ways, some of them substantial.[7]

SUBSIDISATION AND CROSS—SUBSIDISATION

These terms are relevant to another use of 'public service': the idea that some subsidisation should be implicit in the running of the railways. As we have said 'cross-subsidisation' in the loose sense of the term first became a feature of railway operation because it was a way of putting a check on monopoly advantage, but it has become a tradition valued for its own sake, now that there are no monopoly profits. The public service tradition in our first sense — paying too little and relying too much on the spirit of public service — has had a consequence here. It has meant that many of the best railwaymen, again like missionaries or social welfare workers, expect their activities to be uncommercial. A doctor of missionary temperament would not be happy if the job given him by the Church Missionary Society was to set up in private practice in Cairo and extract the highest possible fees, from wealthy Egyptians. Similarly many railway executives, brought up in the public service and paid as public servants, are not happy when required to be out-and-out commercial profit maximisers. They are used to thinking, and want to go on thinking, of the railways as a benevolent institution, disposing of funds, helping transport underdogs, 'taking the rough with the smooth', as having a duty to provide transport services for everyone — the Robin Hood complex — though in some instances there may be another less attractive but understandable motive: the knowledge that either profit or consumers' surplus maximisation will mean a smaller railway system — loss of jobs, power and prospects.

The case against the public service approach is that the results are not in general worth the money spent — the profits or consumers' surplus forgone. And this is not surprising because the broad pattern of railway subsidisation was fixed in the past. Even if there were once good reasons for approving of it, circumstances have changed. Few charities are wise to spend their funds as they did a hundred or thirty years ago. The causes — the type of railway-user — subsidised by charging fares below cost do not usually deserve or need subsidy. Unfortunately what begins as a concession is quickly regarded as a right. It was said it was foolish to make the Sultan of Turkey the present of a fine horse, for if you gave it to him on one birthday, he would be aggrieved and murderous if you did not give him another on the next, and the year after, and so on. But when one thinks of the other things this public money, which must amount in terms of resources used to some tens of millions a year, could be spent on (the improvement of hospitals, education and even the mere reduction of taxes), the benefits it actually realises pale into insignificance.

And it is, in every respect that matters, public money. This is not fully realised by a Micawberish Government which makes too much of an incorrect distinction between subsidisation and cross-subsidisation.

As long as a nationalised industry breaks even or makes a profit, it can indulge in as much cross-subsidisation as it pleases instead of passing profits on to the Exchequer or to the public by lowering prices. But as soon as there is a deficit, the Treasury changes its attitude. It asks if the non-paying services and investment are worth subsidising. This is illogical; for if, in the first place under profit maximisation, it is not worth subsidising by the Exchequer then it is surely not worth the Exchequer forgoing profits for it. And, in the second place under consumers' surplus maximisation, if it is not worth subsidising by the Exchequer it is surely not worth sacrificing consumers' surplus and average cost pricing to it.

A thorough overhaul of these subsidies is needed and it would seem logical if the necessary investigation was made for and the necessary decisions made by the Government. It would be logical if there were profit maximisation because then it would be the Government which would be forgoing the revenue. It would be logical if there were consumers' surplus maximisation because it was the Government that decided it was the policy most in the public interest, and therefore it should appraise the value of any modifications of the principle. Furthermore cross-subsidisation under consumers' surplus maximisation, to give it the strict sense of some consumers being charged more than average cost so that others might be charged less, does seem at the very best an anachronism. Why should country-dwellers' transport be subsidised by town-dwellers? Why should coffee-drinkers, say, be subsidised by tea-drinkers, or house-buyers by dog-owners, or the buyer of any one commodity or service by the buyer of another? If it is decided to subsidise any class of transport-user, this is a political decision taken by the central Government to further some end of general social policy, and therefore it would seem reasonable that the cost should be borne by the taxpayer. All these are reasons for adopting a policy towards subsidisation which has become much more widely accepted very recently: subsidisation should be by the central Government. Under profit maximisation this would look no more than a difference in book-keeping — profits would go to the Exchequer and some would be returned as a subsidy for specific purposes — but this difference would reflect a difference where the decision is taken. It should also remove one of the greatest obstacles to intelligent discussion. The present method of book-keeping, and the poor knowledge the railways have of their costs, means it is difficult to know who is subsidised, and even more difficult to know by how much.

In these four chapters an attempt has been made to face the criteria with the facts of railway existence: to sort out the implications of the criteria and the inadequacies of the facts. It is certainly a major handicap to the solution of the transport problem that we really do not know the probable profitability of investment in the railways. Although there must be some doubt because of future technical developments in transport, much of our uncertainty could be removed by such means as have been suggested in these four chapters: if the Government could make up its mind what it wants the railways to do, if the railways could improve their costing and their methods of programming investment so that the issues and the estimates become sufficiently intelligible for public discussion and rational decision. If these could be done the railway problem should be soluble for it is relatively easy as an economic problem. Much more intractable is the problem of the roads to which we now turn; and that of establishing competition or coordination.

POSTSCRIPT

The 1968 Transport Act did attempt to eliminate any tendency towards cross-subsidisation, strictly defined, within the railways. The railways were not to carry any passenger or freight traffic unless they judged it profitable. There were to be no specific subsidies for freight since it was argued that there was no obvious social case for preferring one method of freight transport to another. It was held in the public interest that freight should go by the most efficient means. Since cost was not the only relevant factor but also reliability, security, absence of delays and of breakage among others, the importance of which varied between consignments, it was held that normally the consignor had to be the judge of what was the best mode of transport for his goods. Public policy should be directed to ensuring that road and rail costs did better reflect the economic cost of transit by the different modes (though even so road-users were required to make a contribution to general taxation that rail-users were not); and also providing consignors with better information to help them choose the mode best for them. Then, as since, it has been argued, that there is an environmental case for subsidising rail freight (though in principle the same ends could be achieved by taxing road freight). This implies there is a reduction in social costs from transferring freight from road to rail especially from heavy lorries. While there may be some cases where there will be such a benefit, there is no general presumption that this will be the effect of transferring traffic from road to rail or that the sum total of any genuine environmental freight subsidy would be large. The greatest environmental impact of vehicles, especially heavy lorries, is within urban areas. This is where they add to congestion and cause most nuisance from noise, air pollution and vibration. In most cities the probability is high that a vehicle moving from its origin to a goods yard will go further and pass through more congested streets on average than one heading for the inter-urban trunk routes on the urban fringe.

A system was introduced by which the railways could be grant-aided for keeping open unprofitable passenger services. The arguments here were partly political and partly economic. There seemed a greater environmental case for keeping unprofitable rail passenger services going, especially commuter services in the large conurbations. The argument developed from that used in the economic evaluation of the Victoria Line.[1] Because urban roads are underpriced relative to urban rail services (since the former neglect the marginal social costs of congestion) a break-even or profit-maximising pricing policy in rail will be inefficient. It will shift traffic from rail to road causing congestion there which is neglected in the rail pricing policy because they are social costs. Outside conurbations, congestion arguments are much less relevant to retaining unprofitable rail lines. The usual case is either hardship to those deprived or more straightforwardly political — the unwillingness the political process has shown to close lines even where the hardship caused was demonstrably small.

Regulations and Restrictions
The same 1968 Transport Act also removed many of the existing restrictions. The railways have more freedom to develop their properties subject to ordinary physical planning restrictions. They may also use their workshops to produce for customers outside the railways.

PART III

THE ROAD PROBLEM

8   THE ROAD PROGRAMME

It is more difficult to make economic sense of the road than of the
railway problem, to make the bricks and build with them than to build
with bricks already made. There, in the railways, we already had an
industry, organised nationally and accustomed to think and plan as an
industry, with its assets legally determined, with annual reports and
accounts and its function powers somewhat, though in certain respects
loosely, defined as those of an economic enterprise. Here we have a very
large number of authorities whose relations are statutory rather than
economic, none of them giving more than part of their attention to
road construction and maintenance and whose criteria tend to be
arbitrary and indefinite. What are the costs of the road system? We
really do not know. We have not even a consolidated set of accounts to
tell us. What is the revenue of the road system? Again we do not know.
We know what is raised in motor and other taxation but, as was argued
in Chapter 1, we do not know how to treat this sum: as entirely
charges for the use of roads, or as part special taxation and part charges,
or wholly taxation which happens to be levied in these ways. Many
decisions of principle must be made before we can fashion the road
system into an economic enterprise. These decisions are principally of
three kinds: who are the road-users; what are to be accounted costs and
benefits of the system; and what are to be accounted the assets of the
system. Until these last two have been decided we cannot set up a
profit-and-loss and a capital account, respectively, of the system.
Therefore the critical apparatus we have used so far does not
at present work when applied to roads. Cross-subsidisation has no
precise meaning. The distinction between a public service
(provided generally free or at a price below average private cost)
and a public enterprise making charges which at least covers
this cost, is blurred. And we cannot easily distinguish between the
public service principle here (the subsidisation of the road-user
from sources outside the road system) and cross-subsidisation
(the subsidising of some road-users by others). Neither have we
rates of return we can sensibly use. Nevertheless, although we
cannot be precise in our use of terms, there is something to be
said for looking back at the history of the administration of our
roads to see what have been its characteristic defects so as better to
be able to appreciate and criticise what we have at present.

THE CONFLICT OF INTERESTS

In the past roads have been administered on what can loosely be called
the public service principle, usually involving some cross-subsidisation.
Certainly those who have paid for the roads have not generally been
the same people as those who have benefited from them. To go back
no further than the sixteenth century, the upkeep of the roads was the
responsibility of the parishes through which they ran. The law obliged
parishioners to work six days a year on the roads, though from 1670
those who could afford it were able to make a payment instead.
Parishes elected an unpaid surveyor who was responsible in his year for
maintaining the parish roads. Justice of the Peace, clergy and doctors
were exempt; consequently in country parishes the office commonly
fell to a small farmer or tradesman who could be fined heavily if the
work were not done, but who had little authority in practice except his
own personality and perseverance to make his fellow-parishioners do
their duty. The system might have worked had it been in the interest of
the parish to maintain its roads to the standard required, but those
who benefited most from the roads, especially the main roads, were
frequently not resident but merchants, officials, troops and others
passing through who, possibly, had no business in the parish; or gentry
travelling between their estates and London or a provincial capital. The
law intended that the roads should be maintained for them – the
administration of justice, trade, the defence of the realm – but more
parishes were satisfied with a lower level of maintenance for their
own needs. The use of a road as a storage place for manure or stones
could be the most important for a farmer at that period. As wagons and
carriages with iron-rimmed wheels became commoner in the seventeenth
century there was another cause of conflict. The traveller wanted hard,
firm roads for the sake of vehicles and horses' hooves. The local people
tended to want soft roads on which to walk their sheep and cattle to
market without risk of laming them. Not surprisingly, most roads were
ill maintained. Fortunately for the surveyors, unfortunately for the state
of the roads, the local Justices of the Peace to whom surveyors were
responsible tended to be sympathetic with local interests and not
enforce the law.

Towards the end of the seventeenth century and into the eighteenth
century the roads worsened, as the industrial revolution sent more
traffic on to the roads. References to the appalling state of the roads
were commonplace in literature and letters in the eighteenth century.
Early in the century Defoe wrote of 'the terrible road, Baldock Lane,
famous for being so unpassable that the coaches and travellers
break out of the way even by force, which the people of the country
not able to prevent, at length placed gates, and laid their lands open,
setting men at the gates to take a voluntary toll, which travellers

always chose to pay, rather than plunge into the sloughs and holes, which no horse could wade through'.[1] This was shrewd of the people of Baldock Lane. It paid them to neglect the roadway where they could not levy tolls to make travellers enter their land where they could. In 1736 we hear that the road from London to Kensington was infamous and, in 1750, the quickest way from Horsham to London, because of the state of the roads, was by Canterbury. Commerce, principally, demanded an improvement and because it was beyond the administrative capabilities and political possibilities of the time to devise something more efficient within the framework of public administration then existing, the only alternative was private enterprise: the turnpike trust.

The first was at Wadesmill in Hertfordshire in 1663. Their heyday was from the middle of the eighteenth century to the 1830s, when there were some 1,100 trusts collecting tolls on and administering about 22,000 miles of toll road. The experiment was not a great improvement. If substituted a conflict of interests between road-user and turnpike trust for that between road-user and parish. Though the parties were different, still those whose responsibility it was to maintain the roads had not the same interests as those who used them; and the users suffered once more. The tolls the trusts could charge were fixed, but they could increase their profits by ploughing back as little as they could in the maintenance of their road. The administrative techniques of the day were insufficient to check their incompetence and speculation. There were no audits of what they were doing, and no limits on their borrowing powers. One highway was frequently divided among several trusts of greatly differing competence and integrity and travellers abroad after 1815 compared our main roads unfavourably with the highways Napoleon had built.

For a short time there was another experiment, the voting of sums for road construction by Parliament, of which the great example was Telford's rebuilding of the Holyhead Road, now the A5, between 1821 and 1836 to replace the old road which had been mismanaged by seventeen turnpike trusts between London and Shrewsbury and nine more thereafter. But there was still a conflict of interest: between the Parliament that voted the funds and the nation that used the roads. The Holyhead Road was chosen for drastic improvement not because it was the most important highway for trade, but for administrative and military reasons as the main road to Ireland. In the past when there was a conflict of interest between national government and the ordinary road-user over the priority to be given to road improvement, the commonest reason was that a national government tended to give priority to military and administrative needs. The roads the Romans built in Britain were of little use for trade and other ordinary needs of

172

the civil population. Their straightness meant they often went directly through lonely, dangerous forests, marshes and wastes forbidding to travellers who were not soldiers. They were not routed so that the traveller could spend every night safely in a village or town. Their straightness also meant they passed by villages and towns which were not militarily or administratively important and this also diminished their general usefulness so that the unmilitary traveller tended to continue to use the old pre-Roman tracks. The motive behind the roads built by Napoleon, Mussolini and Hitler was primarily military and administrative. This determined the route chosen. Now that these motives matter less, the factor making for a conflict of interest is frequently prestige and grandeur, which in this country has meant that impressive rural motorways are built before the less prestigious widenings, re-alignments and other roadworks needed to reduce congestion in towns which are usually more valuable to the road-user.

The early nineteenth-century experiment did not reform many roads and did not last long. Canals, and later railways, were also a response to the demand for better communications. The quick penetration of the country by railways from the 1840s made the roads of little importance except for local transport. Turnpike trusts went bankrupt and gradually disappeared. There was a return of a kind to the old local public service tradition. Roads, like police and fire brigades became the responsibility once more of local authorities acting by arbitrary, and low, standards of road maintenance. There were some changes in administrative structure but they were not the first importance. An Act of 1835 abolished statutory labour and enabled parishes to raise rates for roads. An Act of 1862 enabled parishes to club together in highway districts with Highway Boards which would, if they chose, employ paid officials. In 1888 county councils were established and took over the responsibility for the main roads of the county unless urban authorities chose to continue to maintain their main roads with the aid of a county grant. In 1894 the parish and the highway district were replaced in the country by the rural district council. By 1894 there were 1,800 authorities with responsibility for roads: county councils, county boroughs, borough councils, urban and rural district councils and various bodies in London. But the pattern was still one essentially of local responsibility and expenditure financed by rates. The central Government had virtually no powers and found practically no money. Until the end of the nineteenth century this state of affairs was not unreasonable. There was no conflict of interests, for almost the only period in the history of the roads, since the local people who paid rates were by and large at one, and in agreement, with the local authorities that maintained the roads. The efficiency of these authorities of course varied but there was a

173

certain uniformity in what was required of them and what they did. Maintenance meant the occasional tipping of stones on to bad places in the road to be hammered by the roadmender and ultimately pulverised by horse, carriage and cart; and it meant very little more. No new roads of importance were built — except to serve new building. This was the time when the railways felt they were destined to be the most important means of travel for ever; and that, for travelling any distance, roads were as obsolete as were canals.

First cyclists and then motorists cracked the railways' pre-eminence and re-established the conflict of interests. Again the conflict was between local people and local authorities on the one hand and the long-distance traveller, mainly the motorist, on the other. As in the sixteenth, seventeenth and eighteenth centuries, the power and the purse were the local authorities, and the motorist had no way of influencing the behaviour of local authorities except in so far as he was a nuisance. The nuisance he caused was the dust ploughed up by his wheels that blanketed the hedges and smeared the houses alongside roads travelled by motor vehicles. It was apparently a severer nuisance than it is now easy to imagine. This situation had the makings of compromise in it. As a general principle motorists were ready to pay for better roads, local authorities to improve them if they were paid to. This was the basis for the setting up of the Road Fund in 1909 financed by increasing the small duty on vehicle taxation imposed in 1903 and by a new duty on fuel. The Road Fund was administered by a Road Board which was created to dole out the Fund's income to local authorities. It was intended to be used for road improvement and new construction only. Maintenance was to be paid for in the old way out of rates.[2]

What was achieved in 1909 was an independent agency to make the motorist's wishes felt. It had no power to compel local authorities to spend money on roads, but it could hope to persuade them to do so by giving them the money out of the Road Fund. If it had worked it would have been an admirable arrangement, a model for those we will need to consider when considering how various kinds of road-users can make their needs felt. Just as an industry arises to meet a new need — a demand, say, for a popular car — so the Road Board and its Fund can be represented as a similar attempt to cater for a new need: the need of motorists for a better road. But the analogy breaks down. We cannot assume that the amount paid into the Fund from taxation was all that motorists would have been willing to spend on better roads. The amount was of course arbitrary. And second, as it happened the Road Board, presided over by an ex-general-manager of the North-Eastern Railway, cannot plausibly be said to have bought quite what motorists would have been expected. The Board made grants to local authorities for the resurfacing of the road system with tar macadam. So the dust problem was settled and local authorities were satisfied. But on principle the Board did not, except exceptionally, build any new roads, or make any other kind of improvement to old ones. The Board's philosophy was that straightening roads, the improvement of sight-distances, the elimination of hairpin bends, realignment and similar improvements were unnecessary if the motorist drove carefully, that is, slowly enough. So the only experience this country has had of an independent road authority — without authority but with a long purse — failed. The Board, though not the Fund, was wound up in 1919 and was replaced by the new Ministry of Transport, founded in the same year.

RECENT DEVELOPMENTS

Since then there have been a number of developments. There have been outstanding advances in engineering, so much so that it is hardly exaggerating to say that the major engineering problems of road construction have been solved. In policy and administration, there have been changes but they have not been as fundamental. Road authorities in general have more power and fewer obligations than they used to have. The Unemployment (Relief Works) Act of 1920 gave them the right of compulsory purchase of land for road-building. In 1925 the Roads Improvement Act gave them the right to prescribe building lines along roads. Since then the planning powers of local authorities have on balance increased and this has affected their power in respect of roads. On the other hand their obligations have been relaxed in some respects. For example the 1959 Highways Act abolished the law which dates back at least to the 1285 Statute of Winchester that the inhabitants of an area have a duty to maintain roads in that area. This means that the authorities are now able to allow obsolete roads to decay out of use. And there are now fewer road authorities. The rural district councils lost their road responsibilities in 1929, these passing to county councils, but there are still more than a thousand local authorities with highway responsibilities: county councils, county boroughs, metropolitan and municipal boroughs, and urban district councils. It would be wrong to conclude from their continuing existence that local authorities are still the force in roadbuilding, improvement and maintenance, as there has been a shift in power from the local authorities to the central Government.

When the Ministry of Transport was founded in 1919 it continued what was essentially the methods of the old Road Board, though in a more elaborate manner. Road censuses were the basis of a classification of the nation's roads in 1922-3 into Class 1(A), Class II(B), and unclassified roads. The Ministry made grants of 50 per cent to the first

175

and 25 per cent to the second. In 1927-8 the percentage on Class II roads was increased to 33⅓ per cent. In 1929 the grant on Class I roads went up to 60 per cent, on Class II roads to 50 per cent. Higher grants towards the construction, improvement and maintenance of roads were a means of persuading local authorities to build, improve and maintain, when this was thought desirable as a matter of public policy (or, as it happened, to keep up the level of payments on roads in the 1920s when depression made local authorities retrench). But the Ministry still had no power of forcing local authorities to act. The sovereignty, so to speak, remained with them. The change was occasioned by the Trunk Roads Act of 1936 which made the Ministry, for the first time, a highway authority in its own right, by giving it 100 per cent financial and administrative responsibility for about 4,500 miles of trunk roads. In 1946 more trunk roads were transferred to the Ministry. There are now (1963) 8,500 miles of trunk roads, and 145 miles of motorway (by the Special Roads Act of 1949) for which it and the Scottish Home Office are directly responsible. By comparison there are nearly 190,000 miles for which local authorities are still responsible, though not only do the 8,500 miles of trunk roads represent most of the more important roads, but the classification of roads is the Ministry's prerogative,[3] thus, if there were a road of sufficient importance for Ministry and local authority to conflict, the Ministry could 'trunk' the road. The Ministry could make its will prevail except in county and metropolitan boroughs where there are no trunk roads as the law now stands – a trunk road becoming a Class I road at the boundary of the county or metropolitan borough. Here there could be a conflict of interest between central and local Government over an important road where both have a veto because both contribute; and there have been conflicts, notably in London over the intersection of the Cromwell Road extension and Hammersmith Bridge Road. The Ministry wanted a flyover: but the LCC as the highway authority in London argued that they had more important uses for the £2m. (25 per cent of the cost of Class I road borne by the local authority) elsewhere and that they preferred a roundabout. This is an exception to the virtual supremacy of the central Government, which could, if desired, be altered easily enough by legislation.

PRESENT POLICY: THE GRANT SYSTEM

Yet it can still be maintained that these changes, which have left the Ministry in a position of greater power absolutely, and in relation to other roads authorities, have hardly touched on what matters most, the conflict of interests between road authority and road-user. This has become vastly more complex since the simple old days of local people versus motorists, so that huge groups of conflicting interests, hostile passions, of scarcely reconcilable aims, and vehemently opposed forces are engaged. Our roads authorities have scarcely begun to work out the principles on which the weight to be given to these conflicting interests should be settled, except in a most arbitrary, thoughtless fashion.

Take the system by which grants are made. All maintenance, improvement and new construction of motorways and trunk roads is paid for entirely by the Ministry of Transport. Local authorities get a grant of 75 per cent of the cost of any maintenance, improvement and new construction of Class I roads, 60 per cent for Class II, 50 per cent for Class III; and they bear the whole cost for unclassified roads. All roads fall into one of these five categories. The grant depends on the classification. The classification depends on the Ministry. What is the principle behind the classification? The apparent answer is density of traffic: the more heavily trafficked a road the higher its classification and grant. It can be argued that roads on which traffic is light are more likely to be used by local people; and therefore it might seem as if the point of the system for making grants is another attempt to solve in its modern form, the old conflict between national and local interests. However the idea behind the classification is not quite as simple because the same traffic densities are not everywhere used to assign roads to one of the five categories — 'you can get a trunk road like the Great North Road or the London-Birmingham Motorway and then you can get one running up the West Wales coast. The difference between the two on traffic volume is enormous.[4] The implication would seem to be that a road which might rank as a trunk road in West Wales would be classed lower in a more highly populated part of the country, though its traffic density were the same. The chief engineer (highways) at the Ministry of Transport went on to say that discrepancies of this kind were commoner between roads of the same class in Class I and Class II in various parts of the country than between different trunk roads. This means some local authorities get more money than others for roads of the same traffic density which appears in practice as a concealed subsidy to the more sparsely populated areas. We might try to rescue the principle by arguing that there is likely to be a higher proportion of non-local traffic on a trunk road on the West Wales coast than on a similar road in the West Midlands, and this is why a bigger contribution should come from national funds. The trouble with this suggestion is that it may be true in some instances but it is quite as likely to be false in others. As a generalisation it will hardly stand. Almost certainly there must be some subsidisation concealed here.

There is a more fundamental objection to be made to the principle of classification. The point of a general rule of classifying roads according to traffic density is presumably to attempt to reconcile national and local interests: the heavier the proportion of national traffic, the larger the contribution from national funds. Now this might have made sense from the sixteenth to the eighteenth century, through the nineteenth up to 1909 when petrol taxation was introduced, but as it stands it does not make sense now. All petrol taxation goes to the Exchequer. The local motorist on the move consumes neither more nor less petrol for the distance he covers, and therefore pays neither more nor less in fuel tax than any other motorist. Justice would suggest that a local authority should get a larger grant for a road, the higher the proportion, in some sense, of long-distance motor traffic (and possibly long-distance cyclists, if these were not insignificant) using it; and therefore, conversely the more a road is used by local people other than by movement along it in motor vehicles, the larger the contribution should be to it from local sources. This is because (except for parking where there are meters) people do not pay directly for these other uses as they pay petrol tax whenever their vehicles move; and as most of these other road-uses are likely to be by local people, there is a case for meeting them from rates.

To rescue the principle as a way of trying to reconcile the conflict of interest between local authorities and other road-users, it must be reformulated: the less motor traffic there is on a road the more likely it is to be used by local people for purposes other than vehicle movement. The principle may seem plausible, to take the example of unclassified roads, for unclassified urban streets which are used for parking, waiting, loading and unloading, by children playing and by pedestrians. In some sense these are likely to be a greater proportion of the uses of a small urban street than of a town street with a higher classification; but even in towns the argument looks less impressive when we think of the percentage grants involved. Are we to suppose that motorists do not use unclassified urban streets for driving on at all — otherwise why are their costs borne entirely on the rates? Or that main roads in municipal boroughs are only used by motorists on the move — otherwise why are all their costs borne from national funds? The commonsense attitude might seem to be to assume that these cancel each other out — the local authority makes up on the grants it gets on the more highly classified roads what it loses on those with a lower classification, but towns and villages vary greatly in the proportion of the different categories of roads they possess.

Therefore there is an element of arbitrariness which works in favour of some local authorities and against others. The principle is still less plausible for unclassified roads in the country. Even if we allow for (local) cyclists, farm carts, herds of cattle and pedestrians which use the more than 60,000 miles of rural unclassified roads, it must be the case nowadays that these are usually mostly used by motor vehicles. To suggest that their entire cost should always be paid from rates is surely illogical. The only way out of the dilemma would now seem to be to argue that motor vehicles on unclassified roads do not pay enough in petrol taxation on the petrol they consume while travelling these roads, to meet the costs of the road, and that in some sense which is barely intelligible this is particularly true of local motor traffic, otherwise why require a contribution to this end from rates? There is no evidence that should be generally true for unclassified rural roads (or urban streets for that matter). Rather the reverse, since these are often the sort of road which is not heavily used where one would expect the tax on petrol consumed on them would cover their costs. We do know that Class III rural roads, which are not dissimilar from unclassified rural roads, are almost certainly roads on which road-users are paying out more in petrol tax than the roads currently cost,[5] and therefore it is probable the same is true of many unclassified rural roads. However even if the facts were in favour of this interpretation of principle, this would not explain why *all* the costs should be met from rates.

These are not all the criticisms which could be made questioning the sense of the present system of making grants, but they are enough to establish that it is a muddle, and a failure, if, as seems likely, it ever were meant to be just — an attempt to divide costs fairly between national and local authorities. It has escaped detailed criticism in the past not because it has reconciled opposing interests successfully but because its very complexity has obscured the issues and the interests. In short, it is illogical, inconsistent and arbitrary. Before the grant system grew to its present luxuriance, it was fairly plain what Governments had in mind in shaping or continuing the policy governing road administration. From the Dark Ages in 1909 the leading principle of road administration, save for the turnpike trusts and the few experiments like Field Marshal Wade's roads in the Highlands and Telford's Holyhead Road, was, as we have seen, that local people should maintain the roads at their own expense and labour, in effect as a tax — or subsidy to the minority of the nation that used the roads frequently. The principle of the 1909 Fund and Board was that an annual sum, admittedly arbitrary in amount, should be spent in the motorist's best interest by a body which was meant to have it at heart. I have been able to discover no consistent principle or policy behind the present grant system. The grants do not represent the amount of money which is meant to be spent on various types of roads in the interest of the long-distance traveller or alternatively in the interest of all motor traffic as distinct from what is meant to be spent on behalf of other road-users; or if either of these is *meant,* there are serious imperfections in practice. The system is not obviously fair between local authorities and in particular it appears to subsidise local authorities in more sparsely populated areas.

PRESENT POLICY: INVESTMENT

It is not only the ideas controlling the allocation of grants, the incidence of taxation, regulations and subsidies — which relate to the use of the existing road system — which need attention, but also investment. Here there has been a great clarification of issues in recent years which is still proceeding. There is the problem that there are many highway authorities. The Ministry is of course only solely responsible for working out priorities for investment on trunk roads and motorways; where it makes grants it has to act in collusion with the local authority, both having the power of veto unless the Ministry were to decide, as it has not had to do for this reason, to trunk a road. Investment priorities on unclassified roads are the sole responsibility of the local authority. It must at times be difficult for Ministry and local authority to decide within the structure of the complicated grant system whether it would be better to invest £10,000, say, in a Class II road where the Ministry pays 60 per cent of the cost or a Class III road where it pays 50 per cent. Here there is the possibility of a conflict of interests. We know little about the system of priorities which local authorities, and local authorities in conjunction with the Ministry have worked out for themselves. (There was a call for more research by local authorities on this from the representative of the Ministry of Transport at the *Conference on the Highway Needs of Great Britain* of 1957.)[6]

We do know something of the principles governing priorities of investment in trunk roads. It will be worth quoting at some length from the evidence given by the assistant secretary responsible for highways administration at the Ministry to the select committee on estimates in 1959. 'You ask how we assess priorities in deciding to start new schemes. We have reports from divisional road engineers on everything which they want to do on their trunk roads. These are being collected for a master plan of trunk roads which the Ministry is drawing up. They put into us reports on the present conditions of traffic, accidents, black spots, etc., on each trunk road in their division. (England and Wales are divided into nine. Scotland is in effect a large single division with staff seconded from the Ministry.) They assess the influence on future traffic there of new motorways, changes in the trunk road system and other developments in the area; and they set out in turn for each individual trunk road the works which are proposed on it and the works which they consider necessary to bring it up to a *suitable standard* for the traffic into the far distant future. We are building up a gradual picture in the Ministry — and it is a gradual process because naturally this takes a lot of time — of what is required on all the trunk roads in the country, and as the DRE's put in their reports they give their ideas on the priority to be attached to the scheme. From this broad picture we have got a pretty good idea already *which are the main roads in the country which are overloaded, where the main industrial traffic is going, and where these two coincide.* Then clearly decisions have to be taken on what is to be done to put them right. This picture which we are building up for the master plan confirms very strongly that the five major projects which the Minister has chosen are the right background for a road programme. *With due reservations,* priority is given to them taking into account the effects on finance, the availability of labour in the areas concerned and the Minister's objective of securing as quickly as possible free traffic flow from end to end of an improved route ... *When it comes to assessing a priority between two schemes costing the same amount and with the same amount of traffic there perhaps we are not yet able to use scientific methods* and it is more a matter of judgement.'[7] The passages in italic type are those which seem especially important or ambiguous. It will be seen that the basic pattern, the cross of motorways, and trunk road improvements (the Great North Road, London-Yorkshire Motorway, Birmingham-South Wales, London-South Wales, and London-Channel Ports) was decided before the detailed reports came in — the Ministry states they have but confirmed its good judgement.

Although there are some ambiguities it would appear that the main principles are:

(1) to invest in roads which are overloaded — that is, where traffic density is high in relation to capacity;

(2) to prefer such roads where the ratio of industrial to private car traffic is high;

(3) and, presumably, where two schemes are equally attractive on grounds (1) and (2), to choose the cheaper;

(4) if they are equal in cost, judgement decides.

Although this is a great improvement on the more haphazard methods that preceded it, it is liable to *bias* the order in which projects are selected in a way which may not always be desirable. To take the second principle first; it may seem sensible to invest first where industrial traffic needs it most, but is this in fact wise? It might be the case that by either of our two criteria (if conditions made possible their expression) that holiday and week-end motorists using

181

crowded roads to the seaside might value road improvement and construction more than industrial traffic; but even if we take the more limited but quite sensible view that when investible funds are scarce, we should invest first to benefit national production, the case for investing in roads where industrial traffic is heaviest is not as strong as it may seem. Production could benefit more if some investment to relieve urban congestion was given priority to enable workers to reach factories and offices more quickly and arrive fresher. Travel in private cars and public service vehicles often has a significance for industry and national productivity. Certainly this industrial bias was one reason why rural motorways were built before serious attempts were made to improve access to cities, and why the London-Birmingham motorway was built first of all.

Second, there is the difficulty that density is not a straightforward concept — a point which could also have been made in criticism of its use in connection with the grant system. Seven hundred and fifty vehicles per hour can mean something very different on identical roads, depending first of all on the nature of the vehicles (size distribution of the flow). If there is a high proportion of trucks this is *effectively* a greater density than if there is a high proportion of private cars, and the figure indicating the traffic density of a road should be weighted for this: for example one three-tonner equals x private cars and perhaps other weights for different sizes of vehicles. (The Ministry of Transport uses the convention that cyclists count ½, cars and motor cycles 1, and vehicles above 30 cwt. 3.)[8] The effect of a different size distribution of vehicles is not just a question of the physical occupation of space but also of relative speeds. The heavier the vehicle on average the lower the speed; and the greater the proportion of heavy vehicles the slower the speed of all traffic and the more a given density of traffic taxes the capacity of a road; but on the other hand the more lanes there are, especially if there is a divided carriageway, the less the effect of the large vehicle on the speed of the small. Gradients also affect the density of effective volume of traffic, since heavy vehicles tend to reduce speed when going up and down hill. A track which equals two private cars on the level may equal four on a gradient. This should be allowed for, either in working out the effective density of traffic or the capacity of the road. Another problem is to select the density of traffic in respect of time since this will normally vary hourly, daily and seasonally. The ideal might seem to be to draw up a calendar showing the traffic volume for every hour of the year, but this would obviously be impracticable. Most figures are derived from a sample traffic census from which it should be possible to work out an average annual volume of traffic, but this may be misleading. Some roads have more fluctuations than others in their intensity of use. And does one want to plan a road in relation to its average use? To take the highest density, it is generally thought, might lead to over-investment in roads with abnormally high and possibly infrequent peak hours.

At this level of analysis we are now considering the choice is arbitrary. A favourite in the United States is the traffic density of the Thirtieth Highest Hour because a (rather limited) number of experiments have suggested that there are on average twenty nine hours of unusually heavy traffic on any road and that the traffic carried in the thirtieth highest hour can in a sense be regarded as high normal.[9] One would suspect that it would be unlikely to be a reasonable approximation for both urban and rural roads, and even if it were, would it be valid both in America and here? Experiments would be needed to find a similar dodge for this country. The method used here is based on the average traffic flow for a 16-hour (6 a.m.–10 p.m.) day in August. Since traffic flow is about 30 per cent above monthly average, annual traffic will be about 300 times that for the 16-hour day in August, which in turn is divided by 365 to get the average daily density of traffic. (If there is special reason to think the August traffic unusually high, this is allowed for from local judgement.) The multiplier, as it is called, has no firmer basis than the feeling of the engineer responsible that it is about right. There is not usually a survey which will show what in fact it ought to be.[10] By these steps we reach a figure for the traffic density of a particular stretch of road. (We will here and later use the word 'stretch' with a specially rigorous meaning as a stretch of road from one intersection to the next (inclusive) which can be expected to have the same traffic flow along its length.)

Density is to be related to capacity. This is or ought to be an unambiguous concept in practice. The maximum capacity of a road, sometimes called its basic or design capacity, can be illustrated conveniently on a diagram (fig. 8.1). The horizontal axis represents the time taken to travel along the stretch of road which varies from the minimum when a single vehicle is on the road to infinity when the road is so congested that movement is literally impossible. The flow of traffic with which we are concerned is the flow in one direction. F_{max} is maximum flow possible. Any additional vehicles will slow down other vehicles sufficiently to reduce it.* The actual maximum capacity of a road will depend on many factors: for example number of lanes, their width, gradients, curvature (because of sight-distances). It will also depend on intersections and the traffic at them, the methods of traffic control used, the timing of traffic lights, the adroitness of police in marshalling traffic, the use of the road for parking, waiting, unloading,

* A practical difficulty is that the drawing of the curve will be affected by the speeds at which vehicles try to drive along the road, but this is a complication we can here neglect.

etc. (Parking, waiting, etc. can if sufficiently extensive be regarded as effectively removed lanes from a road or if less extensive as an obstruction slowing down the flow.) It is also necessary here to allow for the probable size distribution of traffic also since this will affect

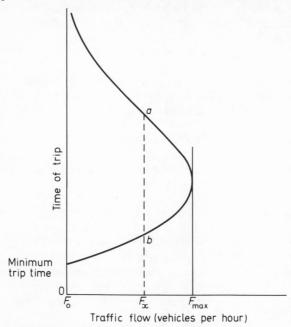

FIG. 8.1: Graphic illustration of the maximum capacity of a road in terms of time of trip for a vehicle

the road's capacity. To generalise the factors determining the capacity of a road are of three sorts: the physical (long period) characteristics of the road; traffic control and other (short period) regulations which affect its capacity, and the nature, principally the size distribution and speed of the vehicles using it (Long period is used, as we have used it before, to mean that investment would be needed to make a change, short period that a change could be effected without investment.) Given perfect knowledge of these factors it is possible in principle to work out mathematically the capacity of a stretch of road.[11] In practice the capacity figure for a stretch of road will be an approximation.*

A method would be to use a formula such as this one which originated in Michigan

$$C_p = C_1 \times A \times W \times T$$

*It can be seen that a given flow (F_x) may be associated with a slow *(a)* or a faster trip *(b)* depending on congestion (see fig. 8.1).

184

where C_p is 'practical capacity' – to all intents and purposes the capacity measure in which we are interested. C_1 is the design capacity for a 12ft-wide lane straight and on the level, a figure presumed to be standard for all roads of a given type – for example three-lane, dual carriageway: 2,000 v.p.h. A is the percentage decrease in capacity caused by sight restrictions (curvature) in that particular stretch of road. W is the percentage decrease in capacity caused by a less than average width of lane. T is the percentage increase caused by the proportion of tracks using the road (C_1 is calculated on the assumption the road is only used by cars). It is easy to see that this is some way away from a perfect measure of capacity, not allowing as it seems for gradients, intersections, frequency of parking, etc., among other things (though it is fair to add that officials are asked to revise the results achieved by this method for condition of the surface, accident experience and roadside friction). Whether it would be worth going into more detail is not something about which it would be sensible to dogmatise.[12]

Let us suppose that we can map a traffic density and a capacity figure for every stretch of road in the country. The traffic density is the best approximation to the hourly volume which is judged (average annual hourly flow, thirtieth highest hour or similar) to be the most significant for investment purposes. The capacity figure is the best practicable approximation to the maximum capacity figure (fig. 8.1). We have now a means of working out investment priorities. The ratio of capacity to traffic density is worked out for every stretch of road: C_p. Unless the stretch of road is operating at maximum flow, the *priority member* will be less than one. Stretches on which flow is less because either more or fewer vehicles want to use the road, will have priority numbers less than one. It is therefore necessary to separate the congested roads from the rest. The ranking of stretches for investment purposes will work as follows. The highest priority will be given to the congested road with the lowest priority number (the most congested road). Ranked below this will be the congested roads in descending order of congestion, ascending order of priority number, to roads numbered *one*. Beneath these will be roads ranked in descending order of priority number until at the bottom there will be the road with the lowest traffic density in relation to capacity. There are nine objections which can be made to this type of method of settling priorities.

(1) It is grounded too much in the present, whereas it should be looking into the future. The relevant traffic density is not the density now but to come. This is only relevant to the priority of projects if the volume of traffic is expected to grow at different rates on different roads. Otherwise, to scale up all priority numbers by the appropriate

percentage may emphasise the urgency of investment. Although there are always difficulties in the estimating of future demand, this should be no harder here than for any other project. Future demand can, and often does, replace present demand in calculating the priority numbers.

(2) It does not allow for generated demand: that is any demand generated by the making of the investment. An improved road will attract traffic from other roads, possibly from other means of transport; possibly it will increase the use of transport as an alternative to other occupations. (A new road might attract additional users – leisure traffic – from watching television for a time and to some extent perhaps permanently.) Although in practice various traffic density/capacity measures do not allow for induced demand, they could be modified to do so as for any other component of future demand, as described above.

(3) The criterion does not enable us to determine what we want to stop investing in roads, because it does not indicate the satisfactory relationship of density to capacity. What is a satisfactory ratio? It is generally thought to be faster than the maximum flow along the road; but to go for the ratio which would give the maximum speed for traffic would also present a problem since the flow of traffic which would make possible the highest speed would generally be *unity,* each extra vehicle tending to slow down those already on the road. What is done usually is to take some rather vague notion of 'practical capacity', the lower volume level, the traffic density is not great enough to cause any *unreasonable* delay or *undue* restriction on the driver's freedom to manoeuvre. As traffic volumes increase beyond practical capacity, a high traffic density directly results.'[13] If one has not a criterion – such as our basic criteria – which is able to give a more definite indication when it would not be worthwhile investing more, perhaps this kind of vague subjective feeling is the best that can be said in the circumstances. Unfortunately some conception of 'practical capacity' is often used as the denominator in the priority number-ratio given above instead of maximum capacity. This has the advantage that all investment projects can be ordered directly, the highest priority number first. It has the disadvantage of being arbitrary in itself – since what is 'unreasonable' and 'undue' is a matter of opinion. And it makes possible and probable a certain irregularity of judgement, since every surveyor sending in his report on the state of the roads for which he is responsible has had to decide the 'practical capacity' for each road, and there tends to be a vested interest for him to keep his practical capacity as low as possible in the competition for his share of the investment funds available.

(4) Another disadvantage is that there is no way of comparing even approximately the rate of return on investment in roads with that on other investments.

186

(5) As it stands it does not allow for differences in the cost of investments. A stretch of road which would cost £1m. to put right and another which would cost £10,000 would have the same priority number and therefore the same priority. In fact, of course, cost is never ignored. It is just not always introduced in a systematic manner. Another reason why the urban schemes, where one would expect a high priority to have been indicated by this kind of criterion, have been preceded by rural motorways and similar projects, where one would have expected the priority to be lower, may well be cost considerations: a rough decision not to invest in projects of more than a certain cost, while keeping a number of projects in motion. To try to avoid this kind of tampering with the system of priorities, one method would be to express the fall in the ratio of traffic density to capacity expected as *a rate of return on the capital invested*. (Say for example that investment in a particular re-alignment is expected to increase maximum capacity from 1,000 to 2,000 and volume from 750 congested to 1,250 uncongested. The change in ratios will be from ¾ congested to ⅝ uncongested. If we arbitrarily assign a negative value to the first and a positive value to the second we can deduce a total change in ratio of ¾ + ⅝ or 1⅜. Let us say the length of the road improved is one mile. Then the benefit is expressed as 1⅜ per mile. Let us suppose the cost is £10,000. At this point we have to establish an arbitrary relationship. Let us say that 1⅜ per mile change in ratio is to be reckoned 1⅜ per cent of £100,000. Since they are incommensurables it would not matter if we said it was 1⅜ per cent of £100 or £1,000,000 or any other amount providing once we have decided on the relationship we stick to it through all subsequent calculations. Then the return, measured, in this way is 13¾ per cent on £10,000 as it would be 11/80 per cent on £1m.) Thus we can express this criterion as a rate of return on investment and so integrate cost with the other factors allowed for in determining the order of priority. The highest priority would be given to the project showing the highest rate of return by this method, subject to the limitation that no road would be improved to a standard higher than practical capacity for the traffic expected.

(6) It is often said that the traffic-density/capacity-type method does not allow for choice between alternative methods of improving a road. For example, there might be two different ways of re-aligning a road, one more expensive than the other. It is the case that those who use such methods (and this would appear to be true in the country) do have arbitrary standards of construction. A bridge to carry a certain amount of traffic will conform to certain specifications which are often thought to allow an excessive margin of safety. And it is often queried whether as satisfactory results would not be achieved at less cost

by lowering the standards without any harmful results.[14]   Again this
is not a necessary result of the method of calculating priorities *if* these
are expressed as a rate of return, in so far as the differences in the cost
of investment are reflected in the capacity of the road — in our
examples, a newly aligned road. We can tell by this method which are
the most worthwhile investments and combinations of investments to
lower the traffic-density/capacity ratio until finally all roads are
operating at practical capacity.

(7) And this disposes of another objection often made which is that
this method cannot allow for interdependence, that is *complementarity*
of investments. To take a simple example there is a road with two
bottlenecks. To remove one would increase the road's capacity slightly
(say ½ per cent) and to remove the other would have a similar effect
on capacity (say ⅜ per cent), but to remove them both would have a
much greater effect than the sum of the two taken separately (say
2 per cent). The investments are complementary. However, the very
expression of the problem in terms of rates of return shows that this
difficulty can be resolved within the framework of this type of priority
system, provided it is decided to express the ratios as rates of return.

There are two other sorts of objection which are more fundamental.

(8) The first is that this procedure omits any reference to other
costs besides the actual cost of investment which most people would
regard as relevant: for example maintenance, accident, and police costs
among others. Neither does it allow for the present condition of the
road. Suppose there are two possible road investments alike in every
other respect except that one at present costs more to maintain than
the other (or the accident and police costs are higher). Then among
the benefits of an investment should be counted any reduction in
such costs. Assume we have two projects. One gets a higher priority
rating than the other, taking into account all the factors previously
considered; yet the second road, to make an extreme case, has higher
maintenance, accident and police costs which would all be considerably
reduced by the proposed investment. Again most people would agree
that these should be allowed to count and to affect priorities. But how?
It is here that our criterion seems to be bursting at the seams. A
common method adopted in the United States is what is known as
traffic sufficiency rating and is obviously arbitrary. The original
Arizona method adopted by twenty-two States uses a points
system which rated a stretch of road according to its adequacy for
daily traffic allowing 35 per cent of the marks for condition, 30 per cent
for safety and 35 per cent for service (and incidentally making no
allowance for peak traffic or the cost of improvements). The King's
County, California, method awarded up to 40 points for geometric
design, 25 points for physical design, 15 points for safety and 20 points

for service. Then the score won by a road is weighted by what is known as an 'economic ratio'. $E = M/C$, where E is the economic ratio, M is the annual maintenance cost expressed as a proportion of C (the annual construction cost). F was also calculated, the 'feasibility' factor or ratio of earning capacity (yield in taxes or tolls) to construction costs. In both cases the higher the ratios the higher the priority. The ultimate priority was given by $P = EF/A$ where A is the score already mentioned expressed not as a percentage but as a decimal fraction.[15] Not much inspection is needed to see that there is an astonishing amount of arbitrariness in this apparently scientific formula. And there are very many other variants of this procedure.[16] Why give safety a maximum of 30 per cent in one case and 15 per cent in the other? Unless one has some underlying principle (such as one of our basic criteria) with which to weigh these various costs, we should not be surprised if the individual judgements which in one case rank the importance of traffic density to capacity high, in others rank it lower. Such sufficiency ratings do not prevent arguments at a rather meaningless level; since it all revolves around the percentages to be adopted and is not concerned with any deeper principle.

(9) The last objection is on the demand side: that this method of assessing priorities ignores differences in value of improvements to different interests concerned. For example, we may imagine two stretches of road identical in every other respect and with the same priority numbers. The traffic using them is composed of roughly the same proportions of private cars and commercial vehicles except that in the one case the commercial vehicles are preponderantly vans and in the other heavy trucks. (The effective density is, in the same way, on the basis of 1 heavy truck to 4 vans.) In every other significant respect the stretches are the same and equally over-loaded. Common sense would suggest that it would be wrong to deduce that it does not matter which is invested in first. What is omitted from the calculation is the possibility that the road improvement might be worth more to the vans than to the trucks. Every trucker knows that value does not usually increase in proportion to weight and that small vehicles can carry proportionally more valuable cargoes. It may well be the case that the more valuable traffic would be prepared to pay more for speed. Here we have a conflict of interests which the priority system has no way of deciding because equal weight is given to same effective density irrespective of any differences in value. Similarly there is no way of deciding the conflicting interests of any road-users — parkers, motorists, pedestrians, etc. — except where these are faithfully reflected by differences in effective density. Those in the United States who devise Traffic Sufficiency Ratings have also realised this and tried to adapt their procedures, but arbitrarily. For example the North

Carolina system allows 10 points for each school, 7 points for each active store, garage filling station or combination of these (irrespective of size), 3 points for each cotton gin, cotton mill or small plant, 3 points for each bus passing in one day, 3 points for a mail route, 3 points for each industrial bus passing daily, 3 points for each daily milk pick-up milk route, 1 point for every two vehicles and 1 point for every family dwelling; the total for family dwellings being divided by the mileage of the road on which they are situated.[17] This is used to weight the priority given to road investment. Again one can say that such attempts to give weight to differences in the value that roads have for different road-users must be arbitrary unless they are based on some underlying principle.

What we have done in this section is to refine the traffic density/ capacity criterion in successive stages so that it has become closer and closer to an economic criterion as defined in Chapter 3 and used in Chapters 4–7. At each stage it has been argued that further refinement was probably worth while because of the limitations of the criterion as it stood, and evidence for this has been the reaching of those responsible for formulating and using such criteria towards more comprehensive formulae allowing progressively for such things as weighted traffic density, speed, hourly, daily and seasonal fluctuations, more exact calculations of capacity, future including future induced demand, a cut-off definition of practical capacity beyond which investment is not desired, allowance for investment and other costs, complementarity of investment and differences of valuation on the demand side. If the criterion is refined so as to meet objections (8) and (9) it can be nothing but an economic criterion in the sense of Chapter 3 – being a set of principles which makes it possible to weight consistently all factors on the cost and demand sides so as to yield the appropriate rate of return – or to put the same point in another way: there is a basic criterion except where explicitly modified by subsidy or regulation.

This is the case for reforming our methods in Britain. We simply cannot tell how crude or sophisticated the traffic density criterion used by the Ministry of Transport is, from published material for the Ministry, unlike American highway authorities, is not accustomed to being explicit on these matters; and it was the misfortune of the select committee on estimates which investigated trunk roads that it did not ask as penetrating questions as the select committee on the nationalised industries which investigated the railways. I believe however that there is no highway authority anywhere which has got as far towards comprehensiveness as to express this kind of criterion as rate of return on investment. An improved method (a consumer's surplus rate of return) has been devised by the Road Research

Laboratory, to be discussed in Chapter 11, but it has not yet been *used* much.

If we are to attempt to resolve the many conflicts of interest in any except the most arbitrary *ad hoc* traffic sufficiency rating manner is it is necessary to adopt an economic criterion. Then we can start at the other end: by pursuing the implications of the criterion into every corner of the problem. Some of the conflicts which matter and which cannot be solved sensibly by the old methods are:

(i)   *between motorists and pedestrians,*

(ii)   *between vehicles in motion and parkers,*

(iii)   *between long-term parkers and loading and unloading,*

(iv)   *between private motorists and commercial vehicles,*

(v)   *between private motorists who wish to travel at different speeds,*

(vi)   *between private motorists who are prepared to pay more to be able to travel on a less congested street and those who are not,*

(vii) *between different sizes of commercial vehicle, particularly between the very large truck with trailer and other motorists,*

(viii) *between other motorists and the public service vehicle: bus, coach, tram, taxi, etc.,*

(ix)   *between road-users and the National Health Service as expressed in the cost of accidents,*

(x)   *between road-users and other uses for land,*

(xi)   *and between roads and other uses for investible funds.*

In principle the issues involved in all these are capable of being straightened and solved if we adopt one or other of our basic criteria (or a similar criterion). As before, in Chapters 9-11 we are going to pursue the implications of assuming profit and consumers' surplus maximisation. Many might be prepared in principle to accept either one or other of these as an intuitively acceptable criterion governing the use of and investment in roads. We will follow the criteria wherever they take us, remembering however that it is possible to modify them by regulation or subsidy wherever we should wish to do this.

CRITERIA

We will assume that it is only the road system with which we are concerned. The application of the basic criteria would be somewhat different if there was any question of running the roads and road transport as a single economic entity. There was a movement in this direction in 1947 when the bulk of roads goods transport was nationalised, but there has never been any question of nationalising all road passenger transport, making, as Krushchev once suggested, the nationalised taxi replace the private car. Because of the right given to firms to carry their own goods in their own vehicles (the 'C' licence) there was substantial competition in goods transport also. But even in so far as road transport was nationalised there was no attempt to integrate it with the road system as a single economic entity. There was even then the asymmetry between road and rail that is more marked now. Most of the problems arising from the fact that the railways provide track and services while the road programme provides only track fall to be dealt with under coordination and competition in Chapter 12. In this chapter and the two following we will consider solely the economic issues involved in running the road system and let the asymmetry hang.

Some may wish to argue the unimportance of cross-subsidisation in the road system even if they are willing that total receipts should cover total costs. I have nothing to add to the arguments against cross-subsidisation on the railways in Chapter 7.

Few of the defects from which the road programme has suffered since 1945 can be blamed on its form of organisation. The argument for establishing a national roads authority is considered separately in an appendix to the chapter. There it is argued that some change in organisation will almost certainly be needed. We will however talk of a roads authority in the body of the book simply for convenience without begging the question of its form — whether it is one or many (that is, its degree of centralisation) or indeed whether it is the Ministry and local authorities trying to implement one or other of our basic criteria, with the minimum of reorganisation, or the kind of authority advocated in Appendix 4.

The basic criteria to be considered are the same as for the railways. The definitions of the subsidisation and cross-subsidisation are the same. Profit maximisation does not present any special conceptual problem but it does present a practical one. A profit maximising roads authority could extract a very high profit indeed by making a separate bargain with every road-user; asking the question: what would you pay rather than not be allowed to use the roads at all? It may be assumed there is no question of this happening. A constraint must be imposed in practice on profit maximisation, since unconstrained profit maximisation we can safely assume would be politically intolerable. What constraint? A roads authority would possess more monopoly power than the railways. Most of this would arise because it would control the access to property and there except in a Jules Verne world of subterranean tunnels and helicopters it would have no rivals. If a man cannot reach his home or his business by any other means than by road it can be presumed he would be prepared to pay a very large proportion of his total consumers' or producers' surplus for the privilege of access to them. If he tries to avoid the extortioner by

192

moving it does not profit him because the same authority controls road access everywhere. If the authority is decentralised this may profit him a little because of competition for his residence and business between regions; but he would still be in difficulties. If price discrimination were ruled out this would not make much difference since the service of providing road access to No. 9 and No. 11 Acacia Avenue can plausibly be represented as the provision of different services with considerable elements of joint costs. It would not make so very much difference if all-or-nothing bargaining were prohibited so that road-users bargained spearately for the use of the roads for different purposes: access, travel, carriage of goods, etc. since it would still be possible, quite apart from problems of definition, to make a large profit on access. All this may seem to exist in a fantasy world; and certainly the road system if it is run to make profits does present problems for the establishement of competition which the railways do not. In the strict sense it is not feasible to imagine the road system being run commercially. But it would not be worth while trying to consider what form constraint on profit maximisation should take for the road system alone because it is part of the wider problem of establishing competition or coordination in transport. Further discussion of this problem will therefore be postponed to Part IV. In the next chapter a principal topic will be the discussion of how the present system of charging for the use of roads could be improved so that it permits a more rational charging and investment policy by either criterion. In Chapter 11 the application of a consumers' surplus investment criterion for road investment will be considered in some detail. It therefore will not matter much that we postpone the problem of deciding constraints on profit maximisation.

It also follows from our argument that as on the railways there is a case for entering any subsidies separately in the books of the authority. Any type of policy required can be implemented by these means without confusing the books of the authority and in particular muddling subsidies with cross-subsidy.

There is at present one form of subsidy which seems perfectly distinct from other payments for road construction and properly earmarked. From this point of view it would seem to be a model for both rail and road. This is expenditure under the crofter county programme. Since 1936 the Government has paid the whole cost of reconstructing certain local authority highways in the Highlands in the special interest of the crofting community.[18] This is an overt subsidy.

It is more difficult to generalise about the incidence of cross-subsidisation than it was with railways, because of problems connected with defining the costs of the road system to be considered in the next chapter, and also of relating revenue to cost. There may be some places where by chance the road system does maximise its profits with its present methods of charging for the use of roads; but there are many places where it does not. If we turn to cross-subsidy in relation to the consumers' surplus policy, there are certain hypotheses which have been put forward. Urban road-users pay less than the cost of providing roads for them and are therefore subsidised by other road-users and the rest of the community, but this judgement certainly depends on what are defined to be the costs of providing roads in towns. Users of long-distance trunk roads and motorways are subsidised in the sense that it has long been the case that the Ministry of Transport and local authorities have preferred to invest in these when by either criterion it would have been more profitable to invest in piecemeal improvements in congested areas.[19] Users of Class III rural roads, also, it has been said pay more than the cost of providing these roads.[20] But further consideration of the extent of cross-subsidisation can be postponed to the next chapter. All that we need say here is that the adoption of either of our basic criteria implies the elimination of cross-subsidisation as better costing and demand analysis shows up its existence.

It will also be assumed that any regulations imposed on the road system will either be in pursuit of the criterion adopted or will be the kind of factory, public health and similar legislation and regulation applied to all similar commercial enterprises. Regulation for safety will similarly either be regarded as in the motorist's best interests as defined by our criteria or as part of a general policy. The effect of regulations upon the competitive ability of road and rail will also be considered in more detail in Chapter 12.

And last, if there should be any reader who thinks we should consider the implications of a pure consumers' policy for roads in which no charge was made but the entire cost borne from general taxation, perhaps he will be persuaded of the sense of charging for the use of roads by these arguments. The invention of the internal combustion engine and its consequences have had four effects:

(1) Road transport has become again an economically significant form of transport. This has greatly increased the amount spent on roads. The more spent the more important it is to see that it is spent carefully.

(2) The general impression is that not enough is spent on the roads. Although we may hope that public policy will change and that funds will be as freely available in the public sector as to any sound commercial firm, this is unlikely to happen soon but as long as funds available for investments are limited by a fixed Government budget, it is the more important to see that they are used as profitably as possible.

194

*(3) It used to be argued that roads benefited everyone equally,
therefore everyone, through taxation, should pay. This has always been
a rough approximation to the truth, since one of the prime causes of
inefficiency from the sixteenth to the eighteenth century was that those
long-distance travellers who mostly used the roads were not in general
the same people, the ratepayers, who kept them. Why should a
parish work and pay principally for the benefit of those strangers who
passed through it on the highway? Yet the case that everyone benefited
more or less equally from roads was more arguable up to the invention
of the automobile than it has been since. And it also used to be
argued more plausibly that it cost much the same to provide roads for
everyone: pedestrian, packhorse, wagon or coach. Therefore any means
of paying for roads through general or local taxation, or of constructing
roads on the principle of the same standard everywhere for
everybody, is more certain to imply cross-subsidisation now.*

*(4) The revival of the road system has produced substantial
competition in transport again: with the railways. Economic methods
are needed in the road programme to decide the relative merits of
investment in road and rail and to avoid the waste which might result
from neglecting to make the comparison.*

SUMMARY

The conclusions of each section of this chapter have been:

(1) The conflict of interests endemic in the road problem was
not solved by the public service principle as it used to operate in the
finance and administration of the roads up to 1919, except during a
comparatively short period during the nineteenth century.

(2) Since 1919 effective power over road policy has shifted from
local authorities to the Ministry of Transport.

(3) The administrative changes of the last forty years have not
solved but rather obscured the conflict of interests which has during
the same period become much more complicated. The system of
making grants to local authorities for maintenance, improvement and
construction of roads, for example, has no sense to it.

(4) The meaning of the density investment criterion used by the
Ministry of Transport is not definite. There are several objections to
the use of such criteria and as they are met, this kind of criterion
begins to approximate to the type of economic criterion already used
in this book.

It is argued that it is worth trying to run the road system as an
economic enterprise by a consistent criterion since this will help
clarify and make possible the solution of the various conflicts of
interest active in the road problem.

(5) The basic criteria to be used in Chapters 9-11 are the same as were used in discussing the rail problem. The definition of cross-subsidisation, subsidisation and regulations are also the same.

After these preliminaries we are able to set about considering the problems of formulating charging and investment policies on the roads.

POSTSCRIPT

The Conflict of Interests

Responsibility for the roads system remains fragmented. The fragments are the headquarters and decentralised divisions of the Department of the Environment, the Scottish and Welsh Offices, and the departments of local authorities set up to administer various aspects of road construction, improvement and operations. They are not organised as 'economic enterprises' with their own equivalent to profit and loss accounts, and balance-sheets. There is no information whatever for any of them, or indeed for different classes of road, on the relation between costs and the 'prices' road-users pay through taxation. Not even in the crudest sense can one discover which, if any, are in 'deficit' or how 'profits' vary. There have been no published attempts to discover if the 'benefits' from their operations exceed costs. No backchecks have been published on particular investments – e.g. motorways – to establish if the investments were justified in economic terms. Even where rates of return have been calculated, it is far from clear how far they have influenced investment priorities. It was only in 1973 that for the first time an inspector allowed the economic case for a motorway to be considered at a public inquiry. No one knows how much investment has been authorised promising a lower return than the minimum acceptable to the Treasury. There is no available information on the marginal return on investment for each authority responsible for investment, or on the programme as a whole. Because the railways were again in deficit and required immediate attention, the 1968 Transport Act concentrated on these and related problems. At the time it was felt that probably most highway investment, at least outside cities, could have been justified, but this could not be demonstrated, because there were no indicators of highway economic performance, even ones as imperfect as the pre-1968 indicators of railway performance. The economic irrelevance of the information it produced protected the highway system from an assessment of its performance; and it seemed administratively impossible to undertake a searching review of highways' policy and organisation at the same time as one of the rest of the transport sector. Such a thorough examination of the management, procedures and objectives of the highway system was the next priority, but for

196

various reasons this has never taken place. Therefore it remains impossible to achieve a logically consistent and coordinated transport policy (see the postscript to Chapter 12). By contrast, very great progress has been achieved in improving the economic tools of highway analysis: in devising methods of effecting road pricing and in developing very much better as well as feasible methods of investment analysis. (See the postscripts to Chapters 10 and 11. Some further thoughts on the problems of establishing a National Roads Authority are in the postscript to Appendix 5.)

Recent Developments

In 1967 the system of classification changed. Trunk roads were retained. A new class of Principal roads was created, roughly equivalent to the former Class I roads. Class II and III roads became unclassified. For all except trunk roads the local authorities remained responsible and there have been attempts to give them responsibility for more trunk roads that have declined in importance or have been replaced as national routes by motorways. In 1963 I overstated central government's power to reclassify a road. Whatever the statutory position, local authorities seem able to resist any 'de-trunking' which increases their financial responsibility unless compensated for this.

Present Policy: The Grant System

Despite changes in detail, most of the criticisms remain valid. Since 1967 trunk roads have continued to receive 100 per cent capital grant. Principal roads receive 75 per cent capital grant. Their maintenance and all expenditure on the remainder are grant-aided through Rate Support Grant. Those percentages were no more rational than those that preceded them. The 1968 *Transport Act* introduced various grants for public transport with the aim of stimulating public transport investment. They were intended as interim measures until it was administratively possible to have a fundamental review of all transport grants. Their great drawback was that different percentage grants distorted local authorities' choices between schemes with different capital structures.[1] The system is changing again. Transport Support Grant is being introduced which is a block grant to local authorities. Trunk roads will remain 100 per cent financed by central government. The justification for this is that local authorities are central government's agents for the services provided. The expenditure decisions remain with central government. No other roads will receive a percentage grant. Local authorities will be 100 per cent responsible for their financing, but they will get a block grant which they can spend on the highway and public transport projects they select. Because it does away with separate public transport and road budgets it will allow a local authority to spend its transport resources on the mixture of public transport and highways schemes it selects. It also allows local authorities to pay grants to meet operating deficits if this can be justified on efficiency grounds. In principle a local authority can choose not to spend any of its resources on large road or public transport investments but on small schemes, operating improvements and subsidies to public transport. Even so, many of the original criticisms remain valid. How much transport grant a local authority receives remains arbitrary. Since all tax revenue from road-users, except parking charges, is received by the national government, why should not ratepayers receive a 100 per cent grant? The argument against this is that local authorities would have no incentive to be efficient unless they are spending their own money, but the cost of road construction and improvement to ratepayers has not been related to the benefits they receive *qua* ratepayers as distinct from those they receive as road-users.

Present Policy: Investment

The methods criticised in this section are still used in many countries. Particularly in towns, British local authorities sometimes still use what is practically an overload criterion to determine their investment priorities. But in general techniques of highway investment appraisal have improved dramatically over the last ten years. To do this the Highways Economics Unit (now the Highways Economics and Modelling Analysis Division) was set up in 1966 within the Highways side of the Ministry of Transport. In 1967 the Ministry of Transport introduced a first year rate of return method for the evaluation of inter-urban road schemes (Circular T5/1967). Research was done on a more comprehensive approach more in accordance with the principles of Chapter 11 below; and in some respects an advance on them. The methods and computer programmes needed to be relatively easy to use both for designing road schemes and in selecting projects for evaluation. It was not until 1972 that a manual was published incorporating this research and laying down procedures to be used.[2] The methods they describe will be referred to in the Postscript to Chapter 11. At the same time work was begun on the far more difficult task of evaluating urban road schemes in the context of the London and the Manchester area transportation studies. There has not as yet been official agreement on what procedures should be adopted. The estimation of capacity has also become generally more sophisticated, and is based on speed/flow relationships for different roads ot the kind underlying the upward and backward bending curve in fig. 8.1.

Criteria

The crofter roads programme is near its end. It was unique and there

198

has been no development of specific subsidies for highway improvements parallel to that for nationalised transport. Cross-subsidisation is endemic. When there is a fundamental review of highway finance, the case for creating a system of specific subsidies will be strong. There are many road improvements in England and Wales which are made for regional reasons, and while there is no published evidence of this, it is widely asserted that the marginal return on Scottish roads is much lower than in England and Wales. There is some suspicion that the cases of this regionalism are institutional. Divisional Road Engineers have had an expectation of a certain rate of growth in their programme. The return from road construction is likely to be lower in a less developed region. When the returns on road improvements in such regions fall towards zero and there are few justifiable projects, it may seem tempting to adduce regional factors to justify maintaining the scale of a regional investment programme. Until the returns on prospective road investments are regularly published, the geographical distribution of those highway schemes which are proceeded with, though their anticipated return falls below that required by the Treasury, criteria, will be unknown. Neither will it be known how many there are. If the justification for such schemes is 'regional', that is, that they are a way of helping raise regional incomes per head in backward regions, then the principles discussed in Chapter 7 would indicate a special regional grant. Suppose the minimum return required by the Treasury to justify a project on normal grounds, was $B - C = x$, where B are the relevant benefits and C the expected costs, and x is the minimum return required. If the normal calculation of benefits for a given 'regional' project, only yields $(B - C = x - y)$ then the regional grant must at least be large enough to reduce the project costs, set against normal benefits, to the level where $(B - C = x)$.[3] The principal advantage of such a procedure is that it would show what projects are being justified on regional grounds, as well as the size of the grant needed in each case. This expenditure to help achieve regional policy objectives should be evaluated against other regional projects within and outside the transport sector. There would seem no case for a 'regional' highway policy only, unless it can be shown that highway projects would always be more efficient than regional rail or airline projects. One also has to remember that the evidence is weak that transport improvements do make a substantial difference to the level of unemployment or the rate of economic growth in a backward region in an advanced country. One suspects that the return from these regional projects is low in terms of creating increased regional income or reduced regional unemployment.[4] They are therefore to be regarded primarily as methods of redistributing income between regions where again their efficiency as a means of redistribution must be low.

Similarly it would be efficient if there were a separate identification of subsidies to the extent that the justification for more road-building is to employ unemployed resources.

9 THE COSTS OF THE ROAD SYSTEM

Let us now suppose a national road authority — or a network of such authorities — has been established; or even if it is decided to implant the new backbone into the old bodies, that is at least the Government's intention to try to run the road system by one or other of our basic criteria. Before considering costs, what are the assets of the authority? And who are the road-users to be brought within the scope of the criterion?

ASSETS

An early problem for those drafting the necessary legislation should be to decide what assets are to be vested in the authority (or authorities). This is primarily a legal problem and the only relevance is if the ownership of assets should affect the scope of the economic criterion to be used. For example, the following assets might be vested in the roads authority: all public roads and roadworks such as bridges, flyovers, road tunnels, viaducts, pedestrian bridges and subways; pavements, cycle tracks, lay-bys, shoulders, verges and central reserves; the right of way for mains, cables, drains, etc., laid under the roadway and for cables, etc., carried above it on poles or pylons; all capital equipment such as traffic lights, street lighting, and other installations for traffic control — road signs, islands, bollards, etc.; and, last, the land on which the road system is built, and any land bought in advance for future road improvement and construction. (In this chapter and the next it will be assumed that all these are vested in our road authority and appear in its capital account as its fixed assets.) However it would make a difference to the working-out of the road problem if some were vested in other bodies *and* this was associated with a difference in criterion. It would not make any difference to the charges made or the investment opportunities chosen if land were vested in the local authorities, but they and the road authority used a profit maximising criterion. The only difference would be that some of the profit would accrue to the local authorities instead of all to the central Government via the road authority. But there would be a difference if the two had different criteria. This complication will not be introduced into the argument of this chapter because it will be interesting to consider the implications of using a consumers' surplus criterion for the use of the land embodied in the road system, but the case can be argued rationally that the community adopt a profit maximising criterion for the land used in transport — by roads, railways and any other form of transport using land, whatever the criteria used otherwise by railways and the road system.

THE ROAD-USERS

Profit maximisation presents no problem here as the enterprise will try to maximise its profits in all its dealing with those outside it: road-users and everyone else with whom it has transactions — those to whom it sells surplus land or who do maintenance work on contract for it as much as those who drive on its roads.

A consumer's surplus policy for roads does present a conceptual problem. Who are the consumers? It might be argued more plausibly than in the case of railways that more classes of people *benefit* from roads and their interests should be considered. Farmers benefit, it may be said, not just as road-users, but as farmers. Shopkeepers gain or lose from road construction not only because they themselves use roads but because their customers and suppliers do. These are some of the so-called social returns (costs) of road construction which it is often urged should be taken into account. This problem could have been raised in connection with the railways, but in Chapter 7 discussion was ruled out by the assumption that railway-users were the consumers in whose interest the railways were to be run. The problem was not discussed then because it arises more obviously and acutely for the road system. It will be convenient to distinguish four types of 'consumers'.

Road-users
Motorists and other owners of motor vehicles, passenger and goods, who operate or park vehicles on the public highway: motor cyclists and cyclists. We will also assume that the pavements, subways, etc., pedestrians use are part of the road system and come under the jurisdiction of our road authority.

Users of what might be called By-products of the Road System
(a) The roads are also used to convey gas, electricity and water mains. In cities there are other subterranean uses of the road system. Roads are also used for telegraph wires above or below ground.

(b) Another type of case is that of the shopkeepers and other advertisers who rent show-windows or shops in a subway built principally for the use of pedestrians.

(c) A third type still is that of the purchaser of land which was once part of the road system but which has, perhaps, from realignment of a road, become superfluous.

Indirect Beneficiaries who can make their Desires Felt through the Ordinary Price Mechanism

It is often said in a vague way that the benefits to be derived from road improvement are manifold, extending far beyond the immediate benefits to the road-users themselves. Trade will improve. Unemployment will decrease. It will give a fillip to exports. Better roads are good for health. They make possible a happier and less strenuous enjoyment of leisure. They are a benefit to the police, fire brigade and ambulance service and so to the general public because they make for speedier movement of their vehicles. Road improvement generally reduces accidents which are a cost to the community. It has even been argued that road improvement benefits education since there is in some places a relation between bad roads and illiteracy and some have been unwise enough to argue it is a casual relationship.[1]

Advocates of more expenditure on roads have understandably tended to argue these vague benefits as strengthening their contention that the returns from road construction are high: as a goad to highway authorities. The first point to be made is of course that road improvement is not the only or always the best method of achieving any of these aims. For example, there may be other prophylactic investments more remunerative than investment in road accident prevention. Therefore the stringing together of unquantified social benefits alleged to follow from road construction need not carry much weight. The second point to be made is that no special allowance should be made for covering some of these benefits in the rate of return because of double-counting. Many of these 'social' benefits to non-road-users become reflected in benefits to road-users and can therefore be trapped in the ordinary way in calculating a profit maximising or consumers' surplus rate of return.

When prediction is made of the demand expected for a new road or road improvement it is usual to divide the demand into two parts:

(a) a trend in demand which is a projection of the demand for the present roadway and

(b) generated demand expected to be created by the attraction of the new roadway.

Some of (b) represents traffic which is induced by expected benefits to non-road-users who are prepared to *pay* for them. Let us suppose that the effect of building a motorway is to reduce the cost of carrying freight from town X to town Y. A consumers' surplus policy operates and the price is lowered to the haulage operators. If, as one would expect, they are out to make profits, they will not drop their charges by the full amount of their reduction in costs. How much they lower their charges should depend on the elasticity of demand for their services which will in general depend on the extent of competition. If haulage is highly competitive it will pay them to drop their charges more than if it is not. If we now take an example where the cost of an improvement is passed on as an increase in the (average cost) prices charged, we would expect the haulage firms would pass some or all of this increase on to their customers, depending again on the elasticity of demand for their services.

Last, take what may seem to be a crucial case. A motorway would not be built if the interests of the road-users alone were considered; but if the interests of their customers is considered it would. To be more specific let us suppose that the saving in haulage firms' time, wages, fuel, etc., is £10,000 per annum and that the road would not be worth doing unless it earned £12,000. However, the customers of the haulage firms also benefit from quicker delivery to the extent of £5,000 per annum. If their interests are considered then the road should be built. Indeed if they are sensible human beings, the road will be built. No special arrangements or criteria are needed. The price mechanism should be enough. The customers of the hauliers know it will pay them to pay up to £5,000 per annum to the hauliers if the road is built. Therefore rather than the road should not be built they will be prepared to pay this. The hauliers will know that it will be profitable for them if the road is built because of this; and those who are doing the demand survey to establish the profitability of the motorway should be able to find this out. What will be needed is full publicity for all facts about the economic consequences of the motorway. Of course it may happen that the market mechanism does not work efficiently enough. Then the road authority must decide whether it would be in the consumers' interest to demonstrate benefit potential.

The simple fact is that most benefits alleged to follow from road construction or improvement imply that traffic passes along the road as a means to those benefits. The police car travels more quickly and the enforcement of law and order is improved. Trade improves because transport is cheaper because time is saved, or for any other reason. In all cases if it is worth someone's while – here the local Watch Committee or the shopkeepers – to get better roads, they ought to be prepared to pay for it, if they are able to. In so far as they are able, it would be double-counting to estimate the benefits in terms of traffic generated to gain these benefits and to add something extra in for improvement in trade, etc. A rate of return so calculated would be fallacious.

Since it is a fallacy to think that this group of beneficiaries should be accounted for separately, no practical distinction can be drawn between it and the second group. Whoever gets the benefit in the end it is paid for directly through motor taxation, road fund licences, tolls, etc.

Indirect Beneficiaries who cannot make their Desires Felt through the Price Mechanism

It may happen that there are some potential beneficiaries who are unable to make their desires felt by payment because the machinery of payment does not exist for them. This was the rationale of the traditional example of the factory chimney belching smoke. It was a cost to the countryside. The spoilt countryside had no means of making the factory pay for the damage because the law does not allow for the assessment of realistic damages in such cases, or if the law were to allow it, the losers are unable to organise themselves to present their bill or the cost of presenting a bill (using the price mechanism) is too high. Conversely, there may be people who expect to gain from a road improvement, let us say aesthetically, and would be prepared to pay something to this end, but there is no machinery by which they can do this. There is much to be said for making it possible for all sorts of bodies: preservation trusts, ratepayers' associations, municipal councils, or any other person or persons who are prepared to back their wishes by payment, to do so, and to make road authorities allow for these payments in their criteria.

Another example would be a depressed area of declining industry where there is unemployment. Elsewhere in the country there are places where there are more vacancies than jobs. Some of the unemployed have moved out in search of jobs. Others have not. Firms do not move into their area in sufficient numbers because it would not be profitable for them to do so. It is suggested that a new road would have the effect of persuading new firms to move in since it would make it profitable for them to do so, provided they did not have to stand the cost of building the road. Full employment in the area therefore depends on the building of this road. Who will gain from the building of the road? Not the firms because they have to be induced to move. Let us suppose that the chief beneficiaries are the Government and the local shopkeepers and unemployed. The Government would gain because of a reduction in the dole and because of social capital in the depressed area: hospitals, schools, etc. If the families move these will be used less and usually become more expensive to run in relation to the population they serve. Moreover the Government must provide new social capital where they go. It would therefore pay the Government to make a contribution of definite amount to the building of the road.

The exact sum that would be worth the Government's while is capable of fairly exact calculation. It is not at present the habit of the

Government to make this kind of exact calculation in such circumstances. If there were a road authority it would, if it were sensible, pay such a sum to it if this would mean that the road would be built and the employment generated. The second group, the shopkeepers by increased custom and the unemployed by employment, also stand to gain from the road. If they were out to maximise their incomes, the unemployed and the shopkeepers might move to the fully employed areas. Since they would stand to lose when they sold up in the old place, the income they would hope to get in the new area will have to be sufficiently higher than what they have been getting. But in addition they may set a value on staying where they are. Perhaps, to take a case, one man would not move unless his expected income in the town was roughly twice what he was getting in the depressed area. Given that those left behind will sacrifice something rather than move, it will be to their advantage if they subsidise the coming of new industry provided that the benefit in the form of wages and shopkeepers' incomes and non-pecuniary advantages is greater than the subsidy paid. If we take the local council as the mouthpiece of the local people, there is some amount beneath which it would pay them to subsidise, and above which it would not. If asked to pay more than this maximum, the town would rather subsidise the movement of its people away, or remain depressed because the reduction in income from paying so much subsidy would outweigh the net advantages of staying put. If the town is rational there is some amount it would be prepared to pay to subsidise the road-building. And there will be other interests also whom it would pay to make a contribution to the road authority. If the present system of governmental and local authority financing does not permit such payments, so much the worse unless it should be decided to exclude certain persons or bodies from the privilege as a deliberate act of policy.

By the same line of argument there is no reason why it would not be possible to devise a system whereby other social benefits and costs can be reflected in the investment and charging policies of the road system. It may be objected that this sounds harsh — uncompromising nineteenth-century *laissez-faire* doctrine. We do not usually expect depressed areas themselves to pay to increase employment in their area. The Government has taken on the responsibility for maintaining something near full employment everywhere. And the argument we have used so far may seem to suggest that everyone and every local authority should pay its way — potential beneficiaries alone should pay for what they gain and to avoid losses; but this is to miss the point. There is nothing to prevent the Government, or anyone else where this is appropriate, shouldering the payment and *subsidising*, when the payment will appear in the road authority's books as a payment by the Treasury (on behalf of, say, Glasgow) and not by Glasgow City Council — if the Government should decide that that subsidy is in the public interest. In such circumstances one would hope that the Government might calculate what the advantage in money terms of the improvement for which the subsidy is paid is to those who are subsidised. If they do not it might, for example, find that a smaller subsidy to cover removal expenses, etc. of labour moving out would be more appreciated than a large subsidy to industry to move in.

THE NEED TO DEFINE CONSUMERS' SURPLUS

Therefore we have our four groups of consumers, who may be reduced to three, and also subsidisers of consumers.

1. Road-users who pay directly as the machinery of revenue collection allows whether the benefit accrues directly to them or ultimately to other parties (the first and third groups).

2. Those who pay for what we have called by-products of the road system (the second group).

3. Those potential beneficiaries who at present are unable to pay a road authority for what they want but would if they could (the fourth group).

The boundary drawn between the first and fourth groups will depend on the machinery for payment available. And then there are those (public authority or private charity) who would wish to subsidise consumers of any of these four groups.

The question is whether a consumers' surplus is to be defined to cover the interests of all four groups or only some of them. For example, it would be possible to take into account the interests only of the first and fourth groups. They are charged a consumers surplus maximising price and their surplus is reckoned in making an investment. Everyone else is charged a profit maximising price and only what they will pay is reckoned in calculating the profitability of an investment. Or one could imagine that everyone except customers in the second group, category (3), is defined to be a consumer in this sense. That category is omitted because it would seem odd to buy land from property-owners at the market (profit-maximising) price but to sell land, at an average marginal cost price. A plausible argument could be made for omitting category (2), and for that matter (1) also. I do not believe it profitable to try to argue the case for and against the exclusion of various people and institutions from our definition of what is to be reckoned a consumer, since the value judgements implied are sufficiently obvious. What does matter is that the Government should make up its mind on the matter — otherwise the criterion remains indefinite. (One might hazard that the definition of consumers might be the same for road and rail.) It will be assumed here that categories (2) and (3) will be excluded, the rest included, but this will not in fact make much difference to the argument because we will not be concerned in detail with these people; and in so far as it does affect the argument, it can be modified to reflect a different assumption on this point.

Once we have decided who are road-users we are able to proceed. When we come to consider charging, the profit maximising criterion will urge us to set charges so as to raise the highest possible revenue from these road-users. If motorists in their role as movers along the highways are prepared to pay more for a strip of it than they are in their role as parkers — and it is possible to make them pay — then to motorists as movers it shall go. The second criterion tells us that the road system should be used so as to maximise consumers' surplus and that therefore, when there is a conflict of interests, that interest shall win to whom the benefit measured in terms of consumers' surplus is the greater.

THE IDENTIFICATION OF COSTS

The next problem is to decide what are the costs of the road system. As was argued in Chapter 2, what are to be counted as the relevant costs of an enterprise is ultimately a matter of opinion. Most people, I hope, will be ready to agree the first five categories are costs of the road system; though there may be some difference of opinion about police costs. Categories six to ten raise more questions.

Non-renewable Construction Costs

Once a road is built money does not have to be spent again on the purchase of land; the legal costs of land purchase; demolition; earthworks and soil stabilisation — unless and until it is decided to improve the road. Even then the old road often has value as a basis for the improvement. The only factor setting a limit to the life of a road is the risk of it becoming obsolescent. There is also the fencing, ditching, and walling, and other accommodation works as they are called, which have to be done for adjacent property when a road is built, upkeep of which thereafter is the responsibility of the property-owners. A costly example would be the reconstruction of an underground station necessitated by road-building. These are also non-recurring costs of the road system.

The problem of amortisation is exactly as it was for railway track. One school of thought would say there is no need for amortisation because there is no risk of obsolescence. The Road Research Laboratory has said that it is enough to maintain the road intact and that this 'avoids the need to provide for amortisation which is a financial device to repay loans or a provision to cover the risk that the road will not be required, at some future date'. The Laboratory argued in the case in question, the London-Birmingham motorway, that the risk of obsolescence 'seems negligible.'[2] Although there is no apparent risk that any form of roadless transport will replace road transport in the foreseeable future, even if air transport and possibly a revived railway system might encroach on it, we cannot know that this will continue forever. Here nineteenth-century railway experience should make us reflect. The railways believed that they would never become obsolete on the same grounds — the state of technology at the time. We cannot predict that scientific progress will not outmode the road. Another argument is that, in cities, town planning may make the present pattern of roads obsolete. Or it is possible that road-using transport of the future will be of a kind to make obsolete just those assets (foundations, etc.) in this category because, say, road transport of the future moving above or along roads does not require the carefully graded, substantial or safe roads needed at present.

To avoid the railways' error, new roads should be amortised over some period of time. The difficulty is to decide the period. A favourite figure in the United States[3] is twenty five years, but this is influenced by short-term problems of bond financing which ought to be irrelevant to commercial enterprises. (Firms do not expect to pay back their share capital as long as they are able to employ it profitably.) How do we decide when we cannot see far into the future on a safe time-horizon for the amortisation of road investment? A dodge might be to ask a fair number of those concerned one way or another with roads and other means of transport — especially engineers and scientists — for their best guess on this point and to take the average, hoping that any vested interests would cancel if the sample was chosen carefully (My own figure at a venture would be fifty years from now.) The figure could be revised if events should suggest it wrong. It is more important that a period should be chosen than exactly what period is decided on (within a decade).

Renewable Construction and Other Capital Costs

These are either like bridges, fly-overs, viaducts, subways, etc., generally having a physical life longer than 50 years, in which case there is no reason for dealing with them separately from items in the first category, or they are comparatively small installations like traffic lights, roadsigns, etc., the cost of which should be amortised over their expected life, presumably less than fifty years in most cases. There are also capital items such as cars used by the police, vehicles and equipment for maintenance and scavenging, and snowploughs, which should also be amortised over the expected life of the equipment.

Maintenance Costs

The concept we need here is that of expenditure needed to keep the road intact. Of course it may be decided after a road is built that a mistake was made — such a good road was not needed when it may be sensible to lower the standard of maintenance. Decisions like these are akin to investment decisions and do not concern us here. Whatever the costs of maintenance these are plainly costs of the road system to be recovered from road-users. Maintenance costs also vary very much with the type of road built. It is possible to spend more on construction and other capital costs and save on maintenance or vice versa. Sometimes it will be more profitable to do the one, sometimes the other. Maintenance costs fall principally into two categories, (a) those which do and (b) those which do not vary with use. Weather, floods and climate are the principal causes of the latter, and congested traffic, causing frequent stopping and starting, of the former. As one would expect, maintenance costs per mile from this cause tend to be higher the larger the town and the heavier the traffic.

Interest

Interest must be paid on capital invested in roads if the consumers' surplus criterion is used — interest payable on fixed-interest obligations if the funds have been raised on the market. If the profit maximisation criterion holds then, as with railways, debenture or other fixed interest stock can be regarded as a cost of the road system; otherwise the rate of profit is some measure of the success of the investment but is not properly a cost but a surplus.

Costs of Ancillary Services and Facilities

(i) Administrative costs. Some of these are part of the construction and other capital costs of making roads, the administrative costs of making an investment, but there are also current administrative costs which commonsense suggests should be borne by road-users as the administrative costs of any business are borne by its customers. It is at present virtually impossible to make an intelligent guess how large these are. There are *(a)* the costs incurred in connection with expenditure on the roads by the Ministry of Transport and local authorities, and *(b)* the administrative costs of raising revenue.

   (ii) Street lighting. (a) Capital costs, *(b)* current costs.

   (iii) Traffic lights, road signs, etc. (a) Capital costs, *(b)* current costs.

   (iv) Research, performed principally at present by the Road Research Laboratory which is part of the Department of Scientific and

Industrial Research.

(v) The cost of policing the road system. Until 1957-8 an item 'provision and maintenance of police vehicles and equipment for the enforcement of law relating to road traffic' was borne on the road vote and was paid as a grant to local authorities maintaining police forces. It amounted to £471,000 in that year. Since then it has been swallowed up in the block grant given by the central Government in aid of rates. But this is certainly not the only item of police costs attributable to the existence of the road system — which, to put it more rigorously, would be escaped if there were no road system and no road-users. By contrast the railways pay the whole cost of their police force but this is not an entirely helpful comparison as the police have a lesser function on the railways. Roughly speaking they do on the roads what is done by signalmen and others responsible for traffic control on the railways. They have special responsibilities in connection with accidents which mainly fall on the salaried officials on the railways. Some of their disciplinary functions are not dissimilar from those performed by managers, supervisors and foremen of commercial firms, Police, traffic wardens, crossing attendants, employees of the AA and RAC are the operating staff of the road system. Because road-users do not pay all the police costs incurred on their behalf, particularly but not exclusively labour costs, they escape a burden which falls on users of the railways and of most other forms of transport.

An exceptional police cost which can be attributed to particular traffic is the cost of providing escorts for wide and other abnormal loads. This is a right for which the police are not paid. The Chief Constable of Hampshire — a county where one would expect many abnormal loads converging on Southampton — has said that his force provided almost 4,500 escorts between 1955 and 1960, the number growing annually. He estimated the cost at approximately £26,000 per annum: or £29 per escort. This was of course for escorts in the County only.[4]

Whether the best or, perhaps, only the easiest solution would be to follow some American and Continental practice and have separate traffic police is not a point on which I would want to give an opinion. It would avoid the difficult question of deciding what police costs are and are not attributable to road-users. The alternative would be to try to separate these costs and reimburse the police forces for them. This is not done at present in the accounts of police forces and it is difficult to guess at the proportion of total police costs properly attributable to road-users. Because of the many joint costs — policemen and vehicles employed on traffic and other duties, and overheads — attribution would not be easy. However it should be possible to get

211

some acceptable distinction by pressing the question what size police forces would have to be and how much they would cost if there were no road system. There is another problem here which would seem incapable of anything other than a rather arbitrary decision. Police also perform services for road-users which are in no way different from the ordinary services they perform for citizens everywhere, broadly the preservation of life, property and order. In deciding how large a proportion of police costs are ordinary and how much special services provided for road-users, there is bound to be some arbitrariness, but it would hardly seem possible to deny that police do have a special role in respect of road-users and therefore some distinction should be made.

So much for the case for charging police costs. There can be no dispute that there are such costs attributable. However there is the counter-argument that such costs should not be charged which must be considered. When the Home Secretary was asked to consider charging abnormal loads for their escorts, the answer given was that this would violate the principle that no charges should be made for police services on public highways.[5] The police are paid for certain services they perform, for example, at weddings, parties and in front of railway stations. When special constables have been sworn in especially to protect a firm's premises, the firm has paid. In 1925 the House of Lords by a three-fifths majority decided that the cost of a police garrison requested by a colliery for protection during a strike should be paid for by the colliery, because it was the local superintendent's judgement that adequate protection could have been given in the ordinary way without a garrison.[6] The importance of the case was that it decided that when there was a difference of opinion whether a service provided by the police was *special* (to be paid for or not) generally the word of the local police authorities was to be taken. But no law suits have decided that police traffic duties are *ordinary* duties of the police force, which is hardly surprising since until recently there was no possible way in which they could have been charged on the road-user when he did not pay for roads other than through the rates. *Halsbury's Laws of England* say the obligation of the police to control traffic grew out of 'their general duty to preserve law and order and to protect life and property'.[7] It has no statutory basis; and one can imagine how it happened that police, who originally had and were intended to have no traffic duties, gradually came to assume the responsibility and how the extra police cost was borne on the rates. But this history does not in itself seem a good reason for not requiring road-users to pay for the special duties performed for them by the police now that it is possible to charge them through taxation or occasionally directly as when an escort is provided.

212

Taxes and Rates

It is difficult to see why the road system, if it is to be run as an economic enterprise, should be any more or less liable to taxation than the railways; so that what was said about their taxation would seem to hold for the road system also. Similarly it is difficult to see why road-users should not pay rates. Traditionally the owner of a piece of land who dedicates it as a highway is relieved from the duty of paying rates on it; but the tradition is surely irrelevant. If the railways pay rates on their property (this has been an understandable grievance of the American railroads in particular) and all businesses normally do, why should not the road system? The old argument that it would simply be the local inhabitants paying themselves is here as outmoded as it is in its other applications. The fact that rates are not payable can cause hardship to some local authorities. A small town or village, if some part of its territory was given over to a large trunk road, would, if rates were payable on it, benefit as it would from the presence of any other industry, but as it is the larger the area given over to roads the smaller the area on which rates can be levied and, other things being equal, the higher the rates required to yield the same local authority income, which means that this particular cost of the road system falls entirely on the ratepayer. This would only be fair if the increase in rates equalled the increase in benefits received not just for ratepayers as a whole but for specific ratepayers. Another example of injustice would be a city which had to provide a large extent of its surface as roads to transport labour and shoppers to its business centre. The more it improves its streets the smaller its rateable area. Again one might argue that to charge higher rates in the business centre would be fair but unless we can assume that they are the beneficiaries to that amount it will not be just. Surely it is more sensible as well as fairer to rate road-users directly, recouping it in the charge made for the use of the road.

Accident Costs

So far we have been considering costs which there would appear to be a strong case for including among the costs of the road system for charging and investment purposes. Besides the more general argument that they are costs which fall to be paid by ordinary commercial businesses, there is particular argument that they are, or should be, paid by the railways. Accident costs are somewhat different. As far as charging is concerned, principally because of the National Health Service, people are not usually charged most of the costs of accidents. At present it would seem that road-users incur a cost which others in similar circumstances do not. Hospital boards can claim 12s. 6d. from the insurance company liable as an emergency treatment fee for anyone injured in a road accident; up to £5 for further out-patient treatment; and up to £50 for further in-patient treatment. This is the only case of its kind. Ultimately these costs are therefore met by motorists through their insurance policies, which would cost them that much less if the insurance companies were not liable for these payments. However the amounts were fixed in 1930 and have not increased since. The average cost of an emergency treatment is now about £2 16s. 0d; Fifty pounds would have bought fifteen weeks in hospital then. Now it buys less than two; and in fact 50 per cent of road accident cases requiring hospital or out-patient treatment cost the National Health Service more than £50. It has been estimated that the National Health Service would get from £650,000 to £850,000 instead of £350,000 which they now get from the insurance companies if the full costs were recoverable.[8] This may seem a comparatively small sum but if it were public policy that all costs incurred by the National Health Service because of road accidents should be recoverable it would probably be many times larger. (At present the National Health Service is only able in practice to claim for about 15 per cent of cases admitted for further treatment.)

If it should be decided to recover these costs from road-users, one would expect that the sums recovered should be the real costs and not notional amounts fixed in 1930, and also that the burden should fall alike on all forms of transport. Presumably the point of charging at all for road accidents in this fashion is that road-users are held to be, at least collectively, responsible for the accidents that befall them as a cancer-sufferer or an old woman who falls down stairs and breaks a hip is not. If the principle is to be adopted for transport accidents one would expect that it would be logical to extend it to certain sorts of industrial and other accidents. It might also make sense on this basis to make road-users reimburse the Ministry of Pensions for sickness and unemployment benefit, disability pensions, etc. caused by road accidents. It might also be possible to devise machinery whereby private persons who suffer from road accidents might get realistic damages from insurance. In all these cases the most obvious method of charging would seem to be through the insurance policies of motorists. What must be decided is the principle: whether road-users are to pay in this manner as others do not or whether they are to receive the same absolutely free treatment as other people. The present compromise is surely indefensible, especially as the sums that can be collected are frequently not worth the collection. (On average it costs the National Health Service 11s. 3d. to collect the 12s. 6d. fee, £7 10s. to collect the £50 from the insurance companies.) Whichever solution is adopted we can, I think, reasonably represent it as something which does not involve the road authority and is therefore not a cost of the road system for charging purposes.

What might involve the road authority is investment to reduce road accidents. Certainly it often pays to invest for safety, but whom does it pay and who should pay for it? Up to a point there is no special problem here. Commercial firms often invest in safety for consumers or workers because they know it will pay them directly or by creating goodwill. In so far as road-users suffer from road accidents one would expect them to be prepared to pay more for more safety: and if safer roads were to be carried to the extent of leading to lower insurance premia, one would expect people to pay something for that. Initially one might say that a road authority should invest in accident prevention as a commercial firm does. If the National Health Service were to benefit by lower costs from investment in safer roads, then it would be foolish if the National Health Service, or the Government for it, were unable to contribute to road investment to this end. Therefore one would expect that if it is profitable to spend money on making roads safer, it should be possible to devise means by which the various interests could make their purses felt.

To decide when it is desirable to invest, calculations have been made of the cost, indirect and direct, of accidents.[9] Many people will find this profit-and-loss approach repulsive since, for example, it treats the death of someone in the prime of life as positive loss to national income and the death of an older person as a net gain because the latter will normally consume more than he produces during the remainder of his life. Repulsive or not, it is important to be clear about the issues. Let us suppose that it would cost £1,000m. to make our roads accident-free (of course they never would be), but let us make the assumption. Let us suppose further that it would be profitable to invest half this amount, tapping all possible sources of funds from all those, the State included, who expect to profit from the investment. The remaining investment could only be made at a loss. We might even say that it would cost 1 per cent of our national income to do it. And let us suppose that the principal effect of the investment would be to save some 3,000 lives annually. If those who say that a life is beyond price mean what they say, they imply they would incur any cost to save even one life, since an infinite benefit must exceed a less than infinite cost. To take an extreme example, if investing all our national income for ten years would cure cancer would they advise this if it meant everybody existing at starvation level during that period of time?

It is surely wrong to assume that any investment should be made which means greater road safety. The total cost of such investments might be more than the nation is prepared to afford. Furthermore it might give a bias to investment in accident prevention on the roads which most of us would think excessive. There is no reason why investment there should have higher priority than investment to reduce cancer; or even an increase in nurses' wages leading to a better staffing of hospitals and better care of the sick. If it should be decided that a greater proportion of our national income should be devoted to investment in health and safety — than is already invested through the National Health Service — the sensible thing would surely be to have some technically qualified board to decide investment priorities and allocate what is available between competing uses. If it decides that the best use of some part of these funds is more investment in making roads safer (over and above what is *profitable*, in the sense used above) then it should subsidise the road authorities to that extent. This means that when we come to consider investment in Chapter 10 we will only take into account *profitable* investment abstracting from any subsidy the Government may choose to make.

Congestion Costs
We often hear estimates of the amount of cost caused by congestion. Should motorists be charged for the congestion they cause? It is important that we consider carefully just what the issues are.

Let us consider the case of a moderately trafficked street in the centre of a town. Every additional vehicle joining the flow on it finds that the distance costs it more than the one before. This is the effect

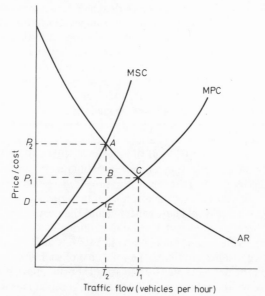

FIG. 9.1: Congestion costs

of congestion. Although the effect of one more vehicle may be imperceptible, the cumulative effect is steady. It costs each extra vehicle more in wear on tyres, brakes and clutch, which is largely caused by stopping and starting. If he is travelling at a speed less than optimum for petrol consumption, his petrol cost will rise. It will take every additional vehicle longer to get along the street and for most of us time is money. This effect of congestion is illustrated in fig. 9.1 by the marginal private cost curve (MPC) showing that the costs incurred by vehicles on a given stretch of road increase the more vehicles there are on the road. The vertical axis measures price and cost, the horizontal, vehicles per hour on the given stretch of road. A vehicle will normally travel along a road if the benefit measured in money terms is greater than the private cost it incurs. If every vehicle paid no more than the private costs incurred by it — petrol, wear on tyres, etc., and time — then the throughput of vehicles would be T_1 and it would cost each of them P_1. On this diagram the marginal and average private cost curves are the same. An additional vehicle on the road will not only put up its own cost above that of the preceding vehicle, it will put up the cost of every other vehicle on the road.

If we make (as we have in this diagram) the simplifying assumption that by and large every road-user has the same costs per mile and suffers equally from congestion, then an additional vehicle on the road will effect the same increase in cost on everyone else. And this is the point of the theory that every road-user should be charged his marginal social cost.

We can draw a curve representing the additional cost that the marginal road-user inflicts on all road-users: marginal social cost curve (MSC). (The relation between the two curves is determinate.

MSC is the derivative of the MPC curve: MSC = MPC x $\dfrac{e-1}{e}$ where

e is the elasticity of the MPC curve.[10] What this means is that one needs to multiply the MPC for an additional unit of traffic by the number of vehicles on the road to find the total increases in cost to all vehicles resulting from the entry of the marginal road-user.) This measures the effect on all road-users on the stretch of road of the entry of an additional road-user: for example the MPC of a particular marginal vehicle might be $2d$. for the stretch of road but the MSC $100d$. if there were already 49 similar vehicles on the road the cost of each of them rising by a like $2d$.

A large vehicle will normally inflict more congestion costs than a smaller one. A stopping bus will by the nature of its operations normally inflict more than an equivalent sized vehicle such as a pantechnicon which does not plan to stop as often. A bad driver will inflict more congestion costs on other vehicles than a good one, etc. And one would also expect congestion to vary seasonally and according to the time of day. It may be possible to make some rough allowance here: for example letting a truck of a certain size count for two private cars; or a bus count for four. But it is quite obvious that though in principle it would be possible to work out the exact amount of congestion costs on a given stretch of road at a given time, in practice it would only be possible to work it out on certain simplifying assumptions that all are affected equally with some rough scale for vehicles of a different size.

When would there be no congestion costs on a given stretch of road? When there were few enough road-users for no one vehicle to affect the cost of travelling to any other vehicle – which as any motorist knows would be very few indeed.

The proposition that road-users should pay congestion costs means again in principle (for we have not yet come to thinking of the problem of how one would charge for this) that every motorist should first pay the marginal social cost, the cost he inflicts on himself and other users; and, second, that the road authority should levy the difference between the marginal private cost, which he pays in operating, and time costs and marginal social costs as a toll, tax or by any means possible. Let us assume for convenience here that it is possible to vary the price charged for a road fairly flexibly. The price a road-user pays ordinarily is his MPC which is P_1. MPC equals average private cost because the actual marginal road-user pays no more and no less than any other road-user. The same cost falls on all. It is the number of vehicles which decides it and it is only in that sense that costs are determined by the marginal road-user. All road-users in our simplified situation pay P_1. It is then suggested that all road-users should pay their marginal social cost. Price rises to P_2 and the number of vehicles per hour falls to T_2. Who benefits from this change? The road authority certainly benefits because it makes a profit represented by the rectangle P_2AED. The road-users who cannot afford to use the road at the new price, those represented by the difference between T_1 and T_2, lose. Whether they use some other road, another form of transport or do something else altogether they must be worse off – otherwise they would not have used the old congested road in the first place.

That this must be so can be illustrated by an example. A man decides to drive into a town to work. He has a choice of two routes or he could go by train. He chooses the more congested road although it is slower. We will suppose its directness compensates for its slowness. He knows what it costs him roughly to travel and he has considered the relevant factors in his mind, one of which may be the pleasure he gets from driving his status symbol to work; he chooses his route, the more congested one, and we may suppose, putting figures in his mind, that it costs him roughly 3s. per round trip; and that he would be prepared to pay 4s. rather than go by the other route, or 4s. 6d. rather than go by train. Then it is decided to pursue a marginal social cost pricing policy on the route he uses. Suppose every car using it has to buy a windscreen sticker which costs 7s. 6d. a week. This puts his costs up by 1s. 3d. a day — he goes to the office six days a week. The cost is too much for him so he goes by the alternative route — the one he does not like as much. No one can pretend that he is better off as a result of the introduction of marginal social cost pricing.

How about the motorist still on the road — is he better or worse off? His private or operating costs have fallen from C to E meaning by this that he is now able to save some time by moving quickly at a lower cost along the stretch of road in question; but he is more than paying for it. Let us take our example again. There is another motorist who uses the same route as our first motorist and for the same purpose — commuting, but he is a richer man. If the cost per round trip, which at 3s. is the same to him as to the first motorist, were reduced to 2s. 6d. by a reduction in the density of traffic on the road, he would be as willing as everyone else to pay 6d. for the difference. (Any motorist who did not would be rather strange since he could not lose if he did so.) However if our motorist and every other motorist using the road were prepared to pay no more than this, nothing would come of a marginal social cost pricing policy.[11] No one would pay more than P_1 and the effect of raising the price to P_2 would be to drive *all* road-users off the road. It is only if there are some people who value an average fall in private costs by more than 6d. that a marginal social cost policy would work.

Let us suppose that a marginal social cost pricing policy dictates a price which works out at a cost of 3s. 4d. for our second motorist, and he is prepared to pay it. Why is he and every other motorist who continues to use the road prepared to pay 4d. more than the average reduction in private costs resulting from the withdrawal of $T_1 - T_2$ road-users off the road? There are two sorts of reason. Either they are people who value the reduction in congestion more than the average road-user does (this could be because their cars use more petrol than the average car) or they are the sort of drivers who spend an amount more than average on tyre-wear, etc., or more plausibly it is because the motorist has an above-average valuation of his time. Naturally a rich man or anyone else whose time is important to him would pay more to save time than someone who is poorer or whose time is less valuable. The other possibility is that these are people who gain no more than anyone else from the reduction in private costs, but who would under any circumstances be prepared to pay more for the use of this road than the majority. Only part of the increase in price to them represents an improvement in driving for which they are ready to pay. The rest represents a reduction in consumers' surplus. It is quite impossible to tell how much is one and how much the other *a priori*. All that we can say is that the road authority benefits from increased revenue and that some road-users benefit because they get an improved route the benefit of which is more to them than the increased price they pay for it.

We now have some idea of the point of charging road-users the congestion costs they cause. If we were prepared to set aside the problems listed in Chapters 2 and 3 and adopt marginal cost pricing, marginal social cost pricing would have immediate validity as a means to the end of optimising the allocation of resources. On AC pricing assumptions if all the benefit goes to the road authority it is simply a method of increasing the road authority's revenue. If some of the benefit goes to a certain proportion of road-users then it is a method by which the authority can price off the roads poorer road-users or perhaps discourage those wealthy road-users who value their time insufficiently to pay more. It is a method of rationing road-space: rationing by price. Here is a case where it is important to decide what are to be counted costs and what not. Do we want a system of pricing whereby those who value their time (for it is time which is the chief factor) are able to price other road-users off the road: to the detriment of those road-users, and to their own benefit and the benefit of the road authority's funds (as for example a restaurant may put up its prices to keep customers out so that those who remain and pay the price can eat their meals in less congested surroundings)? There will be an overall efficiency gain (which incidentally in principle could be used to compensate the losing road-users) because of the elimination of welfare losses elsewhere in the economy as discussed in Chapter 6.[12]

It will of course be obvious that the problem of charging for congestion costs does not arise for a profit maximising road authority. It would set a price to maximise profits; and the optimum toll will be more than AE (in fig. 9.1) because it will be determined by the intersection of the MR and MSC curves. A consumers' surplus maximising road authority would not logically charge for congestion costs if it was forbidden to make profits.

Alternative Use Value

If a private firm thinks it would be more profitable to employ one of its assets, a cotton mill, say, as a broiler house, it is generally agreed that it is right and proper for it to do so; and indeed it would not be doing its duty by its shareholders if it did not. And if it were more profitable for it to sell the asset to some other concern that could use it more profitably, and reinvest the capital realised or possibly distribute it to shareholders again, it would be proper for it to be sold. In short any factor of production including labour should earn in its present occupation at least as much as it could earn in its most profitable alternative use, and it is irrelevant whether the most profitable use is within or without the organisation to which it belongs. Every asset and person employed therefore has what is termed an *'alternative use value'* or *'opportunity cost.'* In noticeable cases a firm which does not employ its assets so is ripe for and deserves a takeover bid.

We took it for granted that it is equally sensible of a nationalised industry to behave in the same way. It is a logical deduction from the criterion of profit maximisation that if a building site would be more profitably used as office block than as station, an office block it should be. If the railways were to be run as a consumers' surplus concern the principle still holds though its measurement is slightly different. The railways should employ an asset where it yields the highest possible consumers' surplus. If it were sold and the capital realised were worth more than its capitalised value to the railways, then it should be sold.

It is generally in the national interest that factors of production should be employed in their most profitable use. National product and income will be the higher for it. This is a sufficiently plausible presumption for it to be reasonable to ask anyone who denies it in a specific instance to show cause why. (To do this he must introduce and substantiate a new criterion. The strength of his case will in part depend on the acceptability of his criterion.) Few people would deny this in respect of private and nationalised industry although they might argue that certain uses of land and other assets should be subsidised. (For instance the most profitable use of a certain building might be for flats letting at high rents, but it might be decided to subsidise it as temporary accommodation for homeless families.) We have argued before that there is no general case for subsidising transport and that in towns and cities in particular road-users should ordinarily not be subsidised. It follows therefore that assets should be employed in their most profitable use in transport, according to the criterion adopted, but many who accept this principle everywhere else seem to disregard it utterly when they discuss the road problem. The principal results of neglecting it are waste and a further confusion of the town planning problem.

The only asset belonging to the road system with significant alternative use value is land, but land embodied in rural roads has practically none since the cost of converting it to other uses will usually be prohibitive. Most farmers would not be keen to take a stretch of road even if it were offered them as a gift. Old railways may have value as a site for roads but not vice versa. Occasionally, even in the country, bits of the highway system will have a value for building, but this will be unusual since new building naturally requires more roads, not the destruction of old ones. The same will be true in suburbs and throughout many villages and towns. To take a case: there is an urban street in a residential district fringed by houses set back behind front gardens, the street is wide enough for a lane on either side which is used for parking but could be used to extend front gardens by ten feet. How much would property-owners be willing to pay for additional garden? Probably not enough to cover the costs of breaking up the road, altering drains and mains, and rebuilding the pavement ten feet out, let alone outbid the value that part of the roadway may have for parking. For this reason the alternative use value of land embodied in the road system will more often than not be negligible.

However there are areas where bits and pieces of the road system have potentially a very much higher value: the centres of large cities, most particularly London. And it is in London we may most usefully pursue the consequences of the notion that land should be employed in its most profitable use. Because of a complication to be raised when we come to land costs, it will be convenient if we assume that the land in question (generally about eight to twelve feet next to one kerb or possibly on both sides of the roadway) is most profitably used by road-users for parking, waiting, loading and unloading, etc. If he were able, a developer would often pay a high price for an extra strip of land to add to a property he is rebuilding. Even if no more than the size of two parking spaces, the extra office, shop or factory floor-space that can be built because of it will be remunerative. And, if development is not immediate but expected in, say eight years, the development value of that bit of the road system will be its value eight years hence, discounted back to the present at the ruling rate of interest. Until development happens the most profitable interim use for it may be parking – just as one finds derelict sites in cities used for car parking pending development.

Profit maximisation and consumers' surplus maximisation commit us to the view that if it is more profitable to the road system that such land should be sold or leased for building rather than retained for parking – making any allowance for any expected increase in its value as traffic increases – then to a developer it should now or eventually go. This may seem absurd: fantastic to think of selling up part of an inadequate road system for building which will itself need more parking space rather than less. This is to mistake the problem. We need more space for car parking but the present street parking involves a wasteful use of land which would not be tolerated by any private firm. A car parked in the street occupies land on which could be built several storeys of building. Suppose we have a section of the street, a kerbside parking space thirty feet by eight feet, say, adjacent to a property being redeveloped as a six-storey office building. If the developer could buy this piece of the roadway, rebuilding the pavement eight feet out, he would be able to provide, allowing for wells and recesses, etc. for light and ventilation, rather more than an extra thousand square feet of office space. Even when we consider only the site value it is unlikely that car parkers using the site would pay in total a sum equal to the value it has for this extra office accommodation. When the alternative use value of land is taken into account it must often be the case that it would be cheaper to provide off-street parking in multi-storey garages above or below ground than to continue in the same wasteful way allowing vehicles to park and load in the streets. In such circumstances – to anticipate charging problems for a moment – a profit maximising road authority would fix parking charges for its parking spaces to maximise its profits. It would sell or lease land where profitable, and private developers who believed that they could provide parking facilities more cheaply than the road system could build the car parks required. Private firms might also be encouraged to provide parking facilities for their staff and also facilities for loading and unloading. One would expect that as buildings came due for redevelopment this would effect a considerable change in land utilisation. Street parking would largely disappear in city centres or would be limited and very dear. Loading and unloading in the streets would be uncommon except where firms were prepared to pay the economic prices asked. The road would be used only for traffic movement to a much larger extent.

The same result could be achieved by a consumers' surplus maximising authority though the method would be somewhat different. Such an authority would charge people who use the street for parking, loading, etc., either on an average or marginal cost basis as discussed earlier (Chapter 6). Therefore one would expect the price to the motorist of street parking to be less than that of off-street parking provided by commercial firms. However it would still be profitable to the road authority to sell many of these street parking areas. This would in itself be a considerable hardship to parkers and others who would now have to pay profit maximising prices, but the road authority could plough back the money realised from such sales in building off-street garages where parking space was to be sold at the lower price; and in subsidising the building of garages in otherwise private development projects. It might be argued that this was in the interests of road-users, within the competence of the authority, and possibly among projects yielding a high consumers' surplus rate of return. Whether the road authority did or did not invest in off-street parking, one would expect a less wasteful use of valuable urban land. If it did invest the difference would be that the garage proprietors' loss would be the road-users' gain and vice versa.

Alternative use values are important. Their neglect is responsible for much of the waste and confusion present in existing road and town planning policy. They are costs in the sense that if the use of a given road was discontinued, the real resources concerned would be saved in that the land would pass into its next most profitable alternative use; whereas if it had no profitable alternative use, the resources would be wasted. But they are not costs in the ordinary sense of payments which must be made if the road is to be provided. They are in the nature of profits or rent and though relevant to the use of land, and in deciding investment they are not relevant to charging. A profit maximising authority will charge as much as it can get irrespective of whether this sums to an amount equivalent to the alternative use value or greater.

Land Costs

It is often argued that road-users should pay rent like anyone else for the land they use, as for example by Sir Charles Goodeve, F.R.S.: 'Most people forget that the enormous network of roads owned by the Government has a very great value in monetary terms. It is right and proper that Government should draw a revenue on this asset, perhaps 5 per cent per annum on the total value. It is difficult to determine the value of roads and to arrive at a fair revenue. My guess is that this at 5 per cent would itself exceed the total taxes on road transport.'[13] The problem is to value the land. You cannot put a value on the road system in a country area because if there were no road system the value of the surrounding land would be much diminished. You cannot put a value on the road system of a city because a city without roads would be practically valueless, as would roads without a city. This is a case of *joint demand* or as it sometimes is called *complementarity*. It was meaningless to try to attribute joint costs because the answer was 'none' to the question what costs would be saved if mutton was produced and not wool. Similarly the answer to the question what value would remain if there were no roads is likewise 'none' and it is therefore pointless to try to attribute value to roads on their own. Towns and roads together have value. Apart they do not. To ask the value of the land embodied in the road system is a meaningless question.

From this it is frequently deduced that there is no economic case for asking road-users to pay for the use of land, except when it has been bought for their use (the first category, p.208) and then it should be the purchase cost which is relevant and not any appreciation in value. The value of the road would not go up if the value of its environs did not. They are interdependent. This is not the last word because although the attribution of value where there is joint demand is impossible, there are two ways of escaping its implications.

The first is to extend the category considered under alternative use value (the ninth category, p.220). There we carefully avoided this problem by considering only instances where there was an alternative use value for the land and no joint demand. The land used for parking, loading and unloading, etc. has a value which can be attributed to it. If the city were deprived of street parking facilities it would not become valueless especially if the change happened over a long enough time to permit the construction of off-street parking facilities. Indeed we have argued that it should increase the value of the city by encouraging a less wasteful use of land. The only use of the road system for which this joint demand problem arises critically is its use for movement. To deprive city or countryside of the wherewithal to move traffic and pedestrians would be to reduce its value to almost nothing. This fact is not significantly altered because there are occasionally alternative means of travel — railways, canals, rivers and coastal shipping. The railways for example would not be worth much in a roadless countryside. The fact of interdependence must be accepted.

Movement excepted, there are uses of the road system's land where a value can be attributed and the value in question is the alternative use value. Under category nine above we considered some of these but we now can pursue the matter further for there are 'parts' of the road system, not mentioned as yet, which have alternative use value. Once again those instances will normally only occur in the centre of cities.

Most streets are open to the air. Tunnels under rivers and underpasses are almost the only exceptions. This is technologically unnecessary and may be unprofitable economically.* To take an extreme case, suppose the alternative is either building a new urban motorway from Shepherds Bush to the City of London or a road tunnel. We may well find before long that it is cheaper to build the tunnel even allowing for the difficulties caused by existing underground installations and the cost of lighting and ventilation. If it did not pay as far as Shepherds Bush it might as far as the Edgware Road. And the reason of course would be the value of land, the price that would have to be paid for sufficient land to build new roads on the surface.

This argument is not only relevant to new roads. Let us imagine that property developers, private or municipal, would pay enough for Fleet Street to more than cover the cost of building a tunnel under it to carry the same or perhaps a greater volume of traffic as is now carried on the surface. Or, what is perhaps a more practicable

*I am indebted to Sir Roy Harrod for this suggestion.

suggestion, suppose developers would offer enough to build on top of Oxford Street. Imagine that as London grows this type of development becomes more profitable, such that perhaps fifty years hence all roads in the West End and the city are either underground or above ground but built over. In 1960 about £379,000 was paid in New York for 'air rights', the right to build over a sunken highway which had been constructed, and this was not the first scheme of its kind in New York.[14] In Omaha a seven-storey parking garage has been built spanning a street.[15] And nearer home we have the road from High Holborn to Theobalds Road where two blocks on either side of the road are linked by a bridge building six floors high.[16] We may conceive a future in which the first stage is throwing buildings as bridges over our roads so that these are still mainly lit by natural light and not ventilated specially. When the value of land rises further it would be profitable to enclose roads in some areas completely and build over them providing artificial lighting and ventilation.

Some may be appalled at the thought of this possible transformation, but even aesthetically might it not be an improvement on what we have? We hear much about the advantages of separating pedestrians and wheeled traffic. This might be one way of achieving it with very little interference with the price mechanism. Imagine Oxford Street and the streets surrounding flanked with shops as at present with a roof perhaps forty feet from the ground. Traffic would not be affected by rain, fog or bad visibility. Lighting could be the same high standard day and night. There would be ventilation extracting exhaust fumes more effectively possible than natural currents of air do at present.*
One parks one's car in a garage and mounts an escalator out of the road system and into the world of buildings towering above it. If there is no interference by subsidy and regulation one might find the buildings all higgledy-piggledy, no further apart than the need for light and sanitation would insist and entered only from below. But if there were judicious interference, the space between the buildings on the roof of the road system might be used for pedestrian walks, and more ambitiously there might be small squares and other open spaces from which the noise of the traffic roaring beneath could not be heard. Occasionally the old might be preserved in the midst of the new. One would descend into St. Paul's Churchyard from which the traffic

*The designer of the Crystal Palace had a somewhat similar vision and advertised without much success for subscribers to 'The Victorian Way; or Sir Joseph Paxton's splendid design for a Girdle Railway and Arcade Boulevard with shops and houses attached, all under a Glass Roof similar to the Crystal Palace with a roadway in the centre, and double railways on the drawing-room and attic floors — trains every two minutes and a half — forming a salubrious inclosed circle of pure country air through ten miles of the densest part of the metropolis, crossing the river three times on magnificent bridges and rendering foreign climates unnecessary to invalids.'[17]

had been diverted from the pedestrian concourse on the city's first floor. Would such a city lack all such advantages? Would it be worse than the waste of open motorways open to the sky which have obliterated central Los Angeles?

However the point is not that adoption of either of our two criteria necessarily implies a city like this, but that we should be prepared to sell 'air rights' unless road-users are prepared to pay sufficient for the amenity of having the sky over their heads for it not to be profitable for the space above them to go to an alternative use. Or if local authorities or central Government should be prepared to subsidise road-users to keep the streets open — as I have suggested they might want to do where there is a special aesthetic or historical value, as at St. Paul's or Trafalgar Square.

However much we cabin and confine the road system by being prepared to hand over bits and pieces of it if there is a more profitable alternative use, there will remain a residue — what is necessary for traffic movement where joint demand continues to prevent valuation. Various dodges have been proposed. A Dutch Government report has suggested that this land should be valued at replacement cost — the cost of purchasing the land if it had to be purchased today — and charged for accordingly.[18] The fallacy is that since there is no question of replacing the land on which the road is built there is no reason to argue as if it did have to be replaced, and imputing a replacement cost to it. And there are many other dodges based on similar fallacies.

This particular problem does not in fact affect us. The profit maximiser gets as much as he can for the use of roads and in practice this will mean that because his monopoly power is greater he ought to be able to expropriate a large proportion of the appreciation in land values which now goes to the property owner (and this whether he charges property directly for access to roads or road-users indirectly). The effect will be to reduce the value of land used for building relatively to land used for roads. Contrarily the consumers' surplus maximiser will not attempt to charge for value in the road system as he did not charge for alternative use value. Any appreciation in land values will go as at present to property owners. The problem only arises when, as at present, all the benefits from the increased prosperity of a town accrue to property, and the road authority does not want to act as a profit maximiser. It is unlikely a road authority would act as a profit maximiser unless deliberately designed as a mechanism for the expropriation of rent. But this does not mean that what happens now is indisputably right. Economics cannot give the road authority a principle to decide how much benefit should go to property and how much to its own land. We are agreed that a town would be worthless without roads, and roads are valueless without the town they serve. Because the road authority does not charge a rent element for its road system, all the increase in value accrues to property owners. It is as if two men were needed to row a boat across and one man got all the money. Even if we allow for the levying of rates on property the situation is strange, but if a road or local authority should decide to increase the charge for roads in order to get some of the benefit for itself it must decide what proportion it thinks it should get; and this is a pure value judgement and nothing in economics can help it reach a more just decision.

SUMMARY

In this chapter it has been argued that both the determination of the assets to be vested in a road authority, or authorities, and a decision who are to be reckoned consumers if the policy is to be consumers' maximisation, can have economic importance since they can affect the scope of the criterion adopted and therefore the implementation of the policy.

The various cost categories of the road system have been considered. It has been argued that it is reasonable to include the following in the costs of the road system to be counted for charging and investment purposes: non-renewable and renewable capital costs; maintenance costs; various costs such as general administrative costs, the proportion of the costs of police forces attributable to traffic control street lighting, traffic lighting and other aids to traffic control, and research; and also interest charges where appropriate; and taxes and rates. Accident and congestion costs were treated differently. It was argued that the fundamental point about charging for accident costs is a prior decision whether road-users should be required to pay as a matter of public policy. It was pointed out that the present situation appears anomalous. And it was argued that although it was proper to invest in the reduction of traffic accidents in so far as it was profitable to do so (a concept which was explained in this context) any additional investment must be regarded as a subsidy or cross-subsidisation, if the funds are provided internally to which the road system had no more obvious claim than many other investments which would lessen sickness, disability and death. It was argued that congestion costs were irrelevant to both our basic criteria or rather that in so far as people are prepared to pay for better roads they are subsumed in different ways within them. The proposition that road-users should pay the congestion costs they cause, it was argued, was equivalent to the proposition that some road-users should be able to price others off the roads and/or the road authority should be able to make a profit. Last, the nature of alternative use values and land costs was examined for the road system.

POSTSCRIPT

The Road-Users

In 1962 those responsible for highway investment had a limited conception of the 'consumer' they were acting for. There was the road-user assumed to value costs and time savings — not that these savings were normally measured. There were those who might experience accidents as vehicle-users or pedestrians. There were those whose land was acquired for road improvement and who were net losers on the terms on which land was acquired. There were others whose interests were given weight, for example, farmers for whom costly underpasses were built so that they might continue to drive their cattle from one field to another, even under a motorway. During the 1960s those responsible for highway investment have been pressed to consider other interests: those whose land is not acquired but who are affected by noise, vibration, air pollution, visual intrusion and neighbourhood severance. In principle any environmental impact of a highway improvement is coming to be judged relevant.[1] There has been recognition that those whose property has been acquired have been undercompensated in the past.[2] Some of the problems of reflecting these interests in a highway investment criterion will be discussed in the postscript to Chapter 11.

Deciding to broaden the number of interests considered does not determine the form of criterion to be used. One possibility is that it is the interests of road-users that are to be maximised subject to the constraint that no one else is to be worse off as a result of highway investment. This constraint satisfies the condition that economists call Pareto optimality, which is that some at least should be better off and none worse as a result of a change.[3] It would imply that all affected adversely by a highway improvement were fully compensated.

It might often be more efficient for a highway authority to redesign an improvement to reduce its negative environmental impact, rather than simply pay cash. A policy incurring greater costs but also greater benefits than one which satisfies Pareto optimality, that is, one which makes someone at least better off without making any worse off, may be more efficient and yield greater returns. The same point is raised in the chapter in regard to accidents. One can imagine a highway authority engaging in optimal highway environmental and safety policies rather than regarding the avoidance of uncompensated negative impacts of non-road-users as a constraint on its behaviour. If so, it would be more than a highway authority. It would be taking positive action to reduce pollution, noise, accidents and other environmental impacts. There are often disadvantages in giving the same agency multiple objectives. Besides, many of the strategies that could be more efficient in affecting the environment are not normally within the responsibility of highway authorities. An alternative would be to develop agencies to operate safety, anti-pollution, and other environmental programmes covering a wider field than either highways or transport.

The Identification of Costs

The discussion of costs here was taken further in *Road Track Costs*.[4] There is an excellent discussion of the principles governing the valuation of a human life by Mishan.[5] There has been a large literature on the theory of congestion pricing since 1962. An excellent, extended treatment is in Walters.[6] The relation between road pricing and land use has also been studied and throws more light on the inefficiencies that result from road charges failing to reflect congestion.[7] A city that introduced road pricing would find that land values near the city centre would rise, because central streets would become less congested but dearer to use. Those land uses which set a high value on accessibility would tend to cluster in the centre and because reduced congestion increased their accessibility, the value of a central site to them would rise. Hence higher central land values, though it is difficult to predict to what extent land values would rise. Uses valuing such accessibility less would be the more inclined to decentralise. Congestion means less efficient use of land.

In the early 1960s two important books pioneered a greater understanding of the relationship between the demand for land and transport in cities.[8] If one asks why land values are greater in cities, greater towards the centre of cities and greater in large cities than in smaller, it must be because those who use land there obtain benefits that more than offset higher land costs. While those who live and work in cities may derive some non-pecuniary benefits from urban living, in general workers in a large city must earn higher incomes to compensate them for their higher housing and transport costs if they are to feel at least as well off as in a smaller city. (Transport costs are higher because the larger the city, in general the longer and more expensive the average journey to work. This is itself a consequence of the land value profile of larger cities. See Alonso and Wingo, op. cit.) Since urban firms must therefore pay higher wages, other things being equal, their urban location must have advantages to enable them to meet higher labour and site costs and yet earn as high a rate of profit. Among these economies of agglomeration are reduced transport costs from being in the centre of a large population. For freight the advantages of a central location have been eroded by congestion so that the least cost location for a firm in an urban area is rarely any larger at its centre. What are still adduced as benefits of a central location in a large city are the advantages of 'face-to-face' contact for certain kinds of activity. The clustering of

230

financial institutions in the City of London or Wall Street is explained by the advantages to them of such easy contact.[9] For an urban area as a whole, the relation between transport (accessibility) and land values is complex. A reduction in accessibility would certainly lower land values. On the other hand radial improvements in transport would also lower land values, other things being equal, because faster journey times mean that a larger area would be any given journey time from the centre. But as Alonso and Muth have shown, other things are generally not equal. A reduction in radial journey costs per mile tends to be followed by an outward movement of population acquiring homes at lower densities. Therefore, the demand for land, and land values, may actually increase as a result of such transport improvements.

Given that land is a scarce factor, there are many causes of rising land values. Transport is one, but it is difficult to decide empirically its influence relative to that of other factors. Many nations try to tax appreciation in land values through property taxation, betterment levies and other devices. Land nationalisation is the most extreme attempt to expropriate increases in land values for the community. In principle, taxing road use could be a way of expropriating some part of the increase in land values because of this interdependence between transport and land values; but there are important efficiency aspects. As has already been argued, if the effect of taxing congested road space would be to raise journey speeds towards the optimum, this would raise land values through increasing economies of agglomeration. If there were already optimal road pricing, raising the road price further by a tax would lead to a less efficient use of urban land and therefore lower land values. Taxing road-users as such is a less efficient means of expropriating increases in land values simply because its allocative effects will be greater than a well-designed tax upon economic rent. It remains true that nothing in economic theory can help decide what proportion of increases in land values a Government may decide to expropriate, but economics does help to evaluate the efficiency aspects of different methods of expropriation. It remains common in transport planning to double-count land value savings and savings in travel costs and time savings because it is not appreciated that most changes in land values reflect a transfer of income either from (1) road-users to land-owners or (2) one set of land-owners to another. (1) The first case may be exemplified by a situation where workers commuting to a firm benefit initially from a transport improvement but because the firm is now able to draw from a larger labour market because it has become more accessible, there is less need for it to raise wages to attract labour. But when its lease is renegotiated the benefit is now transferred to the land-owner and it is the improvement in the accessibility of his site which is ultimately the beneficiary of the transport improvement.

231

(2) An example of the second case would be where a transport improvement increases sales at one transport improvement and raises land values, but only at the expense of lower, or more slowly increasing land values elsewhere, at shops which have lost sales.

Earlier I argued that some road-users would be prepared to pay more for a less congested road because they have above average valuations of time. The considerations of the last paragraph make it clearer how structural changes in the city could reinforce the benefits received by those with an above average valuation of time. They may benefit directly from less congestion. In the long run they will also benefit from changes in land use, especially at city centres, which are a response to the stimulus given to economies of urban agglomeration by higher central city speeds.

The argument distinguishes between consumers' surplus maximisation with average cost pricing (where one would not charge congestion costs) and with short-run marginal cost pricing.

10 CHARGING FOR THE USE OF THE ROAD SYSTEM

To decide what charges should be made for the use of the road system, the various categories of joint and attributable costs must be distinguished. The theoretical framework required is that set out in Chapter 5 and Appendix 3. The aim of the road authority would be to produce, in effect, a map of the road system showing the costs attributable to various parts of it and to be recovered from those parts if possible. These are:

(1) Short-run costs which would be escaped if a particular vehicle did not use the road;

(2) short-run costs of particular flows of traffic or categories of road-user which would be escaped if these did not use the roads;

(3) long-run costs attributable to particular flows or categories of road-user;

(4) long-run costs joint to different flows or categories, probably best treated as costs joint to a section of road ('section' will be used to mean any length of road, perhaps fifty yards, possibly a mile or two, which it is practicable to regard as having a uniform cost along its length and to be indivisible on economic grounds);

(5) a small category of costs will be those joint to an administrative area of the road system;

(6) still smaller costs joint to the road system as a whole.

Those are likely to be the most important categories of costs from the point of view of constructing a charging map of the road system. Because little research into road costs has been done, especially in Britain, with this intention this chapter will be more tentative than the parallel argument on the railways. Its purpose is not to criticise what is done but to give an outline of what might be done.

ATTRIBUTION OF COSTS FOR CHARGING

Short-run Costs Attributable to Particular Vehicles

Research has been done in the United States on the most important cost in this category: highway maintenance due to wear.[1] The heavier the vehicle the greater the wear on the road. Wear is more than proportionate to the weight of the vehicle responsible. Up to some weight, x, there is a steady increase in wear, thereafter a marked increase. Ultimately for every road a sufficiently great weight will destroy it. As one would expect the exact shape of the function and the points at which it curve bends (x) will vary between roads, bridges, fly-overs, etc., depending on construction and the load for which it was designed.

Wear also increases, the more the curvature of the road or the steeper a slope. The difference between the wear caused by a lighter and a heavier vehicle increases with the steepness of the gradient. For example, if a car causes half as much wear as a three-ton truck on the level, it may cause only 25 per cent of the wear by a three-ton truck on a hill. American research has gone further than these generalisations into the effects on highway maintenance costs of: different types of vehicles; different speeds; different kinds of road; different climatic conditions. These would have to be reworked for Britain. In some respects it should be easier because climatic conditions and the quality of road surfaces do not vary so much.

If it were decided to charge for congestion costs on a marginal social cost pricing basis, this would also be a cost attributable to particular vehicles. One would have to attempt to work out the marginal social cost on particular congested roads allowing for differences in traffic density at different times of day, from day to day and seasonally wherever these were relevant.

The only other cost in this category would appear to be the comparatively trivial cost of providing a police escort which could be attributed directly to the abnormal load concerned.

Short-run Costs Attributable to Particular Flows of Traffic

These are a small proportion of costs, the most important would probably be for police. The cost of policing a busy section of road cannot be attributed to all the traffic using the road but is a joint cost of the traffic using it while the police are there and which could be escaped if there were no rush-hour, weekend or holiday congestion. Similarly the police costs caused by the parking offences and other needs of stationary vehicles are the joint cost of those vehicles, since by and large one could only dispense with police for this purpose if there were no stationary vehicles. The cost of traffic wardens is a joint cost of the parking meters they serve. The only other costs might be insignificant, for example, the current costs of street lighting which could be avoided if there were no night traffic and which are therefore attributable as a joint cost to such traffic.

The remaining groups of costs are long-run: escapable over some period of time (see pp. 208-9). If the revenue received in respect of a section of road or a facility does not equal the long-run cost of it, it may still be profitable to keep the road open or provide the facility in so far as no real resources would be saved by closure.

Long-run Costs Attributable to Particular Flows of Traffic or Types of Road-user

The most obvious are the costs of laying mains, sewerage, etc., incurred only on behalf of the undertakings concerned. Similarly, the costs of pedestrian bridges and subways are attributable to pedestrians, of cycle tracks to cyclists. Footpath costs should also be attributed to pedestrians as they are only useful to road-users as pedestrians, whereas the costs of the road surface which is used by moving and stationary vehicles of all types and by pedestrians crossing cannot be attributed to the one kind of road-user only.

Long-run Costs Joint to a Section of Road

These are costs which canot be attributed to particular flows of traffic or which it would be unprofitable to attempt to attribute. In the United States these costs are often allocated on what is known as the Kentucky or Incremental Cost Principle.[2] A United Kingdom example of the use of the principle and its limitations is for bridge costs. Bridges and fly-overs over motorways and trunk roads are built in this country with a clearance of 16ft. 6in. Surveys have shown that roughly 10 per cent of commercial vehicles are more than 11ft. high. This means that if it were not for this small proportion of traffic (possibly 4 per cent of all vehicles) bridges could be built safely with, say 11ft. 6in. clearance, which would make considerable difference to construction costs. The extra construction costs are attributable to vehicles more than 11ft. high. Since there are virtually no vehicles more than 13ft. 6in. high except double-decker buses (14ft. 4in.) this proportion of extra cost is attributable to them only. (The fact that clearance is 2ft. 2in. more than the highest vehicle using trunk roads and motorways must either be a costly mistake of the Ministry of Transport or a prediction that vehicles will get higher.) Clearly the incremental principle here and elsewhere is relevant to investment, but not necessarily to charging, a proposition examined in Chapter 4. Once the bridge, or whatever it is, is built, no real resources are saved by the exclusion of a particular category of traffic, for example, double-decker buses from motorways, so that the asset cost is joint to whatever uses it. The only problem arises when, pursuing a consumers' surplus maximisation policy, charging what the market will bear, brings in revenue more than equal to its cost, and the surplus must be returned to users as lower prices. As was argued for the railways, the choice of the principle to be used for lowering prices must be a value judgement. One possible solution is to charge long-run average costs and this would be equivalent to the Kentucky method. Others were discussed (p. 140). Whatever the policy adopted it seems important it should be the same for road and rail.

Costs vary greatly from one section of road to another. These costs should be expressed as a discounted sum of annual charges. To do this some assumption must be made about the period over which roads are to be amortised. Suppose we assume it to be fifty years, every section of road on which money had been spent on improvement or construction during the last fifty years would have some annual sum set against it to be recovered from road-users. Other sections on which there had only been maintenance expenditure during the last fifty years would have no such cost attached to them on our map of the road system since it would be assumed that their construction costs and any previous improvement costs had been depreciated to zero. (The choice of fifty years for this purpose is of course arbitrary. It must be since there has been no formal provision for interest payments or depreciation in the past (see p.209).

Rates and taxes and any sums charged as rents might also be expected to vary from one section to another.

When all these costs are summed for each section of the road and any others which are relevant we have the variations cost to be recovered *if possible* from users of the various sections of the road system.

Costs Joint to an Administrative Area
There may be costs joint to some larger area than a road section: for example administrative expenses or certain police or maintenance overheads.

Costs Joint to the Road System
Last, there will be some overheads of the system which are not worth attributing further: principally, one would expect the central expenses of the Ministry of Transport and road authority if there is *one;* and the cost of research mostly performed at present by the Road Research Laboratory.

When as many of these costs have been identified as would be profitable a costing 'map' of the road system could be drawn up.

METHODS OF CHARGING: CONSUMERS' SURPLUS MAXIMISATION

Once this organisation of costing data has been completed, it must be related to possible methods of charging. Some readers may already have felt the information it has been suggested the road authority should try to go was too ambitious, because it would not be possible to reflect refinements in costing by subtle enough differences in charging. This was not a problem for the railways where the price of a ticket or a rate could be altered without much difficulty but the use of the roads cannot be sold like groceries or theatre seats or seats on the railways. One cannot imagine a ticket collector and turnstile at every garage door,

and the right to use the road for every journey sold separately, or a ⌐
of ticket inspectors out to see no one used the roads for a purpose
other than that paid for. Most road-users must be charged indirectly.
Nevertheless these indirect methods of charging could be improved to
bear more relation to the costs incurred. To use an analogy, the present
situation is as if coal was sold at the same price per ton for all qualities
and whatever its price of production and transport. The situation we
are aiming at is like one where there is a different price per ton for
the main grades of coal with some allowance for difference in the
costs of production. So for roads we want to reach a charging system
which will make some distinctions between road-users according to the
costs they impose on the road system. There will be some averaging
left if only because it would not pay to be more refined. It will be
convenient to elaborate the system appropriate to consumers' surplus
maximisation (average cost pricing) first.

Petrol Taxation

This is almost certain to be the centrepiece of any charging policy.
It is easy to administer and virtually impossible to evade. Its greatest
merit is that petrol consumption measures some of the variations in
highway costs mentioned in the last section, attributable to use of the
road by a particular vehicle: maintenance costs due to wear and
congestion costs. There are in fact three principal aims which can
determine the level of petrol taxation of which the first and third,
and the second and third would seem to be compatible under
British conditions but not the first and second. In other words it
would seem impossible to use petrol taxation to reflect both
maintenance *and* congestion costs. Let us consider the three purposes
in turn.

First, as the wear on the road effected by vehicles increases, petrol
consumption increases. Petrol consumption will be higher on poor roads
and up hills. Not only does the difference between the wear caused by
vehicles of different weight increase the greater its gradient, the difference
in petrol consumption increases similarly. Much has already been
discovered about the factors determining petrol consumption: type
of vehicles and type of road.[3] Unfortunately petrol consumption is
not a perfect measure of wear inflicted. The chief defect is that a rate
of petrol tax which would charge private cars the maintenance costs
roughly attributable to them would let heavier vehicles off too lightly.
One way of attempting to remedy this would be to do what has been
tried by the State of Kentucky: to impose a surtax of two cents per
gallon on fuel used by motor vehicles with four or more axles.[4] If it
could be made to work in Britain it might pay to have more than one
rate of petrol surtax for different sizes of vehicle. The obvious method

would be to dye the petrol to be consumed by different types of vehicle various colours and levy heavy fines on vehicles found using petrol of the wrong colour; but it was found very difficult to ration petrol effectively by this means, commercial users being required to use coloured petrol which was unrationed, private users being restricted to ordinary colourless petrol on the ration. The alternatives to a surtax on petrol consumed by heavier vehicles are vehicle licences, purchase tax, weight-ton and tyre tax (see below).

Second, petrol taxation can be used to reflect congestion costs. Congestion and petrol consumption increase together because of greater fuel cost per mile as speeds fall below 20m.p.h. and there is an increase in fuel consumption with the increase in the frequency of stops a vehicle makes. A study in Boston found fuel consumption on average 50 per cent higher on congested streets and much higher on some.[5] A Los Angeles study calculated the effect of making five stops per mile — at traffic lights, intersections, etc. — on fuel consumption: at 25m.p.h. a 68 per cent increase.[6] Comparable British experiments have produced similar results.[7]

If the rate of petrol taxation were raised high enough it could be used as an instrument of a marginal social cost pricing policy to price vehicles off congested streets, but the level of tax needed for this (it has been suggested that it might be between five and ten times more than the present UK tax rate a mile) would be far too high a rate to recoup maintenance costs in uncongested areas. To avoid this it would be necessary to charge different rates of petrol tax in congested areas and outside them, which in practice would mean that petrol stations in large congested areas — for example, the metropolitan area, Birmingham, etc. — would have to sell petrol at higher prices. But it would pay many motorists to go to buy petrol in low-tax areas. Suburban and ex-urban traffic commuting from low-tax areas would never buy petrol at the higher rates and so would not be deterred at all from using city streets. Some other method of taxing congestion must be adopted if it is decided to charge for congestion, for example, vehicle licences, purchase tax, windscreen stickers and meters (see below).

Third, let us assume that petrol tax is to be used to recoup maintenance costs attributable to wear. For this purpose x pence per gallon is charged, in practice probably some fraction of a penny. The tax could be used for another purpose. Let us suppose that the costs joint to each section of the road system are known and it is decided to average these costs over the number of vehicles expected to use each road section. At present there is an annual traffic census based on fifty census points. Either this could be used to make the prediction or something more elaborate could be attempted. At the end of the year retrodiction would be used to see whether the receipts had been greater

238

or less than expected; and the average rate to be collected from
road-users for the next year would be adjusted accordingly. (If it paid
to discriminate between different sorts of road-user on the same
section of road or another criterion was used as for the railways which
implied different rates for different road-users, the policy could be
adapted to reflect this. In practice it would probably cost too much.)
It is very difficult to predict the variation in the average cost per road
section per mile. It would be impossible to charge a different rate of tax
for every variation in the cost. It may happen that our charging
system may not be able to take account of more than two or three
variations in this cost (but see p.248-50 on automatic meters).
However, let us assume it makes sense for charging costs to divide the
whole range of average costs per road section per mile into six groups,
each group being categorised by the average cost which is the weighted
mean of the average costs in the group. Petrol taxation could then be
used to recoup the mean average cost of the lowest gro
y pence per gallon. The difference between this and th
be recouped from sections in the higher group would b
recouped by other means because of the evident impo:
differential petrol tax rates for this purpose.

The rate of petrol tax to be selected would equal x
as explained, x being more than y, but the total certai
present rate of petrol tax, as one would expect, becau
against the present rate is that it charges users on mos
much and the majority of users on a very small propo
much too little. To charge the latter properly, someth
petrol tax must be used.

Diesel Taxation
The chief point here is that a rate of taxation should
is equivalent to the rate chosen for petrol taxation so
gains merely by substituting a diesel-driven vehicle fo
one. A certain amount of work has been done to establish an equitable
rate.[9]

Vehicle Licence Fees and Registration Duties
Although they have not this importance at present, these could replace
petrol taxation as the centrepiece of the system. Average costs of the
lowest group of costs 'joint to a section of the road' which it was
proposed to recoup by petrol tax could be recouped from vehicle licence
duties. (Petrol tax, if it were worth bothering about, would then be
restricted to charging for maintenance costs due to wear.) This would
mean that once every vehicle-owner had paid a lump sum annually or
quarterly, he would thereafter use the roads at a lower price since petrol

taxation would be lower. A lower price for petrol would encourage greater use of the roads. Over the span of a year this has much to recommend it. These particular costs of the highway system — costs per road section — do not go up much if the volume of traffic increases (at least within the course of a year), and if the costs should go up from year to year in relation to the number of vehicles the duty required could be raised annually. (The only effect of replacing petrol taxation by lump-sum duties as far as congested roads are concerned, would be that, whatever method is adopted, the charge made to achieve a certain level of decongestion must be that much higher because the cost of petrol is that much lower, but that is a detail. We have as well thousands of miles of underutilised roads and it would do no harm to encourage more use of these.) The principal disadvantage is that the duty would be high enough to discourage many motorists from owning cars altogether. Because they use their cars infrequently they would pay out more in lump-sum taxation than they do in petrol tax levied on the gallon.[10] It is impossible to predict *a priori* whether the net effect would be an increase in mileage travelled by vehicles or a decrease, but the main point would seem to be that this method of charging would be unfair to these marginal users. When the electricity authority connects a new customer to its system, certain capital costs of installation are incurred which would be avoided if the connection was not made. Therefore there is a case for levying a fixed charge to cover these costs, and charge for current according to the amount consumed rather than recover capital and current costs in a standard rate per unit of electricity consumed. The capital costs are the same irrespective of the amount of electricity consumed. The analogy does not hold for the road system. The fact that a new car is registered in itself does not increase the costs of the road system, neither is it the important factor which determines (or should determine) the level of investment in the road system. This is total vehicle mileage. Other things being equal, a private motorist who intends to use his car only for Sunday motoring does not put up the costs as much as a firm which buys a car for a commercial traveller, which is why it makes better sense to recoup this cost on a mileage basis — through petrol taxation — than through vehicle licence and registration duties. A better system than either from this point of view would be to levy a lump-sum tax in proportion to the number of miles travelled by a vehicle, but that in general would be impossible to operate.

The question then arises what there is to be said for lump-sum taxation. As a general rule one would have thought nothing whatever. There are no annual costs of the system attributable to the registration of a vehicle irrespective of the mileage travelled by it: except the cost of collecting the tax itself. Since the registration of cars is necessary for police and other purposes the cost of the licence should be limited to the administrative cost of providing it.[11]

This is not quite all there is to be said because licence duties could be used to charge certain road-users more heavily because of the greater costs they inflict on the system. The most obvious candidates are the heavy vehicles who do not pay enough for the wear they cause. This is the basis of the tax system in Paraguay where the duty payable is sharply progressive with the size (and also with the age) of the car.[12] This kind of tax can make fine distinctions between the amounts payable for different sizes and weights of vehicle, but it has two disadvantages: it cannot distinguish between heavy vehicles using roads for which they are too heavy and on which they inflict exceptionally heavy maintenance costs and those using roads more suited to them; it suffers from the general disadvantage of this type of duty already mentioned. It discourages some would-be owners from buying a vehicle at all. However this will not matter as much as it would for private cars. One does not expect many people to buy a bus or a large truck for occasional use. Therefore despite its disadvantages this may be the most practicable way of charging heavier vehicles this cost.

On the other hand the disadvantages of using differential vehicle licence duties to charge for congestion costs are overwhelming. A simple device would be to charge vehicles registered in cities a higher duty, and the principle could be extended so that if there were a significant difference in average costs per road section in Wales and Lincolnshire this also could be approximated by differences in duty. The inequity of a system like this is that congested (or otherwise dear) sections of road are not only used by vehicles registered in such areas. Indeed it would pay commercial firms to register their vehicles in a low-duty area if they want to use them in high-duty areas. Similarly, a commuter from the Home Counties would presumably register his car at his home address though he might often use his car in the City. It is impossible that such a system should work acceptably.

So we are left with the proposition that vehicle licences and registration duties should be used, if at all, to make heavy vehicles pay for the extra costs they impose on the road system. (If it is policy to charge joint costs on an incremental or long-run average costs basis the duty could also be used to recoup some of the additional capital costs of the system incurred for heavier and larger vehicles: for example higher bridges, stronger roads, etc.) This would mean that the duty on private cars would be zero and the duty on larger vehicles would be progressively larger with size.

Purchase Tax

As a means of charging for the use of roads, at least, purchase tax is indefensible. There are no capital costs of the system which can be attributed to the mere existence of a vehicle. If one were to use it as the centrepiece of charging policy (and it must be remembered that in 1960 £180m. was collected in purchase tax compared with £355m. from petrol taxation), this would mean that in this respect vehicle-owners would pay the same amount of tax irrespective of the use they made of the vehicle *and of its life.* If one could say that less use of a vehicle means a proportionately longer life, purchase tax might be an improvement on licence duties in this respect, but the relation is imperfect. Vehicles deteriorate with age to some extent however little they are used. The fact that the tax is paid in the first year of a vehicle's life also raises a problem if the costs of the road system should increase or decline thereafter in relation to the number of vehicles using it, while it is possible to increase or reduce the annual licence duty so as to make all vehicles pay more or less as needs be. On all these counts it would seem inadvisable and unjust to make vehicle-owners pay a large share or indeed any share of their contribution to the costs of the road system when they purchase a car.

But of course purchase tax cannot be intended as a way of making motorists contribute to the costs of the road system, otherwise why do commercial vehicles pay no purchase tax at all? Rather it is a way of making motorists contribute a special amount to general taxation, but it would seem that this is not even the best way of achieving that end. If it should be public policy to levy what is in effect a luxury tax on motoring one would expect that this should be in relation to mileage travelled — that is that it should be an addition to the fuel tax and not a tax which falls irrespective of how much a man motors. Furthermore levying a purchase tax encourages motorists to keep a vehicle on the road longer than they otherwise would which is not obviously desirable. Therefore better vehicle licence duties than purchase tax for this purpose since they at least do not have as great an effect in prolonging the life of a vehicle; but better still the fuel tax.

The strongest case for the retention of purchase tax is as a short-term measure to restrict the entry of new vehicles on to the roads until there are the roads for them, but if we should find a way to levy a congestion tax, *and* if we should adopt a way of charging for especially costly roads, this would be a better solution of this problem too since purchase tax has the effect of keeping new vehicles off underutilised as well as congested roads.

Tyre Tax

The last important alternative to petrol tax as centrepiece would be

242

a tyre tax.[13] It has much to recommend it but its advantages over fuel taxation are probably outweighed by its disadvantages. The principal advantages are (1) that tyre-wear is a much closer measure than fuel consumption of the wear inflicted on the road by a vehicle. The convenient fact is that wear on the road is proportionate to the wear on the tyre that hits it. Tyre-wear increases with gradient more than fuel consumption does and is there a better indicator of the wear caused. Making allowance for the number and characteristics of the tyres used, tyre-wear is a better indicator of the wear caused by heavier vehicles also. If it were not for the disadvantages to be mentioned later there would be no question that a tyre tax should replace fuel tax as the centrepiece of the system since it would avoid the need for reinforcing petrol taxes with licence duties or some other tax to get the true measure of this cost. (2) Tyre-wear is also a better indicator of congestion costs. Tyre-wear increases more than fuel consumption on congested streets. The average rate of wear of tyres used regularly on city streets was found as long ago as 1945 to be three or four times the rate at 45m.p.h. in the country (and tyre-wear increases with speed as indeed do maintenance costs rise with the speed of the vehicles using the road). Therefore a tax on tyres would be more effective in reducing congestion than a similar tax on fuel. Since tyre-wear is proportional to wear of the roads the same rate of tax as would reflect maintenance costs attributable to a vehicle could not be high enough to reduce congestion also. Therefore the same difficulty arises as with fuel tax. It could not be used for either the first or second purposes suggested for petrol tax. It could however be used for the third purpose.

The principal disadvantages of the system are administrative and technical.

(1) Research would be needed to find out the correct purchase tax on tyres for every type and make of tyre.

(2) Since there is some variation in the wear got from tyres of the same type and make,[14] it would be fairer if manufacturers could standardise the quality of tyres more than it is profitable for them to do at the moment (as oil companies have standardised the different qualities of petrol). Presumably this could be done but one would want to know at what cost.

(3) It would put a premium on certain forms of 'good' driving, for example, not skidding round corners, not decelerating sharply, etc. (and it would also penalise lazy drivers who do not check tyre pressures frequently, or wheel alignment, and do not change their tyres round etc.).

(4) It would make the valuation of tyres important when a car is sold second-hand.

(5) It might present financial difficulties to some car owners who

found they had to pay a large sum down for tyres instead of a sum, more or less, spread over the years in fuel tax. However it should be possible to buy tyres on hire purchase or even to rent them if this should be a real difficulty.

(6) There is the difficulty that a small proportion of tyre failures are due to glass, and other objects placed on the road. Since these are not the fault of the road authority or the road-user, it is not easy to see how anyone other than the motorist can pay for this mishap. The only sensible way of getting round this difficulty would be if motorists were to insure against tyre failure. As there is considerable information on the causes of tyre failure, this might not be an impossible or even difficult actuarial problem for the insurance companies.

(7) It would encourage the use of tyres which are dangerously worn.

There are countries which tax tyres at a flat rate. If we were to accept that a tyre tax would not work for all vehicles yet it might be possible to levy taxes on the tyres used by large vehicles as an alternative to vehicle licences or other taxes to charge them for maintenance costs. Since the tax paid would be proportionate to use, this would have the slight advantage over vehicle licence duties of not putting the occasional user of a large vehicle at a disadvantage.

The Weight-ton Tax

This is a method of taxing heavy vehicles used in certain American states and West Germany. A daily log, of mileage at least, must be kept which is inspected periodically and the tax due assessed. A more complicated log-book records mileage and tonnage carried on all trips so that the tax-rate can be varied according to the weight of the vehicle and its load. The obvious objection to this kind of tax is the possibility of evasion. The most interesting point about this tax is that it has been tried.[15]

By one or other of these means it should be possible to charge the heavy vehicle. A much more difficult problem is to charge for the exceptionally costly road. A road will ordinarily be in this category (under consumers' surplus maximisation policy), because its capital costs are high, occasionally because police costs are high or there are high maintenance costs not due to wear, for example, flood damage. The other reason for wishing to charge exceptionally more for certain sections of road is of course congestion if, once again, it is decided to charge to reduce congestion. A congested road is frequently a high-cost road on other grounds.

The chief methods worth considering are tolls, windscreen stickers and meters.

Tolls

These have an immediate appeal. The road-user pays for the road as he uses it; they have an immediately commercial look. American experience suggests the best way to get more roads built is to authorise turnpikes. When the total amount of money to be spent on roads is fixed arbitrarily as some proportion of the Government budget then it might be possible to get roads built as self-financing tollways which it would not be possible to get past the Treasury in any other way. But this argument for tollways should disappear if we have a national road authority able to borrow for profitable projects (by either of our two criteria. However is it a profitable method of charging for the use of the roads? Almost certainly it is not — especially if our policy is consumers' surplus maximisation but also even if it is profit maximisation. There are access points on the London-Birmingham motorway on average every seven miles. This is the frequency one would expect on British toll roads and increases administrative costs markedly. If we assume that every access point is to be manned day and night on a three-shift system; that booths and an approach area must be provided; that such entries will need more than one exit and one entry booth to deal with the press of traffic, the administrative costs will be high. One conservative assessment has been that they might be 25 per cent of the *profit maximising* toll revenue obtainable from traffic. And this ignores the loss to traffic — the increase in vehicle operating and time costs — because of the delays caused by toll gates, which should influence the calculations of a consumers' surplus maximising authority and would affect a profit maximising one to some extent since delays would discourage some proportion of the traffic from using the motorway.

In all cases it is worth considering whether there is not a cheaper means of obtaining the same end. (It should also be remembered that at present rates of petrol tax, motorists on rural motorways probably do in fact pay enough in petrol tax to meet the costs per secion of motorway. But this is because the rate of petrol tax generally is too high and because rural motorways will not in general occasion as high costs as will urban roads.)

The most powerful argument against tolls on uncongested motorways is that they will cause inefficient under-utilisation so losing consumers' surplus. Tolls may be a way of securing more efficient use of congested motorways but the costs of operation are still higher. Therefore urban tollways are rarely efficient even under conjested conditions. Although the revenue per vehicle should be very much higher because costs are higher, nevertheless we would expect that (1) there would be many more access points, say, one every one or two miles and (2) we would expect that such roads would be much more congested in rush-hours than rural motorways ever are. Therefore it would be necessary *either* to provide more booths to cope with the rush-hours, which would be dear because of land costs, if for no other reasorn; *or* enough booths would not be provided and vehicle operations and time costs would go up because of congestion around the access points.

There may be more of a case for tolls on certain bridges and tunnels where costs are very high and administration comparatively easy. The facts would have to be established in every particular case.

Windscreen Stickers

An alternative to tolls in towns is to levy a special tax on vehicles using city roads. To surround a city by a circle of tollhouses would be impracticable. It would tempt motorists to infiltrate by back roads unless there were a tollhouse on every road, which would be prohibitive. A further disadvantage is that it can only be used on urban motorways, whereas all or virtually all urban streets are expensive from the point of view of the road system and some higher charge is generally desirable for the use of them. Differential vehicle licences based on residence have already been ruled out as impracticable. Another possibility is special licences or 'windscreen stickers' — in effect licences to use urban streets. This device has been suggested by Mr. A. A. Walters.[16] No vehicle is permitted to operate in certain urban areas unless it is showing such a sticker on its windscreen beside its ordinary vehicle licence. The charge for the sticker will vary according to the size of the vehicle and possibly for other reasons: an omnibus or delivery van might be required to pay a higher rate of tax than mere size would indicate because of the effect on other traffic of their frequent stopping; but that would be a refinement of the system. Vehicle-owners who expected to use such streets frequently would buy an annual licence. In certain circumstances it might be possible to buy licences (marked perhaps by a particular colour) which gave permission to use these streets on one given day a week, for example, Fridays only. (If it were not given it would be much more difficult to enforce.) Occasional users would buy a temporary day licence or 'ticket' at some official selling agency before they reach the urban area. It might be practicable to charge a lower rate or no rate at all for those who used the roads during certain hours of the evening and night. Towns which were reckoned to be of sufficient size to warrant such special duties would be treated in this way.

This system has so much to recommend it — administrative simplicity and cheapness — that it may well be the best solution to the problem of charging for expensive urban roads. However it is not without disadvantages.

(1) Although different cities can charge different prices for their stickers, it would be difficult to charge more than one price in one city. Birmingham could be cheaper than London; but not Shepherds Bush or Lambeth than the City of London, whereas the costs may differ enormously between different parts of the same town. This would mean that a sticker system would be hard on someone whose mileage was mostly in the less costly streets around the fringes of the area, and relatively less so on habitual users of the most central streets.

(2) It would be hard on vehicles with a small proportion of their mileage in 'congested areas'; e.g. between Southampton Row and Lambeth.

(3) It would be hard also on vehicles which habitually used roads in several such special areas unless there was some interchange system so that vehicles which had paid their special licence fee for Birmingham could enter London on the same sticker. Either this would make it difficult to have different fees for different areas — since an habitual user of London could get away with buying a cheaper Birmingham sticker and indeed it would pay London users always to buy Birmingham stickers — or it would be necessary to have a complicated system of licences covering two or more such special areas. If a London sticker cost £15 per annum for a private car and a Birmingham sticker only £6 then a combined sticker might be £18 or £20. But this would still, on a mileage basis, be hard on vehicles which habitually travelled through several such areas, doing a few miles in each. Despite these disadvantages it probably remains the best immediate solution of this charging problem.

Parking Charges

These also could be used for this purpose. A surcharge would be added to parking-meter charges to cover these special costs. The surcharge could be graded between parking meters around the perimeter of the central area and parking meters in the expensive centre. It has the disadvantage that vehicles parking anywhere else except at a parking meter or possibly a public car park would escape payment unless all private car parks and even individual private garages were taxed in such areas, a policy which would pose formidable problems. And through traffic would escape payment altogether. Its volume would rise as the streets became less congested. Therefore parking charges have to be far higher to achieve optimal road use than does a meter which charges moving cars directly.

The Taxi Meter

This is another of Mr. A. A. Walter's ideas.[17] A vehicle travelling in a special area is required to have a mileometer fitted. The mileometer will be a simpler version of those used by taxis. When it is in the 'special' area the meter flag must be put up so that the meter will be, and will be seen to be, set working. The meter would be read periodically and a bill sent to the owner. A vehicle in a special area with flag down would be fined. If the meter had its own power supply or motor it could be used for parking charges also. A parked car would also have to put up its flag in certain areas, not necessarily in 'special' areas only. Vehicles making occasional visits to towns which did not want to go to the expense of installing meters would buy a day ticket as under the windscreen sticker scheme.

An advantage of the meter is that it could be used outside the main congested areas. If all vehicles were equipped with meters, very small towns and villages with these expensive streets could put up notices requiring vehicles to use meters. Roads liable to exceptional damage because of floods, and steep hills in a dear group because of earthworks, grading, etc. might also be meter-roads. On some roads where heavy vehicles imposed exceptional costs on the road because of its construction and their weight, only vehicles over a given weight might be required to use their meters. Meters could also be used instead of tolls on motorways and bridges, and would do away with the need for toll booths, extra land and extra staff for toll collection.

Walters, in consultation with a commercial firm, has estimated that such a meter could be sold for £4–£6 apiece, if mass-produced. At this order of costs it would be more profitable for the road authority to provide a free meter for every vehicle than to operate 1,200 miles of toll roads (equivalent to eighteen London-Birmingham, or more strictly Watford-Dunchurch, motorways). But if the cost of a meter were £4–£6 or even twice as much, the cost could easily and should be borne directly by the vehicle-owner as indeed the costs of a toll system are indirectly borne by him in the toll he pays. (The advantage of metering would be that the Government would incur no capital costs, a considerable advantage under the present system.)

Automatic Metering

Recently some experiments have been made at the Crowthorne experimental track of the Road Research Laboratory into the use of guidance cables and detector loops.[18] Guidance cables are cables buried along a road. Simple electronic equipment in the vehicle enables the driver to pick up signals from this equipment which can guide him in fog, and warn him of the proximity of other vehicles. More complicated electronic equipment, like 'George' on aeroplanes, allows

248

automatic driving — the driver not steering, changing gear nor regulating the speed of the vehicle. Looking into the future one can imagine a driver driving his vehicle on to a motorway, switching on this apparatus, and then sitting back to read his newspaper until the time comes for him to resume control at the other end. Other uses of the equipment would be to give talking 'road-sign' messages to drivers, issue reports on weather conditions and congestion, advise on the selection of roads and also of course, link up with the national telephone system. Detector loops are loops of cable laid across the roadway at intervals which have similar uses.

It is unlikely that it would pay to install cables and electronic equipment for these purposes alone for many years. But there is another use to which the equipment could be put which might pay sooner and therefore, though this is not an essential part of the scheme, make the other uses of guidance cables more practicable. It could be used as an alternative to the methods already mentioned for surcharging expensive roads.[19]

Of the several systems which could be used, two are most plausible: First, every vehicle would have a sealed meter. All roads on which a surcharge is to be levied would have cables laid along their length some inches under the surface. Any vehicle using such a cabled road would have its meter activated by impulses from the cable. The meter would be activated at different speeds depending on the frequency of the impulses emitted from the cable. It would be possible to activate the meters of vehicles of different sizes at different rates. To prevent evasion there would have to be severe penalties for breaking the seal of a meter. The meter might be a conspicuous box attached to one of the number plates of the vehicle — with some indication, such as a light from a longlife bulb, that it was working. It would then be possible for police to check if it had been tampered with. The road authority could appoint meter-readers whose job it was to read the meter, which would present certain obvious difficulties; or vehicles could be required to call at a meter-reading station at least once a quarter; or the meter might be detached from the vehicle by the owner and presented when he renews his licence, payment of the bill being a prerequisite of being allowed to take out a licence.

The second method would be to run the road system roughly on the analogy of a telephone exchange. When a vehicle comes on to a cabled road, an automatic electronic device on the vehicle identifies it. This means that some central recording equipment records the time or distance the vehicle spends in a cabled area with equipment not dissimilar from that used to record trunk calls. The road authority then sends in a quarterly bill to the owner of each vehicle. (A tollway in the United States already identifies buses by this method.)

Either of these systems or modifications of the basic principle of either could have considerable advantages. Principally it would make possible great flexibility in charges. If it were profitable to lay cables on the entire road system there would be no special problem of charging for the use of roads at all. But even if its profitable use is confined, say, to the 10,000 miles (out of a total of approximately 190,000 miles) — comprising all motorways and trunk roads and urban roads Class I — it would be possible to achieve considerable flexibility and to reflect costs per section much more accurately than by any other method. It would also be easier to achieve flexibility in other directions. If desired it would be comparatively simple to put rates up during hours of peak traffic flow and down during the evening or night — or at week-ends: whereas the next most flexible system (the manual meter system) is almost certainly confined to a maximum perhaps of two rates (two flags per meter) and zero. It would also reduce the difficulty of enforcement. A cable could be laid on a lonely hill or bridge which was expensive to the road system and there would be no need to police the hill to see that dishonest drivers did put their flags up.

Again the fundamental question is cost. Until recently it seemed this might be considerable but recent investigation by the Road Research Laboratory and Ministry of Transport (reported on in *The Report of the Panel on Road Pricing* suggests that an acceptable system of metering could be installed and operated at a very modest cost. Many commercial firms have prepared preliminary plans of such a system which are ingenious and diverse. The cost of a single loop of cable plus roadside switching mechanism might be, in some systems, as little as £100 or possibly less. A satisfactory system might require as few as one thousand loops of cable for, say, the London area and yet provide an equitable basis for charging which would make evasion negligible. Estimates suggest that the cost of a meter should be less than £10. Would every vehicle have to have a meter? Not if it did not use metered roads. If it was an occasional user it might be possible for it to hire a meter. Would foreign-owner vehicles have to have a meter? Such owners could hire meters as they disembarked; but it might be decided to let bona fide foreign vehicles off.

All that remains in this section is to consider as briefly as possible methods of charging for other uses of the road system.

Parking Meters
These are the obvious means of charging for parking space unless the administrative costs are too great to recoup the average cost charge applicable on a given site, when it would not pay to charge at all.

Purchase Tax on Vehicle Light Bulbs

This would be a method of charging for that part of street lighting costs attributable to vehicles, but the tax might be too expensive to administer.

Traffic Fines

This might be a good way of recouping that proportion of police costs attributable to traffic offences as distinct from traffic control. This proportion of police costs would be recouped annually from fines. It might however be decided on other grounds to levy heavier fines than would recoup this amount but never lower.

Bicycle Tyre Tax

The only obvious way of recouping any road costs attributable to cyclists would be by a purchase tax on cycle tyres since their wear is proportionate to use. Though rough justice yet possibly the best that could be done.

Rates

A difficulty to be faced is how to charge pedestrians for their share of the costs of the road system. It is difficult to see what alternative there is to rates.* They are not equitable. A bed-ridden ratepayer will pay a comparatively large contribution to the road system in this way while at the other extreme a tramp will not. The road authority would have to decide what proportion of costs is directly attributable to pedestrians and what proportion of joint costs are to be recovered from them — on the incremental or some other agreed principle. The bill would be sent to the appropriate local authority.

The only other case for bearing the cost of a road on the rates would, I think, be if a road was built for access to new houses and it was predicted that vehicles using the road would not pay enough in fuel tax, while on it, to pay for it. Then the difference might be made up by increasing the rates on the houses to be served by the road. The same effect can be achieved however by requiring any firm building a house off a main road to build an access road, the cost to be recouped from the purchaser when the house or houses are sold.

Ratepayers should meet no other costs of the road system. It is often suggested that they should but the reasoning seems to be fallacious for reasons already touched on in discussing the present system of making central Government grants for roads. For example, if the effect of better roads to the centre of a city is to bring more shoppers in, it is often said that this is a benefit in part to shopkeepers and in part should be born on their rates. But this is unnecessary. Suppose the improvements are costly and a special tax is paid by

* Except, perhaps, a tax on shoe-leather.

251

motorists using the improved highways, levied by means of
the windscreen sticker or similar techniques. This puts up the
cost of shopping in the city centre. If the shops were to meet
the costs by paying more rates, the cost of shopping might remain
the same as before the improvement or might even be reduced;
but if it is profitable for shopkeepers to pay more rates to attract
custom, they could achieve the same effect by lowering prices.
(If they only wanted to lower prices to shoppers in cars, they
could achieve this in effect by providing free or cheap parking.)
And this principle holds, I believe, for all proposals that
ratepayers should contribute as *ratepayers* to the cost of the road
system. It is the same point made on p.204: 'the simple fact is
that benefits alleged to follow from road as a means to those
benefits.' Then if it is possible to make the traffic pay – motorists,
pedestrians and any other road-user – there is no need to make
anyone else pay. To make all road-users pay the cost *and* to put
a burden of the kind on the rates would be to get some payment
made twice over.

METHODS OF CHARGING: PROFIT MAXIMISATION

One would expect a profit maximising road authority to use
more or less the same methods as a consumers' surplus atuhority,
the difference being in the total revenue gained by the
methods used and in the level at which the various charges are
set. Because a 'commercial' road authority would aim to earn
more revenue, it might be profitable to employ methods which
would be unprofitable for a consumers' surplus authority; for
example, 'meter-ways'. One would expect a single basic rate of
fuel tax set at a height expected to maximise revenue. It would
pay a profit maximising authority to set different rates of tax
in different places or for different kinds of vehicles. But there
are bizarre possibilities of a profit-maximising authority reducing
road quality to increase its profits. It could pay to make road
surfaces rough, where there were not alternative means of
transport, since a rough surface increases fuel consumption
and therefore tax receipts. A consumers' surplus authority would
not lower the quality of its roads to this end since it would
take into account the reduction in surplus caused by it,
but unless a profit maximising one were prohibited from
lowering quality in this way, there would be roads on which
this would pay it, or profit maximisation acting *under no constraints,*
could set charges as a result of separate bargaining with every
vehicle-owner to determine how much he would pay rather

than forgo the right to use the road at all. In Chapter 12 we will consider restriction on the methods which may be used to charge for road services as a curb on a profit maximising road system's monopoly. Given such restraints — for some restraints are, one would have thought, not only desirable but a political necessity — the actual working out of the methods to be used and the level of charges to be set would present no special problems, and many of the observations made in the last section on the characteristics of the various charging methods in the context of consumers' surplus maximisation charging would be relevant.

RATIONING THE USE OF THE ROAD SYSTEM

Some observations were made in Chapter 4 (pp. 91-2) on the policy implied by the basic criteria when all or part of the railway system was running at a loss. This involved a distinction between escapable and inescapable costs. If any part of the road system were unable to cover all its costs, the same distinction would be relevant, but the characteristic condition of the road system is of course the reverse one: more traffic than the roads can easily bear. When this affects one kind of road-user only, this is called congestion. And as we have already argued this is no problem for a profit maximising road authority. A congested road from its point of view is one with more traffic on it than will maximise the authority's profits. It therefore raises the charge it makes. If there should be a demand — at profit maximising prices — for new and improved road facilities, the authority will invest if it is profitable. Since a consumers' surplus authority is committed to covering the actual costs or expenses by the charges it makes, its charges will be lower and the density of traffic greater. It then has to be decided whether it is going to give the opportunity to some road-users to pay a price which will reduce density by eliminating or diverting other road-users.

A somewhat different problem arises when two kinds of road-users want use of the same facility and both cannot have it. This again is no problem for the profit maximiser. If parked cars can pay more for a strip of road than cars in movement will, parkers get it. Given a charging system all problems of this type are capable of solution, not necessarily by research into the facts of the conflict of interests but by the judgement of the authorities concerned. The problem arises for a consumers' surplus authority which cannot use prices to decide. The method logically implied by the criterion is that the facility should go to the interest which stands to gain most — measured by consumers' surplus. The calculations needed are similar to those required to decide between investment opportunities. This kind of conflict is very important in practice and leads to constant controversy so it is worth discussing an example.

Should Oxford Street have been made a one-way street? On the benefit side, there are the savings in vehicle operating and time costs to those in vehicles benefiting from the change. On the debit side are the increases in these costs accruing to other vehicles because these have to go further because of the restriction; and these include the losses to people in vehicles because their shopping is made more difficult by the restriction. Other relevant costs would be the differences made to pedestrians — saving and waste of time principally — by the restriction. A survey could be made on the lines outlined for investment in Chapter 6, and to be amplified in the next chapter, to determine the probability that the result of the restriction would be an increase in consumers' surplus. A private firm makes similar calculations when it decides how to use one of its fixed assets — if the asset is important enough — and if it is not important enough it decides from experience. Even a small number of market researchers working on this problem should be able to produce better decisions than those made on the basis of less information at present. At present however many who argue over these questions are not sure how such a conflict should be decided; but when a criterion has been adopted, the principle follows logically from the criterion. The same procedure — the estimation of gains and losses in consumers' surplus involved — is relevant to all such decisions: one-way streets, prohibition of right-hand turns, the establishment of clearways, prohibition of parking, waiting, loading and unloading, restrictions on size of vehicles, overtaking, the desirability for pedestrian crossings and the timing of traffic lights.

Even if it should not prove profitable to invest in such research to establish the facts in many cases, this should be the principle in mind when the decision is made; and, as a matter of fact, the Ministry and local authorities usually decide with some notion of the general good to guide them — that the gainers should gain more than the losers should lose by a change. The objectionable restrictions are those made in the interests of a minority who gain by it but less than the rest of the community loses: and it is about these that a fuss should be made.

SUMMARY

The principle discussion in this chapter has been of the organisation of costs into various categories of joint and attributable costs, which is relevant to charging for roads; and of the advantages and disadvantages of the different methods of charging for the use of the roads.

It has also been argued that both criteria provide a principle for deciding who should win, when there is a conflict of interests over the use of the road system: for example, whether there should be a one-way street, a pedestrian crossing, etc.

POSTSCRIPT

Further discussions of the theory and magnitude of costs are to be found in Allais, *Road Track Costs,* Meyer and Straszheim, and Walters.[1] There has been extensive research on methods of congestion pricing.[2] While the more elaborate methods of automatic metering have been shown to be technically feasible, the administrative difficulties are still formidable enough to delay their introduction. Because a high proportion of vehicles using any urban areas are infrequent visitors, these methods of road pricing cannot easily be introduced in a small area and then be extended gradually if they prove their worth and are acceptable. There are great problems of allowing for occasional visitors to an area. Even in London while only 5 per cent of vehicles on any day visit London less than once a month, over a whole year some 70 per cent of vehicles fall into that class. Hence there has been more concentration on the economically less efficient but more feasible methods of special vehicle licences and parking charges to reduce congestion.

The development of the argument in this chapter was governed by the two criteria which provided the framework of the book. Any charging principle which starts from the argument that the user should pay for the roads will begin with some estimation of the total costs incurred for the user; and then will attempt to break down the attributable costs by class of user. Most research and analysis has had this ambition. It underlies the Allais report and the EEC transport policies which have been derived from it. Most of the argument in *Road Track Costs* was based on it. As Walters has said and Munby has demonstrated, any notion that users should pay their long-run marginal costs does not have any unambiguous implication for charging policy.[3] Notions of 'equity' have to be brought in to justify long-run marginal cost pricing (itself not unambiguous), or charging according to the benefit received or 'incremental' cost. What was attempted in this book was to derive the implications for road charging of two principles which did not need to appeal in the same way to principles of equity, and which could logically connect charging and investment policy. Provided the form of the constraint were determined, constrained profit maximisation could be a basis for reassessing highway decisions in order to improve their efficiency. So could consumers' surplus maximisation. On highways the main difference between the two was in the treatment of congestion. As Knight had shown many

255

years ago, a profit-maximising road authority under conditions of perfect competition would charge a price to secure an efficient level of congestion.[4] Where it had monopoly power it would reduce the volume of traffic further.

The rationale of congestion pricing is that though road-users are worse off, society is better off. Further analysis might tell us more about who gains from congestion pricing and how. We know that reducing the numbers of cars on an urban road should improve bus speeds and bring net benefits to bus users (even though their bus also pays a congestion charge). Faster journey times on city streets will benefit those who place a high valuation on such times. As was argued in the last chapter, certain land-owners will benefit because their site-values will rise. The substitution effects of introducing congestion pricing will be widespread. So will the benefits. The great disadvantage, which on reflection seems to me overwhelming, of a consumers' surplus charging policy for roads is that it would not deal with the most pernicious problem of the roads: congestion. The social costs of congestion affect a wider universe than people strictly defined in their role as road-user. Because of the importance of these social costs, it would seem too inefficient to run the roads system in the consumers' interest narrowly defined.

Thus it would seem one has a choice: tolerate the inefficiency of average cost pricing, or tolerate the possibility that the highway system makes a profit. If this were so, it would mean that highways are on average produced under conditions of increasing cost.[5] Roads are such heterogeneous commodities that it is difficult to generalise. Because costs are highly dependent on topography and population density, the cost of road improvement also varies immensely. However, as a generalisation, there are likely to be economies of scale in the use of rural roads, especially in undeveloped countries, because a road can hardly be less than a given width and strength if any traffic are to use it at all. On most inter-urban and suburban roads constant returns to scale are probably more likely to obtain on average. In cities where the scarce factor land will be a high proportion of improvement costs, increasing costs will obtain. A highway authority able to differentiate its charging policy from one road to another would be making profits and losses on different roads. In general the higher the proportion of urban roads the greater the profit it would be likely to make from short-run marginal cost pricing. As both Mohring and Walters have shown, if on average there were constant returns and an efficient investment policy, on average no profits would be made.[6] It is in cities that there is likely to be the greatest congestion, even with an optimal investment policy and where efficient pricing would mean 'profits'. If a belief in not making 'profits' were to mean not charging for congestion where long-run costs were increasing, one would expect there would be more investment in road improvement than if short-run marginal cost pricing were adopted, as part of a process of sub-optimation.

The principles referred to in the original text for the assessment of highway maintenance due to wear have been adapted and refined in the United Kingdom by the Transport and Road Research Laboratory.

11 THE CONSUMERS' SURPLUS CRITERION FOR INVESTMENT IN ROADS

Through the course of this book a leading theme has been the development of the notion of the consumers' surplus criterion so as to raise it to a position of equality to the more familiar profit maximisation. Both are useful. Both are about as easy or difficult to use. In Chapter 2 it was suggested that there is already a tradition that nationalised industries should be run in the consumers' interest; that there is strong support for this tradition; and that it was certainly a policy to which attention should be given when formulating transport policy; but that there was a difficulty in defining consumers' interest. The notion of a consumers' surplus criterion for pricing and investment was developed theoretically in Chapter 6. Some alternative forms of the criterion were considered and one selected principally because it seemed to represent what was demanded by public opinion. The criterion implied average cost pricing and a consumers' surplus rate of return to decide investment. Some problems − theoretical and practical − of using the latter to determine railway investment were considered. The argument was hypothetical. No railway has, I think, used the criterion, but it has been used for more than twenty years by highway engineers. In this chapter we will therefore be investigating the criterion further where it has actually been used, and this should better enable us to understand the problems which have been overcome and those which remain. The argument will also be relevant to railway investment, for what can be done on the roads can be done on the railways also. The methods, the procedure and the problems would be virtually the same. I shall have something more to say on this later in this chapter.

Investment in roads to maximise profits, subject to those restraints on the activities of a profit-making road authority which we have to suppose any Government would impose and which will be discussed in the next chapter, presents no new problems. A profit-making authority, if rigorous and efficient, would do as much research into costs and demand analysis as a consumers' surplus authority, and of much the same kind. When it has adequate data it ought to invest as much as and wherever seems profitable, unless limited by Government policy. Then it ought to invest that limited budget in the most profitable manner.[1] Its investment problem is then essentially that of any commercial enterprise and will not occupy us further.

There is a long history to the idea that a consumers' surplus criterion should be used to decide investment in roads and roadworks. It was first put forward in a classic paper by a French engineer, Dupuit, in 1844. Noticed by Alfred Marshall, it was familar to readers of his *Principles of Economics* as an interesting point in economic theory. Towards the end of the 1930s some economists revived interest in it. The interest was mostly theoretical though they believed the criterion ought to be practicable for investment.[2] About the same time a group of engineers in the highway department of the State of Oregon had the idea, it would seem independently, of using a consumers' surplus rate of return to rationalise the State's road programme. They worked out the detail in two studies which have been the foundation of everything that has been done in this field since.[3] Many highway authorities have imitated and improved on the Oregon experimental cost benefit analysis. The first major use of the method in Britain was to calculate a consumers' surplus rate of return for the London-Birmingham motorway, not to decide if the motorway should be built − that had already been decided using the Ministry of Transport's methods described in Chapter 7 − but as an exercise in planning technique, a staff exercise in preparation for actual investment planning in the future. Since then consumers' surplus rates of return have been calculated for other projects; but it will be most helpful, I believe, if we follow the course of the London-Birmingham motorway inquiry in some detail. It was ambitious, an excellent example of its kind, and is well documented.[4] The point of describing how the team from the Road Research Laboratory and the University of Birmingham did its task is that (1) we should get some feeling of the operation required; (2) be able to relate the criterion as it has been used in practice with the criterion that has been formulated theoretically; and (3) to provide a basis for discussing improvements. We will first describe the method used in the London-Birmingham inquiry without criticism or hindsight. Any road engineer or anyone who knows about the London-Birmingham study will find nothing to interest him in the next section. It is only for those unfamiliar with this kind of exercise.

THE LONDON-BIRMINGHAM MOTORWAY

The inquiry began in 1955. It lasted several years and the report was not published until 1960, a few months after the motorway was opened to traffic. It could have taken only a few months if enough men had been available to complete it quickly; and, perhaps, if it had not been the first on this scale in Britain. It cost £20,000, less than a tenth of 1 per cent of the estimated capital cost of the motorway.

By 1955 the Ministry of Transport's engineers had surveyed and settled the line to be followed by the motorway and had planned and designed it, having decided already the number of lanes and access points. There were some modifications later, but these hardly affected the result of the inquiry. The first job of the inquiry was to guess the roads from which traffic would be attracted to the motorway when it was built. It was predicted it would pay some traffic to answer from as far west as the A423/A34 (see fig.11.1) and as far east as A1. To see if traffic benefit would benefit what proportion of traffic would benefit.

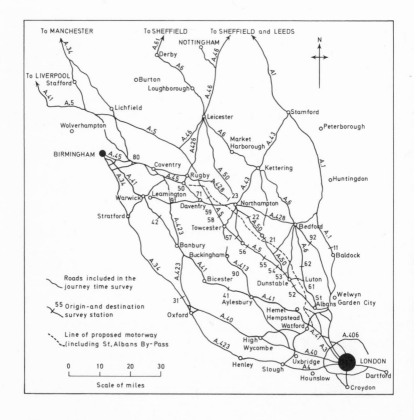

FIG. 11.1: Placing of census posts for the London-Birmingham motorway investigation[5]

and how much they would benefit, interviewing posts were set up on the main roads concerned for an origin and destination survey. These are shown in fig 11.1. The main road nearest the proposed motorway, the A5/A45, from which most traffic was expected to be attracted, had ten of these posts. At the other extreme there was only one on the A34 in Oxfordshire and on the A1 in Hertfordshire. No two posts on the same route were open on the same day so as not to irritate drivers by stopping them more than once en route. At most posts traffic travelling in one direction was interviewed during one day only – for sixteen hours from 6 a.m. to 10 p.m. Traffic travelling in the opposite direction was interviewed at the same post for the same length of time on one other day. Two days, however, were given to each direction at the A34 and A1 posts, to improve the reliability of the survey. There were also interviews lasting one night on the A1 and at one post on the A5 because of the high proportion of traffic travelling these roads at night. Just under 41,000 vehicles were interviewed. The Road Research Laboratory was confident that it could predict with reasonable accuracy the annual traffic flow of each class of vehicle past each interviewing post, using data from (1) the survey, (2) a special traffic census taken simultaneously and (3) general traffic census information (which showed seasonal fluctuations, variations at week-ends and on holidays, etc.). All the interviews were held on ordinary week-days.

As far as possible interviewing posts were established at lay-bys or some other point where it would be possible to draw traffic off the road for interview. Signs and barriers were erected, warning and directing traffic. If traffic was sparse, all vehicles were stopped and interviewed. If it was heavier, a random sample was interviewed. While the two interviewers at a post were interviewing, traffic was allowed to flow past freely. Before the interviews were finished, a policeman would step into the road, slow down oncoming traffic and make it form single file. When the interviewers had finished, a signal was given to the policeman who had orders to direct the next two vehicles, whatever they might be, into the interviewing bay. By this method, vehicles were slected for interview at random. Because the interviews lasted less than a minute, interviews reported drivers were co-operative. Only 0.2 per cent refused to answer the questionnaire. At the same time a traffic census was taken of all vehicles passing in the same direction, so that it was possible to estimate from hour to hour the proportion of the traffic flow that was being interviewed.

Two questionnaires were used. They were much the same. The first, for cars and coaches, asked the driver where he had started and where he meant to finish his journey. A more important question asked whether the last stop was 'for a purpose specially connected with the place,

261

that is, apart from stops for petrol, meals, refreshment and similar purposes' and similarly the next stop for a purpose specially connected with the place. Coach-drivers were asked where they last took up or put down passengers and where they would do this next. The second questionnaire for goods vehicles asked the same question in a slightly different form: where the driver had last taken on or unloaded a part or the whole of his load. The point of all these questions was to fix the last place before and the next place after the interviewing post which the vehicle had to pass through. The second most important set of questions was to elicit the purpose of the journey. Drivers of cars were asked: (1) if they were travelling for 'private reasons'; (2) if the expenses of the journey were paid wholly or partly by their employers or their own business; (3) if they paid their own expenses though on business; (4) if they were travelling to or from work; or (5) if they were making some kind of journey. Coach-drivers were asked (1) if they were privately hired; (2) on a regular service; or (3) being used for another purpose. It was assumed that all goods vehicles were travelling on business. Other data collected were the number of people in car, coach or truck; and the size, number of wheels and axles of goods vehicles.

Together with what was known from ordinary traffic census data about seasonal fluctuations in traffic flows on roads of various kinds, week-end fluctuations, holiday fluctuations and the ratio of night to day travel, it was possible to build up from these interviews a picture of the relevant annual traffic flows. The next stage was to determine the proportion of traffic which would be expected to benefit from using the new motorway. Estimates were needed of the time it would take the various classes of vehicle – car, coach, light, medium and heavy goods vehicle – to travel from beginning to end of their journey using existing roads. The origin and destination survey data were used to find out the journeys which might be expected to gain from transfer. Test cars of the Road Research Laboratory then drove along these routes to establish the average journey time. On most routes, there were only enough resources available to permit one run in each direction, following cars only. On A5/A45, the main London-Birmingham route before the motorway was built, four runs were made in each direction for each of the main classes of vehicle – car, light, medium and heavy goods vehicles. Data collected on A5/A45 for goods vehicles was used to estimate the average journey time for the three classes of goods vehicles on the other routes from the data there collected for private cars. Previous experience of such surveys suggested this was a reasonable procedure.

By these means it was possible to calculate the time taken on the existing road system by vehicles of the different classes expected to benefit by transferring to the motorway. What was needed next was an estimate of the time it would take them if they used the motorway; and to do this, some guess had to be made at the speeds vehicles would drive at on the motorway. At that time there were no British motorways, so that the only evidence was foreign. American evidence suggested that the average car speed on motorways is 55 m.p.h.; light goods − 40m.p.h.; medium goods − 35m.p.h.; and heavy goods− 30m.p.h. By making various adjustments to convert these figures into mean speeds on straight level sections of motorway, and also allowing for certain differences in British conditions, the set of figures shown as assignment III in the second half of Table 11.1 were reached. It was thought, wrongly as it has turned out, that a set of speeds based on American experience might be too high for Britain. The Laboratory

Table 11.1 *Mean speeds on straight, level sections of motorways; observed values in some European countries and values assumed for the London-Birmingham motorway*[6]

Country	Cars	Light goods up to 1½ tons unladen	Medium goods, 2-axled	Heavy goods, multi-axled
Belgium	52	40	38	35
France	52	43	36	35
Belgium and France combined	52	42	37	35
Germany	54	46	40	38
Netherlands	53	45	41	40
Germany and Netherlands combined	54	45	39	38
Assumed on London-Birmingham motorway:				
I	53	42	37	32
II	53	47	42	37
III	53	52	47	42

Table 11.2 *Time saved using proposed motorways, compared with existing roads*[7]

| Journey | Present route | Average saving per journey (minutes) | | | | Extra mileage per journey |
		Cars	Light goods	Medium goods	Heavy goods	
London (central) to:						
Birmingham	A5/A45	30	23	20	12	2
Birmingham	A41	44	33	30	20	1
Birmingham	A40	41	31	28	18	−5
Bedford	*	11	10	10	11	−2
Coventry	*	30	23	20	17	2
Leamington	*	31	23	20	17	1
Leeds	*	−2	−5	−6	−6	4
Leicester, etc.	A5/A50	33	28	26	25	−3
Slough to:						
Birmingham	*	4	−7	−12	−19	13
Coventry, etc.	*	14	7	4	2	5
Luton to:						
Birmingham	*	18	12	11	10	1
Coventry, etc.	*	18	13	12	10	1
Bedford to:						
Birmingham	*	9	2	−1	−6	7
Coventry, etc.	*	9	2	−1	−6	7
Northampton to:						
Birmingham	*	5	4	3	2	1
Coventry, etc.	*	5	4	3	2	1
Average for all journeys assigned to the motorway		16.2	10.8	12.1	9.7	1.7

* Quickest route

therefore looked to Europe. The found no data of the kind required recording motorway speeds — an interesting reflection on the state of road planning in Europe — and sent a team of their own. A radar speed-meter was used to measure speeds at fifteen sites on level stretches of motorway in Belgium, France, Germany and the Netherlands. The results were interesting (Table 11.1). It was found that car speed was roughly the same in all countries. 52—53m.p.h. — slightly higher in Germany and the Netherlands. On the other hand goods vehicles travelled several miles faster in Germany and the Netherlands than in Belgium and France. The Road Research

Laboratory put this down to the greater mileage of motorways in Germany and the Netherlands — the more motorways the more accustomed traffic becomes to them and the faster it moves — and therefore decided that French and Belgian experience would probably be more relevant to British conditions. Even so, the Laboratory decided to make separate calculations for all three sets of speeds: (1) based on Belgium and France; (2) based on Germany and the Netherlands and (3) based on the United States.

Having decided to use these three sets of motorway speeds it was possible to calculate the time gained (or lost) by transferring to the motorway. Comparisons were made of the quickest route between pairs of towns using the existing road system and using the motorway. Part of the table showing the results of this comparison is reproduced in Table 11.2. It shows, for example, that a light goods van would save 12 minutes by using the motorway from Luton to Birmingham. It also shows that the heavier the vehicle the shorter the time saved. The biggest time saving is for a private car going from London to Birmingham by A41: 44 minutes. The average saving in time was reckoned to be 16.2 minutes for cars, 10.8 minutes for light goods, 12.2 minutes for medium goods and 9.7 minutes for heavy goods vehicles. The average additional mileage travelled if the motorway were used was 1.7 miles.

On the basis of the information contained in this table, a traffic assignment was made, that is, a prediction of the traffic that would transfer to the motorway. The form of the prediction is shown in fig. 11.2. It was predicted that all vehicles saving more than five

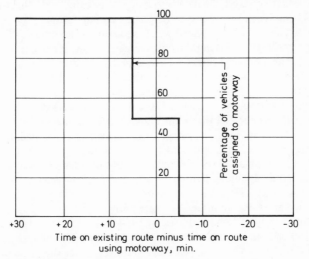

FIG. 11.2: Assignment of traffic to motorway[8]

minutes by transferring to the motorway would transfer, and that no vehicles saving less than five minutes would do so. Although it was recognised that some vehicles which would gain more than five minutes would not transfer and some gaining less than five would, it was held that these should just about cancel out.

By the end of this, the first half of the inquiry, the Laboratory had the following information:

(1) It knew the time saved (or lost) on the routes considered, multiplied by the number of vehicles of the different classes estimated to use the routes.

(2) It knew the proportions of traffic on each route expected to be private cars, light, medium and heavy goods vehicles.

(3) It knew the average occupancy of vehicles and the total extra mileage travelled by vehicles diverting to the motorway.

(4) It had also calculated the time saved by vehicles on the roads from which traffic had transferred, because these roads were less congested than formerly.

(5) Similarly the extra traffic on approach roads to the motorway and the time lost by it had been calculated.

(6) The proportions of traffic travelling for different purposes had been estimated.

(7) A prediction was also made of the effect of the motorway on accidents. Foreign experience suggested that accidents were roughly one third of those on ordinary roads.

At this point the traffic engineers handed the inquiry over to the economists, to convert the data into a rate of return. To do this the various benefits and costs had to be given a money value.

The first benefit to be valued was time savings. The time of all people travelling in working time was valued at their average hourly earnings. The average earnings for coach and truck drivers in this type of employment were taken from the Ministry of Labour Gazette. The figure for coach-drivers' time was used as it stood: for example thirty minutes saved of a coach-driver's time was valued at 51.6d. per hour. It was decided that some allowance should be made for difference in wages paid on average to the drivers of light, medium and heavy vehicles. Data collected from four firms suggested that drivers of medium-sized vehicles (1½ – 3 tons unladen) earned 15 per cent more than drivers of light vehicles and drivers of heavy vehicles 37 per cent more. Time saved by people in cars travelling on business was valued at 9s. 9d. an hour – a figure derived from a London Transport survey of London traffic in 1954. No value was given to non-business time saved at this stage. The time saved by people of each kind was multiplied by average hourly earnings, to get the value of *business* time saved.

The second benefit to be estimated was savings in vehicle use. The quicker the journeys the fewer the vehicles that would be needed to do the same work was the principle here. This was not as unreasonable as it may at first seem. It was argued that thirty minutes saving in time from London to Birmingham, for instance, might in some cases make possible a return journey within the day. In other cases time saved might make possible an extension of a journey; or the making of another journey. Unfortunately no data were available to show the effect of time saving on vehicle use, but it was thought in some cases the time saving might increase utilisation considerably — when, for example, it was possible to make two journeys where before only one had been made and the rest of the day the vehicle was idle — whereas in others it might not increase at all, it was reasonable to suppose that time saved would be directly reflected on average in vehicle use. British Road Services data were used to show that out of 4,000 hours so-called annual vehicle time per vehicle, 600 were spent loading, in maintenance, etc. Assuming that 600 hours would always be spent in this way, it was calculated how many fewer vehicles of each business class would be needed to give the same service when the motorway was built. The vehicles eliminated were valued at their depreciated capital value plus some allowance for maintenance and administrative costs attributable to them.

The third saving was in petrol. Test runs were made with various classes of vehicle to measure fuel consumption. The results were used to work out the value of fuel savings. For reasons we will not at the moment examine, petrol was valued at its price per gallon less tax. The Laboratory was hesitant about the total value of fuel savings. They thought it might be 10 per cent too high — especially compared with the results of twenty-three American tests.

Other components of vehicle operating costs valued were clutch and brake wear. On the best available American evidence it was decided that the effect on tyre wear would be negligible.

The money value of these various savings mentioned so far are given in Table 11.3 for each of the three sets of speed. From them was deducted the increase in the operating costs of vehicles which travelled more miles by transferring to the motorway, and to them was added the extra benefit measured by the fall in operating costs of motorists staying on the old roads now less heavily travelled. Added in as well was the value of the expected decrease in accidents valued by estimating the effect on output, medical and administrative expenses and damages to property. Subtracted from that total were the expected average annual maintenance costs. The rate of return, based on these benefits (and costs) only, is the first set of three — one for each set of speeds — shown in Table 11.4: 3.3 per cent, 3.9 per cent and 4.2 per cent.

Table 11.3 *Estimates of savings in costs (−) and increases (+) resulting from the building of the motorway*[9]

Changes in £ thousands per annum

	First assignment	Second assignment	Third assignment
Saving in working time by traffic transfering to motorway	−453	−624	−766
Reduction in vehicle fleets	−80	−161	−227
Change in fuel consumption for vehicle mileage transferred to motorway	−117	−84	−18
Change in other operating costs for vehicle mileage transferred	−200	−200	−200
Costs of additional vehicle mileage incurred in transferring to motorway	+229	+307	+375
Reductions in cost to vehicles remaining on old roads	−128	−128	−128
Total vehicle costs	−749	−890	−964
Reduction in accidents	−215	−215	−215
Maintenance costs of motorway	+200	+200	+200
Net annual measured savings	−764	−905	−979

Table 11.4 *Estimated rates of return on investments in motorways (%)*[10]

Estimated cost of motorway including interest charges at 5% during period of construction: £23,300,000

| | Rates of return | | |
	First assignment	Second assignment	Third assignment
(1) Benefits enumerated in Table 11.3	3.3	3.9	4.2
(2) *Plus* benefits to generated traffic	3.8	4.5	4.8
(3) *Plus* the benefits of non-business time valued:			
(a) at 4s. per hour	5.4	6.4	7.1
(b) at 6s. per hour	6.2	7.4	8.3
(c) at 8s. per hour	7.0	8.3	9.4
(4) Allowing for the effect of growth in traffic over time at 6% per annum: predicted rate of return in:			
1960		9.9–15.2	
1965		17.6–27.3	

It will be seen that if these were the only benefits considered the rate of return would be less than the rate of interest, say 5 − 6 per cent, one might expect to have to be paid on the capital invested.

The estimates so far concern traffic which might be expected to be diverted to the motorways − the assumption being made as we have mentioned already − that all traffic gaining more than five minutes transfers, and more transfers gaining less; but experience elsewhere shows that the mere existence of a motorway *creates* new traffic: generated traffic as it is called. Traffic transfers to the roads from other means of transport. And there is simply more transport. There is a relationship between journey time and the volume of traffic between towns. When journey time falls, the volume of traffic rises. American and Swedish evidence was used to predict the increase in volume from this cause: 31 per cent of diverted traffic. Since this is new traffic which would not have travelled but for the reduction in vehicle operating costs, it was judged wrong to value this as highly as diverted traffic. Benefits to generated traffic were in fact valued at half the value of those to diverted traffic. (The rationale of this is exactly the same as that given on pp. 146-9 of Chapter 6 where the consumers' surplus of new demand created by the cost reduction is judged to be measured by half the rectangle BCDE in fig. 6.7 in default of better knowledge.)

Counting in benefits to generated traffic brings up the rate of return, it will be seen from Table 11.4 only to 3.8 per cent, 4.5 per cent and 4.8 per cent respectively — still hardly enough to cover interest charges. The next class of benefits to be included made a great difference. Business time saved had been valued. Non-business time had not. Plainly one could almost invariably say that a non-business car-driver would pay to use a motorway something over and above any savings in vehicle operating costs. Experience of toll roads and bridges suggests that this must be so. The difficulty is to decide at what rate to value it. No special investigations were made for the inquiry. Rather, certain alternative assumptions were made. The rate of return — at each of the three sets of speed — was calculated on the assumption that non-business time was valued at 2s., 4s., 6s., 8s., and 10s., an hour. Some of these are given in Table 11.4. The inquiry then assumed that the rate of return for the first set of speeds lay between 5.5 per cent and 7 per cent; 6.5 per cent and 8.5 per cent for the second; 7 per cent and 9.5 per cent for the third.

The fast stage was allowing for future increases in traffic flow not due to the motorway — due rather to the rate of growth of national income. On the assumption that the rate of return based on benefits calculated so far could reasonably be narrowed down further to from 5.5 per cent to 8.5 per cent, it was estimated that if the motorway was completed by 1960 and a 6 per cent rate of growth of traffic was assumed, the rate of return on the investment would be from 9.9 per cent to 15.2 per cent in 1960 and from 17.6 per cent to 27.3 per cent in 1965.

By these steps investment in the motorway was justified — after the decision to invest had been made.

SOME COMPARISONS BETWEEN CRITERIA

The exercise yielded a rate of return, or rather a number of rates of return, because the inquiry did not commit itself to a firm prediction of (1) motorway speeds; (2) the value of non-business time. Rates of return constructed in much the same manner have been used in other countries to decide road investment priorities; and we can expect them to be used here before long for that purpose. There are two questions to be asked: (1) Is it the same as the consumers' surplus rate of return we have described? (2) What is the nature of the difference between it and profit maximisation, if it is not the same?

Comparison with Consumers' Surplus Rate of Return

This rate of return is not quite the same thing as the consumers' surplus rate of return. It is, if you like, an imperfect approximation to it. Apart from any shortcomings in the evidence on which the calculation of the rate was based — with which we are not concerned in this section — there are principally three causes of this imperfection.

The first which may be briefly mentioned is that all the costs which we might judge relevant to the calculation were not taken into account: for example, police and administrative costs. However, *in this case* these are likely to have been unimportant. An allowance was made in calculating the capital cost of the investment for the most profitable alternative — agricultural — use of the land.

The second is the effect of the present way of charging for the use of roads. As it is not an average cost, or indeed a marginal cost pricing policy its form affects the use of the criterion. The Government or road authority has to pay out more in maintenance costs and interest charges because it has a new road to maintain and finance. It will get less in petrol tax from traffic diverted to the motorway and from traffic staying on the old roads because of the drop in fuel consumption. On the credit side there will be the fuel tax paid by the new traffic generated by the motorway, which would not exist if the motorway had not been built. Let us suppose the net effect of changes in fuel consumption is a fall in revenue in relation to the costs of the road system. If the Government or road authority had been breaking even before the motorway, it would afterwards be making a loss and our consumers' surplus criterion would dictate raising charges until the loss was wiped out. In these circumstances the consumers' surplus criterion would give a lower rate of return on the investment than the London-Birmingham motorway criterion which takes no account of the effect of the project on revenue. Conversely, if there was an increase in revenue in relation to the costs of the road system as a result of the motorway, the London-Birmingham motorway criterion should show a lower rate of return than the consumers' surplus criterion. We know however that in this country, the users of rural roads, probably even rural motorways, pay more than average cost — a 'profit' is being made. In these circumstances the London-Birmingham criterion would yield a lower rate of return than our consumers' surplus criterion if the latter is associated with an average cost pricing policy. A price lower on average than that at present charged for the use of the motorway through petrol taxation – *on average* because there may be some classes of vehicle that should pay more – will mean an increase in demand, as virtually any fall in price does; and therefore an increase in the rate of return on investment. This is a second reason for a divergence between the two types of return. Whereas the first, if anything, implied that the London-Birmingham type criterion over-estimates by comparison with the consumers' surplus criterion, here the reverse is indicated.

The third reason for divergence is also important. The inquiry went about estimating the demand for the motorway by summing benefits. The consumers' surplus criterion postulates that all benefits to consumers should be taken into account in calculating a rate of return. First, a decision has to be made who are the road-users to be taken into account in working out the policy. The inquiry assumed that they were, in effect, cars, coaches, light, medium and heavy goods vehicles. No mention was made of the interests of motorcyclists, cyclists, pedestrians, or enterprises that lay mains, etc., under the roadway. Presumably a sufficient reason for omission is their unimportance or even non-existence. Nothing was said of the Government or any other body being prepared to pay towards beautifying the highway or providing amenities of any kind. All this may in this case have been unimportant and, not being in possession of the facts, we cannot say more.

What is much more important and interesting are the benefits that the inquiry took into account for the classes of beneficiary it did consider. The inquiry used the indirect method of measuring consumers' surplus as described in Chapter 6: asking not 'how much would you pay for?' but the exact value in terms of time saved, etc. The question is whether the inquiry succeeded in setting a value on all the benefits that might be expected to be gained by those whose interests it considered.

Let us take vehicles travelling in business time first. We may make the assumption that their owners are out to maximise profits. They will count as a benefit – as the inquiry recognised – any reduction in vehicle operating costs, in the number of vehicles needed, and in drivers' time saved. Is there anything else they might value which the inquiry omitted – any reason why they should be ready to pay more than the sum of the benefits already mentioned? Possibly not. Perhaps the most important omission is any value attached to getting goods, as opposed to people, from one place to another. Over the distance affected by the London-Birmingham motorway this is probably not very important. No one is going to pay a haulier much more for getting goods from London to Birmingham forty four minutes sooner; but over longer distances, say London to Scotland, there may be time savings for goods for which consignors and consignees may be ready to pay something. (I have in mind a man I once met at 3 a.m. in a refreshment bar on the New York turnpike who was a glass merchant in a small way somewhere near the Great Lakes. On the opening of the motorway he found it paid him to drive through the night once a month to New York and back to buy his glass. Strictly this was *generated* traffic but one can imagine how goods already travelling by road might gain increased value by a speeding up in delivery time.) Another factor which might have cash value is greater reliability in deliveries due to the opening of a motorway (or a reduction in urban congestion). Whether these make a significant difference to the benefits attributable to the motorway, and hence to the rate of return, could only be found out by survey and experiment. On the other hand there may be reasons why an over-estimation of benefits occurs. Suppose a firm ought to get £1,000 benefit per annum because of cost reduction due to the opening of a motorway; but in fact it only gets £750. Drivers do not pass on all the benefits — they are not profit maximisers in the interests of the firm. They spend more time in transport cafes on the way, more time loading and unloading, etc. How are we to allow for that? If experience and survey showed that a 25 per cent leakage in commercial benefits of this kind was common, it might be argued that the relevant benefits should be scaled down by 25 per cent in assessing the rate of return. But it might also be argued that though it should be scaled down, something should be added in to represent the extra benefit to drivers whose working lives are made that much more attractive. It might be said that the time saved which is spent in this manner should be valued as an increase in leisure time, valued at the rate used for non-business time. It is also possible that over time, changes of this sort are reflected in the wages that firms have to pay drivers and in the quality of drivers they can get.

A greater problem arises with the valuation of non-business time. What do we mean by *time?* In this context, it can mean strictly, 'how much would you, a non-business user, be prepared to pay for leisure time saved?'; or alternatively, 'having made allowance for any saving in vehicle operating costs, how much *more* would you be prepared to pay to use the motorway?' In other words 'time' is sometimes a residual category, when, pre-supposing that those questioned understand this, we ought to get an answer which allows for *all* the benefits a driver or passenger expects to get from motorway travel: the true consumers' surplus criterion. In the United States it is quite common to slip in a notional 25 cents an hour or so for 'increased comfort and convenience'. The trouble which sometimes makes interpretation difficult is that most people are not used to separating in their own minds the benefits they gain due specifically to time saved, and to any increase in comfort and convenience, to the pleasure of travelling at a higher speed and the many other elements of pleasure or displeasure affecting people's valuation of road improvements. For example, the evidence suggests that many motorists will rather take a much longer route involving a road bridge than queue for a ferry, even though it will cost them more in operating costs and will take longer to use the bridge. There is here something like a pure hatred of queuing or waiting. Yet if one asked these motorists why they made the longer, slower journey, they might well answer 'to save time'. Time has been confused with all the other factors which affect their choice.

Now if it should be the case that the figure used to value non-business time is a figure which only represents the value to time saved, then there will be a larger number of benefits omitted from the calculation of the rate of return which should be included. If in fact, whatever it is called, it is a residual category, then nothing relevant is omitted. (And in that case it would be double-counting to add in another item − for 'comfort and convenience'.) Some empirical investigation is needed to see whether in fact an important class of benefit is omitted.

Summarising we can say that the general tendency of the first cause of the imperfect approximation of the London-Birmingham motorway criterion to the consumers' surplus criterion is a slight over-estimation of the rate of return; and of the second and third causes, a tendency to under-estimation. On balance, the London-Birmingham motorway rate of return is probably less than the consumers' surplus rate of return in the same circumstances, always supposing that conditions were appropriate for its application, for example, that an average cost pricing policy were in force.

Differences from Consumers' Surplus Rate of Return

If we could assume that the London-Birmingham motorway calculation was a consumers' surplus rate of return, there would be no difficulty in giving a general answer to the second question − the difference between it and a profit maximising rate of return. The difference would then simply be analysable in two ways.

First, we would expect the profit maximising rate of return on the same investment to be less if the profit-making authority were not able to discriminate perfectly between road-users in making its charges. The difference between the two depends on the ability of a profit maximising road authority to discriminate between road-users. The rate of return would be the same if the profit-making authority could make a different charge according to the value of the time saved, vehicle use saved, fuel saved, brake and clutch wear saved; and if it could charge road-users on other roads who benefit from the motorway the amount by which they benefit; and charge road-users who suffer less so that more of them should abandon the use of the road system; and so on. This implies a fine degree of discrimination in charging, almost certainly beyond the power of any of the charging mechanisms discussed in the last chapter. (It might be thought that one would, for example, charge motorists at a single rate according to the class of vehicle for time saved: for example, all car-drivers travelling in business time at 9s. 9d. an hour, all drivers of heavy goods vehicles at x pence an hour, etc. This is not so because these are average figures. There are some road-users in each class whose time is worth less than the average and who presumably would be driven off the road (or reduce their use of it) if required to pay at the average rate; just as there are others whose time is worth more than the average and who must be charged more if the authority is to make a profit here equal to the average benefit. Furthermore there is no obvious way in which motorists could be charged according to time saved.) For these reasons one would expect the profit maximising rate of return to be less than the London-Birmingham motorway type of rate of return, in the same circumstances.

Second, besides price discrimination in the ordinary sense it is likely that there will be social benefits and costs which a consumers' surplus maximising road authority will want and be able to take into account but which cannot be charged for — especially benefits and costs which appear to accrue to indirect beneficiaries. Formally it is difficult to distinguish between this and the last case; but the distinction is perhaps worth making. Whether this means the profit maximising rate of return is higher or lower than the consumers' surplus maximising depends of course on what is included and what is left out.

That there should be the difference is really what we should expect of a consumers' surplus rate of return and it should not worry us. Unfortunately, as we have seen, correlation of the inquiry and the commercial rate of return is not as simple as that. We have to face the possibility that the commercial rate of return could be higher than the inquiry rate of return, or what is more likely, that the difference is less than indicated by the two points made above. And this is because the London-Birmingham rate of return is not quite the same thing as our consumers' surplus rate of return.

IMPROVING THE CRITERION USED

The most important improvements must be effected by policy decisions of the Government: to make decisions on who are to be counted road-users for the purposes of the criterion and what are to be accounted benefits and costs of the road system, and to adopt an average cost pricing policy. Unless these steps are taken the present London-Birmingham motorway type of criterion is like one of those fabulous beasts, not all one thing or all another, better than some other methods of deciding investment priorities, but with little in logic to recommend it.

The second most important improvement needed is that such rates of return should be used, even in their present imperfect state. The only point of calculating isolated rates of return is to compare the rate of return with the rate of interest; but this is not the more important function of rates of return which is to compare the desirability of investment opportunities. It should be routine to work such calculations for all road improvements of size. It has already been noticed that the London-Birmingham motorway survey cost £20,000 only, or one tenth of 1 per cent of the cost of the investment. In 1960-61 some £72m. was spent on new construction and major improvement. One per cent of this would have been £720,000. If between ½ per cent and 1 per cent of the annual expenditure of new construction and major improvement were spent on this kind of inquiry, it is likely that it would make a considerable difference to the efficiency of investment; (and would not be more than the percentage spent on market research by many commercial firms).

A third kind of improvement needed is that rates of return should be used not just to choose between different opportunities for investment, but between different ways of making the same investment. It has already been noticed that the route, design, number of lanes, number of access points — and all specifications of the London-Birmingham motorway — were decided before any traffic survey or economic assessment. And it has since been suggested that a two-lane dual carriageway with fewer and differently situated access points would have been a better investment than the three-lane dual carriageway built, even allowing generously for future traffic growth.[11] It is in fact normal that the specifications for new roads and improvements are drawn up on arbitrary engineering standards and not as a result of an economic choice. Hence the criticisms that safety margins tend to be excessive in British road construction: that, to recall one example, bridges are built with unnecessarily high clearance; or the criticisms made of useless and ugly expensiveness of the design of the Chiswick fly-over. It should be normal to compare the rates of return on several different ways of constructing a road, widening it, etc., and to choose the method which promises the highest return.

But looking further to the future there are several topics for research which would make it possible to improve and extend consumers' surplus calculations enormously.

(1) Perhaps the most important is in the valuation of time savings out of business hours. It can make a large difference to the rate of return on a project if road-users' time saved is valued at different rates from 2*s.* to 12*s.* an hour; and we have very little information on this. Most of what we have is American. An experiment where there were more or less parallel tollways and free roads in the United States suggested that motorists showed by their behaviour that on average they would pay $1.20 an hour for time saved – judged by how much they paid to go on the motorway and the time saved by doing so.[12] (Time in this context is clearly a residual category.) Having no tollways this experiment is impossible in Britain, but it can be performed where there is a choice between using a toll bridge or ferry and a longer journey by free road. The difficulty here is that drivers may be prepared to pay very much more on an occasional bridge or ferry than they will per minute saved on a long trunk road or motorway.

To get a figure one might be driven back on direct inquiry, qeustioning motorists of all non-business kinds to ask how much they would be prepared to pay to save time, but this is open to obvious shortcomings – false or exasperated answers. It might be possible to get figures from the study of how much people value non-business time in other contexts; but unfortunately, at least from this point of view, we do not in this country have the excess fare railway expresses, etc., which would make this kind of experiment possible. Another method available is probably that of back-checking. For example, it would be quite possible to repeat the original London-Birmingham inquiry, setting up the twenty three interviewing posts on the previous roads and also some posts on the motorway itself, to try to check whether the predictions made by the inquiry were correct – whether the traffic has transferred that was expected to transfer, whether the vehicles using the motorway are the ones predicted. The method of adjusting the rate of return would be that described in Chapter 6 by a shift in the demand curve. Suppose retrodiction showed that 10 per cent less traffic had transferred than had been expected – this first stage could be established by a traffic count on the motorway – the simplest expedient would be to adjust the rate of return by shifting the demand curve to the left, from D_1D_1 to D_2D_2 (indicated on fig. 11.3), and counting the actual rate of return as the area under the new demand curve expressed as a ratio to the capital cost of investment. Conversely, a rate of flow 10 per cent higher would imply a shift in the demand curve to the right – to D_3D_3. (In reality, a prediction would be made for an increasing traffic volume over time and the back-checking would have to take account of this; but to introduce this would

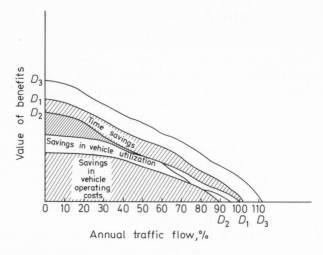

FIG. 11.3: The benefits from a road investment and their relation to a
demand curve

This figure is drawn on two improbable asumptions made only to simplify
drawing: first, a vehicle which gains more in vehicle operating cost savings
from a road improvement will also be one which gains more in other savings —
this need not be the case; secondly the figure is drawn without cost curves.

complicate the example without affecting the argument.) And, if a
number of investments showed a similar tendency, the rate of return on
new investments could be discounted accordingly. This simple
expedient would not disclose the cause of the discrepancy. The
carrying out of a back-checking survey ought to do so. If the figures
for vehicle operating costs are reliable (and they can be tested), any
difference between the volume predicted and the volume of traffic
transferred actually travelling on the road ought to be attributable to a
mistake in the valuation of time savings — both for business and
non-business traffic. If it is much out for business traffic this may be due
to an incorrect figure for average hourly earnings or a mistaken
assumption about the use to which time saved can be put commercially.
Both these are susceptible to further investigation. And if this does not
help, it may then be worth while investigating to see if there have been
any other benefits or costs neglected. Since non-business time can be
regarded as a residual category, back-checking should reveal at once
the value set on it by different classes of road-user, once the other
specific factors such as vehicle operating costs have been allowed for.
(If the data should show that there is a marked falling off in the
valuation of time saved of less than five minutes this might be a
justification for using the traffic assignment curve used by the

278

London-Birmingham inquiry or for modifying it if some other period of time was relevant or if factors other than time should be relevant.) Better still, however, if by observation of behaviour one could find different values of time as one expects there must be for different classes of people: *(a)* of different groups; *(b)* on different kinds of non-working journeys; *(c)* over different distances.

Other topics for research which may be mentioned briefly are:

(2) Work to discover if the wage or salary rate is a fair representation of savings in business time by seeing what value time saved by its employees has for commercial firms and other undertakings. This could be done by sample survey.

(3) Work to estimate elasticities of demand — the amount of traffic generated by different kinds of road improvement. *A priori* one would expect that a large noticeable improvement such as an urban expressway system would generate proportionally more traffic than the improvement of a few intersections scattered over a great city. There must be much evidence on this which has not been collected. Also important and unknown are elasticities of substitution — for example, what effect a change in the relative prices of public and private road transport has on the demand for each.

(4) Work to measure other forms of social cost and benefit on which we have no quantifiable information at present: for example, the social costs of noise, fumes and the effect on property values of traffic.

(5) Lastly, work to discover the influence of transport facilities on the location of industry.

What is most important is that calculations should be made in towns where they are necessarily more complicated. Difficulties of road planning in towns is the complexity of traffic flows, the tremendous difficulty of conducting origin and destination surveys, the need to consider the flows, origins, destinations and time savings of pedestrians, the benefits accruing to parked cars and to gas companies, telephone companies, etc., who lay mains and cables under the road surface. These do not change the essential nature of the problem, only add greatly to its complexity. Origin and destination surveys are feasible but they are usually done in a different way — by the issue of cards to vehicles entering or leaving cities which drivers are required to complete by labelling vehicles as they enter or by interviewing a random sample of people at their homes to determine the pattern of their road-use.[13] The problems of establishing speeds, journey times, vehicle operating costs, are also greater in a city, but already considerable work has been done on these problems,[14] and rates of return have been calculated of the London-Birmingham motorway type.[15] Yet this is most certainly where ingenuity will be most needed in the future.

By these various improvements it should be possible to get a rate of return which is a much closer approximation to the true consumers' surplus criterion. In this section I have not tried to go into great detail concerning the improvements which might be made, only to give some indication of what is needed and what might be achieved without under expenditure of resources if it were decided to run the road programme (and the railways possibly) as a consumers' surplus enterprise.

CONCLUSION

In this part of the book we have pursued a course parallel to that of Part II, but the argument has not been the same because most of the problems have been different. In discussing the railway problem it was relevant to give considerable attention to costs: what the railways knew of their costs; the difficulties created by their comparative ignorance and apparently defective logic. Costs were also important for the rationalisation of the road programme but here the problems were still more fundamental or elementary: what were to be accounted costs of the road system: what variations in cost might be important. Charging problems did not bulk large in our discussion of the railways except that it seemed important to consider what principles should govern charging when there was a deficit. Conversely the related charging problem for the road system was charging where there was congestion. But the improvement of the present methods of charging for the use of roads is essential for a sensible solution to the road problem. The investment problem of the railways which was discussed was largely a criticism of the methods used to formulate and express the railways modernisation plan; and an attempt was made to establish the possibility of a consumers' surplus investment policy for the railways. The chief topic of interest connected with road investment seemed to be the actual working of the quasi-consumers' surplus rates of return used. The last chapter on the railway problem was most concerned, apart from some observations on criteria, with what changes were needed in subsidy and regulation to get conformity to the basic criteria and with the general problems of dealing with subsidies and regulations, problems relevant to the road programme but more important for rail. The corresponding chapter in Part III was concerned with more fundamental, elementary problems: why the present road programmes were illogical, why improvement mattered and why some change in organisation seemed to be needed.

As far as it has been in the competence of the author, the development of the argument has been a process of logical deduction from first principles. We began by considering principles and have broadened into questions of some detail, a progress which may have made the argument grow more interesting to some readers and less to others. It hardly need be said that what has been outlined is not meant to be the last word on the road and rail problems, but a necessary foundation and a general introduction. It has been an attempt to begin at the right end, putting first things first. Many excellent discussions of transport questions are vitiated because it is not clear what standpoint the author is arguing from, what criterion he is using.

In Parts II and III the railway and the road problems have been considered separately. To some aspects of the problem of formulating an overall transport policy we now turn.

POSTSCRIPT

The London-Birmingham Motorway Study is kept as the centrepiece of this study because, though it is now old, there is no easily accessible example of a better and more sophisticated inter-urban highway improvement. Those investment appraisals whose details have been published since have tended to cover more complex evaluation problems than those of inter-urban highway improvement. The majority of inter-urban highway investment decisions remain of a relatively simple kind, even by comparison with the construction of the London-Birmingham motorway. The study remains a good introduction to what is required in such cases and is also a useful introduction to more complex transport project evaluation. As a supplement it is interesting to read a World Bank *ex post* reappraisal of a highway project in Iran which shows the errors that easily creep in and lead to misleading *ex ante* project evaluation, again in a comparatively simple case.

The art of highway project evaluation has developed rapidly in the last ten years.[1] Studies like those of the London-Birmingham motorway have formidable data requirements. Since, attempts have been made to make it easier and quicker for highway engineers and planners to calculate cost-benefit returns in comparatively simple cases. This is necessary if project evaluation is to become a routine and not be confined to projects of special interest either because they are controversial or because they are large. The most important aid has been to make relevant data more easily available so that there is less need for special surveys and estimations of important functional relationships. The American Association of State Highway Officials and the Highways Research Board in the USA, and the Transport and Road Research Laboratory in Britain have produced much data of this kind. There is also information in de Weille and Winfrey. Besides helping the engineer, governments have also wished to standardise data so that they are not faced by returns calculated using different data and so producing inconsistent methods of evaluation. The second aid has been the development of computer packages. In the most useful cases these make evaluations easy for the analysts. To understand how standard best practice has advanced, read the COBA manual.[2] The categories of benefit measured are the same as for the London-Birmingham study and have not changed savings in time, vehicle operating costs and accident costs; and there is no incorporation of environmental impacts. But there has been (1) a vast improvement in the quality and quantity of the data available; (2) in estimating techniques; and (3) in the speed of the exercise. Computer programmes and prepared forms make it easy for engineers to use COBA. Nothing on the scale of the London-Birmingham study is required. The programme user defines a network relevant to the evaluation, numbering each node and link and stating the recorded flow on each link on a 16-hour August day. He writes down other characteristics determining its width, maintenance costs, accident rates, speed limits, gradients and curvature. The user is also required to specify these characteristics for new links and any links or nodes which would go if the road improvement were made. The general proportions of traffic by vehicle type on the network is recorded. For urban roads data with which to calculate speed-flow relations are needed. More complicated calculations are required to specify roundabouts, and traffic signals. Construction costs and delay costs to traffic are to be dated for each year in which they are incurred. All data must be ascribed to a particular year. Given the data, the programme makes traffic forecasts, reassigns traffic from the existing to the improved link, and calculates a *net present value* for the improvement. Much standardised information has been collected and analysed as part of a research programmes over recent years.[3] The COBA procedure is only suitable where the improvement is not expected to affect the pattern, or distribution, of trip origins and destinations, or to generate significant new trips. Then special exercises are required.

The problems of evaluating improvements in the main arterial systems of cities are more complex because of: (1) the importance of congestion; (2) the unrealism of assuming no change in the distribution or volume of journeys; (3) the importance of environmental factors; (4) the importance of predicting impacts on secondary roads; (5) the need to compare private with public transport improvements; and (6) the relation between land use changes and transport. There is an excellent introduction to the urban transport planning process including economic evaluation in Lane, Powell and Prestwood Smith.[4]

282

As well as research to make data more easily accessible and usable, there has also been research to improve the empirical inputs into transport planning. Much the greatest progress has been made in estimating the value of time. Many research experiments on both sides of the Atlantic have been undertaken which are more sophisticated and ambitious than the toll road bridge or ferry experiment referred to on page 274. The principle is the same — to find actual or hypothetical choice situations where the alternatives have different characteristics for the user and then to find what statistical function best explains the choices actually made. The earliest experiments tended to assume that the trade-off was only between time and money: users spent time to save money. From some experiments different values have been estimated for travelling as opposed to waiting or walking time, for different trip purposes, for different income groups and for different amounts of time saved. In other experiments attempts have also been made to try to estimate the value which was set on frequency, comfort and various other factors associated with the quality of the journey rather than its cost or speed. The best introduction is Harrison and Quarmby.[5]

Refinements in inter-urban highways demand forecasting have not received much attention, except where there was comparison with other modes of transport.[6] In cities the problem has seemed much more important because the benefits from investment have seemed much more sensitive to forecasts made.[7] A good introduction to advanced forecasting methods in general is Quandt.[8]

While improvements in approach have been rapid, public opinion on what cost-benefits should be included has outdistanced them and this has been especially true of environmental benefits and disbenefits of transport. Increasing traffic affects those who live and work by a road, and of course pedestrians, in various ways: increased vehicle noise, pollution, vibration, visual intrusion, increased accidents and through neighbourhood severance and other neighbourhood effects. The effects of new roads is, of course, greater especially in cities where high population densities expose more people to these negative environmental effects of road traffic and road construction. There are discussions on the nature of the problem in the report of the United Kingdom Urban Motorways Committee, Foster and Mishan. Dodgson discusses some methodological problems of allowing for externalities in road investment.

The most detailed examination of the effect of pricing policies on the return from a transport investment was not of a highway, but the problem is not unimportant for highways though unanalysed. Tax levels do affect highway use and therefore the return from investment. Deciding on the meaning of differences between profit maximising and consumers' surplus maximising rates of return also present considerable problems which have not been solved.

PART IV

THE TRANSPORT PROBLEM

In earlier chapters we have discussed the problems implied in determining pricing and investment criteria for single enterprises, rail and road. But there are also issues that arise for the whole transport sector, not only rail and road, but other forms of transport also that compete with them. (There is no scientific method of determining what one means by the transport sector. Economists tend to define an industry as a grouping of comparatively closely competing activities. On this basis road competes with rail as, in another sense, do road haulage, private cars and buses; but ships and overseas airlines do not. Sometimes non-transport activities can be closer competitors than other forms of transport. For example the alternative to a journey may often be a telephone call. Thus some writers have argued as if telecommunications were best considered as part of the transport sector.)

Traditionally much discussion has polarised around the twin concepts of coordination and competition in transport: two terms to which we will attempt to give fairly exact meanings. Competition and coordination are the two great slogans of the transport world; and like many slogans, they mean many different things to many people. A superficial history of transport policy would say that the tendency from the earliest days of railway rate regulation until 1953 was towards greater coordination.[1] Thereafter there was a movement back to competition until the mid-'sixties. Such an account puts all the emphasis on centralisation − bigness − and decentralisation as the defining characteristics of coordination and competition; and it does not do justice to the many different ideas that the supporters of coordination, especially, have had in mind. The difficulty about competition is not so much that it is a word to which many meanings have been attached; but that insufficient thinking has been done on how to establish competition in transport. We will begin with this problem of defining and establishing competition.

THE COMPETITIVE SOLUTION

Competition − to maximise profits or consumers' surplus − is not just a matter of indiscriminately freeing some transport enterprises from restrictions they have accumulated in the past; neither is it administrative decentralisation. To achieve profits or consumers' surplus maximisation, the firms in the transport industry should (1) as far as possible adopt the same criterion; and (2) operate in similar conditions.[2] (3) In addition, there must be effective competition between them.

The Same Criterion

The Government must decide on the criterion to be used by public transport undertakings: nationalised airlines on domestic routes, waterways, harbour boards, British Road Services, etc., as well as road and rail. We have argued (Chapter 2) that profit or consumers' surplus maximisation seem the most plausible basic criteria, and there is no need to repeat the arguments that led to that conclusion. If one accepts the kind of argument that was developed in Chapter 2 there is no good reason for requiring some public transport undertaking to adopt one criterion and others the other (subject to one qualification to be mentioned below). The same arguments which persuaded Parliament that a consumers' surplus maximisation policy was the best basis for railway policy, would, one would hope, convince them it was the best for the domestic services of the airlines or the nationalised road passenger transport undertakings; and similarly for profit maximisation.

Parity of criteria would also have an important practical advantage in that it would make it easier to assess relative efficiency and decide investment priorities in the transport sector. By an argument, developed in Chapter 3, it is nonsensical to make straight comparisons between dividends and rates of return on investment which relate to different criteria.[3] (There is a way out of this dilemma in principle if it should be decided to use different criteria: the Government should use the rates of return it thinks fit on different enterprises, and if these should vary, it should make a decision of principle how these rates of return should be weighted to compare efficiency and investment opportunities, but this is at present the kind of choice Governments cannot be expected to make because they have not the experience. Prudence suggests that if we wish to get the allocation of resources right in the public transport sector, it is sensible for all undertakings to use the same criterion.)

Although these arguments indicate the sense of adopting the same criteria, we are at once in a difficulty if the consumers' surplus criterion is adopted. There will be two transport sectors in competition with each other: the public with one criterion and the private with a commercial profit maximising policy. The difference is inescapable. But in practice it is a difficulty which should not worry us too much.[4] There is something to be said for the idea of introducing (consumers' surplus maximising) public firms into

287

competition with private firms.[5] It will be some check — if the public firms are efficient — It may do no harm if profits fall to the level which nationalised firms need to cover their capital costs. (The inevitable consequence of this is that there would be less private investment in transport than otherwise would be the case.) Besides, competition is sufficiently imperfect for public and private firms to co-exist with their separate criteria. However, if it should be decided that this competition is not 'fair' and that it prevents private firms in transport from making adequate profits, there is an alternative solution. Those public firms, for example British Road Services, and B.E.A. on its domestic flights — which are most directly in competition with private firms — could be required to maximise profits. It would then be sensible if they were required to raise money on the market in the ordinary way.

Since the adoption of either of our criteria is logically incompatible with cross-subsidisation, parity of criteria means the elimination of cross-subsidisation throughout the public transport sector, which should be a great improvement in the efficient allocation of resources. For example, the internal flights of B.E.A. are cross-subsidised by passengers flying abroad by B.E.A. This has the effect of making domestic air charges lower and affects the volume of long-distance rail passenger traffic adversely. This is one example of a widespread cause of distortion.

The kind of benefit one would hope to get by the adoption of the same criterion (and the investment and pricing policy appropriate to it) throughout the public transport sector, is an end to the sort of nonsense that said that the building of a new underground railway in London, the Victoria Line, is unprofitable, when it is obvious that the only reason it is unprofitable is that road-users in London do not pay enough for the roads they use — an absurdity which would be eliminated by the adoption of the appropriate pricing and investment policy for roads.

The Same Conditions
The point here can be illustrated by a simple example. A nationalised bus undertaking is not allowed to use any excess space it may have in its workshops to make or repair vehicles belonging to private firms. (There is an example of this in Bristol where the British Transport Commission inherited a large coach-building workshop which it has not been able to use efficiently because of this restriction.) A private firm is able to achieve economies by making mutually advantageous arrangements of this kind with other firms. This sets the public enterprise at some competitive disadvantage which is not justified by either of our criteria or by any obvious principle

of equity. Cumulatively such constraints can amount to a considerable distortion in the transport sector. (Some are in the interest of the public undertakings, some against, but there is no presumption that these cancel out.)

Parity here means first, that there should be equal treatment in respect of liability to taxation. All forms of transport should be taxed according to the same principles. If one pays rates, or profits tax, the rest should. If some form of road transport is taxed exceptionally on a luxury basis, then similar forms of rail, air and other types of transport should be taxed on the same principle.

It also means equal access to capital on the same terms: for example, if the road system finds it harder to get money for equally profitable investment than the railways, this is a serious distortion.

Competition means that all forms of transport should be equally subject to regulations and restrictions where there are any of these. Under a competitive solution one would expect a great many regulations appropriate to an outdated monopoly situation would go. The regulations remaining would be those designed as the framework for competition; and those restrictions in the interest of safety, public health, labour conditions, etc., which are imposed on most firms. It is important that these should fall on all forms of transport equitably — as has not been the case in the past. The chief achievement of the 1953 and 1962 Transport Acts was to make conditions more equitable by removing most of the antiquated regulations on the railways; but there are still disparities to be removed between forms of transport.

Competition also means a fair subsidy policy. If the Government wants to subsidise some classes of transport-users — for example, country-dwellers — they should be subsidised in the cheapest way possible, compatible with the achievement of the objective — whether the form of transport in question is publicly or privately owned. Sometimes the point of a subsidy is to subsidise the means of transport itself — for example, airlines directly or indirectly through the subsidisation of research, or airports for military reasons or prestige.[6] If the Government should wish to distort transport for this kind of reason, of course it can, but it would be sensible if it reckoned in the cost of the subsidy the amount of the loss to other forms of transport because of the artificial cheapening of air fares and the resulting distortion of the distribution of traffic between air and other forms of transport; then it would have a better basis from which to judge if the military advantage or the prestige was worthwhile.

Making Competition Effective

It is also necessary to make sure that public enterprises in the transport sector do compete with each other and private firms. It would be possible to have a single transport authority, monopolistic in form, competitive in behaviour. It would be told by Parliament which of its services were to compete with each other; and it would fix prices and make investment decisions accordingly. The dangers of a monolithic organisation are presumably that there would be insufficient stimulus to competition between its parts and a tendency for it to cover up its mistakes or shelter its declining parts by cross-subsidisation. Apparently the intention behind the 1947 Act was that the British Transport Commission should be competitive in behaviour — providing the best service at the lowest cost. But it would seem that in practice there was some collusion in restraint of competition: 'I may as well make it plain that the Commission encourage a certain amount of competition between their road and rail services. What we do not like is competition at the expense of the Commission's revenue.'[7] That suggests that parts of the Commission were not to undercut each other's prices if this would reduce the profits (or increase the losses) of the whole; and that is not competition. The difficulty of preventing the development of a transport loyalty resulting in such feather-bedding is perhaps one of the strongest arguments for breaking up the Commission. Administrative changes may make it easier to acquire a new habit of competition, but breaking up a monopoly in itself does not establish competition, since it is as profitable, and almost as easy, for separate undertakings to act collusively — enter into price, quality and job-sharing agreements. These pay and in any competition there is a temptation for rivals to sink their differences at the expense of the consumer. The Government will presumably have no greater powers over private firms in the industry than those provided by standard restrictive practices legislation; but if the various forms of publicly owned transport are mutually to compete, whether as separate undertakings or as branches of a single administrative entity, this should be written into their statutory instruments. Competitive behaviour should follow automatically from the consumers' surplus maximisation criterion; but the Government should take into account the order of magnitude of the total profits expected from the public transport sector when it decides on the number of undertakings which are to act competitively. Since greater profits could be made, at least in the short run, by collusion between firms, it would be thwarting the Government's intentions, since, for this reason alone, the industry would be able to make larger profits than the Government had thought desirable.

It is also implicit in the idea of competition that undertakings should adopt what we have called a competitive investment policy. Except for the effect on their own demand estimates, they should not consider the effect on each other's revenue and costs of the investment the propose to make. These are what economists call *pecuniary externalities* and are rightly ignored. If an investment in express buses were to undercut some already existing rail services and make these lower their prices, the reduction in railway profits would in general be matched by a benefit to their consumers from lower prices.

Yet although we have, I think, specified the necessary elements of what most people would recognise as a competitive solution, there are ways it might be improved by administrative arrangement. We can diminish the monopoly advantages transport enterprises gain from the ignorance of their users who do not know the facts well enough to make the best choice of transport. One idea to improve competition is that there should be a national parcels service handling parcels between 15 lb. and 1 ton in weight — small and sundries traffic[8] — with offices and agents throughout the country but no transport facilities of its own, purchasing space from private or public hauliers, or the railway boards, whichever is cheapest in the particular circumstances. It would bargain with transport providers for better terms and services than any single sender of such traffic could normally hope for. Special arrangements are not generally needed for consignors of regular traffic in large quantities. They can get the best terms for themselves. There is a case for another different innovation: a transport exchange analogous to a labour exchange. The occasional user of transport could tell the exchange what he wanted and it would be the exchange's duty to find him the cheapest means of transport for his requirements. Regular users could also use the exchange — in confidence as far as possible — to see whether they could not improve on their existing arrangements. Firms using their own transport could check occasionally to find out the costs of alternative methods.

A not dissimilar idea is that an agency should be set up to administer any subsidy, for example, to country-dwellers.[9] Suppose x million pounds was voted by Parliament for this purpose: there would inevitably be political pressures on the agency affecting the places where it spent its money, but one might hope it ought to be able to spend it in the most economical way — on the cheapest, most efficient form of transport. And one might hope that a small agency would do this more effectively than a Ministry would.

A related idea would go further. Instead of relying on horizontal competition for efficiency (between transport undertakings) it would introduce more vertical competition. For example, all land used by transport might be put into the control of one or more land agencies

—the land on which are built roads, railways, airports, etc. It would be told its criterion. It would then be its duty to lease land to transport undertakings so as to maximise its profits — or consumers' surplus, whichever is the criterion. Transport operators — the authority whose responsibility it was to build and maintain roads, the railway boards and so forth — would have to persuade the authority that it could make the most profitable use of the land in a given instance and would have to produce evidence for its expectations. The land agency or agencies alone would have the right to buy land, and they could sell it, it they thought there was a more profitable use for it outside transport.

All these devices to promote competition are intended, to use a phrase of Professor Galbraith's, to increase 'countervailing power'[10] to set up organisations with sufficient power and knowledge to give each other effective competition. The few devices mentioned above are not intended as a programme but just as a few hints on the kind of thing that could be done to improve competition if thought necessary. Some may feel that these are coordination — rather than competition; but we need to escape from the naive view which equates competition with *laissez-faire*. In a world where there are so many natural opportunities for making monopoly profits, competition has to be established; and it is the Government in the last resort by its policy which makes competition effective.

If the criterion is consumers' surplus maximisation these measures should establish workable competition. What is required is (1) the writing in of the appropriate rules into the statutory instruments of public transport enterprises or a directive from the Minister of Transport to the same effect; and (2) a Committee of Inquiry or Royal Commission to go into the whole question of establishing the *same conditions* for the different forms of transport.

But if profit maximisation is the criterion, there is still the problem of *excess profits*. One definition is to regard these as profits which the Government thinks are intolerably high. But where profits become disproportionately high in one transport mode because its monopoly power is great, it is no longer sensible to ignore the welfare losses that result from this through its overall effect on the misallocation of resources. This should be borne in mind when deciding how transport enterprises are to compete. For example, if excess profits were made by London Transport, one remedy would be to require the underground railways and the buses to compete with each other. In principle it should be possible to do this within the present administrative framework, but splitting the present organisation might be more effective. Fortunately, competition is widespread in transport.[11] The only traffic on which the railways might be able to make very high profits is probably coal. Road haulage is a highly competitive industry. It should be possible to introduce more competition into the road passenger transport industry where there are excess profits. There are scarcely any services where excess profits are likely to be made by airlines or waterways.

The road system is a more certain source of excess profits. In towns many road-users have no alternative means of transport for at least part of their journey. The inflexibility of the charging mechanism would be some check on profits, but even if the windscreen sticker method were adopted and only one price could be charged a vehicle of a given size and type for the use of streets in the restricted area, this could be set high enough to recoup a high rate of profit. If there were metering, the greater flexibility of this could make possible a much higher level of profits. The only reasonable way out of this is to set a ceiling to the rate of profit made by the road system in towns and cities. It would not be politic to directly impose a ceiling to the rate of profit on capital invested, because of the importance of the rent element. Perhaps the most reasonable procedure would be to bring the road system under the direction of the Transport Tribunal already empowered to fix maximum fares and charges for railways and buses in the London area; but to attempt to avoid the past shortcomings of the tribunal by specifying that charges are to cover the costs of the road system as defined in Chapters 9 and 10, plus an element for rent determined by considering the average rentable value of land neighbouring the road system.

A similar method could be used to control the other most important source of potential excess profits in the road system: the money a man could be made to pay for access to his house, shop or business premises. But it would be possible to limit the problem, and in some cases to solve it by restricting on charging. One method would be to prohibit the road system from charging for the use of roads through the rates except in two cases. The first would be that the costs of the road system attributable to pedestrians might be levied in that way (see Chapter 10). The second would be the case where the cost of providing *access* was not covered by the petrol taxation paid by vehicles using the stretch of road in question. In both cases it could be mandatory that price discrimination was not to be practised and that the ratepayers might only be charged the actual costs attributable to them plus some fixed rate of profit. Thus it should be possible to avoid this particular form of excess profit.

By these three methods — defining the area of competition, setting up regulatory bodies with defined powers, and imposing certain restrictions on charging — it should be possible to keep profits tolerable throughout the transport sector; and permit all transport enterprises to attempt to maximise profits as best they can, subject to these constraints.

COORDINATION

Let us consider some of the objections that might be made in the name of coordination to the competitive solution outlined above before considering the policy alternative, coordination, mentioned at the beginning of this chapter.

Subsidisation

There are those who would argue that more coordination, meaning by this more monopoly power, is needed to make cross-subsidisation possible. Though true, it is not an argument we need consider further since our objections to cross-subsidisation itself have been made.

Freedom of Choice

Another argument disapproves of some aspects of the freedom of choice implicit in the competitive solution. For example, both the competitive and coordinated solutions outlined here would allow a commuter to drive himself to work in a city in his private car providing he paid the full costs attributable to him as defined by the criterion adopted. But some might feel that this is in some sense a social waste or simply socially undesirable even then. Similarly they might argue, as certain advocates of coordination used to, that all goods transport should be by publicly owned transport; and that the consignor should have no choice whether his consignment went by road, rail or any other means. This solution would imply the abolition of the right to send one's own goods in one's own freight vehicles — the C licence lorries — at least for any distance. Anybody who thinks that a transport system should to some extent dictate the users' choice of transport other than by the price mechanism will not be satisfied with either of our two solutions which are based on the premiss of freedom of choice; and to impose such a solution a transport monopoly, necessarily working to criteria different from those elaborated in this book, will be needed.

Technical Coordination

A common interpretation of coordination is technical coordination. Examples are cooperation over time-tables and itineraries, standardisation of charging and accounting procedures, integration of delivery arrangements, parcels and smalls and sundries traffic, and the

294

operation of road-railers. Some of these the Commission was developing before the Road Haulage Executive was taken away from it in 1953. In those days it could be argued more plausibly that a transport monopoly was needed to achieve technical coordination because inflexible charges and other restrictions made it impossible to use the price mechanism to the same end. However, technical coordination should take place freely in a competitive situation – if it is profitable. Commercial firms in other industries enter into similar mutually beneficial arrangements without administrative merger.

The only difficulty for policy should be when technical coordination creates an undesirable monopoly advantage and this it should be possible to avoid by legislation. For example, a promising development is the roadrailer, a vehicle which has two sets of wheels, one for road and one for rail. Its use requires a measure of technical coordination between road and rail. If the coordination was between one railways board and a single haulier this would give the two of them a monopoly advantage which they would not possess if the railways were required to give roadrailer facilities to any haulier or private firm with a C licence fleet willing to pay the cost.[12] By such measures it should always be possible to achieve technical coordination without sacrificing competition.

Economies of Scale

But it might be objected that surely the existence of economies of scale could be an argument for a monolithic coordinated transport system. It would be a strong argument against the imposition of a competitive solution on many industries that it would mean forcing the separate undertakings to be a smaller size than would realise full economies of scale. The advantages of mass production are an argument against competition. Fortunately, this is not an important argument in transport because in most branches of transport the optimum size of firm is sufficiently small to make competition effective. There are a very large number of firms in the road haulage industry.[13]

There do not seem to be any significant economies to be gained by bigness. Certainly there is little tendency towards merger and takeover. But even if there were there would still be effective competition from the C licence fleets, from British Road Services, and from other forms of transport. It would be crazy to try to set up another railway system to compete with what we have; but there is sufficient competition from other forms of transport for most traffic. It is unlikely that decentralisation of the railways will lead to any diseconomies due to smaller size, though if the decentralisation were carried much further one would expect them. There are probably few economies which could be achieved by merging public and private airlines, though there are probably several attainable by merging private airlines with each other; but if they merged, competition with public airlines and again with other forms of transport should make for effective competition. Public road passenger transport presents more of a problem. There is some competition in towns with the private car and occasionally the Underground as alternative means of transport. Quite important too is the fact that a steep increase in fares would mean the loss of the short-distance passenger to walking; and, in general, it would be impracticable to charge passengers travelling from one to three miles at a higher rate than those travelling less than one mile. But there are economies of scale to be realised in bus operation which may be incompatible with effective competition. Nevertheless as a generalisation it can be maintained that a competitive solution will not be inefficient because of failure to realise economies of scale.

Elimination of Monopoly Profits
Then there is the argument that some coordination is needed because competition in practice permits some transport operators to make monopoly profits. This is a long-established argument for a public monopoly in transport. If there are natural monopolies in transport then they should be regulated, and ownership is more efficient than control by regulatory bodies. The argument is not as well founded as it was because of the greater competition caused by the development of road and air transport, and as already mentioned the argument is only relevant to the profit maximisation criterion. We have tried to take account of it in developing the competitive solution outlined in this chapter. It is virtually certain that public opinion will require the regulation of the excess profits that occur; but this should not necessitate setting up a transport monopoly. If coordination is defined to include Government intervention to curb excess profits, then it is practically certain that any acceptable competitive solution will include so much coordination.

Avoidance of Wasteful Competition
Sometimes exactly the opposite objection is made. Coordination is needed because of wasteful competition endemic in transport. This was the prime motive behind much legislation of the 1920s and 1930s.[14] It was argued, for example, that the road haulage industry needed regulation. Two many servicemen used their gratuities at the end of the First World War to buy an ex-army lorry and set up as a carrier. Entry continued to be too easy because of the small capital

296

needed. Too many carriers entered the business largely because of the independence given by the expenditure of a small capital sum. An excessive number of lorries competing kept profits too low. Cut-throat competition meant that drivers worked hours too long to be safe. Vehicles were not properly repaired. Regulation of the industry was urged on the grounds of safety; and in 1930 the present licensing system was introduced which restricted the number of road haulage vehicles by fixing the number of licences. The traffic commissioners who operate the licensing system have, in general, kept the number of licences down. Licences are only issued freely to firms − C licences − if these are used to carry the firm's goods only.

In the circumstances of the 1930s there were strong arguments for regulation. Depressed business activity did mean excess capacity. The small capital needed to start a business did tempt in the unwary, and there were bankruptcies though perhaps not as many as tradition reports.[15] It was hard for established hauliers to run safe businesses and make proper provision for replacement. But circumstances have changed. With proper labour laws and safety regulations, there should not be any need for the clumsy apparatus of the present licensing system which has now become a protective agreement, keeping charges artificially high throughout transport. (It is significant that when an application is made for permission to run more road vehicles, it is often opposed by the railways as well as by other hauliers.)

Regulation of the bus industry was justified by the same arguments and others in addition. Free competition among bus companies had meant a chaotic lack of system.[16] Services were irregular and unpredictable, there being few reliable time-tables. Buses indulged in such practices as chasing, nursing, hanging back to get each other's customers. Again one may wonder whether restoring competition now would revive all these old malpractices: especially if companies were required to publish a time-table three months in advance, say, and, except in extreme emergency, be required to stick to it. What one can say is, I think, that the argument for various regulations limiting competition which have persisted from the 1930s does require investigation to see whether they are still in the public interest and if they do not require modification.

COORDINATION OF INVESTMENT

The meanings of coordination discussed in the last section are, I believe, the most important that are meaningful − where coordination in some sense is advocated as a means to an end and not just as an end in itself. But there is this last meaning, *coordination of investment.*

This can also be used vaguely. In the 1930s argument coordination of investment was often demanded as a necessary preliminary to increasing the rate of investment and getting the economy out of a slump. Nowadays those who argue the case for coordination of investment generally have one of two ideas in mind: the first is that the Government can very often make a better decision about investment than separate undertakings whether privately or publicly owned. Very often this is confused with the idea that Governments would use more socially desirable investment criteria — based on a better definition of (social) costs and benefits. We have described a system in which the Government can require the transport undertakings to take certain social costs and benefits into account if it desires; and if this is coordination of investment, then our system permits it. The general proposition, that the more centralised the investment the more logical and the better based on facts, is scarcely plausible. Certainly ministries at present know fewer facts and are often no more logical than nationalised industries. One would have thought that centralisation of investment would often be self-defeating because of the burden of work at the centre and less necessary if the investment criteria are specified from the centre.

The other meaning of coordination of investment is more important. If several industries make their investment plans without reference to each other, they may find that their expectations of the costs of investment, and therefore of the profits they had hoped to make, are defeated because they are competing for and bidding up the prices of the same scarce resources. A simultaneous increase in investment in roads and house-building might be defeated by the size of the building industry, which, let us say, would have been sufficient for either programme separately but not for both together. In this sense there is much to be said for national coordination of investment. This is not a particular problem for the transport sector, and it is plausible that the coordination needed here is not so much between transport industries but between particular transport industries and other industries which use the same raw materials and kind of labour. Electrification of the railways, for example, used electrical resources which might otherwise go to a great variety of manufacturing industry. In this second sense coordination of investment is important and meaningful but it would hardly make sense applied to the transport sector.

The third sense of coordination of investment is the idea that transport undertakings should 'take account' of each other when making investments. Formally this means that they should take into account the costs and benefits (profits or consumers' surplus according to the criterion) of other transport enterprises in so far as

298

is practicable when making an investment. In estimating the rate of return on road investment the Road Research Laboratory takes into account the benefits and costs which accrue to other roads from the building of a new road (Chapter 11, p.269), but does not consider the effect of a new road on the railways (or on canals and airlines for that matter). This one could broadly be described as a competitive policy; the justification being that though both are Government-owned, roads and rail must be in competition to achieve the best services at the lowest cost. By ignoring the effect on each other, the dangers of competition — the risk of loss — are increased and this is a spur to efficiency. The alternative is what we will call here coordination of investment: meaning that whenever the rate of return is worked out on a road, for example, the effect of it on other forms of transport is allowed for as much as possible — whether plus or minus. But as has already been noticed the producer's loss is the consumers' gain. If the railways were to take into account any reduction in road haulage or bus profits from the expansion of their activities, but were to ignore consumer gains from lower road haulage or bus prices, their cost-benefit calculations would be biased. One can go further. If in considering the electrification of one railway line, British Rail were to allow — as any commercial enterprise would — for loss of profits on other competing railway lines of its own which would lose traffic to the new electrified line it would be considering only its own profits and not the offsetting increases in consumers' surplus. Thus to achieve an efficient investment programme, the right aim of investment coordination could be sometimes the reverse of what is claimed: to disallow profit losses where these are matched by consumer gains.

It may be noted that coordination of investment could be achieved by separate undertakings provided they were required to disclose to each other the necessary information; or it might be achieved by a single coordinated transport enterprise. It may also be noted that profit or consumers' surplus maximisation under coordination will not be achieved in the transport sector unless the enterprises: (1) have the same criteria; (2) operate under the same conditions; and (3) subject to any constraints imposed on profit maximisation, act so as to maximise the profits of the whole. Coordination as used here does not necessarily imply the view that public transport undertakings should make greater profits than in a competitive system: a question that is hardly a matter of efficiency at all. They might be required to compete — if profit-maximisers — to keep profits down and yet co-ordinate investment.

Transport in the National Economy

A few points are left for brief consideration. We have described the implications of adopting either of our basic criteria in an environment of competition or coordination. What remains is something about the place of the transport sector in the national economy. If we look at the economy as a whole there are three leading possibilities. (1) It will be a mixed economy. Private enterprise will make profits; the public sector, including the public transport undertakings, will operate by the consumers' surplus criterion. (2) Profit maximisation, roughly speaking, or (3) consumers' surplus maximisation will hold throughout the economy. This is also the order of their probability. We are most likely to have a mixed economy, least likely a consumers' surplus maximisation economy.

If we then ask how these possibilities could be justified, a conservative might be expected to support (1) or (2). If (2), this might be because he saw it a triumph for the profit motive. If it meant the virtual extinction of the public sector, he would see it perhaps as a victory of private enterprise. If it meant that the public sector adopted a commercial attitude he might welcome it as a surrender or conversion of the public sector to the profit motive. But if he were subtle he might see it as a return to a very old idea: the idea that the Crown, or rather the Government should 'live of its own', to use a medieval phrase. The profit-making nationalised industries would constitute 'the Manor of England' to use another medieval phrase, from which the Government might draw the greater part of its revenues. Parliament would determine the extent and general part of its revenues. Parliament would determine the exact extent and general policy of the nationalised sector as it does at present. The point of the change which might have a certain appeal would be to substitute, in part, this method of revenue-raising for taxation, a change which would have the side-effect of making it easier to regulate the economy by fiscal policy. The size of the public sector would depend to some extent on the financial needs of Government. We might imagine an economic system where all industries were run by men of much the same kind, calibre and opinions, the difference being that some were responsible to boards of shareholders of institutions, others to companies and private persons; while all or some of the shares in others would be vested in the Exchequer.

Most non-socialists however might be expected to support the idea of a mixed economy, granted the practical or political necessity of some nationalised industries. Sometimes this may not be disinterested. The consumer as consumer benefits from the low prices of an average-cost-pricing enterprise, and a particular consumer, let us say an important customer of the Coal Board, may feel he has more to gain

300

from average-cost coal prices than as taxpayer from profit-maximising coal prices. Secondly there is the fear of inflationary impetus if the nationalised industries should switch to profit-making, but this will not happen if there are compensating cuts in taxation so that there is no change in total national expenditure on consumption and investment. But probably more important than either of these is the simpler feeling that it is not right for publicly owned business to make a profit.

A few socialists might also welcome (2) the profit maximising economy — if only because they hope to show that public can be as efficient as private enterprise if both are allowed to play the same game. More, one would expect, would welcome (3) the consumers' surplus maximising economy — as something approaching an ideal — if they allowed a place in their ideal for capitalistic production. In a sense this would be the abolition of the profit motive without leaving the economy rudderless. Whoever ran the separate enterprises in such an economy would compete in the (consumers' surplus) dividends they declared. But in the short run one would expect most socialists to agree with most conservatives that the mixed economy is the most expedient as well as the most probable. A socialist might argue that the public sector should adopt the consumers' surplus criterion on the grounds that if there is a public sector, it should not make profits, without going to the extreme of demanding that it should be run as a public service below cost and with virtually no criteria. Or he might take an experimental attitude to the mixed economy, as a way to gain experience of and perfect the details of the consumers' surplus policy. A major reason why it has been difficult to advocate the extension of nationalisation since 1945 has been that there has been no reasonable measure of their efficiency, no yardstick by which a nationalised industry could measure whether it was efficient. Although the consumers' surplus policy does seem the logical extension of what has been attempted since the Second World War, it will take some time and experience to perfect. There are the various difficulties of application we have mentioned. More experience with surveys and calculations is needed than has yet been provided by highway authorities in the United States and Britain. If the use of the criterion becomes a successful routine operation for nationalised industries, then some socialists might feel they had a hard-headed practical alternative to profit maximisation.

The mixed economy, whatever the value-judgements or expediency on which it is based, does seem almost certain to persist for many years to come. What are the effects of having two criteria in the same economy? The most obvious is that transport (and the products and services of other consumers' surplus industries) will be cheaper in

301

relation to the products and services of other firms, than if all adopted profit or consumers' surplus maximisation. From the standpoint of the consumer this will mean there will be some tendency for him to substitute transport for other things in a way which can be illustrated by an example. Suppose we have a firm manufacturing a product which has a component, x. It has always bought this, a bulky commodity, from a supplier some fifty miles away. It has the choice of continuing to do this or setting up a plant to manufacture x itself. If it did this there would be a saving because it costs less to transport the raw materials for x than x itself, but on the other hand there are the capital costs of manufacturing x. Let us suppose profit (or conceivably consumers' surplus) maximisation holds throughout the economy. We will assume that it would then pay the firm to start manufacturing x. Alternatively if the transport sector should operate by the consumers' surplus criterion, charge average costs and forgo profits, this, we will assume, would tip the balance. The firm will continue to get x from the old supplier fifty miles away. Although one would not expect an instance of this kind to be particularly common, overall the difference in relative price due to differences in criteria must have some effect in increasing the proportion of national income spent on transport. (Otherwise we would have to assume that the demand for transport is perfectly inelastic over the relevant ranges.) This is inevitable, but hardly, one would think, a sufficient argument in itself for abandoning the mixed economy in favour of profit or consumers' surplus maximisation everywhere.

There is a similar effect if we look at the economy from the standpoint of the uses of national resources. Relatively cheaper transport prices means a higher demand for transport. A higher demand for transport means a larger transport sector. A larger transport sector means that more people and other factors of production (steel, bricks, etc.) are employed in transport than would be the case if there were nation-wide profit or consumers' surplus maximisation. Again there is the inevitable distortion in the allocation of resources — though to use the word distortion is to show that one is in the grip of an error. It is an error if we try to look at the economy as a whole from the point of view of either one of the basic criteria, but this is just what we must not do if we accept the fact of a mixed economy. Given this fact and the boundary between the two, the 'distortion' follows logically. What is a 'distortion' if we look from the point of view of profit maximisation need not be so from the standpoint of the mixed economy and vice versa.

POSTSCRIPT

If transport undertakings are able to price at marginal cost and follow the relevant consumers' surplus maximisation investment policies, competition will achieve an efficient allocation of resources within the transport sector. If marginal cost pricing were to exist throughout the economy, this would result in a Pareto-optimal allocation of resources in the sense that no further change in the allocation of resources could make someone better off without making someone else worse off. Marginal cost pricing does not exist in the rest of the economy. How important the deviations from it are depends on the view taken of the effectiveness of competition in the private sector and of government's will and success in imposing marginal cost pricing elsewhere in the public sector. If near perfect competition were to prevail, then competition would have brought about an approximation to marginal cost pricing in the private sector, but if one believes that the forces of monopoly are strong, then prices will be substantially above marginal cost. It is very difficult to establish any satisfactory tests of the degree of monopoly among firms since one has to postulate what outputs, prices and profits would be if there were perfect competition and compare these with what actually happens. Few firms possess long-lasting monopolistic advantages because they possess some scarce factor of production or have some technical ability that no rival can imitate. Many secure a monopoly profit through an innovation which competitors then imitate or improve on so that the advantage of the first firm is a temporary one. While some public enterprises attempt to practise marginal cost pricing, this is far from universal. The main difference between the private and public sectors is that one can be sure that if prices deviate from marginal costs in the private sector, it will be upwards if firms are profit maximisers, but also one finds downwards deviations in the public sector, even in some cases leading to deficits.

This poses a theoretical dilemma, though practically the policy alternatives are more limited. In theory there is what economists have called a second-best problem between the transport sector and the rest of the economy. It is possible that introducing marginal cost pricing (or indeed any other single criterion for transport enterprises) could result in a Pareto-inferior result for the whole economy: that is that the welfare losses elsewhere in the economy could exceed the welfare gains in relation to the specific transport industry (as measured in Chapter 6) that must result there from introducing marginal cost pricing.

Comprehensive analysis of second-best effects throughout the economy is extraordinarily complicated.[1] As a result empirical investigations are rare.[2] None have taken place (1974) in transport, though there has been some discussion already referred to of the appropriate theory.[3] Even so, one can make some relatively simple points about the possibility of such adverse effects:

(1) Let us assume that the intention is to *lower* the price of one transport mode to equal marginal cost. Since the price for this transport mode falls, the demand will rise (unless it is an inferior good which is unlikely). Consumers will substitute it for other goods and services. If any of these goods and services are produced at prices not equal to marginal cost, the resulting reduction in demand for them will in general reduce the welfare loss on those products. This is illustrated on Figure 12/1(a) for increasing costs and Figure 12/1(b) for decreasing costs industries. It is assumed in each case that an average

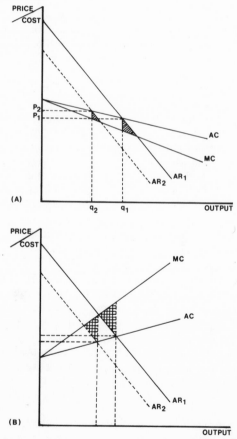

FIG. 12.1 (a & b)

cost pricing policy is adopted though there will be a similar effect for any pricing policy (e.g. profit maximisation) which results in such a divergence between price and marginal cost. The decline in demand is represented in each case by the shift of the demand curve from AR_1 to AR_2; in the increasing cost case the shaded area represents the welfare gain forgone; while in the decreasing costs case they represent the welfare loss. This argument amounts to a statement that in this case there will be some switch in consumption from sub-optimally to efficiently priced products; and therefore there must be an overall welfare gain.

(2) Let us assume the same price change downward to marginal cost in the transport industry but introduce the possibility of complementarity. Thus an increased demand for transport might lead to an increased demand for land in a metropolitan area.[4] Reversing the argument of the last paragraph any such relation of complementarity will increase welfare losses in so far as it results in an increase in demand for non-optimally-priced products elsewhere. The question then is whether the welfare gain in the transport industry is likely to exceed the sum of welfare gains and losses elsewhere in the economy through substitution and complementarity.

This is the important case. The practical question to be asked is whether there is a prima facie case for thinking that there is a relationship of complementarity such that it would be inefficient to lower transport prices to marginal cost. While no doubt there is complementary demand between transport and some other outputs, no research has suggested that any exists where there is a substantial divergence between marginal cost and price outside the transport section on a scale which would be likely to offset the advantages of moving to marginal cut pricing within the transport sector.

(3) Let us take the opposing interesting case* and assume that the initial price is below marginal cost in a transport industry, so that efficiency requires us to raise that price to marginal cost. Then the demand for that transport service will normally fall. Reversing the last arguments, demand will switch to substitutes for that transport service. In so far as these other goods are inefficiently priced, an increased demand for them is likely to increase the existing welfare losses caused by divergence between price and marginal cost. Conversely, welfare losses will be reduced where there is a complementary change in demand for inefficiently priced goods. In terms of fig. 12.1 one is reversing the direction of change. Where there is substitution we must

*There are cases where one cannot be as categorical. In fig 12.2, the shift in demand is such as to lead to an altering of the relative position of the marginal and average cost curves. In circumstances such as these there is no general presumption that the shift in demand is associated with a net welfare loss or gain.

assume an outwards shift of the demand curve elsewhere to result from raising the price of the transport service to marginal cost. Again the relevant question is whether net welfare losses elsewhere will more than offset the welfare gain that must result from introducing marginal cost pricing for the transport service.

What has been said about a transport industry and the rest of the economy also relates to the transport sector itself. Let us assume a two-industry transport sector and further assume that price equals marginal cost elsewhere in the economy. Let initial rail price be above marginal cost, then there will be an increase in efficiency by lowering rail prices to marginal cost unless (i) there is an equal or greater divergence between price and marginal cost on road, and (ii) the demand for road space is complementary to that for rail (which it plainly is not).

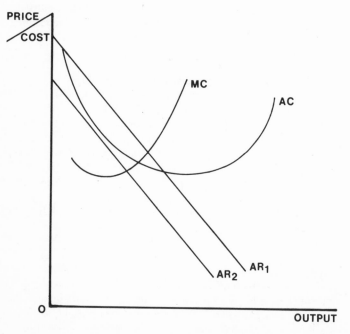

FIG. 12.2

Let us now take the opposite case. Road is assumed to be priced below marginal (social) cost initially and then the means is found to raise road prices to marginal social cost. In a two-sector transport industry on the assumption that rail is the only substitute for road, there must be a net welfare gain if rail were initially priced at marginal cost; but if the

306

divergence between price and marginal cost were greater on rail than on road, the net effect would be a welfare loss despite the gain in efficiency from introducing marginal cost pricing on the roads. As it stands this makes the unrealistic assumption that all the traffic that leaves the road because of raised prices diverts to rail; but some proportion will in fact divert to other transport modes or to other activities not involving transport. Thus to calculate the efficiency gains and losses from introducing marginal cost pricing on roads one would have to establish the divergences between price and marginal cost in relation to these and the effect of any welfare losses on each of the shift in demand to them from the roads.

As a consequence of these arguments it can be seen:

(1) that it is *possible* that it would be more efficient if transport sector prices were not set at marginal cost in the sense that a movement (upwards or downwards) to marginal cost *could* result in greater net welfare losses elsewhere in the economy. While it is possible, economists usually assume that it is not probable. The chances of there being such a net welfare loss intuitively seem less than the chances of there being a net welfare gain. The practical conclusion to be drawn from this is to assume that any policy which can achieve greater efficiency within the transport sector should be attempted; and that no such attempt should be deterred by the remote possibility of adverse second-best effects in the rest of the economy.

(2) One might argue similarly that any move towards marginal cost pricing within the transport sector is desirable in that the probability is that the welfare gains will exceed the welfare losses, even though other transport services are priced at prices that diverge from marginal cost. But the issue is not as clear-cut. Where transport modes are close alternatives, the probability that the net welfare losses will exceed the gains is the greater. For example, let us suppose initially that both long-distance train and domestic air services are losing money in the sense that prices are below marginal cost on each. A policy which raised air fares to marginal cost so that most of the air traffic switched to rail might well result in a net welfare loss. In such circumstances the often-heard argument that transport modes should use the same criteria is likely to be the more powerful. But where there is less competition the argument in general is less powerful. As the amount of road traffic declines for which the railways are an effective competitor; so the probability declines that introducing marginal social cost pricing on roads, without similarly introducing marginal cost pricing on rail, will result in an overall welfare loss. This is because on most roads and for most classes of traffic a change in road prices will not lead to appreciably greater use of railways. Road transport has become so much more important than rail transport.

We can as a result of this argument produce some working rules, Where transport modes are close substitutes for each other, the distorting effects of using different pricing criteria for each is probably greater than the benefits to be gained by equating the prices of one only to marginal cost. The most efficient solution would be that both should adopt marginal cost pricing; but failing that it is probably better that both should adopt the same criterion. Thus if in cities public road and rail passenger services were priced monopolistically above marginal cost, it is probable there would be some efficiency gain from pricing road space, and therefore the private motorist, above cost. This is because in many cities private and public transport are close substitutes but also because in this case the divergence between marginal private and social costs caused by congestion means that any relative distortion between road and other competing transport prices will cause unusually high welfare losses. Similarly, it is probably important that road haulage firms, whether privately or publicly owned, should use the same pricing rules as should rail freight operations in so far as they compete with these.

Conversely there are many non-urban journeys, particularly relatively short ones, where there is no effective substitute for the use of road space. There introducing an efficient pricing policy — marginal cost pricing — is more likely to be important — especially if the demand elasticity for road space is high — than achieving any kind of parity between road and rail.

Therefore the argument of the original requires qualification. It assumes that the 'competitive' situation was typical and that as a result it was obvious there would be a more efficient allocation of resources if transport modes, rail and road in particular, adopted the same pricing criteria than if one were to adopt marginal cost pricing and another pricing policy which diverged more from it. The decline in the railways and the growth of road traffic since 1963 reduces the force of the arguments I used in 1963; but with hindsight even then I suspect I was giving the traditional policy of coordination of criteria in transport more weight than its effect on the efficient allocation of resources deserved.

The Same Conditions
The 1968 Act made some move towards equalising conditions as here defined by harmonising regulatory burdens and subsidy provisions; but further research is required to establish the benefits and costs of regulatory and subsidy policies to make it possible to increase their efficiency in achieving government objectives.

Making Competition Effective

Revival of the British Transport Commission was resisted in the discussions leading to the 1968 Transport Act for reasons similar to those given in the text. It was hoped that coordination of policies, criteria, regulations and subsidies could be achieved by the Ministry of Transport. There were also attempts to promote new arrangements to help consignors of freight traffic to make efficient transport choices. A major argument for setting up the National Freight Corporation was that it could give potential customers a choice between road and rail haulage. This was because it contained the British Road Services and other nationalised road haulage, and acquired from the railways a large part of its smalls and sundries business, and all its freightliner operations. It was hoped that the NFC would develop a concept of the public interest which would enable it to give disinterested advice whether to send traffic by road or rail, even if in some cases the most efficient form of transport was by a rail method — e.g. company trains — which were operated directly by British Rail and not by the NFC. From this standpoint the hope was that the NFC would become one kind of Transport Exchange as mentioned in the original text. The NFC freightliner and smalls and sundries companies were transferred from British Rail partly in order to stimulate efficiency through countervailing power. As far as it is possible to judge, both have been successful. The transference of some responsibility to passenger transport authorities in major conurbations for subsidising unremunerative passenger services had a similar motive. There has been no move towards creating one agency to subsidise rural transport inside or outside the Department of the Environment.

Transport in the National Economy

Observations made in the first section of this postscript apply. But to summarise the arguments as I now see them. On efficiency grounds the traditional economic argument for marginal cost pricing remains strong. While in particular cases second-best considerations might indicate that a particular move towards marginal cost pricing had overall negative effects on efficiency, no one has been able to calculate the sum of such welfare losses and gains in the rest of the economy, to prove which way the second-best arguments tend. Since *a priori* arguments suggest that in most cases a movement to marginal cost pricing in one industry will not result in greater net welfare losses elsewhere in the economy than the direct welfare gain in the industry in question, it is reasonable to assume that a movement towards marginal cost pricing in the transport sector is likely to result in positive overall welfare gains. Within the transport sector, the presumption is less clear, particularly where the elasticity of substitution between one transport mode and another is high. Then one can argue in particular that increasing prices to marginal cost as is required for example on congested roads, could have an overall net welfare loss because of diversion to rail if there is a marked divergence between price and marginal cost on the railways. Then there is some force to the traditional arguments which suggest that on efficiency grounds it is more important for efficiency to establish equivalence between pricing and investment criteria on different modes than it is to make prices on any one mode along equal marginal cost if there are marked divergences on different modes. As was argued in Chapter 6 the notion of equivalence has to be analysed more rigorously. If price is above (or below) marginal cost on one mode then the comparative demand elasticities on each are relevant to determining the divergence between price and marginal cost on the other which will result in the most efficient allocation of resources between them. But this kind of argument has most force where competition is greatest. More than in 1963, there are now areas where competition between modes is comparatively unimportant. Thus in many nations, if a choice has to be made between a situation when a loss-making railway and the road system (through ignoring congestion) both price below marginal cost; and one in which the railway continues to price below marginal cost but the road system introduces marginal social cost pricing, one may well prefer the second on efficiency grounds because the railways' ability to compete has diminished so greatly by comparison with fifty or even twenty years ago, that though there will be welfare losses where there is diversion to rail, their magnitude will be relatively small. (The converse does not hold. To raise rail prices to marginal cost — if that were what was required

310

on the railways — might lead to an overall net loss in efficiency if it were not possible at the same time to introduce marginal cost pricing on the roads. This is because road is competitive for most, if not all, rail traffic.)

In the first edition of this book it was argued that it might be impossible to introduce marginal cost pricing on the railways. The major reason was non-economic in that it was argued that experience suggested that where marginal cost pricing implied deficits, governments commonly required average cost pricing so that no loss was made. As a matter of practice this remains true. Governments allow nationalised industries to make losses and even force them to do so, but not because of a wish to introduce marginal cost pricing. The most usual reason is a political reluctance to raise prices, often reinforced in times of inflation. However this argument seems less important than it did because of the arguments advanced by Dr. Joy that railways are not decreasing costs industries if they pursue optimal policies on track. They can adjust their provision of track to a much greater extent than used to be thought. Moreover congestion is often important on railways because there are usually some bottlenecks. Therefore it is less clear that marginal costs fall with output. As a result it might be possible to price at marginal cost on railways, providing it is pursuing an optimal investment and disinvestment policy, without incurring a deficit.

Marginal cost pricing has proved far more difficult to introduce on the roads and the failure to price reflecting congestion is a major cause of inefficiency. It may be possible to overcome the administrative and political difficulties which have so far prevented the adoption of marginal social cost road pricing or even of close approximations to it through the efficient use of parking controls and traffic restraint. Thus whatever may be an optimal pricing policy on rail, it may well be the case that it is not practical to effect the same policy on the road system. Where competition and the divergence between price and marginal social cost and price is greatest — e.g. in congested cities — this may be a powerful argument for subsidising rail transport so as to get an efficient relative price ratio between road and rail. This is the main basis of the case for subsidising urban public rail transport. A similar argument may lead one to subsidise buses, or improve their quality, relative to the private car, but again only where congestion leads to a substantial divergence between marginal road cost and price. This tends to be greater for individual travelling in a car during the peak than in a bus because the greater occupancy factor for buses outweighs the fact that one bus causes more congestion than one car.

By comparison price often exceeds marginal social cost on inter-urban roads. It is usually argued that this rarely leads to much diversion of traffic, especially freight, to rail because quality is more important in influencing modal choice than price.

In conclusion, while it remains important to coordinate pricing and investment criteria for particular flows of traffic, there is perhaps less general need to achieve coordination between road (overall) and rail (overall) than the argument of this book suggested. However the need to adopt and use explicit pricing and investment criteria for rail and other transport modes and to do the same for roads, given the constraints on what pricing mechanisms are feasible, remains as important as it ever was.

13 SUMMARY OF CONCLUSIONS

The leading argument throughout this book is that there are certain policy decisions which must be made by the Government if a logical transport policy is to be possible. Chief of these is the selection of what we have called the 'basic' criterion – basic because the Government may wish to depart from it for particular reasons, such as by subsidisation or regulation of particular interests. I argue that marginal cost pricing and the investment policy associated with it are not acceptable bases for policy, for several reasons but principally because it has effects on income distribution which happen to be politically unacceptable. Therefore this favourite economist's prescription must be replaced. The problem of finding an acceptable criterion was defined as one of finding policies supported by some weight of public opinion. This question is usually considered in the context of nationalised industries in general, not of transport in particular. Two alternatives are suggested:

(1) That the public transport undertakings should be required to maximise profits, possibly subject to some constraints on the amount of profits they are allowed to make.

(2) That they should be run in the consumers' interest.

Various possible exact formulations of the second policy were considered and that selected was named *consumers' surplus maximisation*. This was defined to imply average cost pricing (of each good or service provided) and a consumers' surplus maximisation investment policy. Two alternative assumptions were made about the relations between transport undertakings: competition and coordination. It was argued that there was a case, in the interests of the allocation of resources, equity and logical consistency, that public transport undertakings should be required to adopt the same basic criterion. Therefore solutions to the transport problem were considered as deductions from four basic criteria: profit maximisation under competition; profit maximisation under coordination; consumers' surplus maximisation under competition; consumers' surplus maximisation under coordination.

The rest of the book has been concerned with seeing how the criteria might work. This has meant consideration of three kinds of problems; places where it was necessary to draw out the logical implications of the criteria; places where it was necessary to supplement the criteria with additional judgements; and last, the

313

problem of trying to make them fit the facts so as to indicate how they might be used to make sense of transport policy.

It is difficult to make definite recommendations about railway policy without better costing. Some description of the inadequacies of railway costing in the recent past was given. The problem of the correct treatment of joint costs under profit and consumers' surplus maximisation was analysed; and the appropriate charging policy was defined. The right charging policy when in deficit was also considered. The chief conclusions about railway investment were that in the past the presentation of the modernisation plan and its revisions had been misleading and had made it impossible to test whether they proposed sound investments or not. It was argued that investment proposals should be set out clearly, that they should take proper account of risk and time, and should distinguish clearly between investments which were supposed to pay and those that were not. The chapter on consumers' surplus maximisation on the railways was mostly concerned with making the criterion more definite and workable. It was argued that it was possible to make this criterion as explicit as profit maximisation, and once accountants and decision-makers were used to it, should hardly be more difficult to use.

The first argument on road policy was that present methods of investment charging, and the grant system were ill considered and confused, the result of historical accident; and that there was a case for organising the road system as an industry with a set of accounts and a well-defined criterion. The solution of the road problem had to be begun at a much more elementary level than the rail problem for that reason. It had to be decided what the costs of the road system were and this depended as much on the Government making decisions on what were to be accounted costs of the road system as improving knowledge. If consumers' surplus maximisation is to be adopted there is the problem of deciding who are to be accounted beneficiaries of the road system. There is the particular costing problem of deciding whether road-users are to be charged for congestion they caused. The nature of this question was examined. It was also argued that the question of the alternative use value of roads was important especially in towns. The chief problem of charging was to find a more flexible method which would make it easier to charge people more accurately the costs they occasion. Various methods from differential licence duties to electronically operated meters were considered. The point made was that it should be possible to devise a system of charging for roads much more flexible than the present system of taxation whose shortcomings were examined. Then it would be possible to require a road authority to maximise profits though it was argued that some constraints on this power would almost certainly be desirable politically.

At the same time it should be possible to make a consumers' surplus charging policy flexible. The chief investment problem considered was that of actually working the consumers' surplus criterion so that it became more useful.

In the last chapter various definitions of competition and coordination were considered. It was decided that the most interesting difference between the two was the notion that investment should be competitive or integrated. The case for and against competition by this definition was set out.

Throughout this book I have tried not to indicate any preference for one or other of the basic criteria. My conclusion is that it would be an improvement in public policy if any one were adopted, and that it is an important *political* decision which it is to be.

POSTSCRIPT

How do the criteria wear with the years? One might have wished to develop an analysis of running British Railways to maximise workers' surplus — not, however, because there has been any obvious enthusiasm in that direction. (The same possibility hardly arises for the road system — the labour content is so low.)

The realisation that there would not be substantial scale economies on the railways if an efficient investment (and disinvestment) policy were pursued means that short-run marginal cost pricing probably would not imply a permanent deficit. Thus in general consumers' surplus maximisation, marginal cost pricing and 'breakeven' should be compatible.

Because the services where railways have significant monopoly power are few, profit maximising on the railways may be determined by market forces and approximate to short-run marginal costs, provided it pursued an optimal investment (and disinvestment) policy. As defined in this book, the consumers referred to in a consumers' surplus policy are those who use the railways. In this context there is no reference to externalities. There would therefore have to be substantial monopoly for there to be marked practical differences in the consequences of adopting either policy on the railways.

There will be greater divergences between (1) profit maximisation, (2) average cost pricing consumers' surplus maximisation and (3) marginal cost pricing consumers' surplus maximisation on the roads, because of increasing long run costs in cities. Whichever criterion was adopted, more efficient pricing requires either progress towards the use of the methods of road pricing that have been developed or the greater use of profits for road pricing. The difficulty with profit maximisation thereafter would be the monopoly power inherent in road provision.

It would require the imposition of various constraints to reduce monopoly profits, and any system of control to this end would raise all the difficulties one ordinarily finds with regulatory bodies. Consumers' surplus maximisation on the other hand is already becoming recognised as the standard highway investment criterion. Its related pricing policy presents more of a problem. Average cost pricing as defined in this book would not deal optimally with the substantial inefficiency of congestion. Whether short-run MC pricing would mean profits or not depends on the kind of highways considered. Deficits are most likely on sparsely used rural roads where congestion is no problem. Even combined with an efficient investment policy, MC pricing in congested urban areas will almost certainly imply profits.

It may not be possible to coordinate transport policy by requiring these two modes (and others) to have the same criteria. The reasons may be political or because of the practical limits to flexibility in pricing, especially in road pricing. If so, the outstanding question is how great would be the inefficiencies that would result from this. On this both theoretical and empirical research is needed.

APPENDIX 1   A NOTE ON MARGINAL COST PRICING

Figure 6.3 illustrated the effect of marginal cost pricing, under two conditions of variation of cost with output.

It is vital to stress that marginal cost (MC) pricing is a means to an end. Unfortunately people have used different language to describe that end — the maximisation of national (real) income, national real product or dividends and the maximisation of consumers' and producers' surpluses. (Or, to put it another way, the object is to make the (social surplus) rate of return on the nation's capital as high as possible.) To avoid confusion we will describe the end to which MC pricing is the means as the maximisation of real income. As was indicated in Chapter 3, believing this is a desirable policy means assuming that money is a cardinal measure of welfare independent of its distribution between persons and over time. One objection to MC pricing is that decision-makers might normally be expected to neglect social costs, equating marginal private cost and price; but this is, of course, not an objection to the principle but to a faulty application of it. The problem then is one of redefining MC so that the right end is achieved: the rule should be marginal social cost (MSC) pricing. The Lerner rule, the most convenient formulation, then becomes: if marginal (social) cost is less than price, increase output; if it is more, decrease output; if it is equal to the price, continue producing at the same rate for then the right output has been reached.[1] If national income is not maximised, then the Lerner rule is somewhere not being observed — for they are logically implied by each other. When it is realised that MSC pricing is a means to an end, it is easier to refute or allow for many criticisms of the policy.

One type of criticism is that the use of the principle is ambiguous, even if every decision-maker in the economy tries to make MSC equal to price:

(1) Decision-makers do not have complete knowledge of the future. They cannot know all effects of a decision. Therefore they cannot take into account all social benefits and costs when they determine MSC. Therefore there is no reason to suppose national income will be maximised.

(2) In so far as they necessarily look into the future, uncertainty affects their decisions in another way. Not only will they not have complete knowledge of all the effects but they may disagree what those effects will be because, faced with the same evidence, their

317

predictions of the future – and therefore their estimation of price and MSC – will disagree. Their actions will vary accordingly. It follows that the outcome – the national income achieved – will depend in part on who makes the decisions.

(3) Furthermore they are not equally ignorant and, because their opinions vary, the outcome will be one not foreseen by any one of them (unless there is one dictatorial decision-maker).

But although all this means that an economy may never in fact maximise national income, in the sense that if it had known more, earlier, it would have made different price and output decisions (chosen different values of MSC and price), this does not invalidate the principle but merely illustrates an inevitable consequence of ignorance. Any principle of behaviour is as likely to mislead. Given any principle decision-makers must do the best they can, and society can try to choose decision-makers who are least ignorant and make the best predictions.[2]

There is a slightly different class of criticisms. It is often said that it is not clear whether MSC pricing implies making price equal to long run (LR) or short run (SR) MSC. It is sometimes said that this is a matter of choice, and therefore the principle is ambiguous for another reason (for example, Wiseman[3]). This is false. The implications of the principle *for pricing* are ambiguous. LR MSC has nothing to do with pricing. SR MSC is the ultimate generalisation of the economic maxim that 'bygones should be bygones'. Hence SR MSC: the cost of producing the extra unit of output consumed. A price lower or higher than this is wasteful. To take the traditional example of a train. While the train is not full, the SR MC of carrying another passenger is virtually zero. When full it is the cost of running another train, but *as soon as* the extra train is provided it falls to zero again. In this example the SR MC, and therefore the price, will always be zero since *either* there is no more room on the train and no one else can be carried *or* there is room on the train and it costs nothing to carry another. But to take the example of a machine wearing out. As it ages the SR MC of its output rises until the machine is replaced, when it falls again. When the old machine is being used the relevant LR MC is that of installing the most efficient new machine to do the work but once it is installed the relevant MC is the SR MC of the new process (Lerner[4]).

It therefore seems that SR MC only is relevant to pricing, though qualification must be made. It is often said that it is not *practicable* to charge the instantaneous SR MC price of a thing (Graaff[5]). If this means that the cost of varying SR MC is greater than the benefit of doing so, not only is it impracticable but illogical to vary it since national income would be less if it were not averaged to some extent. The cost of variation is a SR MC of SR MC pricing and must be taken into account

318

in determining the total SR MC. Finally, to make **any** statement that some LR MC should be paid for by consumers — which many impure marginalists seem to do without realising what they are doing — is to tack on an income distribution qualification of pure marginalism.

Put in that way MSC pricing is safe, but there is a related point which does introduce ambiguity into the criterion. MSC pricing is a pricing criterion. What is the related investment principle? The Lerner rule is correct but neglects to draw a distinction between short period and long period changes in output. Short period changes are achieved by adding or subtracting variable factors of production — long period changes by investment. Even so, the Lerner rule can be taken as an investment principle up to a point. When LR MC is less than SR MC, invest until lowest possible SR MC equals price. But there are two cases where this will not do: (1) When the investment must, on technical grounds, be in some indivisible plant or factor, (2) when capital is scarce. In both exceptions the cause is the same. A decision must be made *when* and in what order to invest. Because the rule does not apparently deal with this situation, it is sometimes said (Wilson[6]) that MSC pricing does not imply an investment criterion. The logical answer is that the end, maximisation of national income, does. But completing the criterion in this way does make clear why the criterion can be interpreted variously according to the time period over which national income is to be maximised. We cannot sum an infinite series. Therefore we only set out to maximise national income over some finite period. The length of the time period affects the decisions — the values of SR MC and price, the pattern of investment over the period. One would expect that the governing factor in its choice would be the distance into the future over which the decision-maker felt he could make non-random predictions (Graaff[7]), modified by the social time preference discount rate.

So far the criticisms are not really objections to MSC pricing, since they could be made to any principle, including profit and consumers' surplus maximisation; but it is perhaps surprising how much space has been taken in the literature by objections which are directly or indirectly based on a demand for certainty or a failure to complete the criterion by incorporating the investment criterion which is logically implied by it.

The more serious objections to the principle, which relate to income distribution, are of two kinds. For one reason or another it is objected that money is not a cardinal indicator of welfare independent of distribution of income between persons or over time. There are possibly three variants of the objection which are worth considering separately. First, it is objected that the effect of the change on income distribution is undesirable, on what can be called moral, ethical or political grounds.

If there are certain income distribution effects which are thought undesirable, these can be ruled out by imposing constraints on national income maximisation: for example, nothing shall be done which will reduce the share of national income going to miners; nothing shall be done which will not increase the share of income going to the poor (a defined class) by more than that to the rich (another defined class). One onerous form of constraint is to demand that all changes are what economists call Paretian: that they make no one worse off while making some people better off. The difficulty about this constraint is to find changes, new policies, which meet its requirement. Virtually all policies, Acts of Parliament, etc., do make someone worse off. Certainly the policies considered in this book will make some classes of the population worse off. But it is clearly important to consider the income distribution effects of any policy to see if they are to be judged (by those in a position to decide) a sufficient bar to a particular exercise of MSC pricing.

The second objection is more far-reaching — not an objection to a particular change, but to the income distribution which happens to be implied by national income maximisation. It is easy to give examples. One indeed would be that it would be better to increase the income of the poor both at the expense of the rich and of aggregate national income — just as it might be said that it was worth while to sacrifice some economic growth (growth of national income) to make a more cultured society — which implies an income distribution — a distribution weighted towards the beneficiaries of culture.

A third kind of income distribution argument which is really a special case of the second raises a particularly knotty problem. One implication of MSC pricing is that there are certain industries which have to be subsidised — all those with increasing returns — where MC is less than average cost. These are the industries with overheads. Provided SR MC are paid for by consumers, the rule has nothing at first glance to say about the source of payment for these overheads, even whether they need be paid for at all as bygones. But this is not quite true. It is possible that a building is an overhead of a particular firm, but if the building industry is to keep going, it must be paid the SR MC of its production, otherwise its output will be suboptimal and likewise in all industries throughout the economy. The only goods which do not have to be paid for are the irreplaceable or non-replaceable goods. But the principle does not state from what source these payments are to be made, whether from an excess of price over MSC or from taxation or in some other way. Sometimes it is suggested that the making of such payments will infringe the marginal conditions (Meade[8]) but this is a fallacy which comes from first thinking in terms of the marginal conditions, irrespective of finding these

320

payments, and then imposing a system of fund-raising on it. This is illogical. The point is given that certain funds have to be raised to pay the SR MC of industries other than final goods industries, and there must be a way of doing this which will be most efficient.

This disposes incidentally of another kind of objection to the principle. But the objection we are concerned with here is to the pattern of taxation and subsidisation, which we will assume is entailed by the income maximisation policy. When the system of taxation which is implied by national income maximisation is in force, it is possible it will include some excise taxes which would result in some disturbance in the initial equalities between MSCs and prices (in the interest of the more comprehensive definition of social costs and benefits); but, whatever the distribution of taxation, it is likely there will be some subsidisation of decreasing costs industries implied. There will result a relative cheapening of the prices of such industries in relation to those of increasing costs industries: the income distribution in favour of the purchasers of the goods and services of decreasing costs industries. Apparently the notion of a world where this happens and people only pay the SR MC of the goods they buy offends many people's sense of equity. 'Many people find very disturbing the tranquil acceptance of a permanent net loss in a production unit or in an industry as of no consequence at all as long as the rule is obeyed. Anyone brought up in a capitalistic society feels 'instinctively' that something is wrong when outlay exceeds income and there ought to be a rule against it . . . this feeling is nothing but an illogical (though easily understandable) transference from the capitalist economy . . . On the lower level this transference is based simply on the individual's interest in keeping solvent . . . It is irrelevant where the purpose considered is not the profit or the solvency of any individual or group or enterprise, but the optimum use of society's resources . . . At the higher level, one symptom of perfect competition is that there are no losses; consequently this is thought to be a condition of the optimum use of resources. On this level abnormal profits are also taboo for the same reason and it has led to the proposal of a rule to make p = AC. This syllogism falls to the ground because the optimum use of resources is *not* identical with perfect competition' (Lerner[9]).

That it is wrong to make a permanent loss is sometimes backed up by an argument which in its usual simple form is spurious. This is that if businesses are allowed to make losses there is no test of efficiency and investment. In practice defective knowledge and imagination may make this true, but in principle it should be possible to make a shot at estimating the *social surplus* rate of return which is relevant as a test of efficiency and investment. The problem is exactly the same as that which we are meeting in this book in finding a criterion

321

and an *ex post facto* test of efficiency and investment for consumers' surplus maximisation, though social surplus maximisation is obviously beset by more problems of defective information. But to argue that there is no test of efficiency, that a business run at a loss for this reason must be inefficient because there is no incentive, no yardstick of performance, is false and illogical. It is again to mistake the means for the end (Wilson[10]). A better supporting argument is one that would tell us as a matter of fact that *profit maximisation* would maximise national income and a loss-making policy would not. This is a simple argument that the cost of SR MC pricing, in industries where this implies losses, in terms of efficiency and economic growth is greater than the benefit. An argument of this kind is latent in much modern political and economic thinking, which assumes that, to macro-economic problems, there are more important solutions which will increase the rate of growth of income than trying to impose MSC pricing. For one reason or another it is commonly assumed that MSC pricing is irrelevant or positively dangerous because of the disruption it would cause. This begs the question whether use of some approximation to a social surplus rate of return would not be the answer. Nevertheless the argument is plausible. I would argue that we should gain more experience in the use of consumers' surplus calculations before we go on to use social surplus maximisation calculations plus MSC pricing. There are therefore arguments both from equity or rightness and from efficiency against the income distribution effects implied by the subsidisation of increasing returns industries which is a logical implication of MSC pricing. I do not happen to share the first dislike. I find I can imagine a world in which permanent losses are made for this reason with tolerable enthusiasm; but the fact that society does not, seems to me final for the time being. The second argument I also find fairly convincing pending further development of the use of non-commercial rates of return.

Any income distribution modification of MSC pricing can be imposed as a constraint on national income maximisation: 'maximise subject to the constraint that . . . ' But there is another way of incorporating any such modification which can be made formally equivalent to the first. This by weighting costs and benefits; and excluding certain categories (giving them zero weight) so as to achieve the same income distribution effect. (An absolute rule not to diminish the income of x then implies giving infinite weight to a downward change in x's income.) The point of noticing this is that if one has a universal criterion that is a unique criterion (well-defined welfare function) applying to all economic decisions, this can be expressed in terms of *some* MC pricing rule (Bergson, Nordin[11]). Under the appropriate modifications to allow for the required constraints on income distribution, MSC pricing becomes alternatively MC = MR pricing or AC pricing.

The last objection to MC pricing, on which a group of criticisms are based, is that national income will not be maximised unless MSC pricing is adopted universally (Little, Graaff[12]). That this must be so, is obvious. The question is: what inference is to be drawn? If some decision-makers are using *known* rules other than MSC pricing, then it is possible for other decision-makers to compensate so as to maximise national income, given the policy of the first class of decision makers. The problem is, however, usually posed in another form. Given profit maximisation and/or other criteria than MSC pricing throughout the rest of the economy, will MSC pricing in the public sector improve the allocation of resources and maximise national income? One argument which has been used in favour is that making price equal to MC is a step in the right direction in industries where products are being sold at less than MC. This was Little's[13] argument in relation to fuel, where MC is or was generally more than AC, hence he could argue 'there is no doubt that this would result in relative prices and relative marginal costs being more nearly equal for a large majority of all pairs of products'. Unfortunately MSC pricing would often mean a reduction in the prices charged for transport — for example on roads, except in congested areas, and on railways, again except where there is congestion on the railways — so that one cannot use what is an implicit proportionallity argument for MSC pricing here.

A second argument which is used is that it is important to make relative prices equal to relative marginal costs where goods are close substitutes (Little, Mishan[14]); that is, in this case, that MSC pricing should be adopted throughout transport. Logically it can only be assumed that this would lead to an optimal allocation of resources in transport if MSC and benefits are defined purely in relation to transport — all other social costs and benefits being excluded from the calculation. On this basis MSC pricing would be a different animal. One might call it marginal transport cost pricing. And this would imply what I have argued is unacceptable on other grounds: subsidisation of decreasing costs transport industries by increasing ones. In so far as this meant a subsidisation of country road-and rail-users by users in congested areas, this *cross subsidisation* might be acceptable politically; but in as much as it would mean, as I suspect it would, subsidisation of road-users by railway-users, it would not. There are two points to this argument. The first is the straight argument for parity of criteria between close substitutes: a case I have myself argued elsewhere. It is generally illogical to adopt one criterion for one branch of transport and another for another, but this does

not imply that the criterion should be MSC pricing. It only implies it
should be the same criterion. The second point is that if one cannot
define the optimum in relation to the whole economy, there is
something to be said for defining it in relation to the transport world;
in which case it would not be MSC which would be relevant but MT
(transport) C. But, although such a policy should maximise real
income in relation to transport, there is no reason why it should affect
the maximisation of national income more favourably than some
other solution, such as profit maximisation or consumers' surplus
maximisation. Another argument which is used is that movement to
MSC pricing in some parts of the economy may actually lead to a
decrease in national income because of the existence of complements
(Lipsey and Lancaster[15]), to which the retort usually is that
complements are rarer than substitutes (Farrell[16]). My feeling here is
that the complementary demand is very important in transport. The
demands for land for transport and other purposes are frequently
complementary rather than alternative. Although there are necessarily
many cases where a change in the price of transport will lead to the
substitution of something else for transport (for example, the
substitution of office machinery for commuter labour, or the tranship-
ment of equipment in bits requiring less transport but higher labour
costs, rather than fully assembled), transport is commonly a means
to an end. A fall in the price of transport will increase the demand
for a great many things from seaside holidays to expense account
lunches. In short, the Lipsey and Lancaster argument is a substantial
objection to the assumption of MSC pricing in transport.

Therefore it seems to me unproven as well as implausible to argue
that there would be better allocation of resources in the economy
because of MSC (or MTC) pricing in transport. It is reasonable to
wonder what effect profit maximisation (the existence of monopoly)
has on the maximisation of national income. Although in principle
it can be seen how the distortion (plus or minus) could be measured,
this has not been done satisfactorily. Similarly one can know how one
could go about measuring the effect of adopting consumers' surplus
maximisation, or having a mixed economy where certain sectors use
profit maximisation, other consumers' surplus maximisation and yet
other MSC pricing; but these are measurements which are inevitably
beyond me. On *a priori* grounds I challenge anyone to make a case
for MSC pricing or indeed for profit or consumers' surplus
maximisation or a mixed economy on the grounds of achieving a better
allocation of resources and a higher rate of economic growth. At present
there is equal though not invincible ignorance.

The conclusion seems that we cannot argue a case for MSC (or MTC)
pricing on the grounds of allocation of resources; and that given equal

324

ignorance there, there are two reasons against adopting it as a basis for the solution of the transport problem.

(1) The income distribution policies implied by it are politically unacceptable (but that if we make industries charge prices which prevent losses, this is not MSC pricing but something else: namely some approximation to AC pricing in increasing returns industries).

(2) We cannot do without a rate of return to decide investment problems where capital is scarce or capital investment is significantly indivisible. The social surplus rate of return is what is logically entailed by MSC pricing but is not capable of being used by us in our present state of knowledge. It would be better to begin by trying a more limited criterion (though drawing an exact line between a social and a consumers' surplus maximisation policy is a matter of fine practical and value judgement (see pp.202-8).

POSTSCRIPT

Boiteux demonstrated the equivalence of SRMC and LRMC pricing; Mohring, and then Walters, showed its applicability to transport pricing.[1] If congestion pricing were introduced to optimise the use of capacity, the SRMC price of a seat in a train will *not* always be zero. As volume increases it will rise to a level where it is profitable to invest in capacity expansion. The significance of this is that congestion pricing diminishes the cases where a marginal cost pricing enterprise will make losses. Congestion is significant for efficiency both on road and rail.

Boiteux showed that an SRMC pricing enterprise will not make an overall loss unless subject to long-run increasing returns to scale. Because land-intensive, both railways and highways, particularly in urban areas, are more likely to show diminishing returns to scale if MSC pricing is adopted, and therefore earn a profit. The apparent exceptions to this generalisation are under-utilised rail and highway track where production indivisibilities make it impossible to provide less than a quantum of rail or road. Normally these will be rural and most important in an undeveloped country. In a developed country most under-utilisation of rail or road track is a result of mistaken over-investment in the past. Should long-run equilibrium be achieved, there is less need to worry how to finance deficits on either road or rail.

As indicated in the Appendix, imposing income distribution or other constraints is a maximisation problem with an additional constraint. Given a determinate social welfare function, in principle the efficient set of prices can be calculated. Baumol and Bradford have recently reviewed the literature on the efficient prices which would maximise the sum of consumers' and producers' surplus (or real national income), subject to the added constraint that government revenues are to be large enough to meet the deficits of all enterprises arising from MC pricing under conditions of increasing returns.[2]

_As they point out, the efficient solution has in principle a long history. Although 'a wide variety of output combinations and sets of prices can then be chosen, each of which would just meet the net revenue constraint,' only one is efficient, given the net revenue constraint: 'the surprisingly simple optimality rule . . . asserts that Pareto optimal utilisation of resources in the presence of an absolute profit constraint requires (considering the substitution effects alone) that all outputs be reduced by the same proportion from the quantities that would be demanded at prices equal to the corresponding marginal costs.' This implies that outputs for which demand is more elastic shall have prices nearer marginal costs than those for which demand is more inelastic; and as the authors point out, the result is analytically similar to that for ordinary price discrimination. They also show that the same result is true for a multi-product public monopoly under a break-even constraint. One can object to this pricing rule on the grounds that the income distribution implications are unacceptable *as between consumers,* but the assumption must then be that it is politically unacceptable that those consumers who value a commodity most in the sense of having collectively a relatively inelastic demand for it, should be charged a higher price relative to those who value the output less, having a relatively more elastic demand. To take a railway example, this would mean charging long-distance freight traffic a higher price relative to marginal cost than short-distance freight or passenger traffic because the first were more 'captive' — the elasticity of substitution for them of other modes being less. This is, of course, rather like charging what the traffic will bear, the policy that has emerged from the 1968 Transport Act. Similarly on roads such a policy would mean charging a higher price relative to marginal costs where substitutes were relatively poor — for example on rural or local roads. Without fully appreciating it, my argument for a different consumers' surplus pricing rule was based on the possible political unacceptability of the distributional implications of such discriminatory pricing. The objection still seems to me tenable, but far less important than it did because of points (1) and (2) above. If SRMC congestion pricing, and comparative absence of economies of scale, in an efficient transport enterprise mean that marginal cost pricing can generally be adopted without long-run deficits appearing, then it follows consumers' surplus would be maximised by enterprises adopting an SRMC pricing policy (except in so far as they might be required to earn surpluses to finance deficits elsewhere in the economy). In such circumstances it becomes less important to consider what the pricing rules should be *if* there were long-run scale economies; and *a fortiori* less important to consider pricing rules with distributional implications other than the efficient discriminatory pricing rules given by Baumol and Bradford. Thus if I were to write this book again I would have found it easier to define a consumers' surplus maximisation policy as one which combined the consumers' surplus maximisation investment rule with SRMC pricing. The difference between profit maximising and consumers' surplus maximising price and output policies (aside from the treatment of externalities) would have depended on the potential monopoly power of transport enterprises.

Market imperfections could also justify not adopting marginal cost pricing in transport (though average cost pricing would not then lead to a more efficient outcome). The literature has analysed this kind of second-best problem and as my Appendix asserted, the crucial argument is whether the adoption of marginal cost pricing in transport might lead to a decrease in overall consumers' and producers' surplus because of the existence of complements. Theoretical analysis suggests that the conditions are unlikely to occur where it would be worth searching for optimal second-best prices. There has been no empirical estimation of the importance of distortions in the transport sector.[3]   As Meyer and Mnookin say, *a priori* theorising suggests that the problem would be most important if an economy were dominated by a sector with a high degree of monopoly into which transport is an important input. They do not consider whether this could be true but as I said in 1963, the interrelation between the demands for land and transport could in principle be the cause of such a situation. There is a complex pattern of substitution and complementarity between the demand for land and for transport. Recently there have been several important explorations of these relations but without as yet demonstrating whether the importance of transport in influencing land rent, especially in cities, could be such that it would be worthwhile attempting to determine a second-best efficiency price for transport as a whole.[4] There has been more study of imperfections within the transport sector, particularly in cities between private and public transport, but not formally in a second-best framework. The sensible conclusion would seem to be that until it is demonstrated that there are strong grounds for thinking that second-best prices would be substantially more efficient to compensate for market imperfections, one assumes the distortions unimportant.[5] This is a different conclusion from that I came to in 1963.

APPENDIX 2 A NOTE ON PRICE DISCRIMINATION

Price discrimination is rare outside transport but has been common within, and is still important. An enterprise discriminates if it charges different prices to different customers for the same commodity. This must be distinguished from the provision of different commodities at different prices, though in practice distinction is not alway easy with borderline cases since intrinsically similar commodities may be differentiated in order to make discriminatory charging more successful. Let us take a borderline case where the difference is rather obscure. There are two seats in passenger trains. One is in a mainline express and the other in a local stopping train. Although the actual seat and train are identical in all their physical characteristics, the railway is not providing the same service in both, because the costs of providing accommodation on expresses and on local stopping trains are different. It is not price discrimination to charge differently for the two. But we can imagine another example which is. One railway line serves two firms and joins them to their market. Both find it cheapest to send their products by rail. The railway has something of a monopoly. Both firms require exactly the same form of transport — goods wagons— and it costs the railway the same per ton-mile to carry their products. There is a canal a distance from one firm so that it will not pay more than x pounds per ton-mile, otherwise it would send by canal. The other firm is not as well placed. Until the railway charge rises to $2x$ pounds per ton-mile it has no competing alternative means of transport. In other words its consumers' surplus is greater than that of the first firm when they are charged the same price. In these circumstances it would pay the railway to charge each firm the highest rate their traffic would bear — in the one case x pounds and in the other $2x$ pounds per ton-mile — thereby maximising the consumers' surpluses and appropriating them. This would be price discrimination in most industries; it cannot happen, because competition will prevent it. Let us imagine a firm with many customers. As one would expect they vary in consumers' surplus. The firm tries to expropriate the surpluses by charging discriminating prices. It would pay the customers who buy cheap to act as a middleman and sell to those who were intended to buy dear. They would undercut the discriminating monopoly and reduce its profits. Price discrimination is possible only where there cannot be resale, a condition which normally cannot obtain unless what is sold is not a commodity but a service. A railway and a highway authority can often act as discriminating monopolists because they provide non-transferable services.

If we return to fig. 3.1 we can formalise the point. The triangle, *DEF*, represents the consumers' surplus gained by those consumers who pay *KE* but would be prepared to pay more. If price discrimination is possible an enterprise will maximise its profits if it can charge each consumer the maximum he will pay. This means that the price the firm will charge, if it can, for, let us say, any unit of output x is determined by where a perpendicular from x intersects the demand curve. There are consumers who would purchase the goods or service at a price above marginal cost but would not pay as much as *KE*. In simple profit maximisation it would not pay to let these consumers have the commodity at less than *KE* because of the possibilities of resale. If resale is not possible than a discriminating monopolist can get some more profit by selling to these people at the highest price they will pay as long as this is above marginal cost. He will therefore maximise his profits if he sells the marginal cost output.

It follows that a producer is not maximising his profits if he does not practice price discrimination where it is possible for him to do so. This is a logical implication of profit maximisation. However, there are two controversies which arise over it. Both are *ethical* and can only be resolved by value judgement.

(1) It is sometimes asked whether it is right to charge different prices for the service given at the same cost to different customers. The argument against is usually that it simply is not fair.[1] I have nothing to add to this issue, but should it be decided by Government that price discrimination is not fair, then it is perfectly possibly for it to prohibit nationalised industries and other public enterprise from practising it. (Formally this is a constraint on profit maximisation.) Whether in practice it can enforce the prohibition is another matter; and whether the nationalised industry can *always* distinguish price discrimination and price differences reflecting costs is another. There are bound to be border-line cases. In the rest of this book it has been assumed that price discrimination is permissible; but it would be perfectly possible to adapt the profit-making criterion appropriately. For obvious reasons price discrimination is not relevant to consumers' surplus maximisation.

(2) It is often argued by railways in distress that they ought to be allowed to discriminate to cover cost. The points at issue are quite simple. The first is whether a railway operating at a loss should be kept open. If it is — and there has been previously a prohibition on price discrimination, which is a reason why the enterprise has not made a profit — the Government has a choice between subsidising the railways or changing its mind and its values, and allowing price discrimination.[2]

APPENDIX 3 OUTLINE OF A COSTING SYSTEM FOR RAILWAY CHARGING

There would have been a danger of burying the third conclusion of Chapter 4 in a mass of detail, but it may be useful to give an impression of the costing system which would follow from the principle advocated.

We are in this context costing to two different ends. The first is to decide the direct or marginal costs which can properly be attributed to a consignment of goods (or a passenger). The second is to discover the costs properly attributable to various elements of the railway system, for example, marshalling yards, stations, locomotive depots, and even trains and tracks, etc., so that we can see if it pays, according to the charging policy adopted, to keep them in operation.

To consider the second question first, we can illustrate what is involved by an imaginary example. Suppose M is a marshalling yard for four stations $A, B, C,$ and D. We will begin by making two assumptions: first, that the cost of the marshalling yard is fixed irrespective of the volume of traffic marshalled; and, second, that there are two flows of traffic from A to B and C to D.

In this simple case it is easy to discover the joint costs of the marshalling yard. We must ask what costs would be saved if each of the flows were discontinued. Let us suppose the total annual cost of the yard is £100,000 and that, if A-B were discontinued, £10,000 would be saved and that, if C-D were discontinued, £15,000 would be saved. Then, by subtraction, £75,000 is the joint cost of the marshalling yard which cannot be allocated to either traffic and which would not be saved unless the yard closed down.

Let us now suppose there is a third flow of traffic from A to C. This complicates the matter slightly, as there is now the possibility of costs which are joint to two flows of traffic together. For example, there may be a portion of the labour force which is needed for A-B and A-C traffic but not for C-D. It would still be needed for A-B or A-C if only one of them were discontinued. We want to discover the joint costs of the yard. We discover, as before, the costs attributable to the three flows of traffic separately. We then ask if any additional costs would be saved if any pair of these flows were discontinued and the third remained. Let us suppose that, if A-B and C-D were both discontinued, £45,000 would be saved annually. By subtraction the marshalling yard costs attributable to the two flows together would be £20,000. Let us suppose that the joint costs attributable to A-B and

A-C are £10,000, and to *A-C* and *C-D* are £5,000, then we have the following list of costs:

Attributable to *A-B*	£10,000
C-D	15,000
A-C	5,000
A-B and *C-D*	20,000
A-B and *A-C*	10,000
A-C and *C-D*	5,000
Total costs attributable	£65,000
Total cost of yard	£100,000
Yard joint costs	£35,000

This is the essence of a perfectly general procedure for distinguishing between joint costs and costs which can be allocated. It is likely that we could break down the attribution of costs further in this notional instance. Let us consider *A-B* traffic only. This happens to be of two kinds: coal and general merchandise. We ask what costs would be saved at the marshalling yard if the coal traffic were discontinued, and discover it would be £3,000. The answer to the same question in respect of the merchandise traffic is that no costs would be saved. We deduce that £7,000 is a joint marshalling yard cost of *A-B* traffic while £3,000 can be attributed to the coal traffic part of it. It may be possible to press the question still further in respect of coal traffic. Suppose that there are two kinds of coal traffic. A regular trainload from a colliery (a single regular consignment) and sundry coal traffic from station *A*. We find that all the £3,000 can be attributed to special labour and equipment needed for the regular traffic which is not employed for any other traffic. We have now in this case found an element in the marshalling yard cost which can directly be attributed as a part of the direct or marginal cost of a consignment. One would not expect this to be very common. In principle one could go on asking our question at a lower and lower level until one came up with the answer that *none* was attributable any further in any direction. Therefore where one could stop particularizing would depend on circumstances. Where one *would* stop would depend on how far it would pay to go on particularising, and on one's charging policy.

Suppose by contrast with our earlier finding that it was discovered that sundry and traffic from *A* was the cause of say, £5,000 marshalling yard costs. It might be decided that it would not pay to press further and see if any part of it could be imputed to particular trainloads or wagonloads of that coal. If it was thought that this was largely a joint cost of all the sundry coal traffic it would probably be more sensible to

331

treat it as an overhead of that traffic. But if it were thought that a large part could be allocated, then there might be something to say for averaging the cost over the sundry coal traffic so that it made an appearance in the direct costs per consignment. Or that might be a case for averaging some part of it and treating the remainder as a joint cost.

We relax the assumption that the marshalling yard cost does not vary with throughput. It was only made to simplify the argument. To find out in advance what the total costs of the yard are likely to be over a given period of time — let us say a year — it is necessary to make an estimate of the number of wagons which will be marshalled. Again we may say that the sophistication of the prediction must depend on what it is worth to be sophisticated. Sometimes a rough guess — 'near enough 200 wagons a day' — will do. In other circumstances it is clearly wise to allow for seasonal, daily or hourly fluctuations or a trend in traffic. Sometimes it would pay to use more sophisticated statistical techniques and calculate a probability distribution. The demand will of course be affected by the charging policy employed. Once a prediction has been made of each flow of traffic expected it is then possible to proceed as before in distinguishing between direct or marginal and indirect or joint costs.

As a consequence of costing a railway system on this method, so far as it is profitable to do so, one will get a picture of the costs properly attributable to marshalling yards, stations, depots, trains, etc. It is then necessary to see whether the revenue which can be matched against costs in each case to make it profitable is sufficient to continue operations. The exact definition of 'sufficiency' will depend on the criterion used. But in general it can be said that the basic procedure is similar to that performed for costing. The question now is asked: what revenue would be forgone if certain facilities and services were not in operation?

This is at least in outline the kind of procedure used by the British Railways when deciding whether it would be profitable to close down a branch line, for example. The suggestion is that this is the logical basis for all costing; and that it is important to make a distinction, certainly for all the more important facilities, between joint and attributable costs instead of concealing them as at present in an average cost.

What items one would expect to find as direct costs must depend on the averaging which it is decided is profitable. If we assume for the moment we are interested in the direct costs of a particular consignment, what we want to know is the additional or *marginal* cost which will be incurred by a decision to accept this particular consignment. As direct costs are used by the railways in a looser sense, perhaps it will be simpler if we slip into economist's language and talk of marginal costs. We can distinguish two categories of marginal cost —

long-run and short-run.

Short-run marginal costs

By 'short-run' here is meant costs other than capital costs though it has to be admitted that there are cases where it is not easy to decide what is and what is not a capital cost. Neglecting that complication there can be divided into two sub-categories which it would be illuminating to call direct and indirect if these terms were not already in use. Instead we will call them primary and secondary.

Primary short-run costs. By these I mean those which accrue directly to the consignment in question. In manufacturing business there is the cost of the raw materials embodied in the product. In any ordinary sense these do not exist in transport and this is, of course, the main reason why joint costs are a high proportion of costs. The most important costs which can be attributed to a consignment of goods are fuel, water and lubricants — which would be saved if the consignment were not accepted. (As their cost is not proportional to the number of wagons hauled there is in fact an element of joint cost here.) Other costs are that part of provision for risk of loss and damage which can specifically be related to the consignment, and some costs which are probably negligible, such as the cost of paper used in documentation, and the wear of track. (It has been said that the only marginal cost attributable to a passenger is the cost of the ticket.)

These are probably the only costs of this category which one would usually expect to find. One would not normally think it worth while working out these costs separately for every consignment or wagonload. There is much to be said for using what may first seem to be a contradiction in terms but which makes perfect sense: an average short-run marginal cost. One might go so far as to say that marginal cost as defined so far could be constant and identical for the system as a whole. If this assumption is badly out, then different average marginal costs could be used for different kinds of traffic.

There will be some traffic which incurs other short-run marginal costs in this category: normally important flows. For example a particular traffic may entail the employment of additional labour *specific* to it. (If it is not specific to it then it is a joint cost of it and some other traffic. It then has to be decided whether it should be treated as an overhead to which both contribute or if it is sufficiently unimportant to be averaged as a short-run marginal cost for both. There are cases where this might be the most profitable policy. Present railway costing policy assumes that this is true, certainly for generalised costing and one suspects for most particularised costing. Short-run costs may therefore be greater for this reason to some extent.)

Secondary short-run marginal costs. These are short-run costs for which the consignment is responsible as cause but which fall on other traffic *specifically*. These are likely to be most important where there is congestion. Suppose we have a crowded marshalling yard where any additional wagon slows down the throughput of the yard. To a large extent the additional cost will fall on overheads, because of their less efficient utilisation. A part however may show up as increased consumption of fuel in respect of other wagons. That is the most likely instance of this cost. Since the cost would be saved if the wagon did not run, it is properly a marginal cost of it.

Long-run marginal costs
These are capital costs specific to a consignment on our assumptions. An example would be the provision of special facilities at a station. In principle it would be possible to make a distinction between primary and secondary here also but this is unlikely to be important in practice. One omission from these marginal costs may seem surprising. In most textbooks one will find an example of this kind. A train carries 1,000 passengers. The marginal cost of carrying the 1,000th is zero since it adds nothing except possibly the cost of the paperboard of his ticket to carry him. The marginal cost of the 1,001th passenger is the cost of running another train. This is good argument but not useful. First, it would never be practicable to assess separately the cost of a 1,000th and a 1,001th passenger so as to set against them different marginal costs (and it would only on very rare occasions be a worth-while costing exercise for goods). Second, it would never occur that there was one additional passenger (for if there were one, or possibly ten, they would be squeezed into the first train). There will be several passengers for whom the cost of providing the train is a joint cost. One would normally expect that the joint cost incurred by the passenger on the second train would not be very different from that incurred on the first train. As far as charging is concerned it would very rarely, if ever, be practicable to charge different fares on the two trains. But charging apart, the point is whether it is worth ascertaining separate costs for the second train and for the first, or whether it would be better to average the costs of passengers travelling by both trains. Whichever policy were adopted it would not involve the attribution of a marginal cost which would properly fall into one of our categories.

APPENDIX 4   THE CASE FOR A NATIONAL ROAD AUTHORITY

The fundamental shortcomings of the present system of administering and financing the roads cannot fairly be attributed to defects in its organisation.[1] Neither can the fact that there has been insufficient investment in roads for many years. Like the railways the roads were starved of new capital for investment from the end of the Second World War until 1955, and for the same reason: the low priority given by the Labour and Conservative Governments to investment in transport. Like the railways also, when the investment programmes began, there were difficulties because there had been insufficient preparation by technical and economic research. The method of assessing priorities for investment was crudely non-economic at first chiefly because of a lack of the relevant economic data on costs and demand. The road programme was also emerging from a long period, of course a much longer period than the railways, during which economic considerations had been of little importance. It, too, had to develop a new approach rapidly to what it was doing. Like any nationalised industry the programme also suffered, and still suffers, from a shortage of key men; but whereas the railways, as a nationalised industry, could have paid more to attract the men it needed, the road programme has been subject to Civil Service and local authority scales of pay. There is also doubt whether the road programme has not been influenced by technical at the expense of economic factors in deciding the quality of road-building; but this could also be alleged of some nationalised industries, and has been alleged, as we have seen, of the railways.

A widespread criticism is that it is unnecessarily slow-moving, and this defect is commonly attributed to it being mainly the responsibility of a Government Department. There are four or five years between the first intention that a road should be built or rebuilt and the start of work on it. One critic, a county engineer and surveyor, has listed the routine thirty-one statutory stages a scheme has to go through during the time of preparation.[2] The Ministry point of view would seem to be that these are essential if the rights of the individual are to be protected.[3] Road investment entails land purchase and frequently considerable rearrangement of the patterns of living and working near the new construction. Preparation must be slow enough to allow for the formulating and hearing of objections. Although it is arguable the Ministry is typically bureaucratic and departmental in its caution, this is not something on which it is easy for an outsider to give a firm opinion. Besides, even if the period of preparation were shorter, this would have made no difference to the amount of road-building accomplished. There are enough schemes to be going on with, given the amounts of money provided by the Government for investment. What delays there have been in getting investment done, have been caused principally by inexperience of large-scale road construction and scarcity of labour and other physical resources. And even if it is assumed that it is desirable the period of preparation should be shortened, and that in time its length will be a factor constraining the amount of investment in roads, it is not obvious that as drastic a remedy as fundamental reorganisation is needed.*

Treasury control over expenditure would appear to be more detailed and hampering, at least, on paper, than it is over the expenditure of the British Transport Commission. The road programme is bound by most of the restrictions set by the method of accounting used in public departments. For example, if it spends less than expected under one sub-head of the money voted to it by Parliament, and wants to spend more under another sub-head, it has to get Treasury permission to do this; but this permission, it would seem, is usually granted. There are other difficulties of the same kind but there has been the beginning of a revolution already in the Government's own attitude to its methods of financing and accounting. In the past it has been a problem, greater for the road programme than for the railways, that money for investment was voted by Parliament for only one year ahead. Local authorities and the Ministry now have some security they will be able to plan five years ahead.[5] There are likely to be other similar changes which will make it easier for public business to be carried on efficiently soon, if the report of the Plowden Committee on *Control of Public Expenditure* is acted on.[6] One possibility is that we will no longer have the penny-wise over-meticulous checking by the Ministry of all plans sent up from below, simply on the grounds that *public* money is being spent. It is possible that a great many of the difficulties of implementing the road programme will disappear.

Another argument for turning the road programme into a kind of

---

*Col. Lovell, the most persistent critic of the present organisation, gave us an example of how quickly preparation could be made, a by-pass built by him for the Air Ministry in West Riding which took only one year to prepare, because the Air Ministry was faster and less exacting in its procedure. But if one *Government* Department can do this there seems no *prima facie* reason why another could not.[4]

nationalised industry − a national road authority* − is that it would be more efficient if centralised. Authority is exercised by the Treasury, the Ministry of Transport, county councils, county borough councils and by some municipal boroughs and urban district councils with a population of more than twenty thousand if they care to claim the responsibility under the 1929 Local Government Act. There are therefore a large number of authorities with road responsibilities but this in itself would hardly be a cogent argument for establishing one authority, especially when the general tendency on public policy is to decentralisation.

The significant arguments for reorganisation as a nationalised industry, a national road system, centralised or decentralised are, I believe, as follows. First, symmetry with other transport systems: There is something to be said for having the same sort of organisation for road and rail to emphasise that they are in the same kind of business. It is unfortunate that the central administration of the road programme should be part of the Ministry while the administration of the railways is separate. The investment plans of the railways are inspected by the Ministry to check that the planning is sound and in the public interest. Who checks on the planning of those in the Ministry of Transport whose duty it is to establish the more important priorities in the programme − to see if their reasoning is sound and grasp of facts adequate? But by itself too much weight should not be given to this argument.

Second, coherence within the organisation: Sir James Dunnett, formerly Permanent Secretary to the Ministry of Transport, has said 'I can hardly conceive that the Government would yield this responsibility to another body without requiring that body to maintain itself from revenues derived from user charges. This is, of course, a familiar enough concept in other countries, but you will observe that it costs nothing to drive along M1.'[7] Without going into the question here of whether in fact it costs nothing to drive along M1, undoubtedly there is an administrative separation between (1) the revenue earned from motorists and other road-users, and (2) the sums of money spent on roads and associated services which are voted by Parliament under different heads to different Ministries or by local authorities. The Ministry of Transport's duty is to administer expenditure only. It has no duty to relate the costs of providing roads to the revenue raised from different classes of road-users. No one has that duty. Most of the charges for the use of roads are

*A national road authority has been demanded by, among others, the British Roads Federation, Mr. G.J. Ponsonby, Reader in the Economics of Transport at the London School of Economics, the journal *Municipal Engineering* and Sir Herbert Manzoni, Birmingham City Engineer, and indeed at least as early as 1901 by the Roads Improvement Association.

taxes and local rates, which are determined on quite other principles. It is impossible to deduce the cost of operating the road system — or any part of that system, for example the trunk road system — for the public accounts. The relevant amounts are scattered among the votes for several departments; and in many cases they are concealed in subheads which include other costs. The least that is needed are consolidated accounts of the road system. These would naturally take the general form of the accounts required from a nationalised industry. (Whether they should be national or regional accounts is another question.) But this would not be enough. If the road system is to be run economically, on either criterion, costs should be related to receipts. At present it is almost always not possible to ascertain the cost of a particular road on the revenue from taxation and rates attributable to it. Whatever the form of administration and accounts it is necessary that the road programme should be operated as an economic enterprise or as a group of interrelated regional entities. This would mean itself a revolution in the present methods of administration. The road programme might be administered departmentally as a public enterprise as the General Post Office is. It would not be of the first importance whether this is the solution chosen, or it is separated and organised as a public corporation, if it were not for the first argument above. Symmetry does seem to suggest that if a reorganisation is needed to establish the road system as an economic enterprise — charging, costing and investing logically — that it should become a public corporation.

POSTSCRIPT

Since 1963 the British Road Federation[1] has pressed most for a national highway authority, its main motive being to secure a hypothecated source of revenue, like the US Highway Trust Funds, and therefore to increase dramatically highways expenditure. If a body were to be set up with hypothecated revenue which would earmark substantial funds for highway expenditure irrespective of the return from that expenditure, it could only worsen highway financial discipline.

An argument against any national roads authority is that property acquisition for highway development is not something which can be delegated outside central or local government. As opposition to the environmental effects of highways becomes greater, it is harder to imagine highways being removed from politics — as the BRF would seem to wish, though this might be easier if compensation were Pareto optimal. The right answer to the criticism of delays — often repeated since — is that most of them result from public inquiries and other processes to help protect the public and individual rights. Pareto optimal compensation might make it feasible to omit some stages but not otherwise. Indeed the delays have grown, such has been the resistance to urban road-building.

However, the efficiency problem remains. From experience it seems that there are disadvantages both to the nationalised or 'arm's length' relationship and to embedding an enterprise in a department. The first gives the Minister advice from civil servants whose future is not bound up with the interests of the organisation they are advising on. Even though there are administrators passing in and out of the highway divisions of the Department of the Environment, advice to the Miniser on the roads programme comes from those, mainly engineers, whose responsibility it is to operate the programme. To have the Director General, Highways, as the Minister's prime source of advice on the efficiency of the roads programme is as if he were to be advised directly by nationalised industry Board Chairmen without civil servants, administrative and professional, acting as intermediaries. It is not human to expect disinterested, self-critical advice from civil servants whose prime function is managerial. From this standpoint it would be better if the highways were devolved so that they came under the same kind of scrutiny as do the nationalised industries. It might be possible to imagine this within a department. But to devolve without establishing investment, pricing criteria and financial targets, would mean that the highways would be under even less financial discipline than they are now.

NOTES AND REFERENCES

The following abbreviations are used in these notes and references:
AER   American Economic Review.
AR: 1950   *British Transport Commission, Annual Report and Accounts,*
   etc.   H.M.S.O.
BOUIS   *Bulletin of the Oxford University Institute of Statistics*
BRF   British Road Federation
BTC   British Transport Commission
BTR   *British Transport Review*
CHNGB   Institution of Civil Engineers: *Proceedings of the Conference on*
              the Highway Needs of Great Britain (1958)
EJ   *Economic Journal*
HRBP   *Proceedings of the Highway Research Board, Washington, D.C.*
              (Annual publication)
JIE   *Journal of Industrial Economics*
JIT   *Journal of the Institute of Transport*
JRSS   *Journal of the Royal Statistical Society,* Series A
JTEP   *Journal of Transport Economics and Policy*
LBR   *Lloyd's Bank Review*
MRBR   *Modernisation and Re-Equipment of British Railways,* BTC (1956)
MT   *Motor Transport* (weekly publication)
OEP   *Oxford Economic Papers*
PA   *Public Administration*
PQ   *Political Quarterly*
QJE   *Quarterly Journal of Economics*
RES   *Review of Economic Studies*
RNTU   Ministry of Transport: *Reorganisation of the Nationalised*
              Transport Undertakings, H.M.S.O. Cmnd. 1248 (December 1960)
RR: 1950   *Department of Scientific and Industrial Research:* Road Research,
   etc.   H.M.S.O. (annual publication)
RRLN   *Road Research Laboratory Note* (these are occasional mimeographed
              papers)
RRTP/46   T. M. Coburn, M.E. Beesley, D.J. Reynolds, *The London-Birmingham*
              Motorway: Traffic and Economics, H.M.S.O. (1960)
RUBA   American Association of State Highway Officials: *Road User Benefit*
              Analysis for Highway Improvements (1953)
SCE:TR   *First Report from the Select Committee on Estimates: Trunk Roads,*
              H.M.S.O. (10 June 1959)
SCNI:BR   *Report from the Select Committee on Nationalised Industries:*
              British Railways, H.M.S.O. (11 July 1960)
WBR   *Westminster Bank Review*

INTRODUCTION

1. In D.L. Burn, *The Structure of British Industry,* Cambridge University Press
(1958), vol.1, p.106.

2   There is an informative account of technical development on the railways by
    C.J. Allen, *Modern Railways, Their Engineering Equipment and Operation,*
    Faber (1959); and a collection of essays which is an excellent introduction to
    the comparatively new science of traffic engineering edited by E. Davies, *Roads
    and their Traffic,* Blackie (1960).
3   Sir James Dunnett, *SCNI:BR,* Q.5. For the change in the Ministry's attitude
    generally, see evidence given on 27 January, 4 February and 25 May 1960.
4   See P.B.D. Massé, *Les Choix des Investissements,* Paris Dunod (1959);
    R.N. McKean, *Efficiency in Government through Systems Analysis with
    Emphasis on Water Resource Development,* Wiley (1958); J. Hirshleifer *et al.,
    Water Supply Economic Technology and Policy,* University of Chicago (1960).
5   *MT* (5 November 1960). The important *RNTU* (December 1960) also put
    organisation first.
6   The opinion that the juggling approach to organisation is practically worthless
    is held by many of the best political scientists especially in America: see
    Chester Barnard, *The Functions of the Executive,* Harvard University Press
    (1938); also Professor W.J.M. Mackenzie's excellent article, 'The Study of
    Public Administration in the United States', *PA* (Summer 1951).
7   Edmund Burke, *Reflections on the Revolution in France.*

Postscript

1   R.E. Quandt (ed.), *The Demand for Travel, Theory and Measurement,*
    Heath Lexington (1970).
2   C.D. Foster, *Politics, Finance and the Role of Economics: An Essay on the
    Control of Public Enterprise,* Allen and Unwin (1972).

CHAPTER 1

1   Sources: BRF *Basic Road Statistics* (1963).
2   For an early statement of the case against postponing roadbuilding for the next
    slump, see G. Walker, M.E. Beesley and A.A. Walters, 'Transport Policy and
    Investment in Roads', *WBR* (May 1953).
3   *Hansard* (1 July 1955), col. 667, Qu. in the BRF *Basic Road Statistics* (1963),
    with other information on the history of the fund.
4   *Hansard* (26 April 1926), col. 1714.
5   Diversion of road taxes to other uses has been prohibited by constitutional
    amendment in twenty-one states in the USA since the Second World War.
    D.M. Winch, *The Economics of Highway Planning,* University of Toronto Press
    Press (1963).
6   For example C.T. Brunner, Director of Shell-Mex and B.P. Ltd., reported in
    MT (29 October 1960): G.K. Newman, Secretary of the Road Haulage
    Association (23 March 1961), reported in *MT* (8 April 1961).
7   Qu. *MT* (14 May 1960), p.13.
8   W.H. Glanville and R.J. Smeed, 'Basic Requirements of the Roads of Great
    Britain', *CHNGB* (1958); also D.J. Reynolds and J.G. Wardrop, 'Economic
    Losses Due to Traffic Congestion', *Proceedings of the 5th International Study
    Week in Traffic Engineering* (1960).
9   See M.E. Beesley, A.J. Blackburn and C.D. Foster "Investing in Urban Road
    Improvement" *Economics* (1963).
10 Figures are from Economic Commission for Europe, *Economic Survey of
    Europe in 1956,* Ch.5, Table 8. ECE, *Annual Bulletin of Statistics for
    Europe; 1958* U.N. (1959). Table 15.

11 See G. Lonnecke, 'Heavy Freight on Motorways', *BTR* (April 1960), pp.504-5.

12 BTC, *MRBR*, p.5.

Postscript

1 *World Road Statistics,* International Road Federation (1973). Again there are problems of comparability with the figures given in Table 1.1.

2 C.D. Foster, 'Transport and the Urban Environment, in I. Heggie (ed.), *Urbanisation and the Environment,* American Economics Association, Macmillan (1973).

3 H.M.S.O. (1968).

CHAPTER 2

1 Some non-socialist writings have been by Lord Brand, 'Nationalisation', *LBR* (1949); E. Goodman, *Forms of Public Control and Ownership,* Christophers (1951); R. Kelf-Cohen, *Nationalisation in Britain,* Macmillan (1958); but more notice was taken when a section of the Labour Party questioned the desirability of more nationalisation: for example Hugh Gaitskell, 'Economic Aims of the Labour Party', *PQ* (1953) and *Socialism and Nationalisation,* Fabian Tract 300 (1956); Crosland, *The Future of Socialism,* Cape (1956).

2 'The Economic Setting', *PQ* (1960), p.265; also Crosland, op.cit., Chs.1,22.

3 See J.H. Smith and T.E. Chester, 'Distribution of Power in Nationalised Industries', *British Journal of Sociology* (December 1951).

4 *Conflict Without Malice,* Odhams (1955), p.172.

5 See D.N. Chester, 'Nationalised Industries', *Three Banks Review* (December 1952).

6 See D.N. Chester, 'Notes on the Price Policy Indicated by the Nationalisation Acts', *OEP* (January 1950); W.A. Robson, *Nationalised Industries and Public Ownership,* Allen and Unwin (1960), p.66. The airlines are not required to break even. It was assumed they would make a loss.

7 Editorial comment in *PA* (Summer 1949) where this passage was quoted from S. and B. Webb, *A Constitution for a Socialist Commonwealth,* Longmans (1920). See also Sir Frank Tribe in the same number.

8 P.S. Florence and G. Walker, 'Efficiency under Nationalisation and its Measurement', in *Problems of Nationalised Industry,* ed. W.A. Robson, Allen and Unwin (1952).

9 W.F. Robson, *Nationalised Industry and Public Ownership,* Allen & Unwin (1962), p.156.

10 *RNTU,* paras.2, 7, 48.

11 D.N. Chester, *PA* (Spring 1952), p.46.

12 G. Walker and H. Maddick, 'Responsibility for Transport', *PQ* (1952), also F. Milligan, 'The Consumers' Interest' in Robson, op.cit. (1952); M. Stewart, *Consumers' Councils,* Fabian Research Series 155 (1953); P.S. Florence and H. Maddick, 'Consumers' Councils in the Nationalised Industries', *PQ* (1953); Robson, op.cit. (1960), pp.246ff.

Postscript

1 R. Pryke, *Public Enterprise in Practice,* McGibbon and Kee (1971).

2 S. Holland (ed.), *The State as Entrepreneur,* Centre for Contemporary European Studies (1972).

3 B. Ward, *The Socialist Economy,* Random House, N.Y. (1967), Chs. 8, 9, 10, 11. J. Vanek, *The General Theory of Labour-Managed Market Economics,* Cornell University Press, 1970. E. Furuboth, 'Toward a Dynamic Model of the Yugoslav Firm', *Canadian Journal of Economics* (May 1971).

4 E.g. P. Dasgupta and A.K. Sen, *Guidelines for Project Evaluation,* U.N. (1972).

5 For the theory of the treatment of income distribution in cost-benefit analysis, see S.A. Marglin in A. Maass and others, *Design of Water Resource Systems,* Macmillan (1962), pp.62-86; A.M. Freeman, 'Income Distribution and Planning for Public Investment', *AER* June 1967); and M.C. McGuire and H.A. Carn, 'The Integration of Equity and Efficiency in Public Project Selection', *EJ* (December 1969). For application in transport see *Commission on the Third London Airport,* Papers and Proceedings, vol.7, H.M.S.O. (1970); V.C. Nwaneri, 'Equity in Cost Benefit Analysis – Third London Airport', *JTEP,* (September 1970); C.D. Foster, 'Social Welfare Functions in Cost Benefit Analysis', in R. Lawrence (ed.) *Operational Research and the Social Sciences,* Tavistock (1966).

6 H. Leibenstein, 'Allocative Efficiency *versus* X-Efficiency', *AER* (June 1966).

7 R. Pryke, op.cit.

8 *The Nationalised Industries: A Review of Economic and Financial Objectives,* H.M.S.O. Cmnd.3437 (1967).

CHAPTER 3

1 One will find this discussed in detail in any elementary economics textbook: for example Stonier and Hague, *A Textbook of Economic Theory,* Longmans (1957), pp.102-3; Cairncross, *Introduction to Economics,* Butterworths (1960 edn.), p.260.

2 A.C. Pigou, *Economics of Welfare* (1932 edn.), pp.24-6. Time preference can be expressed as a *rate,* for example, if someone would as soon have £1 this year as 21s. a year hence, the *negative* rate of time preference is *minus* 5 per cent, of 19s. it is *plus* 5 per cent. However, time preference is a term which is often used irrationally and ambiguously. On this see A.K. Sen, 'On Optimising the Rate of Saving' *EJ* (September 1961), sec. 1.

3 J.R. Hicks, 'The Rehabilitation of Consumers' Surplus', *RES* (1940-1), p.116.

4 It has been argued that it is in principle possible to estimate the social surplus effect of any policy. Cf. Hicks, *Revision of Demand Theory* (1956), Chs. 10, 18; also H. Hotelling, 'The General Welfare in Relation to Problems of Taxation and of Railway and Utility Rates', *Econometrica* (1938).

Postscript

1 'What is Producers' Surplus?', *AER* (1968).

2 E.J. Mishan, *Cost-Benefit Analysis,* Penguin (1972).

3 J.M. Currie, J.A. Murphy, and A. Schmitz, 'The concept of Economic Surplus', *EJ,* vol.81 (December 1971).

4 For a review of the problem, see O. Williamson, *The Economics of Discretionary Behaviour,* Englewood Cliffs (1964); and R.L. Marris, *The Theory of Managerial Capitalism,* Macmillan (1964). See E.J. Misham (op.cit.), or for a fuller treatment.

5 C.D. Foster, 'Pecuniary Externalities in Cost Benefit Analysis: Notes on the Treatment of Tax and Surplus' in J.N. Wolfe, *A Note on the Treatment of Taxation in Cost-Benefit Analysis,* Allen & Unwin (1972).

6 The reader interested in the theory should refer to Part 3 of R. Layard, *Cost-Benefit Analysis,* Penguin (1972).

CHAPTER 4

1   *RNTU,* paras. 23-5. For example, 'British Road Services, the Tilling (Buses) Group, the Scottish Omnibus Group, British Transport Hotels, Road Freight Shipping Services and Thomas Cook and Son, Ltd. will each be operated as companies incorporated under the Companies Act with their own Boards.' Neither is the position clarified in the 1962 Transport Act.

2   Report of the Select Committee on Railways (4 August 1881).

3   *SCNI:BR,* Q.305.

4   The information on costing is taken chiefly from the proceedings: *In the Court of the Transport Tribunal, Transport Acts, 1947 and 1953. In the Matter of the Application of the British Transport Commission (1955 No. 2) To Confirm the British Transport Commission (Railway Merchandise Charges) Scheme,* H.M.S.O. (July 1955–July 1956), supported by some subsequent information. I have examined railway costing in more detail in an article *BOUIS* (February 1962); see also H.E. Osborn, 'Transport Costs', *JIT* (July 1959).

5   Sir Philip Warter, chairman of Southern Region, resisted the suggestion that costing was dear, but it was not clear from his evidence on what level of sophistication he was talking about costing. *SCNI:BR,* Q.1725.

6   A.C. Pigou, *Economics of Welfare,* Macmillan (1932 edn.), Pt. II, Ch.18: 'The Special Problem of Railway Rates'; see also *SCNI:BR,* Appendix 45.

7   W.A. Lewis, *Overhead Costs,* Allen and Unwin (1949), Ch.1.

8   A.C. Tait, *JIT* (January 1960), p.228. See also B.A. Coulson, 'Excursion Trains: Some Economic Problems', *BTR* (December 1959).

9   Ibid.

10 See footnote 4 above, p.368.

11 Ibid., pp.203, 696. More recently the position has been reiterated before the Select Committee, *SCNI:BR,* Q.1627.

12 Cf. D. Blee, *JIT* (July 1959), p.141.

13 For the basis of this calculation see my 'Some Notes on Railway Costs and Costing', *BOUIS* (February 1962), Sec.IV. J.R. Sargent questioned the validity of the distinction drawn between direct and indirect costs. *British Transport Policy,* Oxford University Press (1958), pp.35-37. But he went on to argue a policy for establishing competition between road and rail as if it were the right distinction, for which he was rapped by the financial adviser to the commission precisely on the grounds his solution would not do because the BTC's distinction between direct and indirect costs did not correspond to Sargent's between costs and joint costs. H.E. Osborn, 'Transport Charging Policies', *BTR* (December 1958).

Postscript

1   See *Carriers' Licensing* (the Geddes Report), H.M.S.O. (1965).

2   For excellent descriptions of how the railways persistently seem to have taken the wrong decisions or procrastinated in face of their difficulties, see S. Joy, *The Train that Got Away,* Ian Allen (1973), and R. Pryke, *Public Enterprise in Practice,* McGibbon and Kee (1971), Chs. 10 and 11. Both are important contributions to the scanty recent literature on railway economics.

3   See S. Joy, op.cit., Ch.5.

4   See the brief description in L.C. Hunter and A.W.J. Thomson, *The Nationalised Transport Industries,* Heinemann (1973), pp.168-70. Also S. Joy, op.cit., and his 'Pricing and Costing on Railways – A New European Approach', paper delivered at the University of Wisconsin (1970).

5   G.H. Borts, 'Increasing Returns in the Railway Industry', *Journal of Political*

Economy (August 1954); 'Production Relations in the Railway Industry', *Econometrica* (January 1952); and 'The Estimation of Rail Cost Functions', *Econometrica* (January 1960); L.R. Klein, *A Textbook of Econometrics* (1953), pp.226-36; Z. Griliches, 'Cost Allocation in Railroad Regulation', *Bell Journal of Economics*, Vol.3, No.1, (1972).

6 The main evidence is of the persistence of consignment delays in spite of railway efforts to eliminate these. See A.A. Walters and C. Sharp, *A Report on Traffic, Costs, and Charges of Freight Transport in Great Britain* (unpublished); C. Sharp, *The Allocation of Freight Traffic – A Survey* (1967). G.F. Allen, *British Rail after Beeching;* W.R. Cook, *JTEP* (September 1967).

7 S. Joy, 'British Railways' Track Costs', *Journal of Industrial Economics*, Vol.13, 1964; S. Joy and C.D. Foster, 'Railway Track Costs in Britain', *Proceedings of the Symposium on Railway Traffic Engineering*, I.C.E. (February 1968).

8 R. Pryke, loc.cit., shows how railway rates were normally higher than the corresponding road rates without any obvious quality advantage. Inertia must have explained why many traffics continued to use rail.

CHAPTER 5

1. P. Redfern, 'Net Investment in Fixed Assets in the United Kingdom, 1938-53', *JRSS* (1955).

2 Sources: *SCNI:BR*, Report, para.177; *Public Investment in Great Britain White Paper*, Cmnd.1522 (October 1961); BTC, *Re-appraisal of the Plan for Modernisation and Re-equipment of British Railways*, H.M.S.O. Cmnd.813, para.9; *AR:1960*, Vol.1, p.23; *National Income and Expenditure Blue Book* (1963).

3 *AR:1960* (July 1964), p.3.

4 Sir James Dunnett, *SCNI:BR*, Q.1863.

5 Ibid. Q.1874

6 Ibid. Q.152.

7 Ibid. Q.1905.

8 Ibid. Q.1065.

9 Ibid. Q.1934.

10 *MRBR*, pp.31-2.

11 Ibid. p.7.

12 Ibid. p.35.

13 See a shrewd article by J.E. Hartsborn in *The Banker* (December 1956), 'Doublethink about Transport', where this criticism was made. If notice had been taken of it, the Government could have had second thoughts about the modernisation plan before it was too late.

14 1959 *Re-appraisal* op.cit. p.30.

15 *RNTU*, para.9

16 *SCNI:BR*, Q.1065; see also D. Blee, General Manager, London Midland Region, *JIT* (July 1959), p.135.

17 *SCNI:BR*, QQ.1050-99.

18 Ibid. QQ.1871-4.

19 Ibid. QQ.1108-11.

20 Ibid. Annex 1 to Appendix 9; see also comments in the Report, paras.203-5.

21 Ibid. QQ.1945-6.

22 For example ibid. Appendix 29, p.404.

23 Ibid. QQ.1075-7.

24 See M.E. Beesley, *BOUIS* (February 1962), p.35.
25 See S.P. Chambers, chairman of I.C.I., 'Investment and Britain's Industrial Future', *The Listener* (24 January 1957); P.T. Menzies, in the *National Provincial Bank Review* (August 1957); and N. Kaldor, *Economica* (November 1959), pp.287-9 for an assessment of the rate of profit in the private sector and the factors determining it.
26 Cf. Foster, *BOUIS* (May 1960), where the point is developed in more detail.
27 See *SCNI:BR*, QQ.1875-6.
28 Hartsborn, op.cit., pp.769-71. Sir R. Wilson repeated their 'assumption' that fares would go up with costs in 1959 after several more years in which the Transport Tribunal had delayed fare increases after cost rises. *SCNI/BR*, Q.1153.
29 J. Hirschleifer, 'Investment Decision under Uncertainty', *QJE* (Nov. 1965 and May 1966).
30 K.J. Arrow and R.C. Hind, 'Uncertainty and the Evaluation of Public Investment Decisions, *AER* (June 1970).

Postscript

1 See S. Joy, *The Train that Got Away,* Ian Allen (1973); R. Pryke, *Public Enterprise in Practice,* McGibbon and Kee (1971). Even as strong a protagonist of the nationalised industries as Pryke rarely defends the railways. As he detects, it has been hard for top management to impose its will on the regions. The administrative structure and the power of regions was such that they had an effective power of veto. Long before the Modernisation Plan, regional protagonists of steam kept in being investment in steam against the economics. Later regional opposition to closures was a main motive in the Commission failing to effect the closures it planned, long before there was strong political opposition.
2 L.C. Hunter and A.W.J. Thomson, *The Nationalised Transport Industries,* Heinemann (1973), p.138, observe that the 1968 recapitalisation had 'little or nothing to do with the actual value of the railway assets'. The earning power of assets was not calculated exactly, but the costing had not been done which would have made this possible. The value of assets was determined however on the basis of inquiry into BR earning power. Given forecasts of the scale of its activity, it represented a judgement on the size of the capital stock it could service. The present (1973) financial crisis was inevitable from the moment that BR was allowed to invest at an annual rate more than twice as high as it could maintain without a dramatic increase in net revenue.
3 R. Pryke (op.cit., p.296) questioned my criticism of BR's demand analysis in the 1950's wondering if I could have done better at the time. The only reply possible is (1) that some did question it at the time and (2) that it was based on so little evidence and required such changes in trends that it should have been rejected by the Ministry on *a priori* grounds. Since then there has been a tendency for BR to revise its demand forecasts *upwards* to support the rate of investment they requested; all the while the traffic has fallen. This tendency began at least as far back as 1956. See S. Joy, op.cit.
4. Cf. R. Pryke, op.cit. p.337, and S. Joy, op.cit.

CHAPTER 6

1 See I.M.D. Little, *The Price of Fuel,* Oxford University Press (1953), pp.4-6.

'Coal is worth to the economy at least as much as it could be sold for abroad since if it is sold at a lower price at home, this will encourage domestic coal consumption and thereby diminish the coal available for export and export earnings. But we should not deduce from this that it is wrong to adopt an average cost pricing policy at home. We have a choice of policies with different consequences. That is all'.

2 Cf. A.K. Sen, 'Some Notes on the Choice of Capital Intensity in Development', *QJE* (1957), p.569, N.1, see also his much fuller treatment in his *Collective Choice and Social Welfare,* Oliver and Boyd (1970).

3 See R.G.D. Allen, *Mathematical Economics,* Macmillan (1956), Ch.1.

4 K.J. Arrow, *EJ,* (December 1964), pp.1011-2. A.J. Merrett, 'Investment and Pricing Criteria in the Nationalised Industries', *Manchester School* (September, 1964). R.A. Millward in a private communication.

5 A.J. Merrett (op.cit.) analyses the problem (in the absence of congestion pricing) using a demand curve which shifts downwards to reflect the costs of congestion and queuing. To produce equilibrium in terms of fig. 6.4, the demand curve would pass through C with the same effect on cost reduction and consumers' surplus as if analysed as an increased cost to consumers, BC. But he does not make queuing costs a function of the MC and AR curves, so fails to reach a determinate solution, or note the implications for efficiency.

6 A.J. Merrett, op.cit.

7 See R. Layard, *Cost-Benefit Analysis*, Penguin (1972) for several key articles by Feldstein, Marglin and Sen.

8 W.J. Baumol and D.F. Bradford, 'Optimal Departure from Marginal Cost Pricing', *AER* (June 1970).

9 R. Rees, 'Second-Best Rates for Public Enterprise Pricing, *Economica* (August 1968).

10 See, for example, A. Lerner, *The Economics of Control,* Macmillan (1944).

11 T. Wilson, 'Price and Outlay Policy of State Enterprise' *EJ* (1945); see also J.E. Meade and J.M. Fleming, 'Price and Output Policy of State Enterprise *EJ* (1944), p.324.

12 Cf. H.L.I. Neuberger, 'User Benefits in the Evaluation of Transport and Land Use Plans', *JTEP,* Vol.5, No.2 (1971).

13 I.M.D. Little, *Critique of Welfare Economics,* Oxford University Press (1957 edn.), p.179.

14 The complications raised by income effects on a non-constant marginal utility of money are neglected here.

Postscript

1 There is a useful introduction to this question in J.H. Daly, *Pollution, Property and Prices,* University of Toronto Press (1968).

2 Cf. *Railway Policy,* Ministry of Transport, H.M.S.O. (1967).

3 K.J. Arrow, op.cit.

4 See R. Layard, op.cit.

CHAPTER 7

1 I am indebted for the table to Mr. D.L. Munby of Nuffield College, Oxford.

2 *Transport Bill* (1 November 1961), clause 11, Sec.3; see also *SCNI:BR.* QQ.108-15.

3 Reported in *MT* (23 July 1960).

4 *SCNI:BR.* Q.1377. cf. 'By 189 votes to 135 leave was refused to Mr. Baird (Wolverhampton N.E.) to introduce a Transport Act (1947) Amendment Bill to enable the BTC to manufacture and repair locomotives and rolling-stock for use other than by the Commission. Mr. Shepherd (Cheadle) said the Bill had to be opposed on the grounds of the national interest, in the interests of the Transport Commission, and because it was causing grave anxiety in 50 or more private workshops. If the amount of available capacity for making locomotives, carriages and wagons was increased (sic), in a short time there would be a surplus. The BTC was not in a position to indulge in sales of locomotives overseas'. *MT* (20 February 1960), p.9. The Bill got nowhere. The Government did not pronounce on the merits of the case. The 1962 Transport Act made no difference to the existing position, see Sec.13.

5 *SCNI:BR,* QQ.204-7. Sir Brian Robertson argued it would have advantaged the BTC to have been able to export. Ibid. 1367, 1706. The 1962 Transport Act made no change here.

6 For example a case where the Lands Tribunal held that four kiosks on York Station were not rateable as the general public had no access to them without a ticket. *MT* (19 December 1959).

7 See Sir Roy Harrod, *Policy Against Inflation,* Macmillan (1957), pp.186-95; D.L. Munby, 'Finance of the Nationalised Industries', *BOUIS* (May 1959); C.D. Foster, 'The Cost of Financing the Nationalised Industries', *BOUIS* (May 1960).

Postscript

1 For an extension of these ideas on social control of subsidy policy, see my *Politics, Finance and the Role of Economics,* Allen & Unwin (1970), Chs.4 and 18.

CHAPTER 8

1. *Tour through Great Britain.*
2 The best source of information on roads administration from 1900 to the end of the Second World War is Rees Jeffrey's autobiographical reminiscences, *The King's Highway,* Batchworth Press (1949).
3 *SCE:TR,* p.1. The Secretary of State for Scotland has been responsible for trunk roads in Scotland since 1956. The source for the English and Welsh figures is *Roads in England and Wales,* H.M.S.O., and for Scotland, *Industry and Employment in Scotland and the Scottish Roads Report,* H.M.S.O. Both are annual publications. Much useful information has been brought together in *RRLN/69/RFFD* (March 1962).
4 *SCE:TR,* Q.11.
5 D.L. Munby, 'The Roads as Economic Assets', *BOUIS* (November 1960), pp.281-7.
6 *CHNGB.*
7 *SCE:TR,* Q.247; see also pp.2-3. My italics.
8 The Road Research Laboratory has a different convention 'based to some extent on measurements by the Laboratory, on the relative effect of different vehicles on speed'. Reynolds and Wardrop, op.cit. The Laboratory's weighting is: Motor cycles – 0.75; light vehicles – 1; heavy goods vehicles, buses, coaches etc. – 2; pedal cycles – 0.5.
9 *RUBA,* p.6. The evidence was a study of four groups of two-lane highways.
10 D.J. Reynolds, *The Assessment of Priority for Road Improvements,* Road Research Technical Paper No. 48, H.M.S.O., p.4.

11 See M. Beckmann, C.B. McGuire and C.B. Winsten, *Studies in the Economics of Transportation,* Yale University Press (1956), Chs. I, V.

12 J.C. McMonagle, 'A Comprehensive Method of Scientific Programming', *HRBP* (1956), pp.33-7.

13 *RUBA*, p.5. My italics.

14 See Dr. T. Margerison, *SCE:TR*, pp.21-8.

15 H.E. Carlson, 'Adequacy and Priority Ratings for Rational Highway System Planning', *Highway Research Abstracts* (April 1955), pp.20-7.

16 See the bibliography in J.E. Baerwald, 'Improvement Priority Ratings', *HRBP* (1956), pp.38-62.

17 'Rating System for Secondary Roads', *Public Works* (March 1955), pp.168-9.

18 *SCE:TR*, Q.779.

19 This was admitted by a representative of the Ministry of Transport, *SCE:TR*, QQ.737-8. The criticism is of long standing. It was made by G.J. Ponsonby, in his *London's Passenger Transport Problem,* P.S. King (1932), p.70.

20 D.L. Munby, op.cit.

Postscript

1 For a critique of the grants system which takes into account developments since this book was written, see the author's evidence to the Environment and Home Office Sub-committee of the House of Commons Expenditure Committee on Urban Transport Planning. Session 1972-3 (House of Commons Paper 57-I), H.M.S.O.

2 *COBA: A Method of Economic Appraisal of Highway Schemes,* Highways Economics and Modelling Analysis Divison: Department of the Environment (1972).

3 If the minimum acceptable return were 10% and a given project promised 5%, then half the project costs would have to be met by regional grant, if the return on the remainder were to rise to 10%.

4 On this see K.M. Gwilliam, 'Secondary Effects of Road Investment', *Journal of Regional Studies,* Vol.4, No.2 (1970).

CHAPTER 9

1 On this see Shorey Peterson, 'Highway Policy on a Commercial Basis', *QJE* (May 1932).

2 *RRTP/46*, p.58.

3 D.M. Winch, *The Economics of Highway Planning,* University of Toronto Press (1963), p.12.

4 *MT* (5 March 1960), p.4.

5 Ibid.

6 Glasbrook Bros. vs. Glamorgan County Council, *1925 House of Lords,* p.270. I am indebted to Mr. A. Rogerson of Jesus College, Oxford, for this reference.

7 *Halsbury's Laws of England,* ed. Viscount Simonds, third edn. (1959), pp.129, 131-2.

8 *Notes on an Investigation into the Cost of Collecting Income Arising from the Provisions of the Road Traffic Acts,* Association of Chief Financial Officers in the Hospital Service (February 1961).

9 See J.H. Jones, *Road Accidents,* H.M.S.O. (1946); D.J. Reynolds, 'The Cost of Road Accidents', *JRSS,* Series A (1956). The basis of the two calculations was not identical; see also Reynolds, p.402.

10 A.A. Walters, 'The Theory and Measurement of Private and Social Cost of Highway Congestion'. *Econometrica* (October 1961).

11 An economist would recognise this as the kind of situation mentioned by Mrs. Joan Robinson, *QJE* (November 1934), pp.112-3.

12 The rationale of congestion costs seems to have been neglected by most of those who have advocated MSC pricing for roads: for example, A.C. Pigou, *Economics of Welfare,* Macmillan (1920 edn.): F.H. Knight, 'Some Fallacies in the Interpretation of Social Cost', *QJE* (1924), pp.582-606 and A.A. Walters, 'Track Costs and Motor Taxation', *JIE* (1954) and various unpublished papers. Bechmann, McGuire and Winston, however, comment: 'It may still seem odd that every individual should pay more for transportation as must be the case when demand is reduced on the whole. The fact is of course that since transportation costs other than tolls tend to go down with a decrease in flow, they decrease as a result of the imposition of tolls. The remaining part of the expense becomes available again as toll revenue; so that the community can gain where every individual seems to lose', op. cit., p.95.

13 *Journal of the Royal Society of Arts* (October 1960), p.815.

14 *MT,* (27 August 1960), p.8.

15 *Engineering News Record* (1960), 165(24), pp.42-3, 46-7. Reported in *Road Abstracts,* H.M.S.O. (April 1961), p.95.

16 Reported in the London *Times* (9 December 1960).

17 *Saturday Review* (21 December 1855).

18 *First Report* of the Group Appointed by the Ministry of Transport in 1950 to Study Problems of Transport Coordination: *The Total Costs and Proceeds of Taxes,* Government Printing and Publishing Office. The Hague (1958), p.20.

Postscript

1 *New Roads in Towns,* Urban Motorways Committee, Department of the Environment, H.M.S.O. (1972).

2 *Development and Compensation – Putting People First,* H.M.S.O. Cmnd.5124 (1972). The proposals in this White Paper fall short of Pareto optimality, and short of recent American developments in the law of compensation. For a discussion of uncompensated costs in highway improvement, see A. Downs, 'Losses Imposed on Urban Households by Uncompensated Highway and Renewal Costs' in his *Urban Problems and Prospects,* Markham (1970).

3 For a discussion of Pareto optimality see E.J. Mishan, *Cost Benefit Analysis,* Allen and Unwin (1971). Mishan takes the view that it is hardly rational to question that Pareto optimal compensation should be paid in such cases. However, there is another influential principle that someone buying a property accepts a risk that its environment will deteriorate: if there were no risk of uncompensated environmental deterioration the price of the property would have been higher. On this see this author, 'Transport and the Urban Environment'; in I. Heggie (ed.), *Urbanisation and the Environment,* International Economics Association, Macmillan (1974).

4 H.M.S.O. (1968).

5 E.J. Mishan, 'Evaluation of Life and Limb: a theoretical approach', *Journal of Political Economy,* Vol.79, No.4 (1971).

6 A.A. Walters, *The Economics of Road User Charges,* World Bank Occasional Staff Papers, No.5 (1968).

7 See R.M. Solow and W.S. Vickrey, 'Land Use in a Long Narrow City' *Journal of Economic Theory,* Vol.3 (1971), pp.430-47; J.A. Mirrlees, 'The Optimum Town', *Swedish Journal of Economics* (March 1972); E.S. Mills, *Studies in the Structure of the Urban Economy,* Johns Hopkins (1972). The treatment is highly mathematical.

8 L. Wingo, *Transportation and Urban Land,* Resources for the Future (1961);

13 The methodology of an urban origin and destination study has been considered in some detail by R.B. Mitchell and C. Rapkin, *Urban Traffic: A Function of Land Use,* Columbia University Press (1954): a study of Philadelphia. The first urban origin and destination surveys were aimed to decide where it would be most profitable to place outdoor advertising of a type appropriate to various passers-by; for example where an advertisement was likely to be seen by the greatest number of middle-income housewives, etc. There is an excellent account of the methodology of a traffic study of Utrecht by the late Dr. Feuchtinger in *Roads and their Traffic,* ed. by E. Davies; see also an article by H. Hondermarq in the same volume with special reference to Brussels. The most sophisticated so far is the *Chicago Area Transportation Study,* Vols. 1, 2, 3, (1959-62).

14 See the survey by J.W. Gibbons and A. Proctor, 'Economic Costs of Traffic Congestion', in *Urban Traffic Congestion,* Highway Research Bulletin No. 86 (1954).

15 There is an excellent short description of the use of the methods to decide priorities for building urban motorways in Detroit: H.W. Beavis, 'Application of Cost-Benefit Ratios to an Expressway System', *HRBP* (1956).

Postscript

1 E.g..C.D. Foster and M.E. Beesley, 'Estimating the Social Benefit of Constructing an Underground Railway in London', *JRSS,* Vol.125 (1963); reprinted in D.L. Munby, *Transport Economics,* Penguin (1968) and in K.J. Arrow and T. Scitovsky, *Readings in Welfare Economics,* American Economic Association; Ministry of Transport, *Portbury,* H.M.S.O. (1966). Any reader who has the inclination and time to discover how thorough and comprehensive transport project evaluation can now be, should read Commission on the Third London Airport, *Report,* H.M.S.O. (1971).

2 COBA *A Method of Economic Appraisal of Highway Schemes,* Department of the Environment (1972).

3 E.g. on speed-flow formulae, flow measurement at junctions, analyses of junction delays, capacity of weaving sections at roundabouts, vehicle operating costs, the value of time, construction and maintenance costs.

4 A useful account of the urban transport planning process – in all its stages more complicated than for inter-urban roads – is to be found in R. Lane, T.J. Powell and P. Prestwood-Smith, *Analytical Transport Planning,* Duckworth (1971). They have a good description of the evaluation process.

5 A.J. Harrison and D.A. Quarmby, *The Value of Time in Transport Planning: A Review,* ECMT Round Table (October 1969).

6 There is an excellent bibliography of this in J.R. Meyer and M. Straszheim, *Pricing and Project Evaluation,* Brookings (1971).

7 See R. Lane, T.J. Powell and P. Prestwood-Smith, *Analytical Transport Planning,* Duckworth (1971).

8 R.E. Quandt, (ed.), *The Demand for Travel: Theory and Measurement,* Lexington (1970).

CHAPTER 12

1   For some modification of the standard argument see Sir H.O. Mance, *The Road and Rail Transport Problem* (1940), pp.5ff., who indicates some ways in which competition actually increased in the interwar years; see also G. Walker, 'Competition in Transport as an Instrument of Policy', *EJ* (September 1956).

2   On the importance of road and rail price-cost equality or of the same deviation of price from cost for each see Sargent, *British Transport Policy*, O.U.P., (1958). However, the solution advocated here is not the same as Sargent's since he does not specify just what he means by prices 'reflecting' costs.

3   This problem has been faced in practice by the Ministry of Transport when asking for an increase in fares, some local bus companies put forward the argument that their rates of return were lower than the average commercial rate of return. The Ministry commented that this argument did not allow for differences in 'risk and other features'. *MT* (17 September 1960), p.4.

4   It should only perturb someone who believes in some sense that profit maximisation or consumers' surplus maximisation throughout the economy is the *optimum;* or who believes that the present mixture of a private sector and a public sector with indefinite criteria is in some sense an optimum; or who though he does not defend either of those as an optimum, believes the introduction of a definite consumers' surplus sector would lead to a worse allocation of resources. It is difficult to see what arguments he would advance to substantiate any of these points of view.

5   For example, The Labour Party pamphlet, *Challenge to Britain* (1953) which suggested this role for public enterprise.

6   See D.G. Glassborow, *BTR* (December 1959); J.L. Grumbridge, *JIT* (January 1960).

7   Sir Brian Robertson, *SCNI:BR,* QQ.356-8, 367. It is also interesting to note that the Road Haulage Association recommended a 10 per cent increase in charges from 1 November 1960 and this was followed a week later by a similar increase by British Road Services, *MT* (22-29 October 1960).

8   This was suggested by Sir R. Wilson, in his 'Framework of Public Transport', *JIT* (1953), pp.167-8.

9   See Sir H.O. Mance, *MT* (12 March 1960), who made this proposal.

10 J.A. Galbraith, *American Capitalism,* Hamish Hamilton (1957 Rev.. Edn.) especially Ch.IX.

11 See R. Wilson, op.cit. (1953), and 'For and Against Monopolies in Transport', *JIT* (May 1956).

12 Cf. J.R. Meyer *et al.,* op.cit., p.247.

13 There has been controversy over the extent of economies of scale. See M. Chisholm, *OEP* (October 1959 and February 1961), A.A. Walters, *OEP* (February 1961). On this question see also Meyer *et al.,* op.cit., p.261.

14 See D.N. Chester, *Public Control of Road Passenger Transport,* Manchester University Press (1936); G. Walker, *Road and Rail,* Allen and Unwin (1947 edn.).

15 W.M. MacLeod and A.A. Walters, 'A Note on Bankruptcy in Road Haulage', *JIE* (November 1956).

16 Chester, op.cit.; G.J. Ponsonby, *London's Passenger Transport Problem,* P.S. King (1932).

Postscript

1   See the postscript to Appendix 1 for some references particularly relevant to transport. M.J. Farrell, 'In Defence of Public Utility Theory', *Oxford Economic*

Papers (1958), reprinted in R. Turvey, *Public Enterprise,* Penguin (1968), referred to some of the dangers to transport policy if doubts caused by second-best considerations led to lack of sufficient interest in relative road and rail prices.

2 See *COBA,* Department of the Environment, for a description of the method of calculating net present values which reflects this judgment. It is rough justice.

3 B. T. Bayliss, *The Road Haulage Industry since 1968,* H.M.S.O. (1973).

4 Op.cit. See footnote 2 to postscript to Introduction.

5 Road Research Laboratory, *A Guide to the Structural Design of Payments for New Roads,* Road Note 29, 3rd edition (1970).

APPENDIX 1

1 Adapted from A.P. Lerner, *The Economics of Control,* Macmillan (1946), p.64; see also pp.128, 130.

2 Cf. J. de V. Graaff, *Theoretical Welfare Economics* (1957), Ch.8 and pp.193-4 who here I believe makes the wrong comment on the effect of uncertainty on the principle.

3 For example A.N. Henderson, 'Prices and Profits in State Enterprise', *RES* (1949-50), p.17; J. Wiseman, 'The Theory of Public Utility Price – an Empty Box', *OEP* (February 1957), pp.59-62.

4 Op.cit., pp.198-9. Lerner is one of the few marginalists who have been strictly logical in their definition of a short-run marginal cost pricing policy.

5 Op.cit., pp.150-1; see also A.P. Lerner, op.cit., pp.215-6.

6 For example T. Wilson, 'Price and Output Policy of State Enterprise', *EJ* (December 1945). Lerner supplemented his First by a Second Rule – produce in the cheapest possible way (op.cit., p.130) – but this is not a satisfactory investment criterion since it cannot be used to rank investment opportunities and for that in general a numerically determinate rate of return is needed.

7 Cf. op.cit., pp.93-6.

8 *Vide* J.E. Meade, 'Price and Output Policy of State Enterprise', *EJ* (December 1944).

9 Lerner, loc.cit., pp.198-9.

10 *Vide* T. Wilson, op.cit.; see also R. McKean, op.cit.

11 Cf. A. Bergson, 'A Reformulation of Certain Aspects of Welfare Economics', *QJE* (February 1938); J.A. Nordin, *Economica* (May 1947).

12 I.M.D. Little, *A Critique of Welfare Economics,* Oxford University Press (1957 edn.), p.162; Graaff, op.cit., pp.146-7.

13 *The Price of Fuel,* Oxford University Press (1953), pp.*xi-xiv;* also M.J. Farrell, 'In Defence of Public Utility Theory' *OEP* (February 1958).

14 Loc. cit., pp.*xiii-xiv;* E.J. Mishan, 'A Survey of Welfare Economics: 1939-59'. *EJ* (June 1960).

15 R.G. Lipsey and K. Lancaster, 'The General Theory of the Second-Best', *RES* (1956-7).

16 Farrell, op.cit.

Postscript

1 M. Boiteux, 'Sur la gestion des Monopoles Publics astreints a l'equilibre budgetaire', *Econometrica* (January 1956), translated in J.R. Nelson, *Marginal Cost Pricing in Practice,* Prentice-Hall (1964); H. Mohring, 'Urban Highway Investments' in R. Dorfman (ed.) *Measuring Benefits of*

Government Investments, Brookings (1965); A.A. Walters, *The Economics of Road User Charges,* World Bank Occasional Staff Papers, No.5 (1968).

2 W.J. Baumol and D.F. Bradford, 'Optimal Departures from Marginal Cost Pricing' , *AER* (June 1970)
3 A model for the analysis of this problem is to be found in A. Fishlow and P. David, 'Optimal Resource Allocation in an Imperfect Market Setting', *Journal of Political Economy* (December 1961). Meyer and Mnookin have performed a theoretical analysis of this kind of second-best problem in transport, based on this model, *Pricing and Project Evaluation,* Brookings (1971), Ch.5.
4 Wingo, *Transport and Urban Land,* Resources for the Future (1961); W. Alonso, *Location and Land Use,* Harvard University Press (1964); R.F. Muth, *Cities and Housing,* Chicago University Press (1969); see also footnote 8 to Chapter 9.
5 R. Rees, 'Second-best Rules for Public Enterprise Pricing', *Economica* (1968).

APPENDIX 2

1 The point is well argued by Mrs. M.E. Paul, 'Covering Costs by Receipts', *BOUIS* (February 1960).
2 Cf. Mrs. Joan Robinson, *The Economics of Imperfect Competition,* Macmillan (1933), p.206, who argued this point against the railways.

APPENDIX 4

1 The chief sources of information and criticism on organisation are S.M. Lovell, 'The Suitability of the Existing Highway Organisation to deal with an Expanding Programme of Highway Construction' and the discussion following in *CHNGB* (1958); *SCE:TR;* the *Third Special Report from the Select Committee on Estimates,* H.M.S.O. (April 1960); L.J. Dunnett, Permanent Secretary to the Ministry of Transport, 'The Government and Roads and Road Transport', *JIT:* and a chapter by Col. Lovell, 'The Administrative Structure', in *Roads and their Traffic,* ed. by E. Davies (1960).
2 See Lovell, op.cit. (1958) and (1960).
3 Dunnett, op.cit.
4 Op.cit. (1958), p.221.
5 *MT* (22 October 1960), p.1.
6 Cmnd. 1432 (July 1961).
7 Op.cit. p.241.

Postscript

1 *Roads – A New Approach,* British Road Federation (1968); *Roads in Britain – An Organisation Review,* a report by Booz-Allen and Hamilton International for the BRF (1971).

INDEX

accidents, road, cost of, 22, 23, 25, 267

accountability, 51, 77, 112-3

accounting for a consumer's surplus policy, 123

accounts of public enterprise, 21

administrative reorganisation, 14, 35

agency to subsidise country dwellers, 291

Allais, M., 255

alternative use value, 220

Arizona Method, 188

Ashley Committee, 75n

Austria, road expenditure, 26

autobahnen, 173

automatic metering, 248

autostrada, 173

average cost pricing, 131, 127-8, 133; definition of policy: possible unstable interpretation, 128

balance of payments, 144

Baldock Lane, 171

basic criteria, 30, 60-1, 191-5, 313; possible incompatibility, 124-5

Beeching Plan, 83, 83n, 115n

benefit, private, 74

benefit, social definition of, 64-6

benefits and costs, 64; money, measure of, 52; not private, 64

Bergson, A., 322

bicycle tyre tax, 251

Boston, 238

break-even principle, 127-8

British Railways, 161; deficits, 161; financial position, 161; restrictions on property development, 162-3; taxation, 163-4; wage structure, a disincentive, 162

British Railways Board, 7, 8; decentralisation, 12

British Transport Commission, 74, 80

Brook, Henry, 20

Burke, Edmund, 11, 12n

C Licences, 192, 294, 295

California, L.A., 24

canals, 173

Central Transport Consultative Committee, 45

Chamberlain, Neville, 20

Chester, D.N., 44

Chief Constable of Hampshire, 211

Churchill, Winston, 20, 21

coal, 35

comfort and convenience, 274

commercialism, 35, 46

commonsense economics, 52

Communist countries, 62

competition, 34, 55, 193; countervailing power, 292; definition of, 286; marginal cost pricing in private sector, 303, 310; need for Royal Commission, 292; possible within single transport authority, 290; private and public, 287-8; same conditions, 288; same criteria, 287-8; statutory statement, 290; vertical, 291; wasteful, 296

competitive solutions, 284ff

complementarity, 224

Conference on the Highway Needs of Great Britain, 180

congestion, 22; cost of, 22-3

constant utility of income, 68, 122

consumers' definition of, 121-2

consumers' surplus, 192; definition of, 56-7

consumers surplus maximisation, 30, 41-2, 70, 109, 121ff, 236, 258, 300; accounting, 123; accumulated deficit, 91; charging, 126-43; charging principles, 236ff; consumers charged costs, 123; consumers not charged costs, 122;

provision and maintenance of
sheets and ropes, 81-2; risk of
damage or loss, 81-2; terminal
accommodation facilities úsed,
81-2; terminal haulage, 81-2;
terminal shunting, 81-2; the
eight heads, 78-9; track and
signalling, 81-2; trunk
haulage, 81-2;
costs, 75; decentralisation, 74;
deficit charging policy, 74-5;
deficits, 76, 98; disinvestment
between 1937 and 1953, 97;
expenditure based on internal
predictions, 29; based on
international comparisons,
25, 28; decided largely
arbitrarily, 28;
investment as percentage of
national gross investment, 98;
as percentage of public sector
gross investment, 98;
joint costs, 84; objections to
distinction between direct and
indirect costs, 88; outline of
costing system for railway
charging, 326ff; marginal cost
pricing, 315; Modernisation
Plan, 118-20; pricing since 1963,
95; nineteenth-century, 42;
underestimation of receipts,
110; unprofitable branch lines, 49
rate of interest, 115-8
rate of return on capital, 59
rates, 251
rationing the use of the road system,
253
Ratter, J., 104n
real interest, 159
registration duties, 239
regulations, 162ff, 289; definition
of, 158-60
Lord Reith, 13
rent, 22, 53, 54-6; definition
of, 53
reorganisation, 192
Reorganisation of the Nationalised
Transport Undertakings White
Paper, 44, 75;
reserves, 41, 59
reshaping of British Railways, 83,
88, 115n
revenue maximisation, 75
risk, evaluation of, 111-2

road and rail, difference in the
pattern of, 170; relative prices, 28
Road Fund, 174, 179
Roads Improvement Act, 1925, 175
Road Research Laboratory, 22, 190-1
208, 210, 236, 259, 261, 262, 263
roads,
accident costs, 213-6
alternative use value, 220;
benefits, double costing of, 203-5;
breakdown of, 32; building as
corrective to slump, 19, 38;
charges, 28; charging by automatic
metering, 248; bicycle tyre tax,
251; parking charges, 247;
parking meters, 250; petrol
taxation, 242; profit
maximisation, 252ff; purchase
tax, 242; on vehichle light bulbs
251; rates, 251; taxi meter, 248;
tolls, 245; traffic fines, 251;
tyre tax, 242; vehicle licence
fees and registration duties, 239;
weight ton tax, 244; windscreen
stickers, 246;
choice of time horison, 209;
classification, 197 ; conflict of
interests, 171-5; congestion costs,
216; pricing, 255-7;
costs of ancillary services and facilities,
210; joint to an administrative
area, 236; joint to a road
system, 236; country, 23;
expenditure, based on international
comparisons, 31; financed out of
rates, 22; from rates, 178; largely
arbitrary methods of deciding, 18;
no reasons to suppose present
levels desirable, 23; proportions
spent by different countries, 26;
grant systems, 176-80; changes in,
197
identification of costs, 208ff;
improvement evaluation, 281-3;
interest, 210; investment, 180,
198-200 cost of, 23-4;
land, 292; limitations of the
practical capacity approach,
184-5; long-run costs attributable
to particular flows of traffic,
235; joint to a section of road.
235
maintenance costs, 210; Ministry
of Transport, investment criteria,